Squaddie, Blitz and The Bomb

by Barone Hopper

Cover Photo by Gerald Rice

Available:

100 Years of Sanctuary - A Social History (1997)
ISBN: 978-0956991027

Better Court Than Coroners - Memoirs of a Duty of Care (2012)
ISBN: 978-0956991003

Lest We Forget: BCTC Volume 2 - Memoirs from a Duty of Care (2013)
ISBN: 978-0956991010

Tales of a Caremaker (Kindle eBook, 2014)
ISBN: 978-0956991034

Squaddie, Blitz and The Bomb (2015)
ISBN: 978-0956991041

Squaddie, Blitz and The Bomb

Barone Hopper

Potpourri of Memoirs:
Social History

First limited publication – 2015

Published by:
PerseVerance Publications
26 Sandfield Avenue
Littlehampton
West Sussex.
BN17 7LL

email: info@baronehopper.co.uk
web: http://www.baronehopper.co.uk

Printed by:
4Edge,
7a Eldon Way
Hockley
Essex
SS5 4AD

ISBN: 978-0-9569910-4-1

Dedicated to all of you who experienced Cold War nuclear tests, and fallout, during and after atomic explosions; and those families and descendants, who still suffer today...

Squaddie, Blitz and The Bomb – Contents:

List of Illustrations

Blitz

Chapter One – Wartime Childhood

Anderson Shelter, Blitz, 1940. (Source: *PA Images*)

Grey days

It was the run-up to Christmas, a cold December 1954. I was 17 years old, being no way streetwise (as were many teddy boys, in their expensive Edwardian suits and 'd.a.' hair styles – post war spivs). I was ignorant, more than innocent (of what?, you may ask). Institutionalised, after being in care for all the war years, and early 1950s. Living, doing as I was told by any adult – at school, and then at work, in a Fleet Street photo agency.

Stalin had recently passed away in Soviet Russia. But Uncle Joe's influence prevailed, in Europe and Asia of the 1950s. Along with Blitz ruins, and rigid class social mores; doing as we were told – or else.

Going in early to work on my bicycle, past St. Paul's, under Ludgate Bridge, St Bride's remains, and, white-tiled press buildings of Fleet Street: we boys chatted amongst ourselves – of weekend exploits.

It was Sunday night, a BBC television play version of George Orwell's (aka Eric Blair) classic *1984* – set, for thirty years on, one generation ahead. If we, the royal we, didn't arrest the trend, a bleak, science fiction scenario to come would be inevitable. Our generation; wartime blitz kids, just starting out on our working life, and anticipating obligatory National Service callup papers, due at eighteen years old.

I arrived home at night after work, and earlier from school and homework, eager to listen to our radio shows: *PC 49, Life With the Lyons;* was *Dick Barton* still about? – I can't remember. I recall the comedies and dramas, on the BBC Home and Light programme: science fiction – *Journey into Space*, and *The Quatermass Experiment* (remember the scenes of discovery with London Underground). H.G. Wells' books, *War of the Worlds* and *The Time Machine* – and his social working class dramas, *History of Mr Polly*... And, listen to late night Valentine Dyall horror tales, with bleak, black and white, two dimensional sides – them and us – no vision, only imagination.

My new family purchased a small 12-inch square cabinet television. Most programmes (all?) did not start until 4pm, and television now added to our home grown entertainment, of record playing and BBC progs (like night Radio Luxembourg.)

It must have been a Monday morning, in early December 1954. I had received my call up papers and been informed that I was due for National Service in August 1955. The Sunday Night BBC Television Theatre had produced one of their terrific (though always bleak) dramas. This was a science fiction scenario called *1984* – shown Sunday night. I enjoyed it. It was anti-communist, totalitarian state, *and completely resonated with me* – young as I was. Why? Everything seemed so familiar – the location settings, even the dialogue? And I was viewed as one of the proles.

Orwell lived in many of the London addresses I was familiar with. The ruins, the flat dodgy bleak buildings that survived: a world away from the West End and its glamour – and seats of government and police departments. Orwell and his family lived a short walking distance away from us, in Islington, Canonbury N1 – which I was familiar with. And his other London wartime homes (one of them was bombed out, as we were, in the Blitz). John Thompson (1984) Orwell's London.

Early 1950s, my bro and I went to a cinema in Essex Street, Islington, to see *Gone With The Wind*. Much of the street, which went up to the Angel, Islington Green, and Collin's Music Hall, was war damaged. I recall an area of surviving brick building shelters – the area behind, empty spaces, bereft of any damaged remains. Bro and I played, jumping from roof to roof of the air raid shelters...

Family at War

Evacuation 1939:

1. Patrick Creagh (Snr) married..–Died in war. 2. Barone Carl Hopper (b. 27.2.37) m.

3. Olive Manton (m. Butters / Newson) (b. 13.6.18) 4. Emil Moody Hopper m. (b. 3.6.38)

5. Elsie Caroline Manton (m. Moore) (b. 1.1.14) 6. Marian Susan Creagh (m. Gregory) (b. 2.3.38)

7. Lillian Annie Manton (m. Collier) (b.1888, d.1981) 8. George Evans m. (b. 30.7.22)

9. Albert Evans m. (no details) 10. Lillian Evans (b.13.3.16) m. P. A. Creagh.

11. Elsie Manton m. (Evans) (b.1894) 12. Barbara John Smith (m. Stonehouse) (b. 4.2.31)

13. Eileen Ann Smith (m. Choules) (b. 9.5.33)14. Patrick Arthur Creagh (Jnr) m. (b. 14.12.34)

15. Richard L.G. Creagh m. (b. 10.5.36).

1939. *First* Evacuation Day – end August 1939. Extended family congregated at 29 Wall Street, Islington. One branch of **The Manton Family**, descended from Dr Thomas Manton DD (1620-1677) – splits up, as one wartime London family evacuates its seven children. En-route for Northampton. Why Northampton? Gt Aunt Lil later told me of Manton blood cousins living there in the 19th century – but in 1939 there seemed no connection. Photo taken outside Canonbury Railway Station in North London, as a group, never to meet up again. The pic was treasured by my Gt Aunt Lil Manton, b.1888 (7). Seen next to her is her younger sister Elsie Manton (11), *their* two surviving bros (a third Thomas died of war wounds in 1918) ; eldest John Walter Manton b.1885 (my grandfather), and bro sailor George Manton are not in the pic. Memories through *their* father James Leigh Manton b.1849 extended back into at least early 19th century, in London and Northampton; and linked back in time to clerical ancestors in 16th c. Somerset. Who took the photo is not known.

BOMBED-OUT

LEFT: My absent father, always a mystery (*his* father Johanan William Hopper, Austrian artist, parents migrated to Australia sometime c.1900 – or before?). Name, Barone Ernst Hopper, seen above (b.1902- d.1972). Australian or N.Z. born. Lifetime in circus, US vaudeville (as Ole Olsen & Chic Johnson) artiste, & latter years a stage-designer, Pic circa.**1940. RIGHT: 1940**. Our last home. Blitz kids, away, we'd just evacuated, when our home was destroyed by fire during the blitz. Address No 1 Baxter Grove off Wall Street & Ballspond Road, Islington. Empty brownfield site at Coronation celebrations in 1953. The whole area in N1 demolished in 1960s – replaced by flats. **INSET:** *Picture Post.* Vol.9.No2. p9, October 12th.**1940**

1942. Homeless. **Centre,** mother Maude Susie Hopper (nee Manton, years later new surname Dolan). **Left,** author Barone Carl Hopper age 5yrs 3mths. – **Right**, bro Emil Moody Hopper. A rare pic. On back of photo stamped June 4th – bro was 3 yrs old on June 3rd. This was time of yet another family wartime breakup as I was (again), separated, and evacuated fostered out to Heston Middlesex (for a while). 1944 I was moved into an orphanage. My infant bro would be evacuated – without mother–up-north to Yorkshire, till Summer 1945 when he too entered the orphanage.

1950. In the orphanage. My bro posing in the Huts Yard (yards away from where in 1944 I had stood and watched overhead doodle bugs & V2s; and was subsequently evacuated with other kids to South Wales – and, on return, bro joining me in The Homes in Summer of 1945).

1957. Right. H Bomb....British servicemen stationed on Christmas Island in the Mid-pacific 1956-7. **Left** photo shows sappers of 28 Field Engineer Regiment constructing a large distillation plant to receive surrounding salt waters of the Pacific – no fresh water to be had on the coral island. Fortunately we troops were assured that we're safe from all and any exploded 'clean' (triggered above ground or above sea – i.e. not 'dirty' bombs – sic), experimental H bomb thermonuclear detonations. And, we were told ; 'You are perfectly safe from any after-effects from even minimal exposure afterward radiation effects.' (Hmm!) Lucky! I missed much bigger bombs yet to be exploded (with radiation), in the months and years ahead, some over the island itself.

Institution, Evacuee and Orphanage
1937 – 1951

' The necessity of complying with times, and of sparing persons, is the great impediment of biography. History may be formed from permanent monuments and records, but lives can only be written from personal knowledge, which is growing every day less, and in a short time is lost for ever. What is known can seldom be immediately told, and when it might be told, is no longer known.'
Dr Samuel Johnson, *Life of Addison.*

Background

A few years ago I heard an English radio lecturer drily declare that *at least*, 'four to 5 billion people exist on this planet of ours, where like summer and winter we germinate, grow and pass on into bleak, cold oblivion'. I could think of more basic similes. And a billion sounds bald mathematics, too big, like cosmos, to precisely relate to matchstick human beings. Fowler defines our UK billion as a million million – which is 4,500,000,000,000 men, women and children of all ages, colours and shapes alive for a while, then – gone. And there's me, and thee. Where do I as in it belong. Where do *we* fit in this jigsaw of an abascus Universe. And, in truth, *what* am I, if indeed made manikin out of half-life atoms stardust.

Parade all people on earth – alive at one time – all 4.5 billion of 'em, allow one second to see each individual, my abacus of digits reckons it would take 142,694 years to view each individual pcr sc! And as to how long we human beings have existed on earth surely no estimate of untold billions will come close to how many *have* passed into cold oblivion. Avoiding cant, history must include all living and dead mankind, and positively relate to each other. And pursuing minutiae, wear and tear, use, abuse, in peace and war, individuals search, crawl on, or stationary and time-driven, are relatively rich, poor, sick and in need throughout their singular journey. Ruddy, mewling, puking, innocent babe. If lucky, ruddy, mewling, puking not-so innocent aged, survived, lived, until dry ever-staring cadaver we eventually become. My brother and I were born shortly before the outbreak of the second world war...

Welfare 1939

Home Office *Civil Defence* manuals issued before, during, and in the early post-war years included a pamphlet entitled: WELFARE SECTION. This lengthy HMSO pamphlet anticipated the needs of homeless and destitute families, so rendered by war or national disasters. Chapter IV, Billeting, 36, General, third paragraph, said:

> *'No standard of accommodation will be laid down since much will depend on the conditions obtaining at the time when billeting is carried out. Householders will be required in some cases (e.g. for mothers with their children) to provide only shelter and access to water and sanitary accommodation.'*

And so it was at our first evacuation as infants in late August and September of 1939.

Beginning

As a struggling single parent with two infants at the beginning of the war, how did you manage?' I asked my mother many, many years later after growing up. And Ma described (in writing) how it was for her personally, and for thousands of other mothers and their children, in the early days of the war – as evacuees in 1939.

> *'As you know, you were born in a Mill Hill nursing home the bill which was never paid even though a summons was issued against your father. Of course trouble had started before that. Although his money was good at the film studio I'm afraid he gambled. Then when you were six months old I found I was going to have your brother. Then of course things got really bad. He wanted me to have an abortion and put you in a home. When he realised I wouldn't, I couldn't get but little money off him.*
>
> *In the end when your brother was exactly a year old* [June 3rd 1939] *I went into Barnet to the police courts and got a separation. Then we moved, back to London, to 1 Baxter Grove, Islington* [off the Ballspond Road] *in North London, into a couple of rooms.* [Her parents

lived close by, down *The Grove* at 2 Baxter Grove.] *After listening to other people saying it's a shame, two babies not having a father I took him back. But things got worse I'm afraid. War broke out and we evacuated to Northampton but I stuck it for ten weeks and we came back to London. After a while at the time the London Docks was bombed and it got bad in London I thought it best to take you both back to Northampton. That would be early 1940.*

The government was paying 11/- billeting money for us but I'm afraid I got very little from your father. In fact on one occasion we went five weeks without money from anywhere. I used to borrow 5/- per week of the young woman whose house I lived in to get a little food to feed you at least a little. I had to go to the NSPCC in the end because I couldn't get any money from anywhere because it was a case that I had to take to court. This was done but you can't get blood out of a stone. I was getting food tickets from the local council which I'm not quite sure to what value. It was very little and then if even your father did send anything I had to take it straight back to the council. This was because at the time I couldn't go to do a little job as you both had whooping cough and couldn't go to nursery school.

I certainly went to work when I could. Anyway eventually I was asked to come back to London and work in Lil's Café [Lily was her older married sister an ex-film actress less than ten years before, and with two young children of her own] *at Shrubland Road, Hackney at London fields in 1941.*

By the way the house that we had lived in at One Baxter Grove which had two rooms was bombed, while we was in Northampton [the second time] *so we had no home to come back to –* [becoming homeless throughout the war–until 1951–after mother had remarried, to Thomas Dolan, an Irishman from Dublin] *And, so, I was evacuated – alone.*

The café was open 24 hours a day so I had to do the nights which of course wasn't very convenient and money paid me was bad; so after you had had jaundice you went to Hounslow in 1942 until Maud's husband was coming out of the Navy and she wrote and said could I find somewhere for you to go as she didn't think he would approve. I had made all arrangements for you [early 1944] *to go into the orphanage* [Spurgeon's Orphan Homes, Reigate. Surrey]; *she wrote and said you could stay but I couldn't take the chance of her changing her mind again. I tried to get you both together but they only had the one vacancy at the time. Your brother as you know went to Yorkshire in 1943. The WVS helped me there. I had to leave the café as the money I was earning wasn't enough. ... And I then became a London Transport Bus Conductress* [aka clippie] *through most of the war years – and a while after it had finished.'*

First Evacuation – Canonbury N1

'At the end of August in 1939, [Mother continued in her writing], *'we started our train journey from Canonbury Station, Dilly* [mother's cousin] *with her three children* [Paddy, Marion and Mickey Creagh – she would later have two more, Carol and Terry – but her husband a soldier was killed in action]; *and myself with Lily's* [aka Lillian Manton] *two girls* [Barbara & Eileen Smith], *and my own two boys, you two, arriving in Northampton early in the evening. After that it was having to wait and see who would house us. For some people it was easy, only having one or two children. Unfortunately for Dilly and myself it was quite late before we got lucky. Dilly went to quite a nice couple. We were in the same turning. I think the word had been passed around in the pubs as we had to wait until they were closed. Barbara went to one family and myself with Eileen and my two went to another not far along the same road. None of us was really happy. I returned with my children* [my bro Emil and I] *ten weeks later to London, when the London Docks were receiving nightly raids.* [The Blitz.] *Dilly and children had returned even earlier unable to stay away for long. After staying on through The Battle of Britain, we again evacuated to Northampton for a while before returning to London.'*

An iconic print (who took the pic?) of St. Paul's in the midst of the Blitz of 1940 – surrounding ruins still abounded, in the 1950s. We were bombed out during this same episode, our families' surviving, but a short distance away; but left my bro and I, as infants, homeless.
(Source: Daily Mail. AP/AP/Press Association Images)

'*Very well, Alone*'. June 18th, 1940. The fall of Europe. The island of Great Britain, isolated, against Nazi Germany... (Source: *Europe At War* David Low (1891 – 1963). Penguin. 1941)

Blitz – London

The English weekly illustrated magazine *Picture Post* on September 16th 1939 recorded for posterity typical departing groups of young children, and crocodile troops of escorted children in evacuation. One rare family photograph of 1939 was most treasured by Lillian Ann Collier (nee Lillian Manton) – my Great Aunt – until her death at 93 years in 1981. Her description of her life and times was recorded by me on an audio tape shortly before she died. In retrospect we evacuated not once but numbers of times during the six years of conflict. With war inevitable, between June and September 1939 it was estimated over 3,500,000 (out of a U.K. population of, what, 40 million?) became displaced persons, evacuated from their many broken, homes – to designated places of safety. No home. Evacuee, for years to come. Alone.

On the outbreak of war, September 1st, formal mass evacuation of mothers, teachers, children and mobile-sick began out of London and most major cities. My mother and family members are not quite certain whether it was the end of August or 1st of September (which was a Friday) when we first left North London for Northampton. Whatever departure date, by early 1940 along with four out of every ten children and escorts we returned home utterly homesick.

On arrival at our destination in Northampton, landlord and landlady billeters were only expected to provide lodgings paid for out of national funding at a cost of five shillings per adult and three shillings per child (11/- for my mother, my brother and me) which paid rent but not keep. Inevitably, stranded families became dependent on the charity and tolerance of billeters and their community – or became reliant on out-relief food tickets etc., issued by the relieving officer working under the guidance of the *Public Assistance Committee.*

I have very few infant memories of that second evacuation to Northampton. One was being knocked over by a bicycle outside the nursery school my brother and I attended, whilst mother went off part-time charring, whatever, to earn a few shillings. And I have a distinct memory of a meal of sugar-covered doorsteps of bread, mother walking us away from our lodgings, fast, my brother and I crying out – and very confused.

'Come on. Come on boys.' I recollect her saying, our sack or pillow-case full of toys and building-bricks left behind and hanging on a hook by the door. We pleaded with mother to go back and collect them, but we never returned. Years later attempting to relate that time with Mother she said that it was about the time she finally split with my father – and she was flat broke. She returned to Hackney in London with us and took up the offer of a job at Lil's café in Shrubland Road E8.

Anderson Shelter, 1940

In the Blitz, 1940-41. Sat on an Anderson shelter, is my cousin, Marion Creagh, and her watching mother, Dilly, at 29 Wall Street, N1. A row of houses opposite had been recently destroyed by Blitz, in Islington.

1941 – 42 – Homerton E8

I was just three years of age (brother eighteen months younger), and on our return, from Northampton to London, bombed out by the Blitz, and homeless, in 1941 we lodged with relatives (over the Homerton bus garage), in London Fields, and belonging to Aunt Lil's London Transport Café. I recall elephantine barrage-balloons, hoisted puppet-like kites, upon visible thick wires, and all attached to stationary vehicles on the adjacent London Fields. And as an infant, I recall the numerous large mounted, circular, turning searchlights, resembling mammoth front bicycle lamps. There were erected tents on the green and trenches! In front of numerous buildings piles of sandbags. And especially the heavily boarded up buildings and shop fronts, bombed sites, ditches and piles of rubble and dirty puddle holes. And most, the sheer weight of noise, army lorries, tanks, cars, buses and trams. Mother recalls occasionally one event whereupon she lost sight of me on a visit to a relative in Wall Street. And I was spotted around the corner sitting upon a tramline with an oncoming No. 33 tram, singing 'Roll out the Barrel'. That was in 1940, and highlighted the fact that, like many children, I was prone to wander off to explore surroundings (during the wartime blitz) at the slightest opportunity.

Of Lil's Café [1], I have few recollections, except (for some reason) Swiss rolls, playing with kittens and being told I was to go off somewhere (to Hounslow). Mother says I fell into a nearby pond and contracted yellow jaundice. My infant brother and I developed impetigo (ugh!), that awful crust on my face, and yellow iodine treatment. My bro had his head shaved about this time, and taken away into hospital. We were separated. Time passed before, alone, I was again transferred, and evacuated, out of central London – to Heston and Hounslow Middlesex.

After we had returned – for the second time – from evacuation in Northampton, in 1940 – we moved back to heavy blitz-raids on East London. The last major Luftwaffe raid over London (and the provinces) was on 10th May 1941 – Hitler then invading the USSR.

My mother, brother and I (as infants), recall moving to Hackney, E8, rendered homeless by the incendiary bombs in 1940. As harrowing as it was about East London with the heavy bombing raids, my mother would not, in the future, ever want to talk about those devastating times we had in the East End of London, where we remained till 1942. Not until Spring of 1944, and the awful spate of incoming *flying bombs*, when England itself again experienced Nazi warfare, and be under threat of invasion across the moat of the Channel.

Heston

Evacuated yet again (third or fourth time), now mid-1942. One of my mother's three sisters, the youngest, Olive Manton, became a Land Army volunteer and was already billeted with the Esau family in 37 Church Road, Heston at Hounslow, Middlesex, at the western periphery off the Great Western Road out of London. And Aunt Maude (as I called her) Esau and family kindly took me in too, as an evacuee, to be fostered out of central London (especially since bombed out we were homeless!), but *not* with my infant brother who for a while stayed with mother. Indeed, except for our Manton grandparents own tiny terraced house at 2 Baxter Grove in Islington. The small, terrace buildings, where my mother was born, were original brick-makers' cottages, when London was growing in the late 18th and early 19th century. Much of Islington, thereabouts, wet watercress fields, as my Great Aunt Lil recalled from her own mothers' (died 1902) words...We had no formal fixed abode (was displaced, nor would we have a home, for many years).

Mother, on leaving the café, became a wartime bus conductress for London Transport, based at Homerton E8; and subsequently worked with 'Bill' her happy-go-lucky bus driver colleague (sadly long deceased), with whom she shared numerous close encounters during the air raid bombings. I remember Bill (and his family) with great affection – and the silver sixpenny bits he occasionally deposited in my palm when we visited the garage for mother to pay in her fares.

LEFT: My mother, a new bus conductor, 1942. RIGHT: London Transport Staff group, 1943

(Source: Author)

Conscription

My mother, then, Maude Hopper (nee Manton) age 28 years, became a London Transport bus conductor (aka clippie). The London Transport staff group posed outside her bus, at East End, Homerton E8 bus depot: the snapshots were taken in 1943. Mother is second left and Bill her driver, end right... Their bus route, for sometime, was Route 22; from Homerton, to Putney, in West London, via Piccadilly, and through the ruins, in the waste of the Blitz, 1943.

The early days of the war soon took away all the male members of the extended family on my mothers' side. This included all her brothers, cousins – at home, and overseas at the then British Empire; Australia, New Zealand, and Canada – to be specific. I learnt little from my always very embittered mother of my father, who returned from America in 1935. At one time, I did hear that, apart from his performances in night clubs, vaudeville, etc., he had been a member of ENSA – though I learnt little else about him (other than via my mother) and, his days during the war, in England.

About October 1941, our country formally demanded that all its female population (19 to 51 years old) who had already replaced their conscripted menfolk, be themselves formally registered, conscripted to serve in auxiliary, agricultural, or industry and essential public transport. Though women recruited into the armed forces were *not* expected to formally be engaged in battle conditions.

Exceptions to the rule of female conscription included those dependants who were ill, pregnant or singularly with young children – under five years old. Thus, if possible, mother-and-children should not be separated – unless unavoidable – till after they reached five years old (so I understand), the child could then be separated, and sent away in evacuation and fostered – at home – or abroad. And so I, as the eldest, born in 1937, was evacuated on reaching my fifth birthday out of Central London; but my bro, born 1938, though spending some time in London hospitals, would not be formally eligible till 1943 – when he, too, was evacuated out of blitzed London... and mother became a clippie.

My mother's younger sister was conscripted into the Land Army, but I was unclear about her other two sisters' formal roles on evacuation. I recall that the eldest sister born 1911 – and, former actress – with two young daughters, both older than me – too, were evacuated; initially along with mother, bro and I – away in 1939-1940... then '41 and '43 – until post-war in 1951.

London bus driver Bill was one of few adults I recollect in early childhood; with distant memories of my mother's parents. (Father's parents, any paternal relatives – never met them. They were, sadly, *totally* absent – out living somewhere in America, New Zealand, or unknown in New South Wales in Australia). Fond memories of 42-44, Land army 'girl' my Aunt Olive. And of course evacuee host, foster parent (aka Aunt) Maud Esau. And later 44-45 (with Orphanage) evacuee, billeted with foster parents The Rees family in South Wales. ... Until return of mother's brothers, unknown and unseen uncles, (indeed *all* family males except granddad, who was at the Somme in WW1) after WW2 ended. Mother's soldier bros, Len, Jim and Arthur were always good to us after their return but, mostly away overseas, throughout the war and indeed some-time after it ended. But like an occasional tuft of grass or wild flower, I continued to grow (a little) among the bomb damaged waste, brown sites.

Just five, on arrival in 1942 at Hounslow, I settled in at the three-bedroomed semi-detached house of the Esau family. They were fine caring folk from the outset, with two adults, Aunt Maude and Aunt Olive; Maude's three children,

Roy (12 years), Len (10 years) Jimmy (6 years); and the cuckoo in the nest myself the youngest (5 years old). The new evacuation at five years old and I was more aware of surroundings, and the continuous comings-and-goings of people around me. Since this frequent displacing of myself, had become the 'norm' for me, there was nothing to question. No apparent injustice. No inflicted pains. Indeed, because I was treated so kindly by the host family, in memory it was to be one of the only, few, really happy memories of an entire wartime and post-war childhood.

To a small five-year-old boy the Esaus' garden appeared long, large and well cultivated with a builders' yard over the fence at the rear of the garden. A large rhubarb patch was located near the bottom of the garden. Aunt Maude said it can be 'Your own garden patch' – and so the immense large rhubarb leaves appeared able to hide me, underneath its bower; just a naive young child turning its back, placing hands over his eyes and convinced no-one, no-thing, could see them. Independence. The sight of a cat blithely turning its rear and dismissing the world behind it. Reality ever far far greater than the blinkered eyes of a young child – or free-agent cat. Even beyond the war.

London, its close suburbs and the south, and big cities, continued to be bombed on occasions but mostly it was the regular dog-fights of fighters overhead which spewed wreckage and hot, bright sharp pieces of shrapnel about the roads and gardens. After every raid we young children would scour for spent brass bullet cases and pieces of still warm, jagged silver metal shrapnel – there must have been many a bleeding finger resulting from this regular child pursuit.

Yanks

I have zero infant memories of Christmas time; until five or six years old, 1942–43; as an evacuee. All male members of the family, were stationed abroad on active service.

I have one most pleasant Xmas memory; it must have been either in 1942 or 1943. We were at Heston, Hounslow in West Middlesex (later, identified as Great, West London). The food was bland and scarce, but I recall with affection two Xmas presents from American Troops, stationed nearby on our bleak, but stubborn, island aerodrome for Europe.

These unexpected gifts from the Yanks to us boys (no girls in family) were homemade of plywood and other khaki green wood; a largish tank (I was very small for my age) with a gun turret and everything. Most memorable was a gun with noisy wooden ratchets that, as you fired, clacked loudly as the underside turned with a handle, and engaged. It was a toy replica 'Tommy' gun, as seen in American gangster films during the 1930s and 1940s. A brief but fond memory of unknown, unseen Yankee servicemen, in 1943.

Morrison

Morrison Shelter, c.1942 (Source: *PA Images*)

Instructions were given to us children – '*If you hear the siren go, get out of bed and get under it, until I come to you*', which we did each time – and it was frequent enough an exercise. And, collected, we would troop downstairs, into a *Morrison* cage, an indoor heavy iron shelter in their front room. A bit like a coffin, or cocoon.

One vivid night of gunfights and routine bombings we went to the doorway and I was held in someone's arms looking up. Unafraid and wondering, quite excited. I shouted, 'Look. Look. Someone's bailing out.' And sure enough against the crossing pathways of bright searchlights, probing the high skies over the Hounslow district, we saw one, possibly two parachutists floating down – we had no way of knowing whether they were friends or enemy. As ever after crashes or bombing raids it was not just wondering of where (and who) caught the latest possible carnage and, inevitable damage, broken windows, whatever – but the awful prevailing noxious smells that mostly emanated from holes in the road–and roped off with warnings. There was an airfield nearby, Heston, which accounted for much of the local wartime activity and the searchlights source. And several times we visited the site, peering through the coils of barbed wire on its periphery of the aircraft and crews coming and going activities.

In mid-1942 I was five years old and started infant school after being evacuated to Heston, from central London (my bro was too young and had developed impetigo but on recovery was evacuated up to Yorkshire about 1943). My first school teacher was a Miss Fish (I think). I recollect the camp beds daily put out in the playground and our regular inflicted naps under single red Red Cross woolly blankets in the early afternoon. We were given a one-third pint of milk per day. Hence, one could be privileged to be called a Milk Monitor. As an infant, I attended their religious knowledge Sunday school. Though, the Germans included Sundays in their seven day week's raids. On leaving the playground if one had a penny to spend delicious hot potatoes (aka murphies) could be purchased off a vendor selling outside the school grounds. And occasional visits to the local indoor swimming pool; which is all I recollect of that small Heston Infant School in 1942-44.

The fostering Esau family included me in all their games and I gained some self-confidence. They also had billeted my mother's younger sister Olive Manton who was employed as a Land Army girl on a local farm. Together we visited the kind Esaus' relatives, grandparents – and, with my aunt, I briefly visited my mother and our relatives. (All, and it was all, the menfolk, except my grandfather who was too old, were away overseas on active service in H.M. Forces.) But it was, for me, a happy time. (For a short time I belonged ... though it was not to be for long.) And conscious privileges began. I was allowed to stay up and listen to the radio comedy show I.T.M.A., and hear of the delightfully silly adult antics of Tommy Handley and his radio crew. But, change was again due to occur. And in early 1944 the man of the house returned from active naval service and it was stated that I could not stay in this billet – alternative accommodation had to be found. Only one unfortunate memory occurred. I must have been six years old, approaching seven. This huge man in naval uniform demanded that I tie my shoes up (they were boots in those days) – and I couldn't. And tears of fear, confusion and frustration arose – and I suffered a loss of confidence. This was no way his fault. But it pre-empted a drastic remedy.

The Esau family.

I was taken to be medically examined, in 1943–4, at one time in the glare of sun ray lamps (with glasses on) with other little boys and girls. They were two separate events, but child memories relate them together. And it was the prelude to being transferred to a charitable baptist, Spurgeon's Orphan Home at Reigate in Surrey. (Years later mother told me that her employers, the London Transport staff at Homerton in the East End, had been very helpful in her obtaining this final placement.) The husband, a discharged returning sailor, later changed his mind, but mother would take no chances and into the large children's wartime Institution I departed – to my chagrin. What had I done wrong? And so once again I was moved – to my total bewilderment. One of the first outside 'visits' that I would make in 1951–52, and afterwards, was to the kind Esau's, and their back garden.

Institution

Early in 1944 mother escorted me from Heston up to London Victoria Station, and then by train south to Reigate Station in Surrey. As we walked across nearby Holmsdale Road from the railway station , and crossed over into another road, which turned and sloped downward, marked by a busy dairy with horses and carts amid a cacophony of cranking machines, noisy vehicles, defecating harnessed horses and hundreds of rattling echoing glass-filled and empty milk-bottles. Mother and I proceeded down the sloping residential area.[2] At the bottom of the road I saw over a long wooden fence, and through a thick lattice of trees, into a large green field. I was just turned seven years old, and being displaced once again.

A small wooden-gate came into view, uniform with the drab-black creosoted overlapping wooden-struts, this situated at the bottom of a descending road[3] where, in a T-junction, Oak Road crossed its end. As we crossed this adjoining bottom road, and entered a small gate, (mother must have visited before), I entered an enclosed-world I was not to leave for seven long years – through most of boyhood. Small wonder memories, most unhappy, were etched deep on my reception into these Homes. It was in trusting total bewilderment I was then taken around the outskirts of the grounds, a football pitch one large segment. Boys dressed in short grey trousers and white shirts with sleeves rolled up to the elbows, and wearing black boots were chasing each other about a large tree-lined green football field.

A number of buildings came into view; on our right a complex of long low pre-fabricated huts and a concrete courtyard with a low red-brick wall on its periphery. At the top of this field a large – as I remember it – gothic building, with three cedars in front partially hiding it, came into view. Adjacent to this field, known as the Boys' Side, was another large green field – the Girls' Side – separated at some distance, by a pathway and a slight slope with a number of large trees. Another very large building appeared to take up the whole of that top end, and this edifice was white as opposed to the red-brick of the Boys' Side. A sports pavilion could be seen at the very far end, nearby the tall white building and some distance from it, over on the Girls' Side. I learnt the Gothic-like building (in fact, Georgian), called The Dingle; a white building St. David's;[4] and the low buildings simply known as The Huts.

We entered the front entrance of The Dingle after crossing a narrow internal road, and were taken up a grand flight of stairs to meet the Matron in charge. Significantly I remember first being shown around the five dormitories on the upstairs floor, with two small bathrooms boxed between the fourth and fifth large rooms. Boys slept in order of their birth dates and as one of the youngest in the block I was to sleep in the youngest dormitory. The beds were symmetrically lined around the room a small locker adjacent to each bed. The floor was well polished, unmarked by any specks of dust. Each bed had a uniform clean green counterpane with a circular motif engrained 'Spurgeon's Orphan Homes'. Matron said every child must remake his bed in the morning, clean his own bedspace and have both inspected by the staff member in charge. In addition, each child had an allocated pre-breakfast chore which had to be checked before he was allowed to go. This job changed each new school term, a duty list posted on a notice-board on the upper landing. Time to get up was at 6.45a.m. and get up you had to, or it meant trouble!

I cried after mother left and on many then-to-be future visiting days. Come the morning I was let off any chores as time was needed to settle in. I was informed that because of the large number of children it was convenient for the staff to designate each child with a number, and this would be formally stitched onto each personal article of clothing and advisably marked on all other personal effects. I have forgotten my very first number but remember all other numbers from a year later onwards.

Air Raid

Very soon after entering the Homes, I was on the way back from the dining room, to The Dingle when the air-raid siren went. We were given instructions to head directly for the shelters which were the cellar rooms beneath the main Dingle building block. A tattered curtain hung over the downstairs doorway so you could enter it from outside – or from stairs within the main block. I was already now used to this instruction and followed other boys and staff. But, being so close to the North Downs and coastland, dog-fights[5] were quite common and earlier in the war a number of bombs had fallen in the dell close by at the rear of 'The Dingle'. If any alien aircraft were flying overhead, wherever anyone was outside, boys were to throw themselves prone onto the ground. And, if inside a building, one was to hide under the nearest solid-table; again a most familiar instruction. As a young boy I had only war-time memories.

About this time strange whining aircraft would periodically pass overhead. From our ground view, they looked rather like silver sausages. One time a number of lads and myself had just been given some doorsteps (thick bread) and dripping by Mr. Fox, the cook, and re-entered The Yard when we heard one of these German aircraft come up from the south and, standing on garden seats in the yard, we watched it pass directly overhead with its loud staccato noise, and just as it began to pass out of our vision the noise stopped abruptly and after a slight pause, it fell – we all held breath – and a muffled explosion was distinctly heard, landing out of vision.

Big Bertha (howitzer) WW1-like fired shells, drones of the long-range, V2 rocket bomb's effects, were self-evident. Nazi Germany was also exploring the power of nuclear energy, and explosives, placed in warheads of those rocket bombs. They had yet to construct and deliver the full prospects of such terrible destructive powers – in the head of their rocket missiles. Whereas, in the USA, with British collusion, this impossible bomb, The Bomb, was soon to happen. Thankfully, even as I looked up into those then Surrey skies in the orphanage, the June 6th 1944 D Day allied invasion of France subsequently eliminated the sites from where these V2 rockets were dispatched.

A Spring day in 1944 (before evacuation): after gazing up at a noisy airplane-duel dog-fight over the nearby North Downs hills, three of us small boys, standing on a mound of soft clay (which we prized for a plasticine), looked across a *ha-ha* trench, over our home's perimeter fence, across to Oak Road, and beyond over a similar wooden palisade into another enclosed space, where an abundance of loud happy infants' laughter could be heard. They could *not* see it, for they were in, as a raised board faced Oak Road across from us advertised, an enclosed *Sunshine Home For Blind Children*. Together, we three six and seven year olds, estranged by war, lived and survived in institutions, and did not yet know the word. Equally unknown to us, those anonymous blind children and ourselves, were each other's realities. Since separating from my mother, we rarely saw her in the early years; but in the postwar years my bro and I saw her for one Saturday afternoon per calendar month (missing one from time to time) called (as in all institutions) Visiting Day. Each Sunday after morning church we were instructed to write a letter to someone, a relative if we had one. But we did not personally know our mother's address, only that it was somewhere in north London. The carers had possession of such details.

Blind children, during an air-raid, guided by an attached rope, frozen posture, into a downstairs shelter. Source, picture by unknown (not stated) photographer, for 'The Sunday Pictorial' (nd) but probably 1943. Taken from 'The War's Best Photographs', published by Odham's Press Ltd (nd), content suggests 1943.

The Yard

The concrete Yard, adjacent to the Huts, was a focal point for much of our play and formal meet routines. On completing early ablution, pre-breakfast chores, and on passing inspection, I was allowed to gravitate to the Yard, where we were all expected to congregate prior to meals. On the ringing of a handbell we formed up in respective table groups the junior boys over one side of the Yard – and the seniors another. Adjacent to this yard were residential Huts – two low huts, asbestos roofed, for older boys accommodation. Another hut housed two dining rooms and kitchen areas – divided by a partition and door; juniors to one side and senior boys the other. Off centre the dining rooms, were the kitchen and massive sink units. Mr. Fox, was the cook in those days, a stout affable gentleman, whose specialities, to most of us boys, was door-step lashings of bread and dripping and, especially popular, dark raisin-filled soft bread-pudding.

When the hand-bell rang juniors from The Dingle and seniors from the other two dormitory huts would form up in table groups on the yard. The table monitor checked all members were present. Elected table monitors were favoured for when 'second helpings' were called out, and they were allowed to be first in line at the serving tables. But, after we met in formation within the yard, a rigid silence was expected, except for the monitors who would report any obvious absences to the housemaster, in charge at that time. On command continuing in silence, each table group joined a single crocodile line and marched around the outside of the dining room hut. Any offenders misbehaving were either denied second helpings, or worse, would rendezvous outside 'The Office' for a possible caning, telling off, or a gating, depending on the degree of the offence, and the reasons why.

On entering the dining room we had to stand, each behind his chair. All entered, and everyone in the room still and silent, no clattering of utensils, or chattering of eager tongues, and the duty-master would say Grace. We would then sit down until permission was given to each table, then each individual, to collect their fare. Individuals would then join another orderly line to say 'yes' or 'no' to the proffered food items. Again discipline was very strict in those days, and even as a newcomer one soon picked up the social mores quickly – or suffered accordingly.

It was fearful at times, but respect for rules was paramount. The boys' voluntary help was never relied upon to back up matron and masters or cook and engineers, so detailed chores reached all levels. Boys took their turn – especially for the most unpopular tasks in the winter months (but more of this later): washing-up for a small family is one thing, but for upwards of one hundred-plus boys was something else, and after the meal washers-up trailed into the kitchen amid piping hot water.

The furniture and utensils were basic: well-worn wooden tables and splintered wooden-forms, chipped aluminium-mugs and plates. After the war, and sometime later, all of these items would be replaced by a superior quality – much ironically to occasional chagrin; the boys having to polish the chairs on Saturday mornings (a most unpopular task). Splinters in nasty places were a common feature and numerous visitations to the Homes' nurse would result.

Memories are sharp in places, woolly others, but whatever reason (wartime austerity or otherwise), when breakfast cereal appeared with a deficiency of milk, many of us would make for the tea urn to wet the cornflakes. Second helpings were not common, and for certain dishes a personal aversion to fat-on-meat and cabbage-greens ensured I would not be inexperienced in going hungry – for many years remaining a pithy eater.

Food-times, house-rules, and bed-times were soon assimilated, and as new boy I attached myself to new routines. But yet again moves were imminent.

One of those last nights was interrupted by the air-raid siren, and routinely we got out of bed and hastened downstairs into the shelter of the cellar below the Dingle. As we huddled in blankets, the thin hanging curtain at the entrance would, time and again, be lit up by patterns of flash white lightning cast from behind it. And often accompanied by very the loud noise of gunfire batteries from the nearby North Downs Surrey hills. A lady downstairs with us kindly read 'Sunny Stories' by Enid Blyton to the youngest of us children whilst casting occasional anxious glances at the curtain.

South Wales

The Homes had its own residential primary school attached to St. David's, but I recollect nothing of it prior to the next evacuation. Again, very much bewildered, I was one of a large troop of children, soon seen, marching up Holmsdale Road[6] to the railway station. Each of us had an obligatory cardboard box slung over our shoulder with the musty smelling, sticky, black rubber gas mask inside. And on our back a small brown cloth haversack with meagre belongings inside. As we waited on the station platform, a long troop train passed by, its troops leaning out of their windows and waving, cheering at us kids waiting, for our own train, to take us .... where?

We finally arrived in south Wales in the Swansea Valley. As a member of one small group of boys, I recollect sitting forlornly in what must have been a church hall reception centre. A strange woman offered to take me to her family. Her name was Mrs. Rees; she had a husband a coal miner, and a daughter near to my own age, called Joan. They were good, kind, coal-mining folk, and I have pleasant memories of this Welsh family. Of home-made blackberry pies, long exploratory walks in the nearby green hills, discovering the taste of hazel nuts. And of sheep and more sheep, and tales of foxes galore, with wool-fur stuck to fences and supposed dead-sheep given as evidence.

As small townee evacuees we were easy meat to the local bully-boys; few of whom spoke English. I remember two then orphan friends, named Johnny and Philip – the former was certainly with us at Godrergraig. We travelled to a makeshift school at Ystalyfera on the local bus, but I believe we learnt nothing of value, for it was but filling-time-in, till our eventual return to Reigate. The local bullies would sometimes waylay us, but mostly they would wait until we were found playing around the coal mine tips. On one awful occasion two of us were seized by a gang of teenage (or older?) youths, and I being the smallest (seven-years old) was tied up and terrified. I recall being held over a trench of sorts full of tall stinging nettles and, being manhandled, was bullied and, as I could not understand the big boys, I was rendered totally helpless. But rescue was at hand as the generated raucous noise had alerted nearby neighbours whose houses were adjacent to the tips and the waste ground – the Welsh gang of taunting youths fled as help arrived. That was my first (for a while) memorable experience of being bullied by other children. (Odd, later on, back in the Homes I recall going to and fro the orphanage primary school, and playfully throwing myself into holly bushes – but no way would I challenge any nasty stinging nettles.)

The tips at the top of the Godrergraig road I was billeted in were a low range of hills adjacent to a meandering river Tawe on one side and green scrubland on the other, whereon sheep and cows would be grazing. These low hills to us small children were great fun, and the numerous beautiful coloured stones spread around would sometimes be collected by us. As a townee evacuee, I really had no idea that the tips were coal tips, or if told, it had no meaning. When, some months later, we finally left South Wales, I vividly recall secreting one of these very precious stones with lots of colours in a shirt pocket, only for it to mysteriously disappear. It was to be many, many years later, into adulthood, before this memorised fact clicked. So too, when I would read D.H. Lawrence's *Sons and Lovers* for GCE A' level studies as an adult student some twenty-five years later, memories again became vivid of this coal mining area in Wales during the war in 1944–45.

Mr. Rees would return from work, truly blackened, and be scrubbed in a tin bath, the same dull metal bath that we all used. The colliery was not too far away and the large wheels were quite visible from the house. But coal mine or not, I remember, as a small boy, the sheer beauty of it all – a valley in a valley; for we would, on getting off the bus on the main road, literally descend down a winding pathway, part (on one route) graveyard, and down onto the home road, which had a farm at one end where we obtained milk.

As evacuees and 'foreigners' for us, most locals spoke a strange language, and we felt ourselves as *intruders* despite the kind hospitality of our fostering hosts. This was noticeable when Christmas 1944 came for several of us went carol singing to earn a few pennies–which is what we received. Puzzled why we gained little enthusiastic response, it became clear when we attended the local church – and couldn't understand a word spoken, or rather sung. Sat at the back, we remained I think unnoticed, and just waited till we were allowed to go – as children do. I vaguely recollect we sneaked away before its end.

We evacuees stuck together, and during our stay in Wales we became for a while close friends (especially Phil, Johnny and I). Adventures were not infrequent, culminating in one or other of us getting into some bother. One time, four of us were climbing over the roof of a deserted building; three of us descended safely but not so Johnny, who slipped down the drainpipe into a barrel of tar, and into one helluva ruckus. Another: two of us were out fishing in the river Tawe with a small net and a stringed jam-jar, when on our return I took a short-cut and sank deep into what I believed was quicksand (probably mud). I was terrified but luckily escaped through someone pulling me out like a cork. I received a real scolding on my return; but, eventually, a marvellous slice of pie soon put the experience at bay.

Reigate

Our return to Reigate was another sudden move. Again bewilderment, this time joining many hundreds of other children also returning from evacuation. En route, we were put up in a large school in Reading. Blankets were spread on the floor throughout the classrooms–desks stacked to the sides. Amusing to recall, but not so at the time, a bucket was placed in the corner for urination, and some idiot kicked it over. More so, a little boy–small compared to my seven years–crying and upset laying nearby me, suddenly stood up and pointedly wet his surrounds, to our consternation. All was utter confusion to our scrabbled group, with people, strangers, calling out for this and that, belongings and children getting lost. And at the railway station, what seemed thousands of servicemen, inter-mingling ladies, carrying buckets with tea and paper cups, calling out their mission. And noise, lots and lots of confusing noise.

We finally returned to the orphanage in Reigate early in 1945. Thoughtfully, close by the gatehouse in Holmsdale Road, a bunting was hoisted, welcoming our return from evacuation in Wales. Not yet eight years old (we returned early in January or early February for I was eight on the 27th – and remember my cards being placed on a mantelpiece), we were placed in a small dormitory over in St. David's; the only boys temporarily resident over the Girls' Side – I think about a dozen of us. Two doors led into our dormitory, one a passage door leading to toilets, a bathroom and a downward flight of stairs and the exit.

The other door remained firmly locked – girls' dormitories lay on the other side. Young as we were, they were still forbidden fruit; contact as only permissible in the residential school, or from a distance as in the chapel on Sunday afternoons. Senior boys (over twelve) and girls inevitably arranged clandestine meetings, but innocent no less.

In St David's, my identity again submerged, I was given my new allocated number – 72. And all my institutional clothes (no clothes from outside), personal effects – and tuck – were marked thus. The personal so-called prefix, my first name – aka Christian name – was seldom stated by authority. All houses and huts had a tuck-box or basket, wherein sweets, cakes and preserves usually sent by guardians, friends or relatives, were marked with the recipient's number and–usually once per day – a staff member would call out 'Tuck!'–and the highlight of the day arrived. On the whole, memory informs me discipline at St. David's was slightly less rigid than over at The Dingle; but understandable when considering the age range and quantity of young children. One memorable episode comes to me clearly after thirty-five years distance (written c.1980). One of the boys had been caught swearing, I think at the house-parent, having been warned several times of the dire consequence if this continued, he again swore. We boys were all called together to witness his due punishment.

Congregated in the hallway just outside the dormitory, the house-mother brought a bucket of warm water and a bar of soap–carbolic soap. 'This is what happens if you insist on using foul language. Your mouth will be cleaned with carbolic soap!' Under protest the offending boy had his mouth scrubbed with the soap by the lady, over the bucket. We watched with the usual mixed feelings of awe, fear and respect. No way did we feel the act as cruel – it was just part of accepted effective discipline.

The war had not quite ceased and occasionally came a curt reminder. Due to austere circumstances mother had not been able to visit as often as she wished. But following our return from Wales she attended most, once per calendar month, visiting days. Visiting day was on Saturday afternoon – I think the first of the month.

The Surrey branch of the beautiful chalky North Downs hills was so closely sited to The Homes that it was its backcloth. The Downs, well pitted with gun emplacements and numerous fallen, broken aircraft, now enwombed in the ancient polyps. As young boys we were allowed to walk up onto these Downs, though much was encased in tangled rusty barbed-wire fencing and would remain so for years to come. Watched over by dutiful staff we eagerly prodded amongst green tufts and broken chalk for spent .303 bullet cases, these empty brass carcases found in their thousands above the towns of Reigate, Redhill and Dorking.

On visiting days early through 1945 and post-war years, mother took my bro and me on the green 414 bus to Dorking, to visit cousins for tea. On several earlier occasions I had watched aircraft dog-fights over these same Downs at Dorking. In the main, except for an occasional visit to the local Majestic cinema in Reigate, visits to relatives would be the only 'outside' contact till I attended Reigate Grammar School for the last two years. February 1945, and I celebrated an eighth birthday in St. David's and, placed a few cards upon the dormitory mantelpiece. I could already *only* recall a brief lifetime of being in care (knowing no difference), and initially under the charge of one new strange person (not mother) after another–and knowing by experience no different. So too, at this juncture, only of wartime memories since I was too young an infant to recall anything of pre-war years. Yet there would be many more years to pass in care.

A Brother

It was at St. David's, in 1945, while attending a residential school lesson, instructed by our Dr Holt. Dr Holt (or was it Dr Green) had been a personal friend of the American singer Paul Robeson. I was called upstairs to see the Homes Superintendent, Dr Green. Outside his office, in trepidation, I was reassured in confidence by somebody: "It's all right. You have a pleasant surprise in store for you". On entering the room I was delighted to see my mother and, beside Dr Green, also seated, was a small fair haired little boy–a stranger to me. "This is your brother". Astounded, I was told he had been evacuated up to someplace called Upper Denby in Yorkshire, when I was first fostered out to Heston in Middlesex from central London. But in one sense this dramatic introduction was short-lived when he was then placed down the road to the infants' home (he was six or seven years old) called Brooklands,[7] an adjunct of Spurgeon's Homes, of which I knew nothing by experience. For a while we would only meet on subsequent visiting days. It was most bewildering.

Years later, Emil told me how he learnt to read and write, using a black tablet slate and chalk; schooled as an infant in the sports pavilion, near the building of St. David's. And we – close as we became in time – as adults puzzled how we learnt to read and write, but were unable to tell the time at seven years old.

Later in 1945, my brother and I were collected by my mother and taken up to London. We stayed in a small box-room of our grandparents in No. 2 Baxter Grove, Wall Street, Islington – now long demolished and replaced by tower-block giants as housing progress. We were re-introduced to our former home at 1, Baxter Grove at the top of The Grove – a bombed ruin demolished by an incendiary. We rummaged pitifully amongst broken bricks for relics, but already time had erased any conscious memories of this, our one-time abode when we had two parents.

Hiroshima 1945

Morning of July 16th 1945, at Los Alamos, New Mexico in North America, the secret Manhattan Project (aka 'The Gadget'), culminated in the world's first recorded atomic explosion. Within days, US President Truman agreed to use the A Bomb on the Japanese military base of Hiroshima.

The second designated A Bomb was exploded on Monday, August 6th 1945, on the city of Hiroshima: the first on a densely populated city.

The following day, the London *Daily Express* front page on Tuesday, August 7th 1945, headlined:

> *Smoke hides city 16 hours after greatest secret weapon strikes.*
> *The Bomb That Has Changed The World. Japs told 'Now*
> *Quit'. 20,000 tons in a golf ball...'*

Giles Cartoon, *Daily Express,* August 8th, 1945.

That awful, but so true, tawdry fog of war was manifest no comparison with the ongoing, soon smog of 1950s London. That sulphur mote smoke, hiding our London in 1952... The A Bomb had yet to unfold with its awful aftermath of atomic fallout, radioactive, black rain; storms to follow... and, atomic disease... Atomic Bombs would hereafter have no *Clean Air Act* – ever, to erase the horrors to come.

The *Daily Mail* headlined on its front page, on Wednesday August 8th 1945:

> *"ATOMIC BOMB: 1a.m. cable gives first eyewitness stories
> – City of 300,000 vanished in vast ball of fire... Hiroshima,
> Japanese city of 300,000 people, ceased to exist at 9:15am
> on Monday Morning..."*

The *News Chronicle*, Wednesday August 8 1945, front page headline, said:

> *"Hiroshima disappeared in cloud, boiling smoke and flame.
> Pilot tells what happened when Atomic Bomb fell. Last allied
> warning: Yield, or we lay Japan waste... More Atom Bombers
> to take off... (World scientists foresee new era Rockets that
> may go round the moon)..."*

Despite the enormity of that first bomb – and its dire warning to the government of Japan; the military and its head, Emperor Hirohito – Japan was *not* convinced of the war's end. One infamous Japanese general declared never-to-surrender; better that one hundred million Japanese people died, rather than submit to the Allied forces. But, the Emperor did *not* endorse that suggestion.

Meanwhile, the nearby Russian armies, only seven hundred miles away, were on standby to invade Japan (nominally to support ending the war – the USSR had triumphed in Berlin, and Germany, and moved legions of troops eastwards to occupy Mongolia and the eastern ports of Asia).

And, on Thursday, August 9th 1945, another atomic bomb was dropped, on a nearby city, Nagasaki. The Emperor Hirohito cried 'Enough!' to his defiant Generals, and agreed to surrender to the allies – the USA, in particular. He, a God, his word Law. He agreed to a surrender on August 14th, 1945

But, not surprising, the Allied press would *not* be informed till *after* the awesome second A bomb explosion. And, awaiting the outcome of the Hiroshima event, the *Daily Mail* (in those days a large broadsheet), Thursday August 9th, 1945 ran the front page headline:

> "*'All over within a week' says Washington, Russia in: The Final Ultimatum To-Day. Truman to tell Tokyo 'Last chance to escape annihilation'. From James Brough, Daily Mail correspondent – New York, Wednesday Night.*"

The awesome second atomic bomb explosion on a substantial human population was at Nagasaki on August 9th 1945. And so, eventually, the Emperor Hirohito and his Empire of Japan agreed to an Unconditional Surrender to the Allies, the Americans in particular, on August 14th, and formally accepted on September 2nd 1945, on board the *USS Missouri*, signed... to be known as VJ day – which as a young child in our English orphanage, I recall local celebrations...

However. The *Daily Mail*, on Thursday August 9th 1945, had *not* yet heard about Nagasaki. But, to reassure (what very few people could be aware of), that any subsequent radioactive fallout was little, and harmless; an hygienic, 'clean', though huge, atomic bomb. This was recorded on the back page of (that) *Daily Mail*: two paragraphs headed: "*A Death City for 70 years' - US denial. Washington, Wednesday – from Associated Press (AP) release.*"

'A DEATH CITY
FOR 70 YEARS'
U.S. denial

WASHINGTON, Wednesday. — The War Department to-night denied reports that the area devastated by the atom bomb could continue for 70 years to react with death-dealing radiation.

The Department quoted Dr. J. R. Oppenheimer, atomic scientist, as saying: " There is every reason to believe there was no appreciable radio activity on the ground at Hiroshima and what little there was decayed rapidly."—A.P.

Back page *Daily Mail*, Thursday August 9th, 1945.

The US press informant was Dr. J R Oppenheimer (1904–1967), the principal US nuclear physicist who had led the *Manhattan Project,* which preceded Hiroshima and Nagasaki atomic bomb explosions.

Oppenheimer predicted that *"There is every reason to believe there was no appreciable radioactivity on the ground at Hiroshima, and what little there was decayed rapidly"*. Oppenheimer was a firm advocate of the early A bombs, and nuclear power – but, after the true horrors emerged (and in the emergence of an immediate Cold War, intent on maximising atomic weapons' potential yields of destruction in the H bombs), like Albert Einstein, he became fervently anti-nuclear; but, an ungrateful US government branded him as pro-Communist, and broke the man – to whom they had previously owed so much.

Not apparent, at that time, in 1945, but the Allies and the USSR (both intent on their bigger and bigger stockpile, of atomic weapons of mass destruction) refused to recognise the devastation emerging, longterm human illnesses caused by the collective radioneucleotides in the atmosphere. They remained in total denial (nuclear energy was an enormous fiscal investment).

That boast of 300,000 killed at Hiroshima, *alone*... Well, in the next few decades, the USA *alone* ultimately killed, used as guinea pigs, thousands of its own people – always refusing to admit the pitfalls of blast and fallout, nuclear waste, etc... and, wasteland of the war. Officially, World War 2 concluded on this VJ day. Surrender by Japan in September 1945.

Broke, our country was inevitably bleak in 1945... My brother and I were still in the Surrey Orphanage, otherwise homeless. No change in *our* austere way of life – for us, or our relatives, recovering from the London Blitz years. It was time to clean up – at home and abroad. Life went on... meanwhile, austerity for many years to come...

Bro and I would remember that noisy night in Summer 1945 in the box-room, for years to come. It was VJ-day; whilst we lay in bed, and sweated, soaked in our perspiration, we listened to noise of fireworks and bonfires flashing firelight – replacing our already familiar boyhood memories of constant explosions and searchlights. One fire was lit at the bottom of our turning–on our own empty bomb site where we once lived – destroyed during the 1940 blitz. ..

We were to visit this our gran's household, at 2 Baxter Grove, Islington during occasional holidays from 1945 onwards. I recollect gas-mantles, the

penny slot-meter, the large round whitewashed washing-boiler and mangle in
the damp kitchen; granny's iron-tongs kept under the gas-grill ready for coiling
hair after it had been washed in the sink or aluminium tin-bath; and the outside
toilet with its thick wide wooden seat. Someone regularly walked to the Baxter
Arms pub at the corner of The Grove with a jug to collect stout. And Tiddles,
the black pussy cat which we would chase about the postage-stamp square
back yard, walled in by buildings on all four sides, framing a minute inner-
court. But most it was a tasting of affection and caring by relatives...

Unhappily, it was tasting only, for it only made the returns to The Homes
that much more painful to bear. And it was a *long,* long way away – in our
already normal other bleak world. Normal, simplified into that by which one
is already accustomed. But dreams of change would increase from this visit
onwards. Dreams of being re-united with mother (we had no recollections of
father whatever), and of being permanently amongst maternal nan and granddad
and uncles, aunts and cousins, whom we sometimes met on these excursions.
But, with war-poverty and austerity, this would not happen till we were almost
out of boyhood–and well into our teens.

Comics

Just before we returned from our now-dubbed London home to The Homes,
we were allowed to personally, collect our comics ; these child-magazines must
have been expensive, for years, once per month, delivery by mother on visiting
days at the orphanage. They included two complete sets (one for bro and one
for me) of *Dandy, Beano, Hotspur, Champion, Radio Fun* and *Wizard*. Favourite
for sometime was 'Rockfist Rogan' a wartime Spitfire pilot who figured in the
Champion; and 'Wilson' in *The Wizard*. ... Wilson was a super-hero athlete
who endured incredible physical hardships. Both Rogan and Wilson as heroes,
joined a little later by Captain Marvel, remained most enduring and along with
most comic characters represent a media education in ethics and morals. Good
versus bad; and a fighting for downtrodden underdogs, whether under the heel
of Fascist National Socialist totalitarian dictatorships or more insidious
bureaucratic uncaring administrators, the principle was the same.

Whilst resident at St. David's, one of a small group of boys based on the
Girls' Side, this seemed a stilled oasis in a desert of otherwise alien human
activity. For me, a bewildered eight-year old, guided herded amongst a flock

of almost two hundred children in a very large rambling building, itself situated in – to me – very large grounds. There were people I knew by name or passed around reputation, just one or two boys with whom I had been evacuated; but mostly I had no-one I felt safe to confide in – to direct any blatant questions towards. It is absolutely vital to a child in care to be able to gravitate to another genuine caring human-being. But, dealing with large numbers of children and inevitably legion administrative problems, quantitatively (let alone qualitatively) so few persons to handle us, many, many an aching problem and flowing tear passed wholly unnoticed for many if not most years. Exceptions mark new programmes of thought and experience.

One of the Homes visiting local school-teachers, Miss A.J. Barson was a most caring person who greatly encouraged my intellectual as well as emotional evolution. Education was introduced to me as an adventure. Dr Holt, the Homes' principal head teacher a doctor of music (and one time friend of Paul Robeson), passionate in the drawing arts similarly fed my lotus seed and for a while I drew modestly well gaining maximum marks of 'ten-out-of-ten plus-five'–which indicated a special merit. But after their departure with zero remembered encouragement this artistic skill wholly disappeared. The intense desire to learn and explore knowledge "in my own way" thus perpetuated. In effect I was introduced to an escape from total alienation and a stranded oasis in care, already frightened of bullies and heavy autocratic adults and unable to direct frustrations and most numerous questions, questions and more questions.

No. 72

I became moody in temperament, hot-headed – and, in short, a frightened little boy. But a seed of protest and rebellion was now firmly implanted within me. An outlaw in my brain if not demonstrated by so compliant a body. Number Seventy-Two would survive some way. Withdrawn inside. A few months passed and I transferred back to *The Dingle* with the middle age range – I think between nine and twelve years old. I returned upstairs to the younger group. Still we slept in birth-date order and graduated through the Homes' residences as older boys (and girls) left and others arrived. The war was over but immediate post-war years remained austere and discipline severe. For the first time I heard of boys who had run away from the Homes. 'What for?' was my first question; and 'Where to?'. If, as with my mother, you knew there was no-one in a position to care for you full-time or with a home and finance to accommodate your needs ... how or why? At that age I comprehended this as fact – hadn't a lifetime of movement already etched this lesson well enough upon my brain?

It was largely older boys absconding; dissenting, sometimes taking younger boys – perhaps brothers – in tow. I never heard of anyone who didn't return, or be brought back, even days later by the police or by some most angry hurt parent or guardian. For a while punishment was meted out to the bad offenders and after a caning administered by a senior staff member, a lecture followed. Then came the adventurous sometimes horrendous tales of the escapee's experiences in flight. In whispers within the dormitory–for you were forbidden to talk after lights-out – 'We climbed this tree when we saw this light coming up the hill. Thought it was the police.–Hid in a barn --Christ, it was cold–wet – and hungry. We gave ourselves up in the end. Had enough --' was typical of the remarks we received.

In later years I did contemplate running away, but being aware of the heartbreak it would cause my mother was itself sufficient a deterrent–since I could hardly run off to her or relatives. With no destination to go to, running for its own sake seemed blatantly absurd, so I ran inwards into my own hidden domain of dreams and hopes and childish aspirations. Alone.

Sick Bay

Not long after returning to 'The Dingle' I woke up (now in the third of five upper dormitories), my bed situated in the centre of the room. I awoke with the getting up bell and lights being switched on – and groaned aloud. Feeling nauseous, weak and utterly wretched, I attempted to follow my feet's effort to reach floor – and failed. My body moved, or rather fell helplessly horizontally out of bed and onto the floor. I was ill. Matron was called; covered with spots chicken-pox was quickly diagnosed and I was quickly whisked off to our own lazaretto.

The sick bay was housed in a separate single storey building between The Dingle and St. David's, off the Homes' road which linked all the buildings and amongst the prolific woodland that surrounded the rear of The Dingle and filled the convex shape of the dell behind – the outside world, the - other side – atop of the dell. It was heaven to a sick bewildered young lad. Sister Webb and one assistant ran the establishment–and ran it very, very happily. Food was superb in the Sick Bay it being prepared separately and plenty of second helpings – if you were well enough to receive them. And as to personal attention; well... well, you were sick weren't you? One gloried short times in Sick Bay once the crisis was over. Kept occupied.

Books and puzzles abounded and I spent many pleasant hours reading classic tales; adventure stories by G.H. Henty, Rider Haggard, A.E. Mason, Mark Twain and other *Boys Own* favourites. At that tender age of nine or ten years *Rupert* books published by the *Daily Express* remained an easy relaxed favourite bound in their stiff yellow jackets. And we were allowed to listen to *Children's Hour* on the radio – Uncle Mac, or the current serial introduced by a theme from The Nutcracker Suite. Libraries, books – and guaranteed quiet places to read them in undisturbed, an essential fabric to a well run children's home. Riotous outside games are not sought by all, at all times.

It was resident in the Sick Bay that I first met – in isolation, that is, not inhibited by other mores – one or more girls who were also recovering from an illness. My glands were growing along with my brain and experience even if in stature I remained very small for my age. I found girls delightful to talk with; attractive, intelligent – yet beings from another world – but within my known universe. Segregation, already described, prevented any more normal self-explorations. But on my return to the school I would have a renewed interest – that too would grow – and, years and years ahead, cause not a little, considerable tribulation.

Philip

Earlier I described a friendship with several of the boys with whom I had been evacuated to South Wales in 1944-45. One was Philip Heath. Now, Philip had several sisters, and together we would play happily in the grounds. In retrospect, Phil was the only lad whose close friendship I then truly valued – his sisters resident in St. David's were very attractive – was one named Julie? Came another very great shock. Philip and his sisters were suddenly leaving the orphanage. It was rumoured they were being adopted and going away to a far-away country called Chile in South America. They went. Before their departure I made a vow, if in the years ahead I ever got myself married and was fortunate to have a son – I would name him Philip. I kept that vow twenty years on – thanks to my first wife, Sarah.

Ten years old, many moves, too many changes of faces and places, and time and again, the losses of established friends and relationships. Hardly surprising in retrospect that one withdraws deeper finer feelings into oneself. One learns to survive by earnest playing in the games of insisted mores. A child lost amongst children in an adult-orientated world. It would be many years till I was out of this captivity – at least for a breathing...

Cold

A typical weekday in the 1940s, during school term, began with lights on at 6.45a.m. Bed made, washed, bedspace cleaned (polished once per week) and inspected: then, detailed-term pre-breakfast chore. The chore could be cleaning the bathrooms, sweeping, polishing, boot-room cleaning, picking rubbish up outside. All chores to be thoroughly inspected by the house-parent. If the job was not passed, you missed breakfast, or, if wilfully neglected, you were gated and not allowed out on the coveted Saturday afternoon. By far the most unpopular job was the sweeping with a hard broom the Huts' concrete yard during the bitter cold winter months. The very bitter winter of 1947 clearly comes to mind as I was on this detail at that time. This task was further abhorred because if any boy was seen to put his hands in his pockets (because of the cold), then, as punishment those warm pockets (gloves) would be duly sewn up for a limited period (and they were). I fainted from intense cold on more than one occasion during those years.

Men and women getting their coke *rations* from the South Metropolitan Gas Company's depot at Vauxhall, London, February 1947. (Photo by Keystone/Getty Images)

Dick Barton

Indubitably, life in the orphanage was always austere but *never* but a sea of gloom. Television was a distanced scientific invention, and even in those of my early years, when occasionally heard of, television was only for the storybook rich. Radio, and later to be favourite blessing was cinema-magic. One radio show was very popular, played at 6.45 p.m. every weekday evening and relayed through a tannoy speaker, in the boot-room of The Dingle (where tuck too was distributed and semi important 'talking-to's' executed by matron to the boys). That radio show was *Dick Barton Special Agent*. With some amusement, some thirty-two years later in Worthing, doing some research, I came upon the following quote in the West Sussex monthly magazine, *Littlehampton and Arundel Review of May 1948*:

> '"Thriller" Broadcasts under Fire: Although Dick, Jock and Snowy are taking a rest from broadcasting until next September, the question 'Is Dick Barton a menace to youth?' lingers on. Magistrates, clergymen, youth workers, Members of Parliament, Sunday-School speakers, college professors, and parents too, have been condemning or condoning with all the heat and fire of a peace conference'

But, adventure was adventure – and we loved it.

Athletics and sport unsurprisingly were popular with many boys. Football in winter and cricket in summer were the normal mainstays. I was a lousy football player, but enjoyed a game of cricket, being a reasonable fast bowler and slogger. The favourite match was an annual Old Scholars' Day every June. This was a traditional but informal on-going cricket match through the course of the day into dusk, between Old Boys and the Boys; its highlight was dubbed 'Penny on the Wicket' (more money on the stumps if the Old Boy was affluent– even a sixpence). Each time the batter was bowled out, or caught, the winner was entitled to fallen coinage, and the Old Boy chance to remain at the wicket. Most summer weekends there was a match between The Homes and an outside team, the orphanage as host always entertaining the opposing team to tea. Sportsmanship and honest gamesmanship were as innate good manners religiously imparted, always more important even than winning a game at any price. 'It's not cricket' had a very real meaning to most boys in those days. This stayed with me as a social more unconsciously sub-titled English Justice: Fair play.

Labouring this pointed memory: the first lines of poetry I ever learnt were as an eight year old in the Orphanage primary school, taught by Miss A. Barson. By Sir Henry Newbolt (Source: Sir Henry Newbolt (1862-1938) Poem *Vitai Lampado* (Torch of Life) – first verse) :

"There's a breathless hush in the Close tonight
Ten to make and the match to win
A bumping pitch and a blinding light
An hour to play and the last man in.
And it's not for the sake of a ribboned coat,
Or the selfish hope of a season's fame,
But his Captain's hand on his shoulder smote
'Play up! Play up! and play the game!"'

Games

Adventure, games and play. Good versus Evil, whilst the stuff of childhood, it became the very marrow for my adult bones, injustices always a bane, whether suffered at first hand or known to being executed in an area of my concern. But there were other games. One popular game was played between two opposing sides, the more participants the better : it was called 'Release-Oh'. Outside the Dingle building were three large cedar trees. One trunk elected as a base, its roots serving many a friendly game. A chosen side had to scatter and hide from the opposite team. With a count, say 100 to 500, one team had to hide within a certain periphery. Count completed, the home team had to seek out and catch (touch was sufficient) its opponents. When each opposite was touched he was caught, but when found, if he could outrun and remain untouched, he could remain safe. When caught, each captive had to touch the tree base, though captives could link-hands outward and move–as long as the end member touched the home base. Captives could be rescued on being touched by members of their own team who had not been caught. On being rescued, the shout would go out –'Release Oh!'. Interestingly, many years later, working as a social worker with Worthing Scouts and local youth, I was re-introduced to a search game called 'Wide Game' with considerable similarities to 'Release Oh'.

Other games included 'Cockaroosha'– played on the Huts' concrete yard. One member, standing on one leg with arms folded, had to knock down other boys moving past on one leg, trying to hop past to a drawn line on the other side of him. The last one to be knocked down became the winner. And British Bulldog. British Bulldog became – or could be – a very rough game; the object to catch other boys as they ran past to a goal and lift the captive clear of the ground long enough to cry out 'British Bulldog'.

The World Outside

Most life in the Homes was very insular as *Within Our Gates*. The world outside the gates[8], if and when I was conscious enough to examine this fact, revealed precious little to my intelligence and day-to-day perceptions. Excursions outside the grounds were, in early years, wholly limited to mother's brief visiting-day afternoon outings, and rare, with staff, trips to chalk cliffs on the adjacent Surrey, North Down Hills. In later years approximately aged twelve to fourteen, we would go out, unaccompanied on Saturday afternoons, to pictures or go swimming in Reigate's local baths. Or we might go exploring on nearby Wray Park Common and admire the then still-functioning Windmill going into this quixotic building, inside and out. The priory grounds adjacent to Reigate town was a ready source of adventure in that it provided a network of woodland and lake. A firm favourite was popping in to a small bakery and walking out with a still warm slice of freshly made bread and a sliver of melting butter – for one penny; murphies, too, were still available along with hot chestnuts. A visit to local sweetshops was often a forbidden and daring out-of-bounds excursion during any weekday – or any time – without permission. Besides, returning empty lemonade bottles to the shop, gleaned a penny per item to exchange for a stick of black liquorice. All these sweet goodies were tempting, and obtainable outside our gates.

Knowledge of the world, and its peoples, was limited to fantasy adventures and storybook information. In communication media, the radio was largely heard only for comedy or light drama entertainment – if the News was relayed, there was very little we could relate any significance to through our mean experience. School-time information through education was – to the young – but an extension of the storybook information world; after all, its sources were the same as our occasional entertainment: how to differentiate through any conceptual experience?. At school the geographical magazines were a fact of fantasy fascinating information.

The world outside our gates was, in retrospect, very conservative at its face values (we never saw behind closed doors). Except for scouts' bob-a-job, school, and shop encounters, contacts with the general public, life experience was almost totally within the bounds of the grounds. The Homes' world always remained quite austere. The town of Reigate and its neighbouring towns and hamlets in the 1940s and 1950s had little changed for hundreds of years, and many demesnes could boast of settlements pre-dating Roman times. Reigate was such a town, and as a boy this aspect was absorbed into myself as an interest, and in continuity, became English native soil enwombed in my flesh. Not any absolute self identity with Reigate town and its peoples but with a feeling of England and all its finer qualities that it then stood for. This underlying emotion as much part of my existence as the deeper more anguished personal core of gathered experience: nature and nurture. Any self-identity, about existence, remained stable, its solidarity, dating thousands of years and substance, back to creation itself – however that came about. The other aspect was neurotic flesh, pulsing, searching in turns of mood and insight, impressed or depressed – at least animated. After Hiroshima and Nagasaki, the war was officially over; but, as an eight year old, it meant nothing to me — I had only known the Blitz years.

Christmas 1945

Christmas, 1945, was a time of nostalgia, celebration and goodwill. A time of reunion with recent close relations and friends. But, whatever reasons, some orphanage children were unable to go home: they had no other home, for Christmas. And at this time I was one of them. Those first Christmases at Spurgeon's Orphan Homes memories were of a small gathering in St. David's dining room in 1945. The superintendent Dr. Green, matron, and skeleton staff remaining with us, ensured we ate, drank, sang and enjoyed receipt of any Christmas presents. Christmas Eve and tradition demanded we hung our grey socks up on the bed posts for Father Christmas (or friends) to fill overnight: they were rather small to fill. Decorations abounded and atmosphere echoed with local residents as visitors presenting their Christmas carols. There were two main events which excluded the customary first awakening expectations.

After breakfast the care staff would enter with arms full of brown-paper parcels. These were THE PRESENTS sent to the Homes by relatives, friends and well-wishers. The second main event was Christmas Dinner.

I remember that first lunch of 1945; the year before in 1944, I had been in South Wales, but retained no memory of any Xmas dinner of that time – or of any Christmas meal before it. The meat at St. David's was goose, a fatty edged meat (unfortunately, I had already developed a fetish of revulsion towards any fat or grizzle–like Jack Spratt), but, I adored all the roast trimmings. Around each plate was one apple, one orange, a square of dates and a cracker, with paper napkin. Lemonade was the principal drink. A large lit Christmas tree in the St. David's dining hall. After Father Christmas had arrived (the superintendent in disguise) and distributed a gift to each of us children. There were not very many at this gathering; the exact number escapes me, possibly twenty or so boys and girls. A sing-song inevitably organised. A crown event is of one of my peers a small boy David, lifted up, to stand on top of the piano and lead the singing of 'In Dublin's Fair City where the girls are so pretty, I first cast my eyes on sweet Molly Malone.' We all took turns to sing a verse and I hope I sang 'Cockles and Mussels alive-alive-oh' with gusto and appreciation. Each postwar Christmas would be similarly experienced, but fortunately, in the last couple of years my brother and I would go away to a true cockney London Christmas, to 2 Baxter Grove, Wall Street, off the Balls Pond Road in Islington, amongst my mother's relatives. ... Menfolk returning from the war.

One autumn evening in 1947 we had bedded down at the Dingle. I was in a downstairs dormitory, now aged ten years. Boys were forbidden to speak after lights out and Matron had already spanked one boy with the slipper that evening, for talking.

Matron

Our matron as Mrs L. of The Dingle in the late 1940s, was not *The Matron* (Superintendent's wife of The Homes). A formidable mixture of sternness and unexpected bouts of kindness : our Matron commanded respect, even a sort of fear, but certainly no malice. We were talking of oncoming Christmas and who was going where and who expected to remain behind. Suddenly the boy on lookout, the lad who slept close by the doorway, with an uninterrupted view of the hallway, whispered "Skeed", the password, meaning 'Quiet someone's coming'. Silenced. We heard voices in the hallway. And one of the Hut house masters was seen talking to the Matron, talking about our popular primary school headmaster, Dr Holt (doctor of music). He was ill, and the master said he was 'going for the doctor'. After some movement out into wind and rain there was a silence again. In unison. All boys broke into voice and echoed anxiety and speculation as to our Dr Holt's health. Eventually the hubbub caused matron to reappear and, putting the lights on, demanded to know its cause. We admitted hearing of our school head's illness and made enquiry.

Matron significantly sat on a bed and said that, Yes, it was true, unhappily he was very ill and not expected to live. Sadly he died and, despite the war, multiple 'absences' and moves in the past, this 'death and absence' meant something new to me, and prompted a discussion with peers. It was very much a Christian (I knew absolutely nothing of any other global faith), mostly Baptist orientated home; benignly inundated with aspects of religion and morals. Death to me at ten years of age was just something that happened to old people. Youth was eternal – one died only mythically on the radio, in Hollywood epics, or in storybooks. To die was to go to Heaven (I mean – who would go to Hell?) it was all really meaningless to me.

It was wholly unrelated to any directly recollected trauma. People were coming and going all the time amongst adults and some children who just disappeared from everyday sight or went to some other home. I missed Dr. Holt, a medium-height stout benign patriarch – a mixture of father-figure and genius (to me), a brilliant musician, and happily a gentle dependable human being. Gone for ever.

Sunday Best

The following Sunday a slightly later rise, and after breakfast dressed in Sunday-best grey suits – only worn on special occasions. Morning church was always in Reigate or nearby Redhill town. At the beginning of school term each boy wrote his name under a posted list of local churches: the Redhill Roman Catholic; the Methodist in Reigate; Baptist in Reigate; and the furthest (and most popular due to the long leafy lane walk – past the Redhill Tannery), the Baptist in Redhill; and Presbyterian en route to Redhill. In a casual crocodile governed by a staff representative this church visit and out-of-gate Sunday morning walk was a reasonably popular event.

Back to the Homes for dinner and, early afternoon, the youngest children would be supervised in a letter-writing session to ensure regular contact was maintained with relatives and guardians. In the summer months several groups of children could be observed, sat on the earth out of doors, at the rear of the Dingle, in the close shade of the dell woodland. Mid-afternoon a second compulsory visit to church for the younger children, to the intimate Homes' Chapel situated within St. David's. Boys and girls attended this essential chapel ritual, aided by chosen choir members. It concluded with the Latin school motto being sung "*Sequimini Optima*, Sequimini Optima, This is our motto, and this is our aim " 'Follow The Master', echoed a keen sincere Christian tone innate in its organised activity.

In early Sunday evening the older children again filed across to the chapel for 'their' second compulsory service. In later years, looking back, I was convinced that for some time I had compulsorily attended church three times each Sunday. And this fact, combined with my later agnosticism (with God is dead exacerbation) whilst keeping respect for faith and Christianity itself, it barred me from any desire to voluntarily go to church on regular Sundays.

Sweets

Sweets and pocket-money were two subjects dear to every child's heart–and often dear to the parent or guardian. *The 1948 Children Act* had not yet been drafted and its benign (to children) aspects introduced. A voluntary funded institution is much dependant on public philanthropy. In a time of severe fiscal restraint such items as sweets and pocket-money were seen as a luxury to the giving parent figures, if not to the children. One hot summer evening in 1947 I was out playing on the large field in front of the Dingle, chasing cabbage-white butterflies with my grey school jacket, when a loud call from Matron hailed like Bacchus's horn from underneath the cedars: 'Sweets'.

An unexpected treat in a then rare clarion. Boys rushed from all over the boys' side on an expected 'first come, first served' basis. From a large bag were then counted out (it had obviously been worked out how many each) five large well-wrapped delicious fruit-filled centres for each boy. But, first, Matron insisted on our knowing who had donated this offering to the orphanage. We were informed that they had come all the way from South Africa (I do not recollect the details). Somehow, that we should have been thought of from so far away made this sweet offering of a special significance.

Pocket money was largely dependent on what donations visiting friends or relatives left, or sent by postal orders. As expected, most of us received very little in those days (or why else the need to be in residence?). Children received into care, or through court orders, removed on a local authority care order (as later government acts decreed) into a statutory supported children's home, are ensured pocket money on a graduated scale according to age and stage.

Thirty years on, this pocket-money sum may be in excess of what many children in families receive, (but then it is some compensation for being in-care?). The first specific sum I received was ninepence a week (in old coinage, of course). Before leaving the Homes in Summer 1951 this sum had risen to one shilling and sixpence when I was fourteen years of age. The cinema was (remains so) the main recipient of pocket-money – sweets and comics a close second. The Odeon or A.B.C. entrance had also risen from ninepence to one and sixpence for front stalls: ice creams were sixpence it seemed for many years.

Barter

It was customary amongst boys (and girls too) to barter amongst ourselves in order to gain cash (sans pocket money), or indirectly obtain a desired article. Thus, as entrepreneur one could start with a champion-conker and end up with a large Dinky toy, book, or the price of a cinema visit. Bartering was very much a fixture of the children's institutional life rather than an interest or plain supplement to pocket-money. But, in the Dingle, this feature was not so clearly visible as it was as a twelve-year-old onwards in the Huts.

In the years 1950 to 1951, I developed a number of successful business ventures within the orphan grounds – and overlapped them at school. Stamp collecting led from swapping to buying and selling. And, in imitation of the much media advertised stamps for sale On Approval, I bought, sold, exchanged and retained stamps valued on the Stanley Gibbons' stamp catalogue. Film strips (stips – no r – they were called), I purchased and hired out to other boys viewings. Books I collected and bartered, or loaned for a penny fee. And in summer I purchased lemonade powder, dissolved certain sweets, mixed drinks in empty lemonade bottles, and sold the made up drinks in the Huts' yard for a very modest profit.

Shortly before leaving the Homes I learnt two new pocket-money making habits. Sweets were on ration and some boys (better off relatives) at grammar school had unwanted sweet coupons. I would purchase the coupons, buy chewing gum packs – and sell them off for a profit. The large mostly American coloured comics – especially those called D.C. Superman et cetera – were extremely popular. I collected them and hired them out, or bought and sold – whichever desired.

All this schoolboy bartering brought very little real income, though it did give me a whole range of new interests, and for a few years a useful training in salesman experience. It was also typical of small businesses that build up in any institution, with the young – and not solely in an adult world. Although sport was not a principal interest of mine I admired feats of honest endurance and competitive games that give one a feeling of identification and belonging– if only a transient feeling. In 1948 the Olympic Games came to Great Britain– the 'Great' had not yet been internationally censured by (so-called) progress and politic machinations.

My mother, a single parent for some years, occasionally had an interested suitor. And one summer holiday to London our mother's current young man kindly took my brother and me to Highbury stadium in North London – it being our local football ground – to see England play Holland (I think), I cannot recollect the result – only the event. I do not remember many gentlemen who courted my mother whilst I was an orphan resident, but none, in my memory, was ever unkind to my brother or to me. And, in vogue with most other boys and girls in the Homes who had one parent or no parents at all – or one relative occasionally seen – we wished constantly for a re-marriage, for some gallant to whisk us all away from the Orphanage into a world wholly free from want. And, in some luxury.

This subject was a frequent topic for conversation. And, as bartering was opportunity for verbal exchanges, one discovered new entrants to our shadowed world of distanced relatives, this reflected in a sudden new wealth of books and toys displayed by a boy. Or a sudden withdrawal and cut off from supply. However distanced a relative was, occasional contact by letter or visit helped sustain a personal identity, and certainly gave roots to one's existence. Belongings were another proof of identity and a result of exchanges with other human beings. A feeling of identity was paramount. General literature and public media, notably the radio, assisted in moulding our national identity. And whereas I had accented the religious dignity and moral-tone identity of the Homes, its staff members not surprisingly echoed their own attitudes and beliefs–to inform us.

Royal Wedding

1947 was occasion for the Royal Wedding between Princess Elizabeth and Prince Philip (just like a fairy story), but it was memorable for me, for a different reason than might be supposed. I was then based in a downstairs front dormitory situated not far from matron's rooms in the Dingle. The day of the Royal Wedding was a public holiday – or was it on a weekend? I was ten years old and do not remember the detail. But clearly I had had a substantial work detail that had me on my hands and knees scrubbing and polishing the floor of matron's room, and overhearing a commentary on the radio of the Royal event whilst matron was about her duties

Whilst the excitement of the radio commentator could not be ignored, I do not recollect any personally reciprocated emotions – Royalty was so distanced as not of the real world – at least the world that I frequented. But It was after Dr. Holt's death that I had occasion to experience presence of a new superintendent, Mr Addison (and his wife as the Homes' new matron), replacing the affable musician Dr Green.

No Adoption

It was about this time in The Summer of 1947 that my brother and I, somewhat bewildered, were taken away (for a short holiday) to a fostering family in Muswell Hill. In retrospect, many years later, my bro and I recalled visits to Alexandra Palace, and a large fairground – and being spoilt with some lovely meals and some affection (from strangers?). Mother informed us (again years later) that the family wanted to adopt us but she had absolutely refused. Of course we knew nothing about such things, that the government had a policy of orphanage children being sent (offered) overseas for adoption (as my departed friend Philip Heath and his sisters). Or being adopted – at least fostered – in a new family or other children's home – somewhere in the British Empire' colonies (aka Dominions) overseas, to USA, Australia, Canada, Rhodesia, or New Zealand; like the many wartime evacuations. To be child migrants.

Another Dingle boy (about 1949) and I were particularly hurt and miserable about something or other, and indicated our loneliness and frustration by acting out particularly stupid. I cannot recollect whose crass idea it was, but together we bundled some toilet-paper into a cavity in the wall of a downstairs toilet – and foolishly set fire to it. Within moments remorse and fear set in, and I set about putting the fire out with bowls of water, whilst the other lad ran off. The smoke soon brought matron and other staff and boys to the scene of our crime. And, shamefully, I admitted to the outrage. But punishment was to be expected, and although I refused to name my accomplice I was soon warned that 'The Superintendent wishes to see you at... at St. David's'.

I had been summoned to the height of Mount Olympus over at His office in St. David's. Terrified – for I had heard of terrible canings and other punishments for malefactors being given out – tales by other boys. To my utter amazement this strange person, the superintendent, was kindness itself. Far from attacking me with expected, and deserved, retributions he asked me questions about myself. No-one had ever asked 'such personal questions' of me – although I did know other kind people in contact about the Homes. Here was a man, The Man, in known authority over all the boys and girls and staff of the Homes – and he was kindness and understanding itself? All I received was a gating for a month which entailed not being allowed out of the grounds except for formal occasions. Outside our matron I had experienced a new dimension of experience of staff and their powers of control.

Staff

Staff in charge of the infants and babies at Brooklands, St. David's and the Dingle, were essentially female, assisting the matron (a likely euphemism for the senior house-mother—we never learnt their salaried titles) were alternating young women, sometimes senior girls from the girls' side of St. David's. On later moving to the Huts, only the lady who collected the darning basket appeared from time to time.

There was never – to my recollection – any deliberate cruelty and though I felt a wide gulf (I knew my peers did also) which distanced the staff members acts of occasional kindnesses tempered what aloofness we experienced. Mrs.

L. the matron who dominated life at the Dingle was a tall, middle-aged lady with whom I never truly related. Again one must remember the large numbers of children under charge of the care staff.

In contrast the Huts were for the older boys, twelve to fifteen years old and no female staff (to my recollection) ever existed over with the young men– for that was how the Dingle children viewed them, as Young Men. There were several chronologically marked changes that indicated a moving out of puberty (or into it, according to one's viewpoint) and into young manhood.

The move over to the Huts itself was, ritualistically accepted as an acknowledgement, of senior status. And the graduating from short grey trousers to long trousers – a tremendous recognition of being now grown-up. No matter how tall (I was small for my age) a boy was, he wore short-trousers if he was under age. And even after leaving the Homes in July 1951, I still wore short trousers – with old holiday snaps to prove it. Braces for trousers were the norm, and to keep up the thick grey woollen socks, elastic garters around the calves. With white shirts, the orphanage regulation tie – a striped orange and black tie (I think) – equally to be tied around the neck in a regulation Windsor knot.

In the war and post-war years, black boots gave way to black shoes; never, never brown shoes; only well-off people and officers wore those. Echoes of comedian Stanley Holloway ... 'Brown Boots I ask yuh, bra ..brn boots!.'. And all clothing was clearly marked in indelible ink with our allocated numbers. If any article was damaged or lost we were 'in trouble' – and a gating, caning or withdrawal of tuck or pocket money might result.

There were two residential Huts (yes, just like future army huts), the one close by the concrete yard and opposite the dining room hut and kitchens for twelve to fourteen year olds: the second Hut was linked by a covered corridor, and down three or four steps, past a master's office. And then on a parallel the other long prefabricated Hut. The second Hut was for senior boys fifteen years old, and some sixteen years old – still attending grammar school or technical school. 'They', the seniors, were allowed to read purchased newspapers – very adult. Each hut included a single bedroom, at the end and entrance, for one housemaster on current duty. In later years a very efficient Sportsmaster a Mr. B., ran the orphanage cub and Scout troop – the 8th Reigate Scouts; he was not an in-house master. St. David's and the Dingle were converted from previously,Private School houses (a girls' private school). The austere Huts were – all three of them – wartime purpose-built with thin white walls and corrugated asbestos roofs, and stone-tiled floors overlaid with a thick polishable lino.

Early adolescence

Manhood, in contemporary terms, youth to adolescence, was marked by taboo menstruation in the female and the onset of semen in young males, but our growth was in denial, perceived, perhaps, only as covert biological norms. Whilst in the Homes, knowledge of sex, academic and real, was limited to a meagre lesson or two in biology at school. Bed-wetting was a common symptom of emotional disturbance in young children. And with one incidental exception, whilst evacuated to Wales, (I slept deeply and dreamed I was urinating into a barrel, feeling very snug and warm, but awoke sharply to find I had wet the bed) – I was fortunate in avoiding this obstacle. Based in the Dingle, on several occasions I 'dreamt' I had wet the bed and experienced a warm feeling, only to awake very puzzled to find the bed quite dry. There was, however, an area of pyjama-trousers around the genitals visibly thickened like cardboard. They were early spontaneous sperm emissions, for a while only experienced on occasions. There was no-one to talk to about this mystery and I remained in gross ignorance about such personal matters for years. The normal cast into an abnormal happening by ignorance of one's own body.

Flirting with girls was notable at primary school within the Orphanage grounds. For the vast majority of us children it echoed the healthy exploratory ambivalence of now-I-love-you-now-I-hate-you; the Dandelion Game we called it. This so innocent behaviour echoed amongst peers who exchanged love notes and tokens of affection. Sex play was–as such–unheard of and therefore not talked about, even amongst the older children. In retrospect, exceptions in secret must have existed, dependent on knowledge gained by specific life experiences of new children coming into the Homes.

One incident strange to me at the time, still in the orphanage primary school – I must have been about eight or nine years of age – effected by a brash new admission, a confident young girl, Yvonne, we gathered, three of us boys behind a closed door; close by a back-up flight of little-used stairs. As I remember it she dared us to expose our genitals and ridiculously persuaded one boy to urinate in her mouth. Many, many years later I realised that perhaps, it was not urination, in hand, but perhaps early fellatio. Not long after this isolated incident, we heard our attractive class-mate had been expelled. A normal pitch, a harmless exchange called de-bagging in horse-play–in and out of classrooms, sometimes occurred. Girls wore very large black or navy-blue knickers, which were seen tucked-in during P.T. classes. Playfully boys-versus-girls in small groups would chase each other, about school, mostly jesting, to de-bag, but occasionally actually catching a half-willing girl (or boy) who was loosely held, and the knickers or short trousers pulled down to half-mast. And that was all–a sort of British Bulldog? If lucky, a kiss–the height of indecent or cheeky flirting behaviour–and an accolade–a kiss would be exchanged with a then-favourite or playfully forced (but a refusal to bully), on an unrewarded victim. ... Childhood games.

Whilst still at the Dingle I enjoyed an early romance. The girl was about thirteen years old, I nearly twelve, her name was Joy. It was a very innocent affair as we exchanged gifts – I recollect her giving to me a book associated with Uncle Mac, a radio children's programme personality. Together, Joy and I exchanged our notes and kisses at first furtively, and sometimes more boldly. In a small group we went out to the Park close by the remains of Reigate Castle and dungeons. We, four of us, gravitated to the winter iced-over pond and adjacent swings. Joy, a tall girl with dark hair, and glasses, following my own example of 'a dare to walk across the ice' (viz. walk-on-water) ; I succeeded, but she fell in. And with some consternation, I remember her having to remove her stockings. But no serious trouble resulted. And it would be some four to five years further on – and out of the Homes – before I developed any further interest in the opposite sex.

In retrospect, this anecdote does remind me that numerous, clandestine romances did occur, and in view of the residence division of Girls' side and Boys' side – with severe trouble if one was caught 'out of bounds' – it is the more remarkable that such adventures persisted; but in the nature of man, a natural phase of growing-up. The Girls' side was not the only area forbidden to trespass, within the periphery of the grounds, the Dell, the concave woodland area, to the rear of the Dingle, and up to the rear of St. David's, was expressly forbidden.

A forbidden wood.

Clay-pit

The clay-pit, a small area of ground at the bottom of the Girls' side, just within the fence off Oak Road, in a haha hidden by a row of trees and scrubs, was also 'out of bounds'. But this clay, soft and grey like plasticine, was great for sculpting shapes and building garages and obstacles for our Dinky toys to roam in one corner of the Boys' side – the sand pit. Here, in the sand pit, we scraped out bold circuits of roads and villages, and either aped warfare or imagined what outside grown-up civilian life was by acting out through the sand pit playground. Shortly after my arrival at the Homes, some bullies buried me up to my neck in this sand whilst they went off to tea – I was terrified, but eventually one boy relented and returned to release me from this tomb.

Bullies were unfortunately as much a fixture in the Homes as in the schools and other similar institutions. The staff did not encourage bullying by any means, but with such large grounds and so many children, it made this job very difficult. As a lad small for my age, I remained easy meat for bullies, but several times attempted to overcome this by having boxing lessons (of a sort) from a bigger boy. And, able to practice with my brother, I boxed with a little confidence. However, a few years later I would box for a north London school house, and realise I did not want to hit my opponent anywhere in the face–but still won on points by speed and body trunk punches. I retained the movement and agility, but dropped the fisticuffs, thus remaining most vulnerable – and, as I later recall, I became a professional dancing instructor for some years, a prize aided from years of dodging bullies? It was 1949. And so, with early manhood arrived at, twelve years of age, I was transferred over to the Huts – specifically, The Hut. My brother remained for a while in the Dingle before joining me. A new domain.

The Hut

The Hut divided internally into two sections with a large rectangular table in its centre. The legs and underlying surface of the table were made of steel, and bolted to the floor. Years later I realised that it was almost identical to the Morrison air-raid shelter (Anderson shelters were located outside a house), which I had experienced in sheltering underneath, during regular air-raids, at the Esaus' house in Heston from 1942-44. And, in retrospect, I realised that it was not just a large table – but also the hearth-place of that wartime hut. This work-table (for such it was) with its much-polished section of lino, was nailed down on the top and was the Huts' life-centre. Slung over a triangular iron-rafter above the table was a radio extension Tannoy speaker – controlled from the housemaster's room. And during evenings and at work periods on Saturdays it provided much media news and light entertainment.

Each side of the table, and extending down the length of the Hut, were the boys' beds and adjacent wooden lockers. Most of the eighty or so beds were double-deckers made of tubular-iron and metal springs, with mattress and pillow, two blankets, sheets and pillowcase. The standard covering of the green counterpane with circular motif inscribed '*Spurgeon's Orphan Homes*' covered the surface of the beds, as in the Dingle and St. David's. The counterpane was changed regularly once or so a fortnight, as one sheet end pillowcase was changed weekly, top put to bottom, bottom to laundry basket, a large wicker-cane basket sent across to an internal laundry service at St. David's every week.

A few single beds were down the opposite side of the dormitory. I was given an upper bunk almost exactly opposite a door and connecting passage-way to the third hut where the eldest boys resided–remembering the first hut was the dining-hut and kitchens. Down its two steps and to the immediate right was the often-dreaded and much-used Office – a euphemism for the housemaster's all-purpose room–where corporal punishment was regularly administered.

A small window was situated immediately behind the pillow end of my top bunk bed. This window opened outwards, overlooking the concrete yard and opposite the junior end of the dining-hut. But it also opened to a canopy of stars, and very frequently I would gaze and dream upwards towards those entities after the lights were out and silence of the night ensued.

As indicated, from where I lay, a doorway was close by. In addition, one of the two main entry doorways led to an exit – immediate right, and down a concrete step into the courtyard. Adjacent to this entrance was a small annexe called The Boot-room, with numbered allocated wire-baskets – and a hut boy's locker – nightly, polished shoes were kept within his box. This room always smelt very heavily with the scent of years of thick black shoe-polish ; a separate basket providing brushes to polish was set aside for this daily chore. I cannot recollect the exact time to get ready for bed, I think it was around eight o'clock after supper cocoa. Lights out at nine-fifteen p.m. Remembering the age of this Hut dormitory boys, was twelve to fourteen years. Situated to the left of where I lay my head, was the longer section of the dormitory, marked by the huge centre-table. Opposite the table and through an open doorway – the same side as my bed (and, therefore, out of visual sight) through a short passageway and up three or four concrete steps, led to the sinks and baths in the bathroom to the right, and toilets and urinal to its left.

Adjacent to the hut toilets was another external exit into the courtyard. The boiler-room with its thick-blankets of fibrous asbestos was situated close by, but of course in a separate annexe. And was adjacent to our hut's walled-in bathroom. A raised chimney – but not pronounced as in larger institutions – marked the boiler-house premises; this was sited immediately opposite one of the kitchens of the dining hut. A thick water pipe adjoining the two buildings was also covered with asbestos and covering the overhead basket wire, bridging the two hut buildings. Steam regularly marked the boiler-house, coming out of the chimney, and off this substantial connecting pipe.

Also to the far left of where I lay my head, but at the extreme end of the hut dormitory, lay another entrance and exit, it leading down a step and out onto the orphanage main road driveway – connecting The Gate with Holmsdale Road. And to its left to the other end the Dingle; branching off the Dell to the right, and at its end St. David's. Just inside this far end entrance of our hut, a single-bed room housed on-duty accommodation for the hut's housemaster. A regular feature in most children's homes and public caring institutions. I was often grateful for this physical distancing down the far end of the hut; it allowed for a very subdued occasional whispering after lights-out – provided an elected monitor would not report you if "Who's speaking?" was challenged.

I was given, for-to-be the last time, another allocated number. In St David's it was 72; in upstairs Dingle at nine to ten years old it was 56; downstairs in the Dingle I was 2; and I believe my last number in the Hut was 14. Once again all my personal clothing and effects had to have new tabs inscribed with indelible ink the allocated anonymous number.

Post-war London

This move to the Huts in 1949 was diminished by a further change – outside the Homes. My mother had met a new young man named Tom Dolan, an Irishman from Dublin with a strong Irish brogue. He was introduced to my brother and myself on one visiting day as Uncle Tom. Thomas Dolan was born on the 16th July, 1914, in Eire, of medium height at five foot five inches, with brown eyes and a ruddy complexion. As my mother was born on the 2nd of November, 1915, there was little difference in their ages. Uncle Tom at thirty-five years of age became our step-father. The event came as a great surprise to my brother and me as on one visiting day at the end of 1949 my mother literally declared she had a surprise for us and said that we now had a father. I was twelve years old and my brother eighteen months younger. My mother had happily remarried in London.

Though it seemed clear that at last we had our passport out of the Homes, this did not take place for some twenty months ahead. We did go home to North London more often, though as yet we had no singular place to call our home. After past years of occasionally stopping at our nan's and granddad's in Baxter Grove, Wall Street, off the Balls Pond Road in Islington – for a while in 1948 the address of my mother's digs was 44 Buckingham Road, Dalston, parallel to the Balls Pond Road. Once again, we occasionally visited our maternal grandparents, the Mantons, and a new feature was introduced to our new adopted Irish relatives then living in East Ham. We were made welcome and for a few short years ahead they were regularly on our calendar of events.

New Routines

Life otherwise remained the same in 1950. In the hut new routines – similar to the Dingle but more severe – had to be learned. When I first arrived at the huts, my brother and I attended the Holmsdale Road mixed primary school. There were then three other types of school attended outside the Homes' grounds by the boys (and girls). The secondary school (near the Priory grounds); the technical school which I did not attend (I don't remember the location); and Reigate Grammar School (County School equivalent for the girls). On being called in the morning and preparing for breakfast and school, set routines were expected similar to the Dingle.

First the bed had to be completely and smartly re-made, with so-called hospital corners (tucked in at the bottom and the corner folded over at right angles and then double tucked in). The counterpane which was folded down at nights was to be spread uncreased across the bed and up over the pillow, a neat indent line where the blankets met the pillow. And with a single tuck, tucked in at the bottom with the sides exactly even in drop, hanging each side of the bed. The white towel would be properly and symmetrically folded over the end of the bed. Woe betide any offender who just pulled the blankets and sheets back and attempted to disguise it with a smooth counterpane.

Of course, so much the worse if the whole bed was badly made up. These beds could be arbitrarily examined whilst we were away at school. And many a young heart sank when he returned from school to witness his bedclothes either folded back or, much worse, all the bedlinen on the floor and the bald mattress folded over exposing the springs. It meant by implication a visit to the office, and a meted out punishment by the master. I experienced this situation on a number of occasions. Although we had to make our beds over at the Dingle, inspection was never so severe as at the Huts. After the beds were made up, still in pyjama bottoms you made your way to the washroom. The sinks each had a small mirror overhead. And to one side of this room a row of hooks each dangled a flannel with the boy's number upon it. Over the flannels the long row of toothbrushes in a rack, again with your number affixed. How else with eighty odd boys? Hygiene must be always the major consideration.

Each boy had his bedside locker. And within the locker clothes had to be very properly folded and any belongings kept clean and neatly put away. Again, a sudden inspection by the staff whilst away at school might mean an emptied locker – all effects on the bed as mute evidence of your misdemeanour. Just a few years later I was to be called up for National Service, and blandly accepted exactly the same performance with beds and lockers and equipment, just such treatment by NCO's and officers – though with a few refined additions. In the washroom you ensured you washed face, neck and ears well, and cleaned your teeth. Then dressed for school. And your allocated (if any) pre-breakfast job completed, your bedspace and locker dusted and swept, you then presented yourself for inspection to the master in charge.

Methodically the inspecting master would lean your head forward to look for that tell-tale tide-mark revealing an unwashed neck; then the ears were inspected, head to one side and then the other side. Finally the mouth was opened and teeth inspected. Allotted tasks and bed spaces were inspected later whilst away at school. Again, woe betide you if in error, and especially so if a too frequent offender.

Evenings when preparing for bed, the very first task was a thorough clean polishing of each boy's black shoes. This had to include the cracks at the edge of the shoes and the underside soles and heels of the shoes. Mostly these were inspected the same evening by the master, but sometimes he inspected them placed in their baskets, when you were in bed. And a wrathful master might descend on you whilst abed, demanding 'What the devil do you call this ?'

And, after re-cleaning the shoes a meet at the office to unamicably come to terms with this corporal offence.

In retrospect I look back with some amazement at the social reality. Of mostly one man, the master (sometimes with auxiliary male staff help) effectively looking after so many boys – at one time. It was, after all, our home, not a formal punishment abode. Most of us had never ever experienced any family home on any regular basis. And so, with no other so-called normal standard to gauge, why on earth rebel or fight the master and system? Unless, unless you did feel an injustice had been effected. Or else you were suffering from a disturbance caused prior to entry to the Homes, or experienced recently at school, or outside by civilians in the community. Which facts inevitably did happen on occasions.

Movement over to the Hut brought a number of birth-date peers over with me from the Dingle. And though I was acquainted with them all and friendly with a few of them, there was no pronounced friendship – the most equivalent was to be when my brother came over and moved in underneath me. That was special. My brother always appeared much less concerned with goings-on around us, and certainly was more self-confident. In a free for all scrap he – with no holds barred – would have no trouble in asserting a physical hold over me. But come to our boxing and organised activity and I held my own with him. We enjoyed mutual self-respect, and unrealised deep care for each other. Unrealised in that it remained in the main submerged and only came up when we ardently defended each other against others. But mostly I remained as an individual, alone.

Collector

In the hut I developed a whole range of new interests. I became a more pronounced collector. Between the boiler house and the kitchens a passageway was marked by three or four dustbins. And a source of global knowledge: one day, rummaging in the bins I found a number of envelopes with George VI postage stamps affixed. From that day on, and for four to five years, I collected postage stamps – first all countries, then colonial, and eventually Great Britain only. Shortly before entering National Service I sold most of them; the balance just disappeared from home whilst away overseas. Stamp collecting, with 'swaps' and a necessary body of knowledge (geography a natural spin-off), became one institutional club.

One evening an older, sixteen-year-old grammar-school boy from the adjacent Hut introduced me to the game of chess. To his amazement and my pleasure, I learnt to beat him. As a twelve-year old I was learning some things fast. But some things I still learnt the hard way, if I learnt at all. A popular afternoon excursion on visiting days, and on other Saturdays off, was to Earlswood Common, close by Redhill. The common enclosed woodland, and a boat lake, and often had fairs and circus performances somewhere within its perimeter. We walked this trip, passing numerous orchards and fruit trees overhanging the pavements.

Occasional scrumping was a risky temptation, more often done for schoolboy prank than for want of fruit. Sometimes one got caught. Several lads related how they had been chased out by a wrathful gentleman brandishing a shotgun. We were caught once and warned off by a friendly policeman. Earlswood also has a large Institution sited not far from the common. We believed it to be called the Asylum and always gave it a very wide berth. Nervous jokes were exchanged during the excursion trip centred on the passed-on belief that you could only visit the place if accompanied by a green ticket – whatever that implied. As schoolboys we fed on comic jokes and stories where horrendous lunatics always suggested mythical inhumane monsters – never of suffering sick mortals – and so to visit even in the vicinity of the place was to add token spice to the journey. A forbidden corner.

In Trouble

It was forbidden to play with a ball inside the Hut buildings, in case of accidents. But one summer evening, the rain falling too rapidly outside an almost empty hut, the long gap between the bed spaces proved irresistible for two of us lads. I threw the ball extra hard, he missed it, and it crashed through the exit-door window adjacent to the boot-room. I was reported to the housemaster and later, in fear and trepidation, I waited outside the office in my pyjamas – for the meet was after I had prepared for bed. One duty-master, a Mr. G., was feared by a number of boys as being very strict severe in punishment. In the Dingle (under twelve years) it was the slipper or an occasional hard hand slap as the norm disciplinary measure. But amongst the older boys the recognised censure was the cane. Most staff were kind though strict.

Several years before I had occasion to see a master at a then general office situated at the end of the Hut dining room–not for a punishment, but for a telling-off for some minor infringement. As the master spoke in this very small room I could not ignore a small row of canes upright placed in a rack, looking like a small range of billiard cues. The smallest and thinnest was quite fine in appearance. I don't think this range of canes was used very often, but its very presence was a daunting deterrent.

I finally met the petty tyrant Mr. G. inside the hut's office and, after a very severe ticking off, a gating, and – as expected – a deduction of pocket-money to pay for the pane of glass (reasonable enough), came the real punishment. Bending over the desk my pyjama cord untied and trousers dropped, I received several lashes of the cane on my bare backside. Most canings were received on the palm of the hand – as at school (until the law forbade it), and though painful were rare enough an experience. I witnessed Mr. G. swipe several boys around the face on numerous occasions, but, to emphasize, this was the exception, not the rule. A fact we much appreciated. One of my peers with whom I was friendly attempted to stand up to this housemaster on several occasions, but invariably failed as his protests were swallowed up by an insular system – too many children, too few staff.

For two years I attended an outside school, the Holmsdale Road primary school. It was a mixed school but I recollect no experiences whatever with other youngsters at that school. There was an excellent young teacher Mr Yates who, like Miss Barson, had optimistically thought I'd potential and gave a little encouragement. I took the 11+ common entrance examination for grammar school and passed. This accompanied an excellent school examination report, and I received two small book prizes for my school effort. I learnt that adults were very pleased with any display of intelligence by their charges.

Mr. B., one of the Homes' housemasters and a sports master (he owned a small M.G.), was very kind and quick to praise my seeming sudden intellectual achievement. In truth, I had discovered any pursuit of knowledge was a fascinating self-exploration of which (I thought then) one could not only safely assert oneself but, in a way, escape. The problem (as it would later become) was that from the outset there was often a difference between what I wanted to explore and the demands of a curriculum by rote. A balance to be realised? I joined a small group of boys who stood out in a separate group to attend Reigate Grammar School. At a set time each school group would be expected to collect together at the end of the Hut on the drive. And (as an army troop) later again to be formed up on their school playground – each boy had his appearance thoroughly checked before departing for school. The local grammar school had an excellent reputation, and a long academic history. But to an orphan lad it also reflected a rather well-to-do outside world wholly beyond my reckoning. And of which we seemed never wholly accepted.

Bullies

Although bullies abounded in this school, as in every school (to some degree), in fairness I do not recollect any of the Homes' boys being victimised 'because' they were poor and from the orphanage. They received no special considerations or additional support either. It was again, assert yourself, or else! As a small boy, shy – even if a little articulate – I continued to be occasionally bullied, and hated it. Unable to fight my way out of confrontations very effectively – and angry enough not to always want to run – I developed a new ploy which sometimes paid off: to talk my way out of trouble. This little growing area of self confidence juxtaposed the natural growing in evidence in pursuit of knowledge, further exampled by occasional trips into the community.

On Sunday mornings we continued journeying to a local church in the customary double crocodile formation, a similar routine to the Dingle. In the afternoon we were allowed some free time, as chapel visit was due in the evening after tea. I recollect three of us boys paying a visit to a local church[9]– not to join a service but to examine and experience its ancient architecture. Encouraged by the other two lads to talk to the vicar (or who-ever it was?) I persuaded him to allow us to explore the tower of the church. To our amazement he agreed, and pleased with this new social skill we repeated this exercise at the local windmill. And then over months ahead explored numerous other historical places of interest. I was no fist fighter, but was learning to survive by asserting myself through speech – and private learning. It also provided a dignity hitherto denied in anonymity. Settled into the Huts, the weekday school day routines must have been similar to any other schoolchild, visiting out of a children's home or organised institution.

Typical Days

Weekday: up at 6.45 a.m., wash, clean, dress, beds made and bedspace cleaned. Pre-breakfast job inspected. Breakfast parade, meal, school parade, morning school – school dinner (ugh!) avoided where possible – afternoon school – return to Homes around 4p.m. Tea – homework (if any) – private hobbies – clubs – or (as Monday evening) film (i.e. a Laurel and Hardy favourite or similar). Bed-time – wash, and shoes inspection – then bed, with the radio extension on (beloved by all boys); shows included 'Ray's a larf' (Ted Ray show); 'Life with the Lyons' 'Ben and Bebe Daniels and family); 'As much binding in the Marsh' (Sam Costa[10], Kenneth Horne and friends). These were typical of the radio fun we were allowed and enjoyed – then lights out; talking allowed, possibly, for ten minutes then silence enforced by monitors on pain of corporal punishment if broken.

Saturday. The grammar school, up to recently a private prep school, had just stopped a Saturday morning class shortly before my commencement. But work was a norm every Saturday morning in the Homes. Detailed cleaning tasks were allocated to all boys, spread throughout the grounds. And jobs very typical of all institutions, large and small. Most and unpopular was chair polishing work in the dining rooms. Since the war the old chipped wooden tables and long forms had been replaced by more modern furniture. If detailed, every part of the chair had to experience the wax polish provided and the same methodically cleaned off. If any polish remained, it had to be done again – and again and again – until passing inspection.

The worst experience was on one Saturday morning when Mr. G. echoed his disgust by making all of our working party stand on their chairs, hands on heads, for all that afternoon. It was a notable exception, but highlighted the difficulty to please some members of staff. Window cleaning was a similarly unpopular task that could take all day rather than all morning. Sweeping the courtyard I described whilst at the Dingle. The long Hut dormitories and dining rooms were swept by one detail and scrubbed and/or polished by another work group.

An interesting alternative Saturday morning job was the wax polishing of the Hut dormitory floor, and large wartime steel and lino covered Morrison shelter, now work-table surface. It involved a thin spreading of polish throughout the floor, and then the swinging to and fro applications of the heavy metal bumpers with broom-length handle attached. To improve the shine, extra rags were placed under the bumpers. And we were 'allowed' to tie on to our feet some of these rags and slide–to polish in our otherwise stockinged feet. On the table too–a small boy could enjoy a limited skating experience. Whilst overhead – a luxury – the radio tannoy was sometimes turned on to enjoy music while we worked. Saturday afternoons were usually free, if it was not a once-monthly visiting day. The older boys could collect their pocket-money and visit the local cinema in Reigate or Redhill; the A.B.C., Majestic, or Odeon. The younger boys had to be accompanied either by staff or by older boys. My brother and I went out together–when possible to the cinema–a glorious escape from an entrenched routine to celluloid adventure.

Sunday Suit

Sundays I have described, but notably there were no enforced work details on this day of rest, only beds to be made up. It was the day for school clothes to be put away and the Sunday grey suits to be put on in order to present our better appearances to the outside world in visiting their churches and walking through their town community. At the close of the day, the grey suits had to be very precisely folded; the trousers (short or long) properly creased, folded with Sunday braces tucked in, and placed within the jacket–and the whole folded in a *particular* boxed fashion. The Sunday suits when collected would then be examined by the duty housemaster and (as with the shoe and wash routine inspections), if your suit was not properly folded – or worse, was torn or dirty – then this could be a corporal offence and a caning the end result. Like the night-time boot or teeth inspections (only worse), the Sunday night suit inspections I found fraught with real fear – of getting it wrong and of then expected retribution. Due punishment. At least a caning .

The suits were piled onto the large centre work table, and alongside the linen basket where grey woollen-socks in need of darning were to be placed for the Dingle staff over the way to later attend to. The Sunday suits' routine was quite awesome a conclusion to each Sunday. As the housemaster called each boy's number out, it was collected, stacked, and later checked. Intense relief was echoed as the boy's suit was passed and the enclosed Sunday-best tie and customary trousers' braces were also checked out–and inevitable tension, yes, fear, I awaited the check, to an accompanied overhead Sunday evening radio, big band, *Palm Springs Orchestra* or whatever happened to be on from

8.30 to 9.00 p.m. But as post-war years passed by (and, in retrospect, new Children Acts passed allowing more finance into the Homes), tastes of opulence were experienced by us kids.

Opulence

A regular Monday evening Huts' dining-room cinema show became norm for which nine-pence per week was deducted from our new pocket-money, to pay for this luxury, in early 1951. Apart from an easy diet of westerns and comedies (especially much loved Laurel & Hardy films), occasionally a real documentary salvo was displayed. One vivid recollection was a shown documentary of war in the Pacific, and terrifying flamethrowers in action with their victims fleeing from besieged foxholes and caves in mountains. But, as this horror did not relate to any reality of our orphanage past experience, it was viewed as just another fictional movie. But – spared from the reality of such events – the full horror and waste of human fecklessness and immense pursuits of power and revenge, were a sophistication happily out of reach in the closed Homes' institution. As likely it was not, of course, to children, in a real line of fire.

A small orphanage library sprang up, the books stored in a large cabinet in one of the prefabricated Huts dining-rooms. This literary haven was administered by one of the masters, Mr. B.– I think, on a one evening per week basis. From this stock I first read the Enid Blyton 'Five' adventure books. And, in particular, Mark Twain's 'Tom Sawyer' and his close friend 'Huckleberry Finn': it was very easy to identify with such boy heroes.

Once, returned from school, children were not allowed out of the grounds. But in 1950 and into 1951 a certain laxity was to be noticed, and staff were allowed to take selected boys (and girls) out to attend social activities in the community. In school holidays, if you did not go home to relatives or guardians, excursions to the cinema, pantomime, swimming, walks to forest or lake land were experienced. All events helped to slacken the otherwise closed-in feeling of boredom and vexation experienced sometimes within the Homes.

Such outside visits certainly drew staff-and-children closer together. And, inevitably, contacts with the outside also created a taste for liberty and an eagerness for an eventual leaving date. Unknown to my brother and myself, our departure date was drawing close–but not yet. In family home or children's home, occasional illness often comes as an unwelcome visitor. Already I have indicated the Homes' staff tight morals, standards of immaculate general health and hygiene, and thus the greatly diminished risks of major infections and illnesses. But contact with schools and the community also brought in occasional ailments and shared common discomforts.

Whilst living downstairs in the Dingle I acquired athlete's foot, a very painful annoying skin ailment on both feet between the toes. I still had this on entry to the Hut, but following a course of iodine foot-baths by Sister Webb over at the Dingle surgery, it eventually disappeared, never to return.

Another common ailment in the Homes was the acquisition of chilblains on fingers and / or toes. Most schools, dormitories and dining rooms had large cast-iron steam radiators. And suffering from intense cold I was one of many who quickly headed for the nearest radiator – subsequently, red swollen fingers and toes might be the result. Fortunately they did not last long, but uncomfortable Vaseline-coated limbs was a too common instance during winters of the late forties and early nineteen-fifties. Inevitable occasional fractured limbs, and bouts of flu, competed with normal childhood illnesses like chicken-pox and measles. But it was very much to the Homes' credit that general health remained always at a good level.

Following my 11+ common entrance examination scholarship to the local Reigate Grammar School, for a short while, another world was experienced for a few hours every school day. On entry to the first form, I think it was 1949, form-masters still wore black tasselled caps and flowing black gowns – just like masters caricatured in our comics. Latin and French became a normal diet –'Sto Stas Stat','Amo Amas Amat'. And for the two years I attended this school I did very well.

For some extraordinary reason, end of year form placements were engineered by combining summer examination results with an arbitrarily calculated 'average' based on school term work, by the form-master. Whereas the examination marks were clear appraisals, the form-master's remarks it was felt were much dependent on outside school relationships (no chance), and social criteria, rather than proven success at academic school work. But I still came 2nd in exam work, at least. ...

Our own orphanage 8th Reigate Scout Troop was a pleasure, formed within the Homes, and we attended a competitive camp at Surrey Ranmore Common (Walton Firs) circa. 1950–1. This was the orphanage's own Scouting Group, with its own scoutmaster; my brother (in the cubs) and I (in the scouts) were members of the 8th Troop, which performed well, at these outside camps.

Grammar School Pirates

Some time during 1950 I was playing in a routine gym game of 'Pirates' at Reigate Grammar School, which meant boys clambered up ropes and side panels, along Swiss apparatus, over gym horses, and jumped over on to islands (mats placed around the large floor), whilst being pursued by selected opposition. I flew from the top rail of the wood panelling, or rather foolishly jumped, and landed badly on a mat and fractured my left ankle.

Laid up in plaster in the Homes' sick bay for some time, plus several doses of 'flu, I was absent from school for a considerable amount of time. Came the examinations at the summer end of 1951 term – I put in a lot of homework – and to my surprise I came top of the form in the examinations; English, Latin, French, History and Geography all had marks high up in the gradings. But due to my great absence through sickness I was down-graded to second or third place although I was clearly out front through effort in examinations. Worse was to follow later where schooling was concerned. As a school child this seemed most unjust.

It was July 1951 when my brother and I finally left Spurgeon's Orphanage Homes at Reigate, Surrey. For one last time we joined other boys due to go on summer holidays with guardians or parents. Our brown haversacks, battered suitcases and holdalls evenly distributed, we left for the railway station en passage to Victoria Station and our new north London home. For some months previous to departure we eagerly absorbed details of our leaving from Uncle Tom and Ma, and discussed the event with our Dorking cousins.

Miss Barson (who'd accompanied us evacuees to Wales in 1944–5) had recently retired from teaching, following Dr. Holt's demise, in 1947, and settled at her home in Juani, Reigate Road – opposite the Grammar School. For two years I attended this school, my brother joining me a year after I passed the 11+; we were regularly entertained by our elderly friend and mentor, and her equally caring elder sister. They remained the only friends we had made who lived 'outside' the Homes' domain other, that is, than distant mother's relatives.

Absent Father

Our Australian born father, to my personal knowledge, had never made any approach to contact us. (This was *not* true but I did not learn of this till after my mother's death over sixty years later); mother declared that he only showed interest in one child (myself, his namesake) – and unjustly excluded my younger brother at that time. Thus we never could remember our father. We learnt many years later that after divorce he married a Scots lady in London, and despite his being some years older than mother, it is quite possible we have several unknown younger half-brother or sisters. (None were traced.) Another unknown area.

My father was purported to be about fifteen years senior to mother. He was born in 1902; they married in London, at St. Paul's Canonbury, on the 6th January 1935. A rogue (she said) he may have been but all relatives who knew him own to his musical, dancing, and wide creative artistic talents and his immense energy. (I would love to have known him). Mother said father was born in Richmond Australia about 1902 (his father an Austrian 19th century immigrant, with a silver-plate in his head). Father's younger bro Thomas Hopper, and sister Greta Hopper also lived in Australia (or New Zealand). Totally unknown to me. Father left Australia (or N.Z.), at 15 years old (1917?), and ran off to sea. For a time he was a clown with a circus troupe in Spain and Scandinavia. At some time father arrived in the United States of America, it must have been just before the Great Depression in the early 1920s, and before the era of the movie talkies, and advance of the movies and early demise in 1930s of the raw Vaudeville (music hall).

He may have become a nationalised American citizen. (No record is known of any details.) His talent in painting, design, music, banjo, piano, writing, dancing and stagecraft, led him to be a stooge (clown), and writer for American comedians 'Olsen & Jolsen' for at least eleven years and more. On leaving the States for London the comedians several times sent the return fare and expenses to return to work with them but (my mother recalled those offers) he declined and remained, and stayed in wartime London. Here he met and married my mother, on January 6th 1935. Maude Susie Manton was then 20 years old. In those years the early 1930s mother and two sisters worked in theatre land. Her eldest sister Lillian Manton (b.1911) was lifted from West End Theatre usherette to film star, at 17 years of age, a beautiful blonde.[11] And for some years the sisters mingled in and on the fringe of stage and film making, Mother working as an extra for a time (e.g. H.G. Wells' film *'Things to Come'*– extra on South Down filming).

My parents knew 1930s showbiz Binnie and Sonnie Hale, Monty Banks and other actors and actresses, presumably through Lillian Manton's contacts. And following this life-style, mother met father, and after marriage lived in Chelsea (Ma said she remembered the awful rats coming up and being visible on the Thames embankment whilst they were renting at Chelsea). They then, for a while, rented lodgings in Rupert Street, Soho, in the West End of London, when father was performing cabaret as a Russian dancer in a nearby night club. They later moved up to Hendon District (Barnet R.D.) where my father obtained irregular work as a stage designer in the Film Studios. On my 27 February 1937 birth certificate our address says 28 Whitehouse Avenue (adjacent to the film studios) at Boreham Wood, with father's occupation listed as stage artiste.

I was told he lived a hectic life in show biz during the 1930s and 1940s or so I was informed. When mother again (after me in 1937) became pregnant in 1938, he wanted her to have an abortion (she said). Financially times were very hard and another war was clearly approaching. The fragile marriage broke. They attempted to repair it–but it proved unsuccessful and divorce eventually followed. Divorce Court Missionaries (Probation) in North London attempted to persuade my estranged father to assist her financially but he refused (she said), at least on a regular basis. She always refused *any* access to see my brother and me; although we were then placed away in an Orphanage.

Father re-married in the late 1940s (though bro and I knew nothing about this fact for many decades as we remained in the orphanage). He went back into the theatre appearing as Barone Ernst (aka Ernest or Edward) Hopper, in a Chicago 1948 show called *Funzapoppin*, a sequel to *Hellzapoppin*, in the USA, reuniting with his friends, the American comedians Olsen & Jonson. Father was billed (with), ' Billy Kaye and Barone Hopper (musical hall performers from Australia).' Years later I learnt he was briefly married to a Swedish lady, long before meeting my mother. We have no memories whatever of our Australian father and his relatives. Our soon distanced mother later re-married, (in 1949), a Dubliner Tom Dolan who became our step-father, and we were *eventually* withdrawn from the Reigate Spurgeon's Orphanage in July 1951. ... Staying with them till my *Call Up* into National Service in August 1955, later, signing on for an extra year–plus; to be discharged December 1958. Twenty-one years old.

Years later, in the 1980s, I located Abney Park cemetery on Stamford Hill, and found my mother's relatives' plots. Later still, I employed a professional family history genealogist, who found my father's burial plot, in Hither Green Cemetery, located in GZ 856 – close to the relatives' crematorium. He died alone in a care home in 1973; on his death certificate it registered he was born in New Zealand in 1902: a professional artist and theatre stage designer.

Our Lil

1929-30: Time of talkies replacing silent films. At the Alhambra, *The Compulsory Husband*, with *After The Fog*–then, the latter appeared, replaced with Alfred Hitchcock's (first talky comedy) Irish classic *Juno and The Paycock*. Italian Monty Banks to marry English favourite Gracie Fields. Inset pic of Monty Banks & Lillian Manton, my mother's sister, aged 17 years in 1929.

"OUR LIL"—A FILM STAR!

Programme Seller's Rise to Fame.

RIVIERA TRIP.

" Everyone loves her—she's so pretty and has such lovely blue eyes—and I miss her. I'm almost lost without my Lil."

In a small, working-class house, one of a few comprising a narrow back street in Islington, a buxom and cheerful mother of eight children thus referred to her 17-year-old daughter, who a few days ago was helping her with the housework.

Now she is at a palatial Continental hotel in Nice, ' starring " with Mr. Monty Banks, in a new comedy to be called " The Compulsory Husband."

Romance entered the life of Miss Lillian Manton, whose home is in Baxter-grove, Islington, while she was a programme seller at the Fortune Theatre.

This is Miss Manton's own story of how it happened :—

Lilian Manton.

" One night about Christmas time, when I was selling programmes in the theatre, I noticed a man in the stalls watching intently my every movement. I felt extremely embarrassed until he broke the ice and spoke to me.

" It was Mr. Harry Lachman, the film producer, and he asked he if I would like to undergo a film test. At first I thought he was joking, but when he assured me he was serious I said I would, and thanked him.

" The next day I went to the studios. They made me up, and placed me before the camera. I just smiled as pleasantly as I could. That night I returned to my programmes, but soon after I was asked to undergo another test. This time with Monty Banks himself, who was kindness itself in the way he assisted me."

A few days later the lucky girl, whose "off" hours from the theatre had always been spent in helping her mother in their humble home, was signing a contract, and within a short space after that she was speeding with other film stars to the Riviera.

SHE CAN COOK, TOO!

" Proud of her? That I am," said Mrs. Manton, her cheerfully smiling mother, to a representative of " The Sunday News."

" All the same, I hope it won't turn her head—but I'm sure it won't. We are only a poor little family, and Lil was one of my main supports. No mother could wish for a better girl. She can cook lovely !"

At St. Paul's L.C.C. school, Islington, where Lillian was educated, 'ey are very proud of her rise to fame—and you should just hear what her younger twin brothers say about " Our Lil !"

From *The Sunday News*, January 1929, (see also *Daily Mail*, 18th January 1929).

Seventeen year old film star Lillian Manton and Mum, my maternal grandmother, 1929.
Everybody has a past... My Aunt, Lillian Manton, born January 1911, was born shortly before
her grandfather died in 1914 (his wife had died in 1902). My mother, Maude Manton, was
born November 1915. In the mid-late Victorian era, a family fortune was lost, due to a faulty
entail... The film script of '*The Compulsory Husband*', written about 1927-8, a silent film, then
converted to an early 'talky', released in 1929 (publicity photo inset above). Years later, in
1940, Lillian's two children, Barbara and Eileen, were evacuated to Northampton with my bro
and me – they, too returned to London. From 1929, 1930s and 1940s, my mother's family
were involved with the West End stage and film industry. Her sister a film actress; my father,
in vaudeville and cabaret. Gainsborough Film Studio was close by, in Islington, N1. And, in
Borehamwood, there were Elstree Film Studios in Herts – close to where I was born, in 1937
– But, my life had no show biz; only a brief West End dance teaching career, in the 1960s...

Institution

Institutional Care: Examples of British orphan childrens' homes, from 1750s. From the top down: 1. The Foundling Hospital – 'The foundation of this hospital, for the relief of exposed and deserted young children, was laid 16th September, the George II, 1742' (pic. 1810). 2. Royal Military Asylum (Chelsea) 1801. 3. Asylum for Fatherless Children; Reedham orphanage, Purley, Surrey, 1844. 4. 'Lining up to go home.' Foundlings group postcard, 1930s. 5. Beeding Court Mission for 80 children (West Sussex). Postcard, 1913. As always, many, many orphaned and destitute children were left alone as street urchins, or entombed, in care, in a poorhouse, workhouse, or house of correction... Source: largely from old postcards

Dr Barnardo

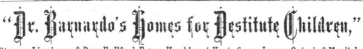

"Dr. Barnardo's Homes for Destitute Children,"

Stepney, Limehouse & Bow, E; Ilford, Essex; Hawkhurst, Kent; Gorey, Jersey; Ontario & Manitoba.

Former Presidents.— { The Right Honourable the late EARL CAIRNS.
The Right Honourable the EARL OF MEATH, P.C.
The Right Honourable the LORD POLWARTH.

President for 1890-91—The Most Honourable the MARQUIS OF LORNE, P.C., K.T.

Vice-Presidents.— { Sir ARTHUR BLACKWOOD, K.C.B.   JAMES RANKIN, Esq., M.P.
The Rev. CANON GIRDLESTONE, M.A.   SAMUEL SMITH, Esq., M.P.
The LORD KINNAIRD.   COLONEL C. E. HOWARD VINCENT, C.B., M.P.

Treasurer.—WILLIAM FOWLER, Esq. (National Discount Company), 35, Cornhill, E.C.

Founder and Director.—T. J. BARNARDO, Esq., F.R.C.S.E., 18 to 26, Stepney Causeway, E.

Bankers.—LONDON & SOUTH-WESTERN BANK (Bow Branch); PRESCOTT, DIMSDALE, CAVE, TUGWELL & CO., Ltd., 50, Cornhill, E.C.

COMMITTEE.

Chairman.—SAMUEL G. SHEPPARD, Esq. (Sheppards, Pellys, Scott & Co.), 57, Old Broad Street, E.C.

Vice-Chairman.—HOWARD WILLIAMS, Esq. (Hitchcock, Williams & Co.), St. Paul's Churchyard, E.C.

C. C. M. BAKER, Esq., B.A., 6, King's Bench Walk, Temple, E.C.
WM. BAKER, Esq., M.A., LL.B., 10, New Court, Carey Street, W.C.
Rev. Canon BARKER, M.A., Rector of St. Marylebone, W.
W. ANSTIS BEWES, Esq., M.A., LL.B., 11, Stone Buildings, W.C.
Rev. J. TRAIN DAVIDSON, D.D., Presbyterian Church, Colebrooke Row, Islington, N.
Rev. NEWMAN HALL, LL.B., Christ Church, Lambeth.
Rev. D. R. HANKIN, M.A., Vicar of St. Jude's, Mildmay.
Gen. R. MACLAGAN, R.E., LL.D., 4, West Cromwell Road, S.W.

Rev. DONALD MACLEOD, M.A., D.D., St. Columba's, Church of Scotland, Pont Street, Belgravia.
Rev. F. B. MEYER, B.A., Baptist Church Regent's Park, N.W.
Rev. H. SINCLAIR PATERSON, M.A., M.D., Notting Hill Presbyterian Church.
Hon. and Rev. W. T. RICE, M.A., Vicar of All Saints', Woolwich, S.E.
Rev. W. L. ROSEDALE, LL.D., Vicar of Middleton, King's Lynn.
Rev. J. H. SCOTT, M.A., Rector of Spitalfields, E.
HEYWOOD SMITH, Esq., M.A., M.D., 18, Harley Street, W.
A. BUTLER STONEY, Esq., LL.D., 6, Stone Buildings, Lincoln's Inn Fields, W.C.

General Secretary.—MR. JOHN ODLING.

In reply, please say how you should be addressed, whether Miss., Mrs., Rev., Mr., or Esq.

ALL COMMUNICATIONS TO BE ADDRESSED TO THE OFFICE,

18 to 26, Stepney Causeway,

London, E.

Telegraphic Address:
WAIFDOM, LONDON.

Letterhead

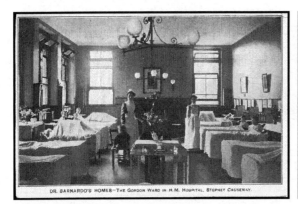

DR. BARNARDO'S HOMES—THE GORDON WARD IN H.M. HOSPITAL, STEPNEY CAUSEWAY.

DR. BARNARDO—"THE FATHER OF NOBODY'S CHILDREN." From a drawing by Alfred Pearse.

LEFT: Dr Barnardo's Homes; the Gordon ward in Stepney Causeway (old Postcard). **RIGHT:** Dr Barnardo (1845-1905) (Old postcard, of a drawing by Alfred Pearse) Dr Barnardo homes, for destitute and necessitous children. First institution established in 1870, in Stepney Causeway, South London.

Above, one of many Barnardo's cottage homes, schools and settlements. Like Spurgeon's, they largely depended on charity – otherwise only the poor law. Source of the previous three pictures above, old postcards.

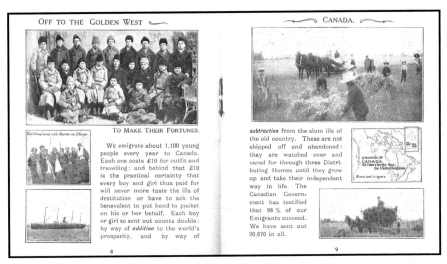

Dr Barnardo's Homes. 1904. Migrant destitute children, sent off to Canada for resettlement. In 1980, Professor Joy Parr of Queen's University, Ontario, Canada, published a detailed work on *Labouring Children. British Immigrant Apprentices to Canada. 1869-1924*; which included data from Dr Barnardo's Homes Annual Reports (in Canada)...

Inset, portrait of Rev. C. H. Spurgeon (1834-1892), baptist minister and philanthropist. His first institution, for boys only (main picture) opened in South London, Stockwell, on the Clapham Road, in 1867. It existed until 1939, when the establishment evacuated to St Davids, Reigate (until 1953, when it moved to Birchington, Kent). Stockwell was bombed during the war.

Boys' side, Stockwell, from 1867.

My great, grandfather's (1849-1914) first cousin, the Rev. Joseph Manton-Smith, was a personal friend of C.H. Spurgeon, greatly assisted in raising funds in the East End of London, for this project. (See journalist Peter Paterson's *How Much More of This, Old Boy...?: Scenes from a Reporter's Life.* (He grew up in Stockwell and Reigate: Five years older than myself – he, too, lived on the boys' side of Reigate, and at S. Wales, St. Davids, evacuation (I did not know him); he left in 1945.) I would leave in 1951...Source *C.H. Spurgeon's Autobiography,* 1900 (four volumes)

> During the past 78 years
> # Spurgeon's Orphan Homes
> **1945**   (temporarily at Reigate, Surrey)

1947-8. Spurgeons Orphan Homes own Cricket Team. Third from left back-row the Sports Master Mr Batson. The seniors in the above photo were all older than myself and left the Homes by 1950 to make their way in life. The Homes sports teams also had outside fixtures with local teams – and the Girls their own teams i.e. Stool Ball (similar to baseball).

1948-9. Football Team. Holmsdale Road Reigate Secondary School. With Mr Yates (my form master) top left.. After the implementing of the 1944 Education Act, older Spurgeons children attended outside the gates of the institution, mingling with local populace in the local Secondary, and (soon my) Reigate Grammar School. Source, 1950s photos of the above in my possession (but photographers unknown).

1950-1.The 8th Reigate Scout Troop at Ranmore Common Camp. This was the orphanage's own registered group (as with the larger Dr. Barnardo's' orphanage) with its own scoutmaster; my brother and I (both in the pics) were active members of the troop, which did very well at outside competitive camps. TOP LEFT: Cooking in the field, 1950. TOP RIGHT: I am last on the left. BOTTOM LEFT: My Bro, arrowed, at centre. BOTTOM RIGHT: The Scouts and Cubs, a worthy, caring institution, for boys and girls. Source, photographs in my possession...

St. David's (Cricket Pavilion on left) Wray Park Road, Reigate, formerly pre-1939 an exclusive boarding school. 1939-1953 circa. In my time, a taboo! Girls' Side, including a primary school, in later years, of Spurgeon's Orphan Homes. Later to become part of the headquarters of Surrey Fire Brigade. Source, photo by author, 1953.

Spurgeon's Orphan Homes in Reigate Surrey. Boys lived on one side of grounds, girls on the other. Photo a posed united pic with other kids, taken on girls side down in front of St. David's house. Bro and I would leave the Homes in July 1951. Source, photo in my collection – unknown photographer.

LEFT: 1953. Homes just vacated. Oak Road side-entrance of Homes on the Boys' side, first entered early in 1944. **RIGHT:** The Huts, Boys' Dining Room, and office (far left, kitchen on right). The Dingle juniors ate in this section, the huts seniors ate in the other half (out of sight). Source, pictures by author, 1953.

Main Gate entrance, from Holmsdate Road, in 1981. The old two orphanage prefab huts still existent. This road led up to the right (out of sight) to the Dingle. The superintendent and his wife (the matron) M/M Anderson lived in the house behind the fence, over to the immediate right.

The Huts, boys' side, age 12–16. 1981. The old wartime Huts–the allotments in the foreground. The old boot room is centre of the pic. The site awaiting conversion.

The Dingle, The Dingle Walk (the Dell) behind it, for boys side, age 7–12. Thirty years on. Two cedars – gone. The Dingle converted. On the right new buildings replace the mounds of the underground cellars, used as Anderson wartime air-raid shelters by us children & staff. ... I remember it well. In 1981 an established HQ for Surrey fire brigade. Source, pictures by author.

Spurgeons Orphan Homes – Departure

Standing (left to right): M. Harbour, M. Birch, J. Greetham, K. Price, M. Tweed, G. Betts, R. McLeish, B. Bailey. Sitting: D. Elliott, S. Hills, C. Dyer, I. Gordon.

Annual Leavers, Summer 1952.

Only months after I had left the institution. The photo culled from the Homes monthly magazine *Within Our Gates* is of the annual summer leaving group of 15 year plus school leavers, and older, Grammar school leavers – all the above children known to me. Eg; David Elliott, sitting first on the left accompanied us (with the teachers and staff including Miss Barson), as evacuees in the last year of the war to Wales 1944–5, as did most of the posed group, which was taken one year after I left for north London, about July 1952. The Homes formally moved to Birchington Kent in 1953, and the Surrey Fire Brigade moved onto the Reigate site.

Years later, Brian (Bill) Bailey (back row), having viewed the online PDF 'draft' of this memoir, on 1st May 2012, sent me the following email from the Netherlands:

Hi Barone,
Greetings from Holland.
I have been reading about your experiences at Spurgeons. It was exactly as you described. I am the B. Bailey in the pic of the group who left Spurgeons in 1952.
I was born in 1937 and was sent into care at Barnardos when the war started. After the war in 1948 mum sent me to Spurgeons.
Thanks for the trip down memory lane, I really enjoyed it. I think I recognise that pic of you when you were ten, but not the name.
Mr G was sacked after I advised my pal, John Taylor, to report his vile threats to the preacher on Sunday, after the service in St. David's Chapel. Mr Holmes and Mr Skardon were much fairer, heh? Regards, B. Bailey (my RAF pals called me Bill, and it stuck).

Het ga je goed.

Post War London

Chapter Two - Post War London

Skylon, Festival of Britain, 1951. (Source: Author.)

Out of Care

It was a warm summer's day, Friday 27th July 1951, when bro and I left Spurgeon's Orphanage (aka Spurgeon's Home) in Reigate Surrey for the *very* last time. We were destined for a *new* home in north London – together, *in a family*. My brother was just turned thirteen years old, and I fourteen years of age. I had lived in this institution (after years of war evacuation) from 1944–51 – and bro from 1945–51... homeless from 1939–51: twelve years.

Ending a lifetime of mostly being *somewhere* in care.

A family... this reality was, for bro and me, unique. It felt strange, yet magical, as we boarded the train at Reigate Station and travelled up northwards; through Redhill and East Croydon to Victoria Station. In close excitement, we inhaled the thick train smoke from the forward engine, tasted the acrid, sulphur motes which trawled backwards funnelling, through tunnels and narrow cuttings, sucked in through the carriage windows opened in the summer's heat. Mother quickly insisted that we grab the thick-leather holed-thong, and pull the window up. But soon we entered the cacophony of the huge London (aka The Smoke) terminus, its atmosphere a constant changing kaleidoscope, indistinct in haze human and locomotive industry.

Victoria Station was the largest of the Southern Railway's terminals, earlier known as a station for the London, Brighton and South Coast Railway. It was constructed with sixteen-plus platforms, so long that two trains stood end to end at each platform. Before its inception, early trains from the south finished at London Bridge, sharing it with the Dover Line. I loved and welcomed its thudding pulse.

Picking up our meagre belongings packed in Woolworth brown sisal-tied cardboard cases, I tucked a well battered cricket bat under my arm as we made for one of the beloved red double-decker London Transport buses out of Victoria. Taxis and private cars were then, to me, believed, only for the rich or famous – and foreign visitors. Not for us other Londoners, as we identified ourselves, although I had resided in Surrey these past seven years.

London town was heart's home.

The Underground did not reach our part of London. Stoke Newington was due north of Shoreditch and Dalston, and south of Stamford Hill and Finsbury Park–all stops on the long Kingsland Road. The closest tube stations were Liverpool Street or Finsbury – both meant buses to arrive at our destination. There were no more noisy rattling Janus driven electric trams, of which I had many fixed infant memories; as route 33, crossing Ballspond Road up north through Green Lanes during the early wartime forties. There was a brief back-shot of a moving 33 tram in the 1944 wartime Gilliat film *Waterloo Road* starring John Mills and Stewart Granger. The celluloid background footage, included authentic shots of bomb damaged ruins in the London scenes.

We boarded a 38 bus at Victoria, via Piccadilly Circus, for Dalston Junction; then, changed to a number 643 trolleybus north, up the Kingsland High Street – its name changing into Stoke Newington High Street, where we would descend, for Dynevor Road; adjacent to Church Street N16 – our destination. As we left Victoria Station, seated up-front on top of the bus, mother pointed across the road to the Victoria Palace Theatre, a local music hall. On a massive outside billboard was faced *The Crazy Gang* – our Uncle George (married to ex-land-army girl Aunt Olive Butters nee Manton, one of mother's three sisters), had until recently worked in this music hall for some years as one of its electricians, after being demobbed from wartime service in the Royal Air Force. Unhappily, he was presently laid up in bed in an advanced stage of tuberculosis. Though almost six years had passed since the war had finished, many broken house-plots remained, hoardings up, with torn wartime billposters quite visible. Our mother's rented house at 1 Baxter Grove was one of the 1940 blitzed ruins – presently, in 1951, an empty brown corner site. The bus conductor counted two paper tickets and punched the fare stages. Mother showed her bus pass. She had been a bus conductress since the early days of the war in 1942. At present it was the 22 bus route, Homerton to Putney. During our school holidays from the Homes bro and I had sometimes travelled with her, 'on duty'. Tales of wartime escapes were already memorised. Best was her description of Bill, her driver's, close escape; his bus stopped, and he got out during a noisy air-raid for a break. Walking away, he bent down to tie a shoelace, and was suddenly blown off his feet: a bomb had demolished his bus behind him, and left its remains parked in a large hole.

As we journeyed on the upper deck of the slow moving London Transport red bus, a panorama unrolled of our sad, kindred, war-torn plains of London. And so recent memories, reflecting bro and my own brief fragmented lifetime. It was also summer term school holidays, though we would soon be changing schools for the umpteenth time to an unknown school curriculum.

In July 1951 London and its media were reflecting excitement generated by the *Festival of Britain* exhibition, built by the Thames, the site, a blitz-flattened South Embankment, near Waterloo Station. We noticed a huge 'saucepan lid' dome and the Skylon, a large elongated cigar-like metal entity suspended vertically and taut against the skyline – seen as we crossed the bridge over the Thames to enter Victoria Station. Bro and I decided to visit this spectacular event by ourselves – a taste of our new found freedom. It was an unreal experience this *going home*. It felt – despite the excitement – just like it was, initially, but a holiday.

Parents off to work, my brother and I began to explore our new London domain. Stoke Newington, formerly Saxon Neutone, Newington, until recent times was a small rural village in Middlesex, two and a half miles north from London, between the City of London and Westminster, and Edmonton.

The local manor house was the one-time seat of Sir Thomas Abney; Dr. Isaac Watts lived therein for thirty-six years. Following the demise of Mrs Abney, daughter of Sir Thomas, last will and testament revealed that this entire estate was to be sold, and the proceeds distributed in charitable donations. And so it was sold to Jonathan Eade, esquire, the monies realised distributed to local charity. The cemetery located close to our new home, unknown at this time, housed – if that's the word – a number of mother's relatives dating back to the mid-nineteenth century. My bro and I dearly wanted to feel we belonged, and learnt that a number of mother's (thus ours too) forebears had lived and been buried in this vicinity, for several generations. Roots...

Black Beauty's Quaker author, Anna Sewell, as a teenager lived in Stoke Newington in the 1830s (as did Edgar Alan Poe) – she acquired her awful injuries at that time. And, contemporary with myself, the adorable Barbara Windsor, our young cockney nightingale, lived nearby (I never knew her) in the 1950s...

For some years we collected our comics in Stoke Newington, *Captain Marvel* et al. And, in the late fifties, I added science fiction magazines – as *New Worlds Science Fiction*... These delightful teenage readings were printed locally by Nova Publications, at 52 Stoke Newington Road, London N16. One issue (pure H.G. Wells territory, issue no. 22) introduced *The Sentinel*, by Arthur C. Clarke – with its 1954 edition cover picturing the 'relic on the moon' – fantastic, in the future, of 2001...

Rocket through Space

 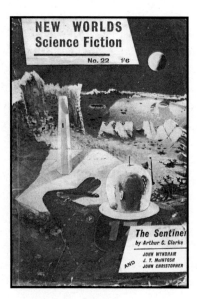

Left: January 1937 (I was born February 1937) cover from English *Practical Mechanics* magazine. **Right:** The 1954 English issue of *New Worlds Science Fiction*, featuring Arthur C. Clarke. Nazi Germany was the first in developing the V1 and V2 rockets in 1944. The USA first to land men on the moon in 1969. Science fiction was becoming scientific fact in my lifetime... I saw the real rocket flying bombs, nicknamed 'doodlebugs', overhead, and the first moon landings on live television.

St Paul's Cathedral

Top Left: St Paul's, by Paul Popper (d.1969) was taken pre-Blitz; through the top cross-lattice enclosure – looking Eastwards. The vast majority of the buildings below were all destroyed during the Blitz, the Nazi raids on London, in September 1940.   (Source: Undated, pre-war photograph, taken from The World's Best Photographs, Odhams Press, 1940, p221)

Top Right and Bottom: Pictures taken by me, at 14 years old, from the very top of St. Pauls cross, looking westwards, the *Festival of Britain*, visible, in mid 1951, ringed by bombed ruins – temporary buildings visible on brown sites... **Centre**: looking northwards to the Old Bailey, from the top of St. Pauls. 1951. (Photo by author)

Roots

Easy walking distance from our 1951 small terraced home 139 Dynevor Road was Abney Park Cemetery of thirty acres–the cemetery opened in 1840. Most of its grounds were originally of an Manorial Estate–attached to Abney House. The house was demolished in 1846. Shortly after the private cemetery was opened, my maternal great-great-grandfather George Manton (1807-1856), a City of London tea dealer at no.8 Eastcheap, purchased a family plot, located south of Abney's internal North Boundary Road – a path side grave at B5, the end of Elm Road. (My Hopper's origins unknown – but, overseas.)

George Manton was buried in 1856, dying of apoplexy at forty-nine years of age; the same year as his own father Joseph Manton, also buried on the site. On George's demise there were four surviving children (two boys, two girls): My great grandfather, James Leigh Manton (1849-1914) was the eldest male heir survivor. But great aunt Lil's father James Leigh was persuaded to sign away an Entail in suspicious circumstances, and thus 'swindled' (great aunt Lil's word) out of a Manton inheritance by two of his uncles, the younger bros of George, named Richard and Nathan. ('Nathan drowned himself in Northampton. Richard fled to Australia and married a rich widow, I heard some years later on' great aunt Lil added.) Richard and Nathan had been advised by a Josiah Beddow, accountant for the firm of tea & coffee dealers. [2] James Walter Manton (her bro and my maternal Grandfather) witnessed his father's signature at the time. A later coincidence; the year before her father's death (July 1914) which would have been in 1913, he received a legacy of £100 from a cousin named Thomas Manton living in Northampton.

An interesting connection. George Manton's rented home in the 1850s was known as Pymmes estate (damaged in the Second World War) up in Edmonton. Aunt Lil said (all of this data recorded orally on a tape in 1980–the year before she herself passed away at 93 years old). How sad it was that when he, her father, and two sisters were in their old age; they would visit Old Pymmes Park's walled-in Edmonton garden. That was their old kitchen garden, and they'd talk of happier times when they were young children, tended by a nanny and servants..

'It was so sad' Great Aunt Lil remembered. 'They'd talk of their departed father George Manton, and of grandfather Joseph Manton's demise in 1856...' Of George's 1850s tea dealer company[3] and the fleet of clippers which was much affected by the soon to be Crimea War, and an abnormally high price of tea. George died an alderman of the City of London and was expected to be a lord mayor of London. About 1853, he was given the freedom of the City of London (at the time of Charles Dickens): its legacy provided for his children. And his son James Leigh Manton, my great grandfather, received his schooling at the Mercers of Holborn with his brother George Leigh; and his sisters Caroline and Marion went to the Freeman's School.

The oldest son James Leigh Manton (my great-grandfather), whose younger bro James Leigh, died in India in or about 1883. James Leigh appears to have been legally, entitled to George's family inheritance – perhaps, also related, backwards through a male lineage, and also connected to an un-named son of Dr Thomas Manton D.D. – the history of my family name remained blank.

Myths and legends. Fact and fiction. At the time in the early 1950s such historic family legalistic detail was unknown to me, and my mother and step-father. And. So what! In reality having such ancestors meant – nothing. It didn't prevent my bro and me from being estranged since birth, and ending up in an orphanage, my mother a relative pauper.

So what!

On an exploratory walk Saturday July 28th 1951 to nearby Clissold Park N16, (off Church Street and Green Lanes, near the Arsenal football ground), mother drew our attention to a recently built block of redbrick flats named *Manton House* located in Church Street. The local library had a picture of him on a wall at the Stoke Newington town hall. Ma indicated the small original church of St. Mary's, situated opposite its modern replacement, another larger edifice. 'He,' Mother said, 'Manton, was one of our ancestors'. Doctor Thomas Manton D.D., Holder of the living of St. Mary's. At his death on October 18th, 1677, he'd been a *dissenter,* a Puritan divine – and Cromwellian minister, Mr Manton, and served King Charles the Second.

'He was buried in the crypt.' mother added. I would pass that church, where unseen our eminent ancestor's remains were one-time hidden – pass the site many, many times. And what a can of worms I began to uncover, when trying to establish just a few London and, other, roots after bro and my complete anonymity, as displaced persons, in the orphanage, such a short time ago.[4]

To us, as teenage boys, this block of flats named after Manton, felt like a borrowed plume, as such genealogy knowledge, bore only a 'so what?' passing interest. As too, interest at zero, that many of our Victorian forebears had lived in this same vicinity. Amazingly our great aunt Lil would, many years later, inform us of Victorian relatives who had lived in Brougham Road, and that she firmly believed one of our forebears actually lived in our now (then) newly purchased home, when it was first erected. How strange life is, in its coincidences. Schoolboy diaries of those early nineteen-fifties reveal that, prior to leaving the Orphanage and for a considerable period after the event, an immense interest in visiting relatives, and enjoying the cinema and theatre, fills date after date of laconic leaf entries.

Initially our new parents couldn't afford us any pocket money, so (as before in the Homes) this had to be earned. And so, from an early date, I commenced Saturday mornings helping out on Unigate milk-rounds; learning to handle the hand-operated power wagons in which you literally pulled the vehicle forward and released the gear and applied the handbrake at the end of the long metal arm. Paper-rounds; two in the morning (up at five) and two after school, on my later-acquired second-hand bicycle – which rewards bought many cinema tickets. And for a period prior to leaving school, I assisted in a butcher's shop, scrubbing out the large out-back deep refrigerator and blood entrail strewn floors and thick wood tables, to sprinkle fresh sawdust to absorb again fresh spilt residue.

In retrospect, I look back with astonishment at the apparent ease with which my brother and I resettled back in a war-torn London. Recalling we had never in our previous brief lifetime ever lived as a nuclear family unit before. Researching childhood diaries – especially few and far between – is an experience not just of nostalgia, but reading of 'another person' a different, most certainly then innocent and seemingly naive human being. To illustrate: the following though banal surface leaf entries for the vital week followed leaving the Orphanage: 26 July 1951. Thurs. Break up for Summer hols. Speech Day. Pretty Good: 27 July. Fri. Leave Orph. Left: 28 July. Sat. Didn't do much. Visit Clissold Park: 29 July. Sun. Was given plastic camera by [step-dad] Dad: 30 July. Mon. Clissold Park : 31 July. Tues. Went to West End : 1 August. Wed. Aunt Olive's: 2 August. Thurs. Went to Festival of Britain. Swimming after: 3 August. Fri. Aunt Olive's. Stayed Home: 4 August. Sat. Morn. went and saw Uncle Arthur at Nan's. Eve Went to Pictures. Main film 'Command Decision' and 'Phantom of the Plains', also 'Jungle Girl, part 3. ' ... A family life. ...

I had experienced a father, stepfather, in a home situation, for the very first time. It seemed just natural a happening, an extension of mother, and if she was happy and O.K., then, without question, there was nothing to fight against. Why? The camera given to me was a small brown plastic 127 film holder, a cheap but effective machine, and very much appreciated as a warm and for some time treasured personal gesture from a relatively strange man, already called 'Dad' in the diary leaves, converted from 'Uncle Tom', our Dublin born Irish stepfather.

Festival of Britain

On our West End of London visits, mostly by bus or trolley-bus, we sat on top to the front or rear end seats where possible, as we studied a sometimes surreal landscape. Everywhere all the bus routes were pockmarked with still apparently untouched broken bombed out buildings. Greenery was emerging among many ruins, saplings, flowers and weeds, moss and abundant tufts of grass. Amongst the flotsam were the inevitable collected pools of often foul water, with human refuse pollution in all its variety, heaped and scattered amongst the ruined panorama. But these ruins were also our cricket and football playgrounds. And scattered, fronting the sites were numerous asbestos prefabs with minute gardens about them.

Aunt Olive, mother's sister, had frequently looked after us in years past holidays, and was held in fond regard by my brother and me. Relatives became our security. *The Festival of Britain* (built on bombed dockside ruins) visit was greatly enjoyed by us as boys, although the mostly economic and technical aspects were lost over our heads. It was the Festival's entertainment aspects which clung, though the high Skylon and broad dome were much admired. Like a huge modern washing machine or NASA space engine, there was a drum room exhibit in which, for one shilling, we placed ourselves, back and flat against its surface. It turned, first slowly, then escalating speed it went round faster, faster and faster. Then slowly on this fairground we felt the floor receded and dropped, lowered away, leaving human participants literally stuck in a frozen posture sucked against the walls, like flies glued to paper. Any movement was difficult and mostly impossible. Clothing, any object, equally grotesquely stuck in its arrested spot, and areas of flesh or underclothes exposed at the time of its fastest gravity-defying speed (Mach's principle). It was fun. There were the three-dimensional films, with colour line and sound drawn graphic animations.

And lots of foods. And engineering achievement displays. *The Festival of Britain* a truly pleasant and optimistic event.

For swimming, we attended the local baths in Church Street, Stoke Newington, near Clissold Park. The house we had moved into was a Victorian built small terraced three-bedroomed property. Initially it had no bathroom, and the toilet was more outside than in, in that it was built onto the house, but you had to go outside, exposed to wind and rain, to gain entry and proper relief. Consequently we had to go to local public baths, a bathhouse in Church Road, and pay sixpence (6d.) at least once a week, for a clean overhaul. And swimming was an extra fun-way of removing surface dirt. 'Saw Uncle Arthur at Nan's', my child's diary note recorded. This uncle was one of mother's brothers, in fact the youngest born in 1921, a tall handsome fair-haired distinguished man – one of many uncles and male relatives' some, not all, servicemen returning from the war.

Uncle Arthur Manton had signed on as a regular moving from his wartime regiment, the East Surrey (his older bro James Manton, Uncle Jim, had been in the Devonshire Regiment, serving three years on the isle of Malta) into the early fifties Royal Engineers; and in his uniform of the sappers was awaiting transfer out to Malaya. ... 'Went to Pictures' reads another diary note, included *Jungle Girl, Part 3*. Postwar 1950s cinema shows usually included two main features; and frequently included a weekly Gaumont Pathe News, a cartoon, and a current serial – and even a short documentary usually issued by the Coal Board or London based Central Office of Information (aka C.O.I).

News Theatres

From day one, at our first post-war arrival at Victoria Station, we saw a news theatre close by the exit of the station, on the east side. Great! We – Bro and I – regularly attended these minute cinemas which had, in the 1940s and 1950s, no main feature; but, the centre piece programme *The News* – documentaries and short features. And, for us, the loved *Walt Disney* cartoons. The programme was ongoing, with no separate performances. Price, one shilling (5p in metric).

Whilst waiting for friends and relatives in the West End, or mainline railway stations, the main line and west end underground stations had a *News Theatre* close by their entrance or exit. They filled in many a waiting out time – out of the rain or time-waiting. The principal news theatres we used were Victoria Station, two at Piccadilly Circus and others scattered about post-war London.

These hallowed places of refuge would soon become continental – with a main feature of X or H censor licence. And disappear, as they were sold out for shops, etc., or as sites for the larger cinema networks, like the ABC cinemas in Leicester Square. The news cinemas bring back many happy memories – of sanctuary and refuge.

Entry cost to early 1950s picture houses was anything between one shilling (5p in post-71 coinage) a ticket, or as the fifties progressed, up to one-and-ninepence for a seat in the back-stalls. Terrific value. I loved theatre and cinema, this affinity and love of books, staying for life, with no guesses where my earned pocket money went.

London Markets

Few people I knew had a television set. And going to the pictures was a staple diet. A fortnight later, my brother and I went to the Gaumont at Dalston Junction, at the top of the Balls Pond Road in Islington; and, for sixpence, enjoyed our first Saturday morning matinee. Already addicted to cinema pictures, a symptom of freedom, for me, on its own: one diary note said, 'saw *The Swiss Family Robinson* and *Dick Barton Strikes Back*' – the latter, if I recollect after all these years, involved Dick, Snowy and Jock fighting criminals who were misusing a new scientific weapon which produced subsonic sounds and killed by shattering exposed eardrums. This was pure cinema magic. A foretaste of nuclear weapons to come. And presently still in science fiction; just!

1951 diary leaves continued: 21 August. Tues. Sold rubbish at 1d. a lb : 24 August. Fri. Sold some newspaper waste etc., at 1d. a lb. Growing up in wartime educated me in conservation in most areas – and in profit, collecting domestic flotsam for re-sale was a common activity. Old newspapers were used by most shopkeepers for goods wrapping paper. In the orphanage, and, afterwards at home cut up newspaper squares were used as toilet paper; or uncut as an underlay for tablecloths. Even better, local shops and horse-drawn rag-and-bone-carts trawled the back streets with the driver's singsong 'Ole-rags-an'-lumber' advertising to pay for your reusable waste.

Our household collected old newspapers (those not used for a coal fire), tied the bundles with string, and bro and I visited a local fish and chip shop in Church Road, where the assistant gave us one penny a pound in weight. A few months later we added to our pocket-money collecting unwanted wooden boxes from shopkeepers, fish or meat or vegetables, and descending to our downstairs minute cellar, broke the wood up into uniform sizes, tied them up in bundles, and hawked our commodity from house to house at 6d. or one shilling a large bundle of firewood. We always sold out. This was an exercise I had learnt well in orphanage life – that is, economic innovation; collecting, bartering and selling. Money was scarce. Pennies turned into shillings.

Parents at work in 1951 inevitably (latchkey teenagers) we were, as to be expected, often left to carry out home chores, and various shopping errands. We had already become acquainted with various market areas (no such thing as supermarkets)–but in earlier days had to always be accompanied. It was fun, a bonus, to explore the London markets and makeshift stalls on our own. Fronting many war-torn building sites were large billboards, often adjacent to temporary tatty huts, but all were thriving buzzing hives of industry.

One early market stall memory was of a shopping journey with mother shortly before the war was over. We occasionally (on holiday from the Homes in the last year of 1945) walked up from our nan's, up the Balls Pond Road towards Dalston Junction. There were lots of billboards in this area, much of it was badly bombed, and as we headed for Ridley Road Market, off the Kingsland High Street, we took a short-cut, passing behind some of these billboards (to us, as little boys), along Kingsland Passage, a narrow 'U' turning, connecting road of sorts, that linked the corner of the Balls Pond Road directly to Kingsland High Street and missing the busy x junction. Human cries competed in every market place, a mostly unmusical medley of loud yet welcome sounds. Such a raucous assailed us as we entered this narrow 'short-cut' passageway and saw constructed a little market of trestle tables, and ground sheets, situate in Kingsland Passage E8 . One stall sold fish and meat, bloodied and smelling most awfully strong as it lay unclad upon wooden duck boards on the ground. Any meat was still a luxury, and required ration coupons. The sale tariff read *'For Sale. Fresh steak'. (No coupons required.)* On display were two main meats: horse meat; and whale fish, unusual features of most English butchers' shops and fisheries but then a not uncommon sale. I had never thought of *horses* as meat before. Though my grandfather had had a great deal to do with them in the trenches – and he a horse lover. [5] And the human subtleties of cow and sheep as all right for eating, but not horse and dog as in the Orient. They were anthropomorphised in the West – pets to man were, it seemed, more sacred in English mores: as revered (beef) cows in India.

Much less the needs of hunger and starvation, and rats – scrubbed vermin – as fleshly food.[6]   We were just emerging out of a second world war. And, as individuals, most of us, remained ignorant of those persons, across the world, for whom even horse meat and whale flesh would be a phantom wanton luxury. As to the luxury of 'choice' enabling a complete refusal of all flesh eating as carnivores and omnivores – well ... ! But at this stage only the social mores of to-eat, or not-to-eat horse flesh; beef and mutton were scarce, and demanded ration card points, and were much too expensive. But my mother forewent all such Kingsland Road market offals at that time.

A little further on, in 51, Ridley Market was reached in our perambulations, a large multi-street market off the Kingsland High Street. This general purposes and groceries market extended the length of Ridley Road – Dalston Lane and Norfolk Road at its easterly end; a railway line of the London and North West Railway and goods depot visible and experienced to the immediate south of the market stalls. I recall my cousin, Barbara Manton, ten years my junior, taking a job in the 1950s, in a betting shop in Ridley Road, owned by one of the later infamous Kray brothers; she said they were good to her and other staff.

I recollect cockles, prawns and eels being sold off the pavement, an open-shop front, in a shop sited in the Kingsland High Street – across the road and opposite the entrance to the always very busy Ridley Market. The live eels coiled in large white enamelled bowls rather put me off, but winkles and prawns were a most popular staple Sunday tea diet. These were sometimes purchased by adults on leaving the pub for their family (must have) Sunday lunch, or collected by us kids sent off on errand. The sea-food was mostly bought off the green-painted 'spiv' carts, regularly seen outside many London pubs on Sunday mornings, as in Southgate Road, which had several such stalls. A pint of winkles–their black-eye caps to be winkled out and off with pins–and a pint of prawns, to be messily stripped of thin flaky scale and mushy head with vacant eyes and hair-like antennae. And the cold fare much enjoyed, sharing with invited visitors for Sunday high tea, with brown bread and butter, lettuce leaf, spring-onion, tomato and radish salad, and specially home made fairy cakes to finish – with the teapot kept filled and kept warm under a usually homemade flowery embroidered tea-cosy

Dalston Waste & Petticoat Lane

A diary note entry for Saturday, 12th April 1952, included: 'Morning: went down waste'. Of all market place names, the Waste must be one of the historically most common (before Enclosure Acts removed public access) with its correct place-name 'public' assertions – an area of land uncultivated or later not so heavily built upon, whereon local people can market their wares for a small fee. Many English villages and townships had communities with peripheral areas of land known locally as the Waste – land whereon Poorhouses and hospitals might in the past have been built. The Dalston 'Waste' was frequently visited on Saturdays, when part time work was not available. The Waste along Kingsland Road (A.10), was on a stretch of pavement and concrete waste, just past Dalston Junction en route to (or from) Shoreditch, between and adjacent to Dalston Lane and Forest Road, and Richmond Road and Middleton Road, at these roads' junction on the Kingsland Road. This local Saturday-only market was open from 8 a.m. to 4 p.m., and sold anything from groceries and hardware to its main attraction, any second and umpteenth-hand clothes, books, and cast-offs of multiple human households. A smaller version of Petticoat and Brick Lane Sunday Market several miles up the road near Shoreditch ; that wasteland then comprised of prolific linked up bombsites, bounded by low brick wall boundaries, where bro and I were frequent visitors.

Close to fifteen... interest in the opposite sex gave unbidden arousal of its secretive adolescent head; one bookstall bro and I always examined sold the then coveted 'naughty' censored Hank Janson (author Stephen D. Frances) books, and risqué pin-up books. (Pornography was largely unknown, let alone on sale, in local street markets in the 1950s; teasing and titillation–risqué was preferable.) I had insufficient funds and wanted two book items, one large, and one small. Tempted beyond adolescent endurance, I purchased the large book and stole the small volume, inserting it discreetly enough between the pages of the larger tome–with a tight body of other local persons around us. But, returning home, my conscience bitterly attacked me. We about-turned and returned to the Dalston Waste stall in the late afternoon, and in peril , I deftly returned the stolen item unobserved (I thought) and safely back onto the stall surface – to my intense relief.

Sometimes on Sundays we visited the Petticoat Lane market, situated in and around Brick Lane, Middlesex Street, and Commercial Road, starting from

Shoreditch Church crossroads. Behind this sacred monument, Arthur Morrison's infamous real-life Jago district 'filthiest of London slums', partially remained. And forbidding whatever crimes 'Thou shall not nark' was gospel in the 1890s, the time of my grandparents' youth, then only two or three miles away, on the A10; remnants of the Jago, at Shoreditch, its peak 50 years before, back in early *Oliver Twist*, Dickens' time.[7]

Most market sites had grown within their developing communities, and many have ancient origins. Petticoat Lane, in mid-Victorian times, was known as 'Rag Fair' and listed as *an Old and Secondhand Clothes Market* – for the sale of the refuse of the Metropolis.'[8] In the 16th century the Chronicler and London antiquary John Stow wrote that Petticoat Lane was formerly called 'Hog Lane'. Erm! Appropriate – or unfair. And Stow remembered it forty years previously, when it 'had on both sides fair hedgerows of elm trees, with easy stiles to pass over into the pleasant fields'. An Elysian view, and a far cry from the Victorian old clothes district that Henry Mayhew described so lengthily 'A vista of dinginess. Dress coats, frock-coats, great coats, livery and gamekeepers' coats, paletots, tunics, trousers, knee-breeches, waistcoats capes, pilot-coats, plaids, hats, dressing-gowns, shirts, Guernsey frocks, handkerchiefs–all are displayed.'[9]

Bro and I travelled up to the Lane either by bus, trolleybus–or bicycle–any vehicle going up to Liverpool Street would suffice. Although we had tried to leave our bicycles locked at great risk, far too often parts would be stolen from them. And more than once I lost an article. A general belief held that a tourist visiting the Lane could have something- stolen at his entry to the Market, and have it offered for sale to them at the other end. We turned off at the top of the Kingsland Road, at the commencement of Shoreditch High Street, and turned into Calvert Street, E.l. Adjacent to the Shoreditch Church, turning around Arnold Crescent into Club Row, where at its end sales could begin from pavement hawkers. Several bus routes terminated at Calvert Street.

The Lane sprawled its market stalls and human hawkers over miles of criss-crossing roads. At the times of our visits–in the late forties and nineteen fifties, there were many sunken bomb sites, with low brick walls around most peripheries. Off the low brick walls' narrow ledges old gramophone records, books and other flotsam could be purchased from obviously unlicensed hawkers.

In the late 1950s, and after demob, I purchased a secondhand graphite 78 r.p.m. copy of English pop star Tommy Steele's *Singing the Blues* together with a Ben-and-Bebe Lyons' record of popular radio and cinema fame – from off the narrow top surface of one of these Petticoat Lane (not Hog Lane) low redbrick walls. No idle boast: these market stall hawkers had long declared that anything could be purchased (or arranged to be bought) from within Petticoat Market – from a pin to a battleship, or livestock, from a canary or crocodile to an elephant. ... I still believe it to be true.

Slightly more distant from our home was the Caledonian Road, Islington, Market, between The Angel and Kings Cross, this market mostly selling groceries and hardware, similar to Ridley Road Market. Shortly after I started work in Gough Square off Fleet Street, in 1953, I added another small market street to my list, alongside Gamages at Holborn – we called it Leather Lane, although other markets of this name also exist in London, as at Bermondsey, 'Over The Thames' (suff-of-the-river) at Southwark side. Its market title is descriptive, and leather and new clothing items were generally for sale on *licensed* stalls. Behind Waterloo Station another general purpose market was sometimes visited by us–when in this vicinity.

Last, by no means least, for there were hundreds of local street markets existing within Inner and Greater London; famous and more tourist generally known such as the Portobello Road Market was in West London, at Notting Hill Gate– close by Ladbroke Grove. This market, though selling the usual groceries and hardware off stalls, also sold antiques; silver, gold, and antique books. Some years later, in 1963, my wife-to-be Sarah and I explored the antique shops off the Portobello Market and purchased her Victorian blue sapphire wedding ring – unknowingly buying an identical model to my own grandmother's. *Portobello* Road Market had already become familiar to me.

In 1961, for a while, I'd lived with a good friend, an Aussie – from Queensland and New Guinea, Keith Buxton (a great mate from my 1959-60, days working at 167 Oxford Street *Arthur Murray Dance Inc* our dance instructor days. And, our later early Sixties *Home Travel* adventures. From where in Earls Court Keith met his nurse-sister Audrey, and wife to be . But all this was of *future* early 1960s, post-army-discharge days' adventures. Together, Keith and I moved from our Earls Court bedsit to new digs at Maxilla Gardens in Nottinghill Gate, and frequently shopped in nearby Portobello market place.)

And so Ridley Road, The Dalston Waste, Petticoat Lane, Caledonian Road, Leather Lane, Waterloo Market, and the Portobello Road – all these London street markets, north of the Thames, soon became regular marks on my local postwar landscape. Supermarkets in the early 1950s were only distantly, viewed on the cinema screen in American films. Large stores – other than in the affluent West End – were, as they remained in the 1980s, Woolworths, Marks and Spencer's, and Sainsbury's: Boots in our locality was then but a busy, minute chemist.

On an errand from home, emerging from Kynaston Avenue, N.16., a narrow alley with an annexe small public garden site (ex bomb ruin) which linked Dynevor Road to Stoke Newington High Street, I came into a very busy two-way main road – one-time high road route of the Romans due North – and I found thereon motor buses, trolleybuses, cars, taxis, bicycles and all the ordinary traffic flotsam of a busy town centre. The two overhead cables, one connected to the trolleybus arm, frequently shaking and sparking with activity, and then familiar metallic noises as its majestic rectangular passenger box, powered by the shaking electric cables, moved on smoothly below – these overhead wires giving one the feeling of being enclosed, within the road space; and wire netted.

On the corner of Brooke Road, opposite, our narrow alley entrance into Kynaston avenue, stood a solid post office looking more like a city bank than a post office. Back on the home side of the road, round to our right, one of the small shops was the baker; three-farthings had to be regularly put aside each day as the price of a loaf. About Ninepence three-farthings appeared to be one shop item, guaranteed to add farthings onto its price. Close-by the baker's, a gap existed between a row of terraced shops, marking another bomb-site, several market stalls, selling vegetables and fruit. I would frequent these stalls for some time to come.

Between Brooke Road and Tyssen Road , close to a white tiled Sainsbury's, was an old small family grocer's shop with a handsome sign painted overhead on white marble-like stone. The grocer's minute store was more cosy and personal rather than claustrophobic. Large square biscuit-tins with a variety of brand names laid neatly stacked to the sides; the top ones all opened end price-tagged. A singular wooden counter indicated the one shop manager and owner, a helpful, friendly, portly gentleman. One biscuit tin placed near the doorway often held broken Peak Frean biscuit pieces – a delicious bargain and offered at a very low price per quarter-pound. This shop's owner in the not so distant future would be moaning at the threatening growth of the new American type supermarkets, and did so to me.

One memorable a feature of this grocer's shop was its floor, each day, liberally sprinkled with fresh sawdust and dried tea leaves. In shopping I was always reminded to keep a supply of farthings to hand as 'increases' often went up in farthings, especially the price of, for example, a loaf of bread (no sliced), say at ten-pence-and-one-halfpenny (two-farthings equalled one half-penny) per item.

Delicatessen

One new facet, for me, (I'd lived in a Baptist orphanage – my mother Church of England, and stepfather a Dublin Catholic – though, true, neither was devout in any church attendances. But the orphanage was quite strict about attending Sunday services and gave me knowledge of 'the scriptures'). I now became acquainted with the faith and Torah of Jewry through new school friends at the Grocers grammar school and their specialised local shops. These special hygienic services were indicated by well stocked provisions grocers' shops called delicatessen, advertising a guaranteed range of kosher items for orthodox practitioners.

New words being introduced to our till recent rural and closed-in vocabulary. On the windows next to kosher were matzos, and strange symbols like Egyptian hieroglyphics or sparse pictographs – these were of course only normal Hebrew or Yiddish advertisements. In real life I had never, till then, experienced any other person who expressed a different culture – and who lived in the same vicinity as myself. The Jewish lads always left school early on Fridays in winter-time. Back at the orphanage there was one small lad who had had a super dark tan and came from Burma – but he was a Christian, which meant, as far as I had learned, 'the same as us'. This new feature of day to day life – in passing – interested, rather than affected us, and added another colour tone to a growing knowledge of human tapestry.

Before leaving the Homes, Mother enquired into local scouting activities. And on the 5th September 1951 bro and I joined the 45th North London (Stoke Newington), transferring from the 8th Reigate (Surrey). For twopence per week I became a senior scout, and purchased a small Lett's *Boy Scouts Diary* for 1952.

A Glimpse of Show Biz

The day after joining the new scout pack, my brother and I journeyed to the West End theatre, the Apollo, to see *Seagulls over Sorento*, starring Ronald Shiner, Gordon Jackson, Bernard Lee and David Langton. We had free tickets – mother worked part-time as a theatre usherette and occasionally obtained free passes.

For some years mother, after leaving school in 1929, had on and off, worked in the West End theatres, sometimes, with two of her three sisters Lillian Manton (the eldest born in 1911), and Elsie Manton (born in 1914). The eldest 'our Lillie' my mother referred to her, as seventeen year old beautiful vivacious teenager–back in early 1928–was spotted by a seated theatre talent scout who, converted Lillian in the *'rags to riches'* mode–from usherette to successful (albeit brief) film actress.

Aunt Lil (not to confuse with great aunt Lil) was a 'girl attendant' at the Piccadilly Theatre, spotted by a Mr. Harry Lachman and, subsequently Lil as a starlet, acted in the comedy *The Compulsory Husband*, with Monty Banks (later a husband of Gracie Fields) an early English talking film–in the role of Joy. It started out as a silent film but converted to a new talkie. (*Singin' in the Rain*, and *The Jazz Singer* – it was not). The film was a second feature, viewed, at the The Strand London *Alhambra* theatre in March 1929 with first feature *Juno and the Paycock*, Sean O'Casey's famous play, filmed by Alfred Hitchcock. A notable double-featured programme. I have a copy of the Alhambra programme– and other ephemera. And its respite, from what must have been gloomy early post-war years, after 1918.

Lillian Manton (and the 2 Baxter Grove Manton family) was a local Islington media celebrity for some time. But domestic pressures (she became pregnant) forced her to withdraw from a very glamorous film career. A spin off from those days, mother and sisters remained very interested in the theatre – for a while friends of Sony and Binnie Hale, well-known 1930s stage artistes, and other notables in the cinema end theatre world. In 1935, mother had been an extra in a film of H.G. Wells *'Shape of Things to Come'* and was given a one liner – which ended, she believed (quite rightly I'm sure) on the cutting floor. But she fondly remembered that crowd scene on the windy South Downs (or was it North Downs) Hills of Surrey.

Mother met our Australian born father about this time in the early 30s– fourteen years older than her, he was for twenty years or so, a successful onstage stooge with the American comedians, Olson and Johnson, later stars of *Hellzapoppin* and other zany comedies. Our father, I thought, was a nationalised American (it's uncertain whether he actually signed the papers which left him as an self-exiled Aussie, according to one relative informant): years later I was unable to trace any record of his pre-war existence in America, Australia, New Zealand, or Sweden ... all places to which he had had attachments, before finally settling in London after the American great depression.

After my parents married on January 6th 1935, the ceremony solemnized at the parish church of St John the Baptist Canonbury, they lived a short time in Chelsea, by the Thames, where, there were enormous embankment rats mother recalled. And then they lived a while off Rupert Street in Soho whilst father worked nearby on a night-club engagement, before they moved up to Elstree and Boreham Wood near Barnet. Barone Ernst Hopper was an Australian vaudeville artist and painter, and stage designer and artist, who also played a variety of musical instruments – and wrote songs. Mother recollected his writing awhile for Jack Payne, one of the big band leaders. But on my birth certificate– at Elstree father was on record as a stage painter (aka stage designer). And his father Johann Wilhem Hopper, too, was recorded as an 'actor' and 'artist'– on mother's January 1935 wedding certificate.

Mother divorced father a few years later, in the late Forties, a casualty of the war, gambling and intense pace of theatre-life; and certainly, background fiscal world pressures like the American vaudeville theatre slump at the coming of The Talkies in 1929 and the Great Depression. Wall Street crash et cetera. And so he'd moved over the sea to London about that time in the early 1930s, and my bro and I would end up in an orphanage. ... But all this was water under the bridge. Though interest in theatre and films escalated for my bro and me. I retained no living memories of my music hall father.[10]

Pantomime

In the early 1950s theatre tickets were expensive, compared to cinema costs of one shilling, one shilling and threepence, one shilling and sixpence – even a shilling and ninepence – depending on which cinema attended . But West End theatre and cinema tickets though expensive–were *not* prohibitive. My 1951 diary recorded *London Palladium* Theatre ticket prices at this time. Stalls: 6/6d. 8/-6d.10/6d. 15/-: Grand Circle 7/6d. 10/6d.13/6d. Upper Circle 2/- 4/-.

Boxes: 15/- 21/- 30/- 31/6d. 42/- 60/-. .Cost of pantomime tickets ranged from two shillings to five pounds.

Bro and I went to see *Babes in the Wood* at the Palladium on January 3rd 1951, and paid two shillings and sixpence for standing room only. The day before we visited the *Princes* Theatre and saw Ethel Revnell in *Old Mother Goose*, where we sat in the pits for four shillings. And, most delightful, on January 5th 1951 we enjoyed Arthur Askey and his daughter, Anthea, with Leon Cortez at the Casino, starring in *Goody Two Shoes*. Arthur Askey was particularly funny dressed as a fairy – with appropriate remarks about his short hairy legs. We paid six shillings. Mother occasionally worked part-time, when not on the buses, at the West End theatre The Casino (among other theatres) as an usherette – but free tickets were not always available.

On December 8th 1951, a diary leaf recorded: 'Went to *Finsbury Park Empire*' (where they had a massive theatre organ, like the one in the Odeon Leicester Square, which rose up from beneath the floor level and, after playing music, descended back out of sight for the film-show to begin). 'Saw Carol Levis, Leon Cortez and others'. Carol Levis was a popular talent scout and Leon Cortez a comedian.

We also frequented the Hackney Empire. Sam Costa had been on one billing, and we went round the back to the stage entrance to get his autograph. Sam was a marvellous gentleman, and before giving us his signature he told us a little about his pop singing days twenty years before and cracked a joke or two; my brother was then twelve years old and I late thirteen – two strangers but treated right royally by pop-star and comedian Sam.

Another memorable autograph hunt was experienced in 1951 at Eastham Empire. One of our new stepfather's Irish blood relatives, his brother Jim Dolan, a baker, and his family, lived in Eastham – specifically at Manor Park. They always made us welcome during our visits and, we soon became acquainted with Irish hospitality. During this period the Korean war conflict was not yet ended and as we emerged from the local underground station, the newspaper hawker's – 'Star, News, Standard' advertising card mapped the awful day-to-day pace of destruction. But, on one regular interlude, we sought out the Eastham Empire we saw *'Old Mother Riley'* and her daughter 'Kitty McShane'– true old-time Music Hall and Film Fun celebrities. 'Old Mother Riley' was a very funny man in old-woman drag, Lucan McShane I believe his name was. They were already well known to us through the comic strips, enhanced in the *Radio Fun* (or *Film Fun*?). Out of his pantomime drag (we never even knew of it as such, as boys, and dressed in a smart suit, Mr. McShane 'and daughter', Kitty McShane, were most charming in giving their autographs. Sadly, these souvenirs were lost years ago. I believe 'Old Mother Riley' died not long after this music hall performance ... And I thank them all.

In retrospect what I most loved in pantomime comedy and drama of those post-war days was the apparently unwritten code, displayed by all the hard-working performers of those years. To have *their audience* and peers to be in sympathy – with them – *never* to obtain cheap and obscene, laughs or jibes at the expense of (to laugh *at them* like Nazi prison guards) poor and however, dis-advantaged, members – among *their* public. And bro and I shared, loved, those precious momentary joys; just as had Dickens' Nicholas Nickleby and his new friend (and unknown cousin) Smike, meeting up with a delightful theatrical travelling troupe, in their flight from infamous Dotheboys Hall).

Collins Music Hall

A year or so later (1952) I added the old Collins Music Hall at Islington Green to my regular visits. A growing teenager, with pulsing glands, visits were mixed in my innocent motives. On the one extreme there were the traditional music hall comedians and skilled artistes, tumblers, etc. And there were the semi-strip performers (like the West End Windmill theatre) with 'art displays'; all or most statuesque nudity (conforming with The Law which its censorship laws of the day demanded) being semi-nude female displays, and never, ever, a pubic hair displayed (like Graeco-Roman white stone statues). I enjoyed both varieties–but mostly went on my own, a little guilty about being attracted to visions of unclad female artistes, and too shy to ever admit to such clandestine interest. But Mother knew: I kept the theatre programmes in the bedroom for souvenirs, and on a return from army leave, now eighteen years of age, they had all disappeared, and were never mentioned.

Appropriately Collins Music Hall remains in my memory for a more traditional fare. Situated at a junction of Upper Street with Essex Street, it was known as Sam Collins's during the Eighteen seventies. Collins was apparently a nickname, for his real name was Vagg. Vagg was a chimney-sweep who became a music hall success as a singer of Irish songs, such as *The Rocky Road to Dublin*, dressed as an Irishman in a green coat, brogues and knobbly Shillelagh.[11]

Great Aunt Lil had many memories of the old Collins music hall. One distinct memory was of her older brother big Jim (my grandfather James Walter Manton) and, herself, visiting Collins's during its heyday early 1900s. She recalled, for me, the time they saw the popular Hoxton comedienne Marie Lloyd.[12]   Marie had, had the curtain brought down on her, long before her music hall act was due to finish. Censorship was sometimes severe, and the watching manager had panicked on hearing her 'smutty talk'. My maternal grandfather (big Jim) too, years later, told me of his own rebel gestures from up in 'the Gods'– the audience sometimes heckling artistes down below.

When I first visited Collins's in the early Nineteen-fifties the dark inside of the theatre had retained most of its internal fixtures from the Victorian age. I noted the photograph of Collins's in *Adcock's History of London* [13] showed a plaque indicating It was rebuilt in 1897. And advertising 'Dramatic Plays Twice Nightly 6.30 and 9'. It was then playing a show called '*The Plaything of an Hour*'–in its 144th week–by the Dorothy Mullard's Repertory Company. One placard, just discerned, advertised Collins's as 'The New North London Drama Theatre'. This picture was taken in the 1920s, with a horse and cart unloading outside the bar, and two ladies in full period garb chatting outside the entrance and exits.

One regular Collins's show I saw in 1952 was called *Casey's Court*, a humorous medley modelled on a local community cast in music and comedy. Included in its repertoire was the raucous *On Mother Kelly's doorstep, on Paradise Row* ... (I loved it) and other well known old numbers. ' Casey's Court' was also the title of a front page English comic paper feature, in either *Comic Cuts* or *Chips*': – I can't remember which.

The gas mantles I saw in the Music Hall in 1952 had mostly, *but not all*, been converted to electricity, but the original fixtures remained. The seats in the pit were plain but padded and comfortable . Upstairs in 'the gods', seating remained as uncomfortable wooden fold-ups, (just like the hard wooden plank seats of London trams, as I recall). The safety curtain retained very old advertisements of Pears Soap, and local traders, who even then were likely long departed, advertised their trade whilst performing on earth. Limited runs.

The theatre bar also opened out onto the street, and triangular green, and served local regulars as well as inside theatre-goers, as a pub. I enjoyed sometimes meeting the stage performers when they were enjoying a pint (though I was too young to drink alcohol) and loved having a brief chat with the artistes (not until years later I learnt *they* could have – in theory – included my estranged vaudeville father, but such ephemera was then unknown to me) whilst they were waiting to go up on the stage. The inevitable bar walls were paved with autographed pictures of many past famous music hall performers and actors. Terrific atmosphere. Sadly, within two to three years a serious fire demolished much of the theatre, and it never appeared to recover; it was one of the many London features changed before I left H.M. Forces in late 1958.

Radio and Television

Back in early Nineteen fifty-one, Sunday the 13th February, with few months to go till leaving the Orphan Homes, I had accompanied the usual crocodile formation of boys and staff member to a local church, where we were shown an interesting lantern slide service, on far-away New Guinea Papuan missionaries. Although radio and film shows were a common feature, so too, then, were hand coloured lantern slide shows.

Shortly, before leaving the Homes, I was invited by a grammar school friend to visit his home the coming Saturday afternoon. His father was a local Reigate Girls' Grammar School caretaker, and lived in the school lodge-house. This was for a special occasion and, although he was not a special friend, as an act of kindness I was invited to watch the Oxford versus Cambridge University Boat Race on television. It was also most memorable for my *first ever* television viewing for one reason: whilst I arbitrarily supported Cambridge, together we watched them lose, as their boat and crew sank below the Thames waterline.

An interesting baptism in television viewing – for me.

Whilst we often listened to the radio: out of the orphanage. September 27th, 1951 Thursday diary leaf recorded: 'Stayed at home all evening and listened to '*P.C. 49*', etc.' At home. ... we would not see our own television, a 12-inch cabinet model, which stepfather obtained on hire purchase, for some months to come. But a diary entry, before that date, said 'Sunday, 2nd December 1951: T.V. at Barker's house (first time)' – and, on the 4th December, I saw Ralph Reader in *The Gang Show* on television.

This new-found friend (albeit briefly) lived with his family in a small terraced house off Defoe Road–named after the famous author of Robinson Crusoe of that name, who had lived awhile in this street. Several years later Barker's family would have to battle over a compulsory purchase order, with the potential homelessness it presented.

Home radio was made of thin box wood with a front fretwork motif and had to be serviced regularly by detaching the back cover. Diary leaf: 'February 6th 1952. Wireless 'busted'. It was the valve'. One of my regular errands had been getting the radio's accumulator recharged. This errand was often combined with another periodic chore – taking the Christmas club money to the pub off Crossways, N.16. I was small for my age and found the heavy thick glass accumulator container awkward – nervous of the acid inside; but no accident ever ensued. It was left for a while with a dealer, and after being re-charged, collected and returned to the radio. The valves were also changed by this shopkeeper. For a small interest rate an authorised pub collected weekly monies from off local working people and paid out at Christmas time, the bonus varying from year to year. Occasionally one heard of Club monies being stolen by a holder, but we were lucky.

Two months out of the orphanage and we were settled in our new landscape, secure sufficient amongst our blood relatives. But when this holiday was over, and initial exploratory excursions ended, we prepared to go to another grammar school. The school – to be our last – was Hackney Downs Grammar School, a few miles away to the east, in E.8., situated adjacent to the green common land of the Hackney Downs, off Downs Park Road. A school for boys only, London maps recall that until lately it had been a London County Council Secondary School. Older maps still showed the premises, as the Grocers' Company School, its emblazoned symbol a loaded camel. Across the road from the school, on the periphery of the Downs, I recollect a substantial number of war built prefabs. These low buildings covered a large area alongside the roads on our way to school. We moved in mid 1951 from an excellent Reigate Surrey School to our down-market blitzed school in the East End of London.

The Grocers' Grammar School

The size of our (bro and I) new school and its accommodation for the six hundred boys, was physically remarkably similar to the Reigate Grammar School we had left only weeks before. The school could be seen in the cup of a Y-junction just north out of Hackney Downs railway station, its branch lines north out of Liverpool Street Station – the old G.E.R. Stoke Newington was two stations on past Hackney Downs. The noise of the numerous passing trains muted through the school's Victorian built brick walls. I recollect the lead being stolen off the roof of the main building one weekend. But then, in the Reigate schools, a laboratory explosion at the Grammar School–and a robbery of the school cups and laboratory equipment at Holmsdale Road Primary, are recalled. Schools are frequent game to child and adult offenders, and accident-prone. Changing schools with some frequency, I could hardly fail to note the changes in the syllabus subjects. And the formal traditions reflected in the sub-cultures of the schools' body.

In contrast, a London Board School 'near Wincott Street' in Lambeth, at the beginning of the Nineteen hundreds, children attended from three to twelve years old, with an average size class of sixty children. The headmaster, on being asked 'How on earth does one manage to teach sixty boys?' had answered: 'You may well ask that – it is impossible to teach them as they should be taught. There are always several backward ones, no matter how we arrange the classes, and it is very hard to give these the extra individual attention they need to bring them on without keeping back the bright ones at the top .....' [14] Which seemed an all too familiar dilemma and highlighted inevitable ˉproblems of too large classes. At this board school poor older girls would often have to bring their infant baby sisters or brothers to school. One description read : '... there sits a big girl with a baby on her knee – a chubby little fellow of about eighteen months ....' [15]

School subjects at board schools taught the 'rule of three ; reading, 'riting, and 'rithmetic ! ... Arithmetic was not known as mathematics in those days; and then there was model drawing, and woodwork for the boys, needlework and cooking for the girls – and for boys and girls physical drill. Assembly was held in the morning, and an assembly held in the afternoon prior to dismissal. Anyone bunking off early would thus have been noticed in early Edwardian times.

A Victorian blood relation of mine, a first cousin of great-great grandfather George Manton's sister (one of two), had married a (Revd) Joseph Manton-Smith (b1844–d.1900) a devout baptist preacher from Northampton and, personal friend of the Rev' Charles Haddon Spurgeon. Ironically, Manton-Smith had assisted C.H.S. in founding the *Spurgeon's Orphanage* in Stockwell, South London back in 1867. [16] Manton-Smith wrote two books called *Stray Leaves* and *More Stray Leaves* in the 1890s. In these autobiographical accounts he described, his lifetime friendship with Charles Haddon Spurgeon and Stockwell Orphanage. [17] He described how he was torn between the music hall and ministry. Manton-Smith was skilled with a 'silver cornet' and other musical attributes, and had appeared in London's East End Music Halls. But ... he joined the Baptist ministry and used his talents in fundraising for the poor, and particularly so, in teaching in charity Ragged Schools (to become board schools) of the East End of London; again, graphic written detail with illustrations – as if by Dickens' Phiz - extent in his books.)

Most noticeable was the near-starvation of so many of the London Board School bare-footed Jago - like children, which philanthropy had insisted that over a hundred of these street urchins be fed – free, 'over at 'Wincott Street'[18] before classes could begin. And ' the near nakedness of many pupils was all too common. ' No problems of to-be or not-to-be school uniforms – earlier schools were not called 'Ragged Schools' for nothing. But soon were formally replaced by the London board schools.

In preparation for our new school in 1951, mother was determined that we should, at first, have a good (common) entrance. School uniform was preferred, but in London optional : in our previous school at Reigate it had been mandatory. Caps, blazer-jacket badges, and ties were purchased – as most of our charcoal grey clothing – by the use of Provident Cheques Clubs. As cut-price interest hire-purchase, with a Co-operative Store, a common method for working-folk Londoners. It was imperative that sufficient rationing clothing coupons were accumulated, although these were about finished – only price of clothing was prohibitive – cast-offs remained more normal. And they first had to be new, somehow.

It would later prove ironic, or should I say academic, when mother would withdraw us, after two years, too early, from grammar school. Because, she said, 'I can no longer afford the school uniforms.' And added that anyway, she couldn't afford to keep us at the grammar school, to where bro and I had earlier won the necessary scholarship, whilst resident in the orphanage. And so we were forced to leave before the all important exams ... (but that's another story) .   The headmaster pointed out the school had a charity box (poor box) of discarded uniforms (we were *not* ragged) but it was to no avail.

Our first morning assembly at Hackney Downs we met in the school amphitheatre, a most unusual feature. A boys-only school, the gym doubled as a swimming bath, the wooden floorboards periodically lifted up by the caretaker to expose a pool below. As with our previous school, the gym was also used as a marshal point, and cadet corps training ground (as at hundreds of other schools). The assembly morning prayers, hymns and nominal headmaster's lecture over, we filed into our new classes. But from the outset there was a notable difference in these assemblies and their Christian ritual – numerous boys were always absent. The school had a very heavy complement of orthodox Jewish boys who joined their own mandatory groups. As the winter nights got dark earlier and earlier, the Jewish lads would have permission to leave early in the afternoon. Before darkness began they were to be home. I was always unclear on the exactness, but their Sabbath was on Saturdays – and appeared to begin with Friday dusk. ... A different life style.

The Grocers' had class groups divided into three grade streams, exactly as had *Reigate Grammar School*: 1a, 1b, 1c; 2a, 2b, 2c, and so on. Back at Reigate it was accepted practice that if a boy came in one of the first three form positions, certainly first or second in the annual school examinations, whilst in the lower streams of the 1c or 2c forms, then he would be promoted and go up a stream in recognition, and for encouragement. At Reigate, in the Michelmas term in 1950, in form 2c I was placed second in the annual Exam in a class of thirty – despite being off sick with a fractured ankle for some weeks. I had achieved a first in Latin with 86%, second in History with 56%, and second in English and English Literature with 71% and third in French with 70%. It was fully expected that I would go up the next year into 3b. But, it was not to be. Moving back up to London, I was placed in the C-stream at least into 3c. But at the new school The Grocers in 1951, I was to be disappointed and wholly disorientated. I moved to 3c and my bro (who had also excelled in the previous school exams) into 2c.

Even more perplexing was the change of curriculum. Back In Spurgeon's (Primary) School in 1946, Arithmetic, English, Reading, Spelling, Writing, History, Geography, Needlework (for girls), Art, General Knowledge and Conduct, were the subject headings. In Nineteen fifty the Reigate Grammar School syllabus was more (academic) extensive: Scripture, English, English Literature, History, Geography, Latin, French, German or Spanish, Arithmetic, Algebra, Geometry, Trigonometry, General Science, Chemistry, Physics, Biology, Drawing, Handicraft and Physical Training.

And, up to London, the Grocers' syllabus headings were reduced: Religious Instruction, English, History, Geography, French, Mathematics, Science, Mechanics or Handicraft, Art, Singing–and Physical Training. This tedious listing revealed, through recorded experience (examination reports), the similarity between the Spurgeon's Primary and the former London board school (pre-1944 Education Act) and, dissimilarity between the Reigate and Grocers' grammar schools.

Notable was the difference in attention to Classics: Reigate pushed Latin– in the first two forms. At the Grocers', Latin was totally absent from the curriculum. And In Reigate, rugger was its principal sport; at the Grocers' it was soccer. I didn't miss rugger, but I missed the accent on Latin, which I had enjoyed. And so at 14 years old, for the rest of my schooling, it was downhill all the way.

Changing schools at any time was fraught with problems. The necessity for new friendships, new teaching staff and new milieu. And, most obvious, the contents of the syllabus curriculum itself. Moving schools at the commencement of the first, even second form term years, gave the staff opportunity to gauge the level of pupil and assist in their catching up. But to move in the third or fourth years, approaching the matriculation, or programmes for the General Certificate of Education, is tempting providence, and probably requires considerable homework; new subjects, different periods of history or new areas of geography, or in substance worse, absolute repetition, work already covered to learn over again but indicating earlier terns of material then already spell-covered and lost to the newcomer.

And the psychology. I found the lack of reward for effort, combined with so much syllabus changes, most dispiriting : although by the end of the first year I was eighth out of the class of thirty-two. My heart was no longer in the work and 'insufficient effort' was a fair appraisal at Grocer's, compared to the previous year at Reigate. 'A very pleasing report ' (mother kept these reports). But it meant nothing – or so it seemed at fourteen years of age. The size of class-forms of the 1950s was clearly, very different from the 1900s board school's minimum of sixty pupils. In 1946, it was twenty-nine (and I was fifth). In 1950 it was thirty (and I was second in the exams).

In mid-1951 when I started at the Grocers' Grammar School there were thirty-three pupils in the Autumn term; thirty two in the next Spring term ; and by the Summer term in 1953 – when I left – only twenty-five pupils in the class. The reason why the class reduced from thirty-three to twenty-five was unknown to me. Even so, I knew myself lucky, as many of the other London secondary schools had classes upwards of thirty-five pupils. This was, of course, before post-war Sixties' comprehensive schools got underway.

Nevertheless, in most ways the school was no different from the thousands of others across the land. Its elected prefects then colluded with staff establishment to keep the peace and social mores. School bullies and absentees (aka absconders), illnesses and private tragedies, juvenile crime – all real-life facets were observed within normal school life. But, overall the Grocer's appeared under adult control. And most children then predicted where they were going straight-away after school life. That is ... they knew their limitations.

The days of the meritocracy were yet to happen in the 1960s. I found there were definitely more poor pupils in the London schools than in Reigate Surrey. There was little difference in the school furniture. Our desks in both buildings were old-fashioned wooden-box-lids with slots for long-ink-pens with nibs, and indented holes with removable porcelain inkwells, still regularly filled by allotted ' ink monitors', and which supplied constant ammunition for caper-soaked ink-pellets to petty offenders. By the end of our second year – July 1953 – biros were becoming a regular feature. And though fountain pens and Swan's inks still lay within most desks, ugly cheap biros had taken over. Cherished fountain pens and standard wooden pen-nibs were abolished in the classroom, in the name of progress. They were already a long way from the white-chalk and black-slates of the earlier board schools; and further still distanced from the tall, white cut-down swan-feathers – known as quills – used by our forefathers.

I was up about 4.30 a.m. to commence the first of the two paper-rounds being at the newsagent at 5.00 a.m. (some papers could in those days go up three to five editions in a day, I was once told – certainly the evening editions) . Home by 7.30 a.m. for breakfast – and away and cycle to school about 8.15 a.m. And after the school day over, and hopefully some homework completed, before leaving school, I cycled to the paper-shop and did two further rounds. But it paid reasonably well and contributed to many a cinema and theatre visit. Newspaper delivery boys, and few girls, had been known, with their shoulder-hung hessian sack carriers, each one advertising a paper since mass media circulation became a common feature. Hard work it frequently was, but there were often odd events, sometimes hilarious, occasionally painful.

London Smog

Diary note of Thursday, 15th December 1951, recorded ' Very Bad Fog'... fog, as a thick mist or watery vapour. No! The fog referred to was the then, often infamous, unhealthy, grey-yellow or black smog, or pea-souper, a sour product of industrial pollution, and aggregate, caused by hundreds of thousands of ordinary household chimney exhausts, undiluted smoke from coal fires, industrial chimneys and car exhaust fumes. (The industrial Black Country up north was not called the Black Country for nothing.)

The London smog was at its worst during the winter months, the freezing cold damp temperature falling below 'dew point'. Moisture, attached to the many billions of clinging nasty polluted dust particles, which then condenses, and fog becomes smog as the dirt sticks. Winter cold and common fog were troublesome enough when combined with early morning darkness – a normal enough hazard on paper-rounds.

I recollect a number of mornings in early 1952 when the smog was so thick, that even with my hand torch literally twelve inches away from my face, the beam could *not* penetrate its thick mesh soup. The nasty bits often entering my mouth. Much as the intrusive sulphur motes from off steam trains. But I knew my way from home to the newsagent well, and literally felt my way down to the paper shop, coughing and spluttering, periodically removing sulphurous motes from my eyes. And lowering the white handkerchief tied around my mouth as a gag to diffuse the smog, and spitting out its refuse. On arrival at the shop the newsagent might have decided it prudent not to make the deliveries. But on one occasion, believing in confidence that I knew exactly where each house was spaced, I departed, still feeling my way along the fences and hedgerows, and guessing the positions of the kerb-stones, using the hand-torch to locate the letter-boxes. Unfortunately, we later learnt that every paper had been successfully delivered – but every one to the wrong house.

Much of the traffic refused to budge during the worst of the winter smogs. But occasionally, an intrepid bus conductor could be seen in front of his vehicle, a walking footman leading the way by torch-light, and inching very slowly, forwards through the murk. On his way home from school my bro had seen one bus career into a lamp-post. Returning from school one winter afternoon on my bicycle, en route through smog to the paper shop for the evening round, I triumphantly pedalled all the way down one normally busy road and arrived

at Stoke Newington High street, but then discovered that I had moved all the
way up on the wrong side of the road. Fortunately I encountered no stubborn
traffic coming the other way.

Unhappily, the smog was not known as a killer-smog lightly. In 1952,
because of smog, many thousands of elderly folk were known to have died
through bronchitis and other complaints. Even the insides of buildings were at
risk. One Saturday afternoon I visited the Vogue cinema in Kingsland High
Street near Ridley Market to see favourite actor, John Wayne, in *She wore a
Yellow Ribbon*. To the hidden audience, as it sat watching Maureen O'Hara
and 'the Duke' on the screen – only twenty-feet or so in front – the beam off
the projector became more and more fogged as the whole cinema filled with
the choking, cold damping smog. Eventually a perplexed cinema manager
groped his way down the gangway and shining his torch at us few film-fan
Duke lovers apologised that, although it was only mid-afternoon, the cinema
must close down. The sparse audience, politely, having their entrance fees
returned.

Our London public was appeased in the unexpected success of the in-power
government's anti-pollution Clean Air Act of 1956 (and 1968), which introduced
definite penalties for wanton pollution of the atmosphere. And soon after, old
father Thames too was cleansed, to such a degree that fish were seen and bred
in the inner-city river stretch for the first time in many, many years. Ecology
was becoming an insidious reality; man-made pollution a recognised problem
that could be reduced – in time. Wow! It was great breathing relative clean air
in city and town instead of that horrible choking fug....

Many public buildings and numerous large statues were seen supported
by much scaffolding, and Londoners about their business would become used
to ducking a spin-off water spray from pressure-hoses as the black-soot of all
too many decades was erased, leaving gleaming white architecture, like porcelain,
emerging from a murky mantle. New houses were to be built, some I noticed
without chimneys, and their sometimes flat roofs house an expensive in a new
form of heating–central heating. The old fireplaces would also make more use
of coke and other smokeless fuels. As a teenage boy in 1951, I'd never known
relative days of plenty, and rationing of all basic commodities was a part of
ordinary day-to-day existence. I was not then aware that the post-war years
were, in some ways, worse than back in the pre-war years before 1939–1945
[19] in respect of the quality of life.

Food Parcels

The appearance at home of unexpected, but most welcome, '*food parcels*' sent from Dublin to us in Stoke Newington had more than a passing significance. New relatives in Eire (the Dolans) periodically supplied us with butter, fat, bacon and a new item to me, black puddings (it didn't register it was coagulated blood) – and other occasional postwar goodies.

And the fact that stepfather worked in a Tate and Lyle sugar factory over in Hammersmith meant the addition of *extra* sugar and treacle supplies on occasions. Erm! . Excellent for my set of sweet teeth. ... But stepfather ¯paid dearly for his many years in the sugar factory with subsequent ill health (no industrial settlements) that eventually brought about his early death. Too much water immersion.

Changing schools, I transferred orphanage bartering skills in a new trading venture and, for a while, was successful in selling sweets at school for a small profit, buying up sweet coupons from boys who mostly had other sources, or no use for them. This income added to my paper-rounds' earnings. During 1951 there were four changes in weekly sweet coupon supplies. On February 25th, the allotted amount went up from five to five-and-a-half ounces; on May 20th from five-and-a-half to six ounces; on July 15th from six to six-and-a-half ounces – this last rise due to a fall in consumption indicated by the stocks of manufacturers and distributors, and not to any increase in sugar supplies. And finally, in December Nineteen fifty-one, Christmas time, the sweet coupons were reduced back from six-and-a-half to six ounces, due to a fall in sugar supplies to manufacturers.[20]

By far the most popular item for sweet trade was chewing-gum supplies. Purchased at four or five for a penny, with coupons, I would re-sell them at a penny each, without coupons. Sweet rationing did not finish until the year of the Coronation in 1953 – specifically, on February 4th, which ended all price controls of chocolate and confectionery. The then minister of food, Major Lloyd-George, reminded us that 'Rationing of sweets began on June 26th, 1942, and had been in force for over ten-and-a-half years with the exception of a short period in 1949; in April of that year sweets were de-rationed by the Labour Government, but the demand was so heavy that rationing had to be re-imposed after about four months.' [21]

But sweets were de-rationed, and a source of income diminished, then ceased altogether, helped by the decontrol of egg rationing on March 26th, 1953. The year before, back in 1951-2, fresh eggs were still *not* in plentiful supply; and dried egg supplies had almost dried up. But, self-help motivated, and on Tuesday, 29th April, 1952 my *Letts' Boy Scouts Diary* leaf recorded: 'Bought eight chicks at 3/6d each. A bargain at 28/-, instead of 32/- (4/- each). Already made the shelter'. The rear of our small terraced house had a small walled-in garden, and to introduce a regular egg supply we built a shed and wired in run, against the back wall (bomb ruins the other side of the wall) having, and feeding, our own chickens and eggs for several years.

One of my domestic tasks was to purchase sacks of 'off ' potatoes, to make the chicken feed, pots purchased from a market stall in the High Street. These nasty spuds were boiled up and, stone grit added for potential egg shells. We took turns in feeding its portion to the chickens. I remember that smell of cooking potatoes as we boiled them up. Ugh! Absolutely foul. Whilst I willingly ate the chickens and collected the still warm eggs, it was stepfather dad who stretched their necks. I could never kill one. But, obviously I did not have to.

Christmas 1951, and my brother and I enjoyed a Christmas at home for the very first time without a return to orphanage life and unhappy return to the Homes (like a sentence in a juvenile prison – which of course it was not), within two seeks of Xmas.

Reference to diary leaf notes illustrated holiday on-going visits to pantomimes and relatives – and sapping, sinking new roots, the base line of our new existence in post-war London. Austerity was still a fact of life. But newer warmth, soaked in a hitherto unfamiliar emotion, of growing affection from others. This new emotion blanket more than compensated for any apparent past deprivation. Bro and I would many years later (both widowers, on the phone, twixt Cape Town and Littlehampton) own to no memories of the romantic fiction of so-called what-ever-it-was '*love*'– during our long childhood. ... More basic. Diary leaf dated 8th January '52 recorded: Tuesday: 'Did a bit of business. Lines made ten-pence-halfpenny.'

New year of 1952 opened with a very cold spat. On the battered school playground quadrangle bitter cold frost had, as usual, produced long sheets of ice in isolated patches. Gleefully boys would queue up to race dangerously onto ice-glassed slides upon otherwise normally uneven concrete surfaces.

Each school I had previously attended enjoyed this icy game to keep warm, as a token spin-off from the bitter wintry weather; prolific colds, chilblains, chaps, bronchitis and influenza; then cut and 'bruised hands, scrapped knees, and for the fallen – bruised bottoms (torn seats of trousers) – joined day-to-day winter maladies.

And that childhood mother's panacea of most cold sores, Vick or Vaseline, was spread on one's protesting skin like margarine. Iodine was kept ˉperversely for the painting of deeper cuts, and added a sticking plaster if available, that would get dirtier and dirtier, and refuse to be pulled off the skin.

To drink one's health castor oil was more common than the excellent thick brown malt, but both, as medicinal precautionary needs, diminished as we grew older. Until they ceased as but a memory.

In class, spidery ink writing remained appalling, but unappreciated: Calligraphy apart, spelling and grammar proved adequate, and speed of flow profitable. Receipt of lines, as ever a reward for petty offence at school, enabled me to write lines for others. I charged three pennies (a threepenny bit) per hundred (or more) scribbled lines. Amazingly I was never brought to task for this extraordinary line of school-work – and profit.

School life was interrupted. On the 6th February 1952. Wednesday. Diary note recorded: '*King died in early morning.*' [1936-52. King George VI] '*Scouts paid all subs, discussed Soap-box Derby car. Did more lashings, etc.*' The Grocers' Headmaster had called hush to our morning assembly in the school amphitheatre, and solemnly announced the death of King George VI. The head then asked us all to bow our heads in prayer for a few moments' silence. But life went on, and to us boys the to-be inevitable royal funeral, and coronation, with its immense festive pomp and ceremony. Royalty meant little, to nothing, to me as a teenager..

March 1952 endured a lot of snow, and the close of the month, Sunday, 30th, noted: 'The Blizzard blew over just about leaving some five to six inches of snow. Some funny things happened to me, in the snow, on the paper round'. My brother gave me a hand on my second morning round because of the 'difficulty in using our push-bikes.' On several occasions thick snow fell off rooftop eaves and landed on top of us filling the paper bags. Once it partially buried me as I got to the top of a flight of steps, and a fall from a Victorian three-storey terraced block almost knocked me out. But we laughed it off, scooped the stuff out of the bag and subsequently squeezed numerous soggy newspapers through letter-boxes and under door-knockers. Not long after this event, another humorous episode added to my experience.

Late afternoon. I'd just completed the evening paper rounds and was leisurely cycling home past some close-by shops, when I observed an attractive youngish lady carrying two shopping bags, emerge from a newsagent shop. Suddenly she let out a cry and, with her, I too stopped abruptly. The lady had dropped both bags, but she had also dropped something else – a pair of white panties (wearing no stockings) were clearly discerned around her shackled ankles.(*This really happened*.) With straight though reddened face, she deftly reached down and blithely, stepped out of the nether garment, putting it in one of her bags–and picking up her shopping casually, walked off. And I, just as matter-of-factly, with straight face (but roaring inside) pedalled on my way. Associations as teenager were legion, but the humour of it, like a picture postcard, outweighed any other adolescent innuendoes.

Twixt January and March 1952, amid the frost, smog, rain and snow, school homework, pocket-money earned pursuits, and scouts, theatre ,and numerous cinema visits, and regular visits to relatives, February 27th had held a chronological milestone for me – my fifteenth birthday. And, as my diary leaf in its mediocrity revealed: 'Fifteen years old today. Scouts – paid all subs. My birthday received five cards and 5/-, 2/6d. from Gran and Granddad.' ... Youth – at fifteen years old, although many children then left secondary school for the labour market – I was at grammar school and allowed to stay on. The labour government in a few short years would make it compulsory for all children to remain at school till they became sixteen years of age.

The week of my fifteenth birthday in 1952 began with Gilwell Work Day on Sunday, 24th February, a special Boy Scout preparation day for the coming weekend's brief camp at Stock. A mid-term school holiday. *Going to the pictures* remained my only then extra mural ambition. And I went to the pictures twice during that week. On Monday it was James Stewart in *Winchester 73*, and a B feature, *Sixteen Fathom*. And on the Thursday my brother and I saw Bing Crosby in Mark Twain's, *A Yankee in King Arthur's Court*; and *The Sign of the Dagger*. I noted in the diary that an 'Anne Malone' visited that same day. Anne a young dark haired Irish girl, was a niece of Thomas Dolan our good stepfather. Sadly a few short years later she would disappear, and still later learn the reason *why* she always seemed so thin. Anne had died of tuberculosis (like my Uncle George) – consumption still remaining a killer disease that had removed many relatives and friends from existence:

'Saturday, 1st March, 1952. Went to Stock at 2.55 p.m. and got there with dynamo trouble approx. 4.30 pm' Which suggests I had cycled through London. Looking back at these leaf notes, I recollect how at fifteen years old, through to sixteen, seventeen and even eighteen years, whilst chronologically I was becoming a young man , I was very much an immature boy. (I was not street-wise.)

The country's media talked about our age group as 'youths' or 'teenagers' as a separate part of its corporate body, but generally growth markers as growing up milestones were still the normative viewpoint with which you evaluated yourself–as others did of you. At fifteen I was viewed as rather small in height for my age, but with years to grow. Genital development was normal, and curly pubic hair had marked me for any school peer doubters to observe in passing at the inevitable after-sports communal baths or showers.

This awareness of my boy's body, The Body, teenage clumsy awkward and, almost painfully shy of its own existence, could be exaggerated in the school swimming baths.

A Hackney Downs (Grocers') 1952 school ruling existed that, for health reasons, all boys had to swim in the school baths in the nude. (Years and years later I questioned my memory – was that really true?) Only the female school secretary would occasionally come near the baths – to our inevitable humour and discomfort–but that was only occasionally. Another norm was regular sudden penile erections and nocturnal emissions. As a boys-only school, opportunities to confront shyness with the opposite sex, with no sisters in the family, and no close peer group neighbours, made difficulties and reinforced my shyness – and shared bouts of occasional bravado. Erections were perceived embarrassingly as related to the taboo subject of sex, rather than a normal active body state. And subsequently it was never ever discussed at home – and at school; only briefly, by a teacher in human biology class under the matter-of-fact heading of Human Reproduction.

Only clandestine references were made to sex, and reflected the normal embarrassed giggles of schoolboys. *Not nice to talk about* – publicly. Books, and photographs – mostly books – the common way of uncovering sex. And I was certainly amongst the proverbial, caught irresistibly reading a banned Hank Janson, or viewing small *Spick, Spam* or *Lilliput*, risqué magazines, hidden behind a Maths or French textbook. Caught and confiscated, a spell of

detention after school with x-amount of lines, and loss of the offending article
– if I was found out.

I recollect a tall well-built boy who spoke with a strong guttural accent
who came from Germany. He sat adjacent to me, for a while, and gave an
occasional opportunity to view saleable items brought in, to make his pocket-
money, by producing a few pornographic photos – graphic details of sexual
intercourse and oddity displayed – at a price. His line of goods paled to
insignificance my own mediocre market of sweet coupons and sweets, doing
lines for others, and selling stamps and D.C. comics. Inevitably, to a class of
teenage boys, this tall lad for a while became its doyen, with his outrageous
evidence of seniority above us, and we glimpsed a sensual ecstatic other world.

The following year the boy became the class rebel, and teamed up with
another boy to become a pair of fervent school bullies, labelled juvenile
delinquents. Our doyen's new partner had openly boasted to us classmates of
his criminal thieving and other activities. And, true to type, whilst the rest of
the class grew to dislike 'the pair' they could never ignore their dominance.
And most of us admitted to fear of their open aggression. In my last school
term, in the early summer of 1953, I recollect our German doyen, who had
become it seemed delinquent, having a confrontation with a schoolmaster in
our classroom.

Chairs were used as weapons as the rest of us were told to move aside.
The master coped adequately with the incident. And although I too (amongst
others) had personally suffered from the pair's bullying, I had no doubt that it
was the weasel-like colleague, rather than the tall German boy, who had stirred
up our previous esteemed colleague. And a covert respect and frail friendship
for the big lad from the earlier days when we chatted and laughed as neighbours
(while I occasionally gloated at the pictures) made me feel genuinely sorry for
his situation. The weasel was later sent to Borstal – but of the doyen I heard
no more.

Few boys were really aggressive, '*all the time*'; most episodes were in acts
of bravado; a showing-off, how independent *they* were of our adult schoolmasters
and parents. And showing to us other boys, *they* were to be feared, that *they*
were no longer to be treated as infants or children: 'Do this – do that.' In fact
we sided with the teachers. And held the bullies in total disdain. But In other
ways, groups travelling together (not necessarily as friends – only friendly)
boys would reflect, even demonstrate, that *they* were now become young adults.

In the second year at Reigate Grammar school, I recalled, at thirteen years of age, arriving in class one winter morning to a giggling furtive group huddled around one curly fair-haired boy who I could hear loudly boasting of some action.

Naturally curious, I stood up on my desk-seat to glimpse the object of such overt hilarity. And saw the boy had his trousers open and was doing something. ... But I hadn't a clue to just *what* it was he was doing to himself. Moving on. A year later a similar episode, whilst travelling in a group of lads by train back from a sports afternoon in Tottenham, I learnt of this hidden adolescent pleasure, but normal, relief of masturbation. (Do normal adolescent girls also masturbate, I thought privately, with no possible way of knowing. Or even addressing the curiosity.) To relieve oneself and siphon off the volcanic swell when it arose spontaneously seemed sensible. And to do it outside and in public was of course no way really acceptable. But to juveniles displays of large erect penises were evaluated as new status achievements, a visible (even risible) sign of daring young adulthood. Masturbation relief was a normal channel of sexual energy release but – and the buts were many – numerous fantasies and fears mixed in with the excitement and biological disclosures of momentary, yet inexplicable, sources of pleasure, and affected one's sudden changing moods.

As a teenager at fourteen and fifteen, I had never seen an adult female in the nude. And, even at sixteen and seventeen, such glimpses were well distanced on a theatre stage, or in photographs (*never ever with pubic hair*) ; or within the–format of a censored H or X-marked film, where I could view with clandestine pleasure – and mentally fantasise – without direct reproach. Such cinema visits were initiated on the 14th July 1952, when at fifteen years of age I saw my very *first* X-film (only for over sixteens); then appropriately a foreign subtitled French classic.

The diary leaf said– 'Saw at Coliseum an 'X' film, *Clochmerle*, starring Simon Michele, and *The Man with My Face* an 'A' film.' – The Coliseum was an old cinema of the biograph type in the Kingsland Road. ... *Clochmerle* was about a French village whose irate mature female populace was actively opposed to a males' public urinal being erected in a prominent place. (Yet its purpose was to accommodate males, with otherwise no urinal facility, needing to otherwise openly relieve themselves, up against public buildings et cetera. A taboo subject – females apparently never had such needs....) It was a *very* funny French farce, and provided much titillation – like English *Carry On* films a decade on – by mere association and playful suggestion.

Only later French films, especially those of the French Revolutionary period – *The Mare's Nest* – and others, would provide occasional glimpses of voluptuous deep cleavage, a bare bosom or even, if lucky, a retreating naked female buttock. Most of these continental films thrived on prolonged exposures of low cleavage–*in colour*. Foremost for me as a teenager was a French actress, Martine Carol, as in the film *Caroline Cherie*, I thought her adorable. Hollywood Doris Day and her peers were, well, like one of the boys really – dubbed tomboys – and not sexy – as her continental peers. Or so I believed. Then.

The distinction between well presented erotica as exotica, and crude pornography (the latter often seemed obscene when it involved ugly violence), was evidenced in books, photographs and theatre. And at school new words as graffiti displayed specific code meanings, or meant-to-be shocking, attempts at confrontation were now included in day-to-day disclosures. But still always furtive–hidden from adults–experiences.

Visits to the school library or the public library, invariably meant a few minutes set aside for privately peaking at the yellow paperback *National Geographical Magazines*. At school, one would discover copies of the NGMs with pages missing, or rudely and mostly too obviously, crudely defaced pictures. Female breasts had exaggerated nipples and aurealae, and the vaginas would be marked out with an additional birdlike nest of pubic hair drawn in up to the navel. And the men–penises would be drawn in erect and massive–and if the artist was adept enough the male and female organs linked together in a believed simulated intercourse. And the words.

Words I had never seen or heard (or been aware of) before, suddenly appeared, and a new secret glossary added to my grammar school vocabulary. Over the cave-like female vaginal organ a prominent arrow would mark out 'cunt', or more often said, in those days 'quim'. Where the origin of these 'rude' rather than erudite, graphic terms came from I never did learn. And the male organ too, designated, to a drawn arrow, captioned as a Victorian or Edwardian forbidden Henry Miller-like 'Cock' or 'Prick' – to establish the daring artistry of some young lad–or imitate a Fielding lothario Tom Jones in the making.

Insidiously all drawings and hastily scrawled graffiti (or so it looked on gaudy billboards, tunnel walls and, especially public toilet cubicle wall-spaces, gave out their crude sexual innuendoes. And I suddenly understood. All this language was in no way to be demonstrated by me at home–or school–and it too, became a normal (however crude) channel of education–though *not* approved by our adult masters. Despite the gathering intensity of these new feelings within me, and the increasing frequency of sudden early morning penile erections, it was *not* towards those femmes fatale that my day-dreaming fantasies were directed–but to safer, often girl-next-door (but just grown up) female models..

And it was not the couldn't-care-less aggressive men that I modelled adulthood upon, but the honourable dependable very-human grown-up man's man heroes, Gary Cooper, James Stewart, Cary Grant and John Wayne. And females, Yvonne de Carlo, Doris Day–and Maureen O'Hara. A diary note for July 31st 1952 read; 'Went to Whipps Cross. In evening saw at Savoy *The Quiet Man* starring John Wayne and Maureen O'Hara'. After a day's cycle ride up to Whipps Cross parkland, the visit to the A.B.C. (cock crowing) Savoy cinema in the Stoke Newington High Street in the evening the day was complete with my two boyhood film heroes, icons, seen together.

School Sport

In school sport for one afternoon the whole class travelled up by coach to our sports field at Edmonton. I travelled up by a school sick-making bone-shaking old charabanc – and, often returned by train or bus. Football or cricket was played. However, I skived from the former as much as possible, bored by the soccer game. ... But having played in the orphanage first cricket eleven for a while, I still enjoyed being a slogger and modestly fast bowler in school matches. I could not dive into a swimming pool, I would jump in, and was a fairly fast over-arm swimmer. Organised boxing – especially to represent one's school house team; well, I only experienced one full boxing match. It was an ironic series of bouts. Due to my sum experience at the hands of a number of bullies over much of my short life, I *loathed* violence in any form. (Sadly, I didn't recognise *shouting* as a potential form of aggression – only a demonstration of it as passion or excitation or hysteria.) But admiration of skills in athletics and other organised games remained with me – as a passive observer.

A boxing match was pressed upon me to represent the school house. And I met my opponent, formally, with some trepidation – in the school gym. He was tall and quite large, a red-headed, indeed a well built lad, quite unknown to me. And I got the impression he too wasn't really keen on our boxing match – but the show had to go on. Boys and masters crowded round the ring, and we took our turn. To my surprise I found I was able to literally dance rings around him, and in moving fast around him he was able to land very few punches. Periodically I would dart in and out, and land one body blow after another–but I deliberately would not, could not, hit him on the face because there was no way I really intended to hurt him. His guard was frequently down as I danced and spun around and boxed into him. It was my determination *not* to hit him on the face, but accept frequently catching him on the trunk, combined with sufficient agility. It surprised me when it was declared I had won easily– purely on points. I refused to fight any other boxing match, as I always thought no blood sports–for me. Clearly I hadn't got what it takes to be any sportsman, (no manly killer instinct) let alone an athletic super-hero. But it didn't bother me since my interests were still growing in other directions.

My sixteenth birthday arrived and mother confirmed that they could not afford to keep me on at grammar school. A requested visit for her to meet the Headmaster achieved little but a gentle rebuke from him that it was a pity to remove Barone before taking any exams–he would have done well at the end of the following school year; might have gone on to University. (I wanted to go to Cambridge.) It must have sounded like a glimpse of cloud cuckoo-land to my mother and stepfather. With continuing austerity, and the need for a little more money to come into the family coffer. But most, it was the gross reduction of costs in attending grammar school. The following year my brother, too, would leave in 1954, one year before exams could have been taken. What did I feel?

Very little really. I was still but a thin child unknowing, in a world at large; with a great gulf existent in the fifties between ... us-and-them– a class distinction, felt *since* leaving the orphanage institution–less than two years before. Asked to write an essay on 'What You Would Like To Do On Leaving School' at an English lesson, I not surprisingly linked up with my passion for visiting the cinema, and suggested I sometime learnt to become cameraman – taking pictures. This interest in furthering camera work was also reflected in the numerous amateur photo snapshots recording our London expeditions. There were many photos taken from the tiny 127 film size; of the Festival of Britain; London Zoo; Clissold Park; and from the top of St. Paul's Cathedral. This amateur camera work combined with frequent cinema visits undoubtedly expanded my educative horizons. It insisted I look and often imagine, what was it about the object; and thought of who and what was being captured behind my cheap camera lens.

At school I had befriended one or two Jewish lads and had been to their homes on a number of occasions. I learnt what a synagogue was, and noted there was one near the top of Stamford Hill, and another on the way to school. A number of Jewish classmates appeared to come from 'well off' families – jewellers, furriers, grocers – and locally a number of photography shops were owned by Jewish proprietors.

Manor Park, in Eastham

We visited Eastham to meet adopted Irish Dolan and Malone relations. And, attending several Irish weddings; adored lively accordion and violins (fiddles) music and dancing jigs. The seemingly often hot-headed arguments and occasional fist fights were somewhat out of line of my family experience. These fights 'not' with the relatives, but amongst their acquaintances. I was most perplexed by the learning; in 1953 or '54, of one of my Irish step-cousins giving birth to a child without arms–a thalidomide baby–of which the public media would soon discover hundreds more casualties in the months and years ahead. And a staunch reminder that some drugs have cumulative effects, and even well-tried and researched term awesome results.

Mother escorted me to a youth employment exchange in Mare Street, Hackney, and the interviewer referred to my then lack of any paper qualifications. The schools had only recently moved over from matriculation exams to the then recently Ordinary level General Certificate of Education Certificates (I don't believe A levels were yet available). Only very well off people (we believed) could afford to graduate with GCE's and experience the realms of a higher education, and even a professional career. Intelligence had nothing to do with it. An interview was subsequently arranged–in line with my school leaving essay subject and amateur photographic experience. There was a vacancy for a photo press messenger at Central Press Photos, situated in 6 and 7 Gough Square, Fleet Street, in the City of London. I got the job, commencement at £2 per week, and began in August 1953. The job's prospects – the interviewer of Central Press alluded – could lead to the world of press photography – but one must start from the bottom, as messenger–and tea boy, and hope!

To Work

At sixteen I reckoned I was becoming a Young Man; after all, I was about to start work. My step-father had shown me how to wet shave on my birthday. And we chuckled in acknowledgement how my fair light down 'bum fluff' would need shaving–about every other month. I was still a boy and knew it. One of my last school out-functions was to attend the Army Cadet School annual camp. The school bullies again made their mark and behind the scenes (without officers' knowledge?) they held a mini reign of terror – the weasel was at the core of this persecution.

One poor devil at the army cadet camp had had his genitals thickly blancoed for fun. I'd heard he'd experienced a great deal of trouble scrubbing the green substance out of his skin pores. My involvement at the camp was cut short by an unexpected emergency visit to the dentists where I experienced for the first (and last) time *gas* anaesthesia. After a bad after-reaction it was suggested that the school military administration send me home a.s.a.p. – to recover at leisure. And I prepared for my first job.

It was with pride that I journeyed *to work* for the first time, travelling by two buses. If I took a trolley-bus I had to change. And the trams had finished locally and soon in London 'altogether' in 1952; the last tram journey ceremoniously exiting down into Kingsway with a full press fanfare. The last London tramcar was, I believe, burnt on January 26th, 1953, a few weeks before I left school.

Leaving schooldays for young adulthood, I knowingly left Opie-like childhood games behind. [22] No more would I thread a boot-polished lace well baked conker and, contest with others, play each autumn in the playground. No more would the beautiful multi-coloured glass marbles rattle and click loudly in a bulge in my pockets. No marbles or cigarette cards to be competed for in play at school and along many a street gutter lane. No more would those cigarette cards be accumulated for 'sets of information'; and be cast against a building wall–to be flicked in turn until your cast-card laid upon another on the ground, and all laid down become yours. And the victor to enjoy the set cards contents of information. And many other games were left behind as a new game in life got under way, with innumerable new rules and regulations, social mores and statute laws. Work. A wholly new set of rules and information.

Entering full-time work for the first time, I recalled the school Head's last lecture to us 'boys leaving school'. Gathered together in the internal amphitheatre, he worldly informed us that: ' Many of you will be learning lots of new words. And be exposed to numerous temptations. Do· *not* be persuaded to pick up the F word, or persuaded into easy ways of making illegal money.'

For some years I had been using *swear* words such as 'blimey' and 'hell' or 'bloody'. And, after one early burst of 'blimey' I had been taken aside by a master whilst in the Orphanage and I was told a tale, a moral tale, as to what could happen if I kept on using this foul word in bursts of temper or exasperation. The master said that; "One time, centuries ago, a godly man was visiting a market place when some incident caused him to momentarily lose his self control. And so it happened. An overhead dark sky was lit by blinding darts of lightning; a storm at its zenith". "Well", he continued, 'The man shouted 'God Blind Me.' And instantly a singular bolt of lightning struck him and rendered him truly blind. You see, 'blimey' is short for 'blind me'". .... and at that time I believed the master. And reckoned that any invective swear word was a derivative of some ancient curse–and was loaded with esoteric potential. In truth as I left school the word 'fuck' as invective had never been heard by me, at home, or recognised at school. But quickly, that word, became familiar much repeated in parlance, and in my presence gather momentum. And only later, on leaving H.M. forces would in its everyday use by me, diminish, until only in fits of pique and in a loss of temper would invective be more than occasionally used.

Gough Square

First job on leaving school was in Central Press Photos situated at 6 and 7 Gough Square off Fleet Street. I approached The (previously Georgian) Square by walking off Fleet Street up Bolt Court, Hind Court or Wine Office Court, from the south side. The Thames-side of Fleet Street. Wine Office Court was bent shaped and included the site of the famous, on the corner inn the 'Cheshire Cheese'. The inn was known to be the one-time haunt of the literary genius Dr. Johnson, of Dictionary fame and, his noble circle of friends, literary critics who too had lived close by.

So too Gough Square, as well as being the home of my firm, the photographic agency, Central Press Photos was competing with other Fleet Street photographic press agencies including Associated Press, Reuters, Keystone and Fox Photos in Red Lion Square. Dr Johnson's original home at 17 Gough Square was where over five years he constructed his *Dictionary* in the mid 18th century.

Another of Johnson's residences was located just off the square, but long gone, and had given his name to Johnson Court.

At sixteen I was not really interested in tourists following old history to the extent of following other lines of tourists, for I had a new here-and-now world of my own to explore–whilst often reminded of recent wartime history, and ancient history, in the immediate surroundings. Travelling down from home by bus, passing St. Paul's Cathedral, down (or up) Ludgate Hill, under the bridge, and up again, into Fleet Street – I could hardly ignore the gradient, or the litter of many bombed ruins on the way to work, and around work itself.

In August 1953, when I began work in Gough Square, buildings surrounding its perimeter stood up tall and stark against the horizon. The north, west, and eastern surrounds were a litter of sunken bombsites marked by peripheral neatened low brick walls (like Petticoat Lane). During the next two years, 1953-55, Central Press staff lads and I would often play football or cricket during lunch-breaks down on these cluttered bombsites off Line Office Court, leading downwards into Shoe Lane.

Dr. Johnson's house at 17 Gough Square was built about 1700 by a London city father who called himself 'Goff', the square taking its title from him. After Johnson left the property it became neglected and was used, for commercial purposes by 'Hailer and Mines General Printers', until 1911, when it was restored to something of its original condition. At the top of the house was one large oblong room called the Garret (aka attic), an area which had suffered severe fire damage during the Second World War, in 1941 and 1942. Two garret roof beams still showed black charcoaled edges as a stark reminder of how close The House came to join the fate of numerous adjoining buildings I then knew as bombsites. The thick brown doorway to Central Press Photos I found in the northeast corner of Gough Square, actually under an archway; the north side, linked to the east-side buildings in the square facing Shoe Lane. Two panels of leaded glass were visible in the pavement and close to the wall; these two subterranean windows indicated my workplace, underneath the square. I was shown downstairs to the darkrooms and a machine room.

Mr. Pope was my immediate boss, a pleasant, dapper, small lively gentleman wearing a light coloured suit, glasses, a raised forehead and slightly balding. He was strict but fair; one essential cog in the Central Press's photographic process. Mr. Pope was principally in charge of four of us messenger boys, aged fifteen to seventeen years old, outside the darkrooms. He was responsible for correct captions being pasted on the back of the 'rush' photos and, then swiftly despatched to all London and Provincial Newspaper buildings–and other press agencies (Mr Prior, and Mr Disney are two photographers names I recall).

On entry I was formally given a guided tour of Central Press by Mr. Pope after I was taken upstairs to meet the executives and secretarial staff. And then on the top floor, to visit the library – as all the darkrooms and apparatus were located in the basement. He then introduced me to my peers, two lads from south of the Thames, and a third from one of the fashionable suburbs – his father a staff photographer for Reuters. A senior staff photographer, Mr. Prior, happened to be present, having just loaded up his cameras and about to depart on a job. Mr. Prior (made me think of Falstaff), a jovial stout gentleman, dressed in dark suit, and needing a walking stick.

Our manager said affable Mr. Prior was one of 'the' selected on rota Central Press senior staff photographers, who had recently taken many of the published press photos in the recent Westminster Abbey coronation of Queen Elizabeth II. Central Press was one of the rota photo agencies given access to the internal coronation service. I was informed that, because there are so many agencies, they rotated by agreement, in attending special occasions (i.e. royal). In the machine room there were four circular drum machines – two blanket driers, and two chromium glazers.

To one side of the machine room, just inside the entrance, was a long raised desk and cupboard with numerous wooden compartments, marked with recognised names of national newspapers, these boxes placed overhead. Two small alcoves were to the side of the machines. In one low rounded dome-like cave there was a wooden trestle table with a wooden form alongside it for seating. In this alcove the captions were composed and typed for speedy distribution. In the even smaller and darker alcove next to it a form seat lay along one wall with a tall filing cabinet – on the seat we young messengers awaited our duties.

In this same dark alcove a battered side table supported a large boxlike camera with huge condensers and bellows–all movable on two narrow wooden rails. In front of the lens (with a brown papier-mache cover over it) a wooden board with four equal lengths of neon light strips were attached, in a square, with a neat row of coloured plastic pins reedy for use in a line along the top of the board. This large camera was for copy work, and within several weeks I learnt to use the glass negative plates set in the double-sided wooden holder. And, having made my copies, entered one of the two grotto-like darkrooms next door to process the results. Although paid as 'messengers', I soon learnt that, we had additional daily tasks and our own rota for attendant darkroom duties.

Adjacent to the machine room, still underground, was the main large staffed darkroom where the photographic negatives were developed and printed. And, via a slot in the wall, a substantial porcelain double wash sink area. Next-door were two more grotto-like alcoves, with thick double-doors, behind which the negative glass and film sheets and, roll films (not many in those days), were processed. Most photographers were expected to develop their own work, but sometimes trusted others were asked to process them. The main darkroom had one entrance and an acute angled slot in one well to despatch freshly developed, fixed prints, down into the large china sink for aluming (if they were double-weight).

And then they were dropped into two very cold water running sinks for rinsing – the better the rinse (provided they were fixed long enough) the longer the lifetime of the pictures. But for 'fast' rushes, long fixing was not necessary, as it was for that day only – to rush to the papers in a hope of beating other Press Agency contenders and make the earliest editions. There were three big enlargers, including one upright, around three walls of the darkroom. Two enlargers were horizontal – larger editions of the copy machine. These had interchangeable lenses for either reducing work – that is, reducing the size from the original – or standard, for controlled enlargements. Blow-ups might be of an action football picture, or a royal appearance on the balcony at Buckingham Palace, or of a cricketer at the stumps at the Oval, or Old Trafford.

I recollect the speed of experienced printers in their exposing and hand-shading (to enhance one area or subdue another), and duplicating the same effect upwards of thirty to fifty times – for each picture. A batch would then be given by the printer, to a developer (me) working with a set of trays, in the middle of the room. And deftly, hand over hand, the prints would be kept moving, watching the leading print for the right density, (and any accidents or bad prints to be thrown out–underneath into the bin). When the prints were developed sufficiently, they would be equally served in the adjacent fix chemical, till it was safe, to exit them out through a slot, down into the sinks for washing. When the prints were sufficiently washed, they would be passed through the hatch, a link window and wooden hatch slide, surface, placed between the sink-room and, the machine room–for drying. Carefully, double weight prints were singly lined up and fed, face down, onto the slightly chalked blanket, to pass under and over the cloth covered drier, and collected as they dropped off the drum. And they emerged, hopefully dry – if not to be re-fed until they were.

The newly dried unglazed print would be passed over to the raised desk surface and the typed captions, one per picture, white pasted on the back of the prints. Immediately–if a rush–a messenger was called and given a run to the newspaper picture editors for potential selection for that day's publication. Eagerly each successive published edition would be checked and marked up. If a print was published, then came a subsequent internal acknowledgement to the photographer and agency for payment.

Next to the narrow sink-room area were two other claustrophobic, small grotto-like darkrooms with arched ceilings (bitter cold in winter) and gritted stone walls–as was the plain decor throughout all the underground work areas. Full one third of each ice-cold grotto rooms had a raised lead-lined sink, with running water keeping it clear of washed out fix chemicals. These sinks were largely used for single weight prints, especially 'private' orders – all due for a shiny, even glazed dry surface. If the private print had a poor glaze: if any pitted areas were observable, or unglazed areas were discerned on the surface. Then quickly, the order would be, sometimes angrily, re-ordered. At my commencement of the job, and for many months to come, hundreds of private orders for the recent 1953 Coronation were being executed.

Also developed in the grotto darkrooms were the 5 x 4 film negatives and large glass plates. Depending on the type of negative determined whether a green light could be used, or – and more frequent – it was processed in total darkness. All darkroom work done by feel and knowledge. The finished work left to wash in the large flat water sink within the cold grotto – under a running tap. By far most common sized glass negatives in use were those five inch by four inch negatives.

The most common size was double-weight ten by eight unglazed prints, for rush distributions to respective Fleet Street Newspaper Picture Editors. Each rushed out pic had to compete with other Agencies–and of course the paper's own staff photographers. And so speed was of the essence.   Other print sizes were produced, but in lesser quantities. Used negatives were eventually placed in transparent bags with each contact print (print the exact size of the negative), and boxed with other unused negatives and filed away upstairs in the picture library archives.

After the initial introduction to the printing staff, machinery, and other rooms, in the underground of Central Press Photos: I was then again, taken upstairs to the ground floor to meet two senior staff members, who controlled the more academic aspects of the work–selecting the right negatives for publication, arranging new assignments for photographers, dealing; with the fiscal accounts aspects, and other more esoteric forms of press office work. And finally at my formal introduction to the premises I was taken upstairs by Mr. Pope to the Central Press library and met, as I recollect, the only female member of staff, a young girl employed in the library. Above this room was the flat roof of the whole building, whereon at times during the next two summers I was to occasionally gaze out upon London and St Paul's–much as Dr. Johnson, in shouting distance, would similarly have done from his garret two centuries ago.

From the outset there were two tasks I had to learn fast. One was the exact location of all the various newspaper offices. The second was the even more important job of how to operate the metal tea urn–and run numerous errands for cigarettes, pipe tobacco, and hundreds of doughnuts and favourite cream slices. Most food and confectionery were obtainable from an incredibly busy small cafe, or more appropriately snack bar, at the bottom of line Office Court and junction of Shoe Lane–past a long row of vacant bombsites. Across the Shoe Lane slope, I could see down and across several more, bomb-scarred sites, and directly into Farringdon Street. It was a downward slope, from Gough Square into the region of Farringdon Street; with Holborn up north to the left, and south to the right, past Ludgate Circus, through to Blackfriars Bridge.

Not so many years ago, certainly in Dr. Johnson's days, the Fleet river ran parallel to the main road. Insidiously it became more and more polluted, and silted up, becoming literally the Fleet Ditch. The infamous Fleet prison on the eastern bank overlooking, now Farringdon Street, the Fleet river. After 1841, the Fleet Ditch at the back of Field Lane was covered over. And later the Fleet was completely submerged, its stream remnant to be found underground on the east side of Farringdon road, in league with the sewer, mouth arriving out of sight under the Blackfriars Bridge. So too the Blackfriars' London Underground subways. I recollect visiting this area and thinking – one time – I would be in, or under, the mouth of the River Fleet. Little imagination was necessary to envisage the tidal-borne Fleet covering the marshes out, and even possibly even up to, Shoe Lane itself. No doubt an archaeological dig would answer this question. Old Seacoal Lane at Ludgate Circus suggested a smelly loading stage of coal fuel, being off-loaded from the Fleet and including, perhaps, a drop delivery at the nearby foetid prison – and even up the hill to St. Paul's.

Getting to know the exact location of all the London national newspapers and the local offices of the provincials took me a little time. One of the big papers, I think the *Daily Telegraph*, or *Express*, had a lift in which you pulled yourself up by rope – or do I remember it wrongly? And there was always a prevailing strong smell of machine oil. And the musk from huge round Bowater bales of unused paper – indicating numerous departed trees. And the ever pervasive noise of clattering typewriters and hastening feet, always in a hurry– all noise of which soon became commonplace markers in visiting Fleet Street and outlying newspaper premises.

Innocently, I asked someone how one got into the print and, quick as a flash, came a standard reply; No Chance – it's a closed union shop. Only relatives or close friends, 'in' people, could become employed in the print. I never learnt the truth of this statement. Another colleague of mine, another Central Press lad, insisted the Docks too (often then on strike) were a closed shop? As nought but messenger and immature youth, I hadn't in honesty a clue what to expect from a first employer. There was no mention by anybody of any need for a union membership.

A year later, when my younger brother started work in the Balls Pond Road in Islington, he was quickly introduced to the importance of union membership by a workmate; and he related to me its frequent in-quarrels. I had no such kind of experience at Central Press Photos. They were good employers for an interesting job. And the money: at the end of my first week I received my two pounds, of which I kept five shillings, and my mother had the balance towards my keep.

It came as no surprise that shift-work and weekend work were normal practice, and that overtime was common. But the low rate of pay meant that even with maximum overtime, the net sum was unrewarding. And so it was the nature, quality and variety of the job itself that gave justification. One shift began about 8 a.m. (though on request it would be earlier). On arrival the messenger's or duty boy's first task was to make up fresh chemicals–opposite from last task of the day, emptying and clearing up the darkrooms; the last job before lights out and ascending the stairs–to cover the machines up with fitted blankets.

Someone would make up the developer and fix for the main darkroom. Another boy would mix the alum bath with its thick clinging – sometimes stinging – viscosity. And then, with often icy water, a measured quantity of hypo-peas would be extracted from a hessian sack and correctly mixed, transferred to the grotto room as required, for private fixes. There were two experienced darkroom printers, and one youngster in the process of learning. The two adults, Sid and Alf, were at Central Press all the time I was there as a boy. The third, learning the trade, soon departed to do his National Service in the Royal Fusiliers, based at the Tower of London, and later a stint in North Africa–the Sudan. Sid and Alf (not their real names) were full of laughs, and, rough play–often playing practical jokes upon us messengers.

Although there were no formal apprenticeships, it was an 'unwritten' expectation that the firm teach as much as permissible to new recruits–from the boy messengers upwards. One game played regularly to newcomers was an initiation. On arrival I was given two tasks. To go down to the snack bar and collect an unholed doughnut; "There is such a thing", it was insisted. But I refused to believe this and merely pretended to go for one. The second practical initiation could have been very time-consuming. Sid said the darkroom were out of special condenser emery-papers for cleaning the glass surfaces. Again I thwarted him, as I already knew enough about the condenser lenses and realised the absurdity of the request. However, not long after my arrival another and smaller lad began, who knew nothing about the camera section, and he was asked to do a tour of the other agencies to see if they had any spare 'special emery paper'.

I did not give the game away. And on arrival at the other Fleet Street agencies which caught on (having done it before), the lad was sent from place to place until he finally caught on that he had been had – but took it all in good part. When rush work, or private work, or copies were complete, there would emerge a short time to fill – and perhaps a tea-break take place. During this important act a favourite gambling game might be played–double or quit. One man could challenge another to toss for a penny coin. "Heads or tails?"–it was tossed. The contender lost or made a penny. But often the amount would multiply to a substantial sum and a cry be echoed "Double or quits?". This game got out of hand for a while and was banned–but was soon furtively restarted.

We oft-times went out in our lunch-break–or after an early shift break. If I had one shilling and ninepence (less than two bob–a florin) I could visit the nearby working men's wooden hut, a shed, serving as a cafe, erected on a bomb site, and north west of Gough Square, close by E. Harding and Great New Street. New Fetter Lane and the old *Daily Mirror* buildings–clearly observed across the Fetter Lane open sites. The *Daily Mirror* would later move to new premises in Holborn. A cup of tea cost twopence at this working men's cafe, the meals superb in value. Sausages and mash was a favourite meal of mine at that time.

After a hasty meal (the workmen's cafe was always filled up), we lads sometimes strolled down Fleet Street and up and under Ludgate Bridge, and then to a small garden shopping area–just past Sea Coal Lane. But we often stopped under Ludgate Bridge, for a little old fashioned entertainment. For us adolescent boys the ' *What the Butler Saw*' , and *'The Maid*' , or any of the striptease numbers of peep show shows, were found in 1930s (end of the pier) one penny green-painted hand cranking machines located in the cave under Ludgate Bridge, which gave much titillation. Then for a lunchtime 'cuppa cha', we walked up Ludgate Hill a little, and, on the left, onto a large temporary, built-on bomb site. In its middle a low rectangular wall enclosing a decorative lawn patch in its centre, surrounded by network of paths and small prefab-built shops. A year later, on this site, I purchased a first pair of stockings for a girl friend. "What size?" the assistant asked. "Eh, eh, I believe she takes a size five shoe", I spluttered. I had a lot to learn.

The summer months of 1954 and 1955 we might have alternatively taken a stroll along the Thames Embankment, a modern built road. Till recent times our Fleet Street was an ancient trackway alongside a sprawling Thames. The ancient City of London finished west, almost above the river Fleet. Roman Watling Street went across a bridge further up at Holborn (Holbourne). London long pre-dated the Romans, a high island fort in a long estuary. Caesar called the river Tamesis. It was his settling countrymen, directing Celts, who showed up on a wooden lined section of the embankment to provide early wharfs–but the bulk of the long Thameside remained as low marsh.

Wren believed it was for a long time a large sandy plain at low water. And he suggested embanking the river and reclaiming a mile and a half of mud flat as new building land. But the Thames Embankment was not constructed till 1860-1870, an engineering feat: 'from Westminster to Blackfriars a great concrete foundation sunk in the river bed, and on this was built the granite wall, eight feet thick, that has so far successfully withstood the wear of the stream .....' [23]   A total of thirty-seven and a quarter acres of land was at that time reclaimed from the Thames mud. [24]

Despite land reclamation, each year Londoners would hear of the threat of Thames floods, for a great deal of London town is built on land *below* the high water mark. Back in 1928 ten people in Westminster were literally drowned in their beds ... ' by the stealthy invasion of the river on the night of Saturday, January 7th ....' [25]

I have several photographs of Central Press lads and myself walking the embankment in a lunch-hour. In one shot I am wearing an over-large double-breasted herringbone styled jacket–cast-off donated by one of my uncles. My meagre first wage of two pounds per week (before deductions) did not allow for any clothes purchase–I did not own a suit. Not until much later when discharged from the army would I eventually, own a suit.

Most of my garments for work and pleasure were made up of odd jackets and trousers. Trousers were usually grey flannels. After a year or so I proudly purchased a large, two-buttoned sports jacket, it was a speckled white, single breasted, with broad padded shoulders. I was still on the long and lean side in build. Another photo of two Central Press lads and myself revealed that wearing a tie was always respectable, rather than expected. Nevertheless, our clothes were mostly cheap, black or grey, and shapeless. At first our haircuts remained school-boyish, 'short back and sides'; in 1952 I paid one shilling, or even one shilling and threepence. And in 1953 it had risen to one shilling and sixpence in our local barbers. But in 1954-55, close to Call Up, I was affected by fashion–at least in the limit of my now three pounds per week wages. It rose to four pounds per week on entry to National Service in August 1955.

A popular Hollywood film actor named Tony Curtis displayed a large shaped hairstyle which many of my peers began to ape. Another description of one large hairstyle was a 'd.a.'–a duck's arse, because the back of the head hair looked just like a shaped 'd.a.'. The style that I adopted was called a 'Boston', a thinned shaped front, but a specific back, razor edged, with a slight rear cliff-edge of hair. One distinct feature in men's hair was the liberal use of greasy White Brylcream as advertised by the ace cricketer Denis Compton. It kept the hair in place, but it left acres of the unwanted sticky grease wherever it touched. And, inevitably, if your hair were shaped and styled it cost more.

Despite shift work I soon sandwiched a few social activities. And as shy as I was, a desire for girl friends was not surprisingly becoming a pursuit. Music was going through a transition, though big swing bands were still popular, great sounds like the Ted Heath band, competed with crooners Crosby, Sinatra and Como; ballad singers like Tennesse Ernie Ford; and especially pop artistes, Johnny Ray, Frankie Laine, and Jo Stafford. And as to dance music–Victor Sylvester, Joe Loss, or real sophistication was Earl Bostic. I had yet to discover real jazz and jive.

My brother and I were determined to learn to dance, so we could better socialise and get girlfriends. For a while we attended a London County Council evening class behind the Odeon Cinema at Dalston Junction. But the singular rhythm of Victor Sylvester, whilst it introduced us to respectable ballroom dancing, waltz and quickstep, did *not* introduce us to the teenage 'in' dancing–jiving. We started to attend a Wednesday evening dance session, not lessons, at a studio called *Barries*, rooms situated over a Montague Burton Tailors in nearby Mare Street E.8, Hackney.

After ascending a steep flight of stairs and paying entrance at the table, a pace back from the top step, we entered a long low-ceilinged room, with deliberate dim lights. And under it a revolving spot-light hung from the centre of the room. Barrie was a well dressed distinguished looking gentleman–in his late thirties or forties, who often acted as referee as well as occasional instructor and knowledgeable disc-jockey. There was no bar– a Hackney pub was nearby for those who could use it.

LEFT: Central Press Photos, 1954. Downstairs. I'm at the back. **RIGHT:** Central Press, outside Buckingham Palace, 1954 (I am arrowed, right). (Source: Author)

Barrie's Dance Studio

Hackney Barries' dancers were divided down the middle of the room and, when *not* dancing, all sat down on chairs around its periphery. Top half of the long room, overlooking Mare Street, was dominated by 'in' cluster groups of jivers–moving an' swinging or indulging to the deep sultry music of the alto-saxophone strains of New Orleans Jazz, Earl Bostic's *'Flamingo'* –which I loved. (Bostic was early fifties pre rock 'n' roll, pre-Haley and pre-Presley–and *before* I later adhered to trad Jazz–*and* had learnt to *really* jive. Indeed in the early sixties I would *teach* ballroom and jive dancing ...). And otherside, lower half of Barrie's room (even– by default) was the more aspiring middle class, grammar school types–of which–bro and I belonged And who didn't *yet* know–how to jive. It was a natural social class division–but *never* a source of rancour. In reality most of the regulars would like to have been able to perform to all or any, dance and dancer, they chose. For most jivers–could *not* do any ballroom dances. As vice-versa. ... Barrie aware of this hollow class irony.

And as host he seldom allowed the room division to be too rigid, and would introduce novelty dances to circulate and avoid embarrassment of being unable to ask of a new partner. (When music stops, you will kiss your partner on the cheek then, change your partner, sit on the floor, et cetera.) The dance studio gathering was almost exclusively for young boys and girls from fourteen years old, up to and including those in their early twenties.

Occasionally new dance steps would be introduced, and then integrated into already accepted dance rhythm sequences. I recollect with amusement a dance step pattern called *'The Creep'*; the boy and girl could, would dance *very* close–hip to hip, and hands supposed, casually, to be draped behind your partner and placed around their buttocks. It was intended, that in *The Creep*, you danced cheek-to-cheek, even cheek over shoulder, casual, shoulder to shoulder, chest to chest–not really hip-to-hip, (but of course they were). And, sexual innovation demanded our natural, not so innocent, tendencies to get as close-to-one-another as possible – yet casual as possible. (In retrospect it was of course the normal social foxtrot – but slouched).

Creepers were a fashionable mode; their thick crepe soles (brothel creepers) and soft suede leather, coloured green brown mauve blue shoes–later immortalised by a new singer in faraway America called Elvis Presley, as *'Blue Suede Shoes'*. And there were the fashionable winkle picker shoes, with their impractical,

Turkish-like seraglio pointed toe caps, a pair of which I had purchased down Petticoat lane. Winkle pickers proved most uncomfortable, their thin soles useless for dancing, let alone walking about the street. As the Creep dance title suggested, you literally 'creeped' *very* slowly in time to the music, a half-beat– or suspended beat–and exaggerated a state of dreaminess. ... That *really* worked.

Youth was aided by a seemingly boundless continuum of energy, with extra red blood corpuscles (compared with a decrease in old age), and very active endocrinal glands. Apart from nocturnal emissions, and now daily morning erections, morning glory was to be a normal lifetime biological curiosity and occasional embarrassment. I began as teenager to experience more erections whilst dancing hip-close with partners, and with profound embarrassment and mixed excitement I would delicately attempt to *not* let my partner know–she probably did. And instead of the proper ballroom convention of holding one's partner, apart, I would have to, reluctantly, attempt to subtly '*unstick*' our joined pelvis. This unexpected teenage development only seemed to reinforce my shyness, whilst inwardly escalating the natural desires. Were teenage girls spared from such heated situations: of periods, I knew little.

Central Press Photos

I decided to find an alternative to being dependent on public transport and the often long-wait for late-night, or all-night buses–even though, for a while, they were actually reducing bus-fares for the working classes travelling in the early morning. And I took to using my bicycle to and from work. Cycling was to become my basic mode of transport in the early 1950s.

My stepfather regularly let one of our bedrooms off, to help pay the modest mortgage, and for a while we lodged a husband, wife and child–the man a very keen touring club cyclist, who introduced me to its weekend rigours whilst I was still at school. As I commenced work the family had left, and the large back room was presently let to a single man who possessed a very large collection of jazz records. '*You can always tell a good number*', he wisely informed me. '*You can hear each musical instrument at play in the band*'. A middle-aged gentleman, our lodger was one-time secretary of a jazz club, and the hundreds of catalogued 78 r.p.m. records stacked about his room must have taken years to collect.

Popular music at fifteen years old remained at a mean level to my still limited experience. My parents purchased their first television set in late 1952

– but most musical numbers were still gleaned from the radio. And titles from teenage peers. When my brother and I left the orphanage, a modest pile of effects of my parents were piled in an unfurnished front room; these included less than half a dozen old gramophone records – one was *Twelfth Street Rag* by Pee Wee Hunt.

A few months later I purchased my very first gramophone record, principally to entertain my young six year old cousin, Derek; it was Max Bygrave's *The Dummy Song*, from 'Educating Archie', a radio comedy show with ventriloquist Peter Brough and Archie Andrews. A Glenn Miller re-make film starring James Stewart, *The Glenn Miller Story* (1954), was enjoyed sometime later, and I purchased a number of republished recordings of Glenn Miller. About this time I obtained my own first record player–and later still became really hooked on *Trad Jazz*, learnt from my associates at work. Artistes like Chris Barber, Cy Laurie, Sandy Brown, Humphrey Lyttleton (soon to go Mainstream). I sighed as I listened, and, wished I could trad jive.

At work, interest in black and white photography (colour photography was very expensive and not used in The Press agencies) inevitably expanded. As messenger boy I frequently went out on runs to various papers, or out as an assistant, carrying apparatus for staff photographers – their photographic kit was often large and heavy. The long black box that housed the camera and huge telephoto lenses, as used for the Oval Cricket Ground; and especially at Royal Family occasions. And there was a heavy shoulder box containing the loaded double-sided, glass negative plates in their wooden slides, heavy indeed. Sometimes I worked in the darkrooms and learned something of the trade.

From a junk shop at the end of Church Street, Stoke Newington, adjacent to a school, I purchased my own first plate camera – a small ancient relic. Unfortunately it was already out of date and from the outset I found it difficult to obtain plates from a local chemist supply. However, it did help me to master some of the basic techniques in black and white photography–and the camera body itself would prove very useful as part of a home-made enlarger–several years later.

A younger colleague at work whose father worked as a Press Photographer for Reuters of Fleet Street obtained a magnificent brand-new duplicate of Central Press's staff worker large Micro Press 5" x 4" cameras – and soon enjoyed a copy of one of his Spring prints in an evening paper. Much advertised were the Rolleifleix, and 35mm Leica roll film cameras – but, they too, were a sophisticated world apart from my cheap camera. I envied my well-off colleagues with their superb kits.

Sid and Alf (not their real names), the two experienced adult printers in the main darkroom, would occasionally teach me something of their magic art. Sid was in his late twenties, and smoked a strong smelling Bruno pipe tobacco. He was tall, lean, with a black moustache. His hobbies were collecting Benny Goodman classical recordings (as 1930s Carnegie Hall collections) – and he was very fit from his Judo classes. After printing a number of shots, Sid would instruct me to put the thin rubber gloves on and move up to the developing dish with adjacent fix dishes. At his word I began to feed the prints into the developer dish, until they were all submerged into the slowly browning developing liquid, (when dark it was time to be changed). And anxiously I would look back to Sid (standing behind me on the duck-board) and, look up at him, for I was small to his height, and when I thought the leading print developed enough would ask his agreement to fix – and feed the prints over to the next dish, and re-commence the hand over hand movements required. Now this procedure required a deal of concentration, but Sid had a rather over-zealous playful (bullying) habit of practising his judo holds and fist punches on me whilst I was attempting to work and producing the developing prints in front of him.

Standing in the semi-darkness on the wooden duck-boards, I would (not surprising) vainly attempt to properly develop the prints while Sid would suddenly move up and begin to punch away at me. It would be churlish to suggest that Sid was being deliberately vicious–he wasn't. He was I believed genuinely, perhaps rather thoughtlessly, unaware of his own strength, and the multiple bruises I would daily take home with me. But, in retrospect, hardly surprising, I was not known as a good darkroom worker (though sufficient), and for a short while I was gently rebuked as the Black Baron–for the number of over-dark prints emerging through the hatch Sid's occasional over-zealous punching episodes were not a good learning vehicle. I was *not* confident working in the darkroom, subsequent to Sid's aggressive tuition. And, in August 1955 when I entered the Royal Engineers on National Service, I still bore numerous dark bruises on my arms, sometime previously inflicted by Sid.

The printers and other C.P. workmates would periodically allow me to view the few clandestine uncensored prints of various film actresses and other starlets taken on jobs. On top of a small cupboard in the main darkroom several large buff envelopes contained prints that were not for public press publication.

There were one or two starlets in the nude, with a peak of pubic hair (then highly censored) and ample naked breasts. In modern parlance there was *no* pornography, rather but risqué photos. One set was of a then popular radio and screen starlet called S renowned for her very large breasts. The photos were rather more amusing than erotic as they looked magnified goose pimples on rather large over-ripe oranges.

At this time one of Central Press's contracts was to copy fashion photographs sent over from Paris, or other foreign parts, and then distributed to the national press. There were many hilarious (I thought as a teenage boy) fashion modes. Tall hairdo's with stuffed birds in minute cages bound in hair, or glass heeled shoes with various bound-in phenomena. And as to some of the clothing styles– surely, I thought, no-one really wears garments like those models? And there were the regular copies to do of the Windmill Theatre girls. About once per month a set of nudes, and mostly semi-nudes, (never any pubic hair regions– they were all posed proper), and in good taste. On some weekends we might be asked to go and collect a parcel from Scotland. Johnny, our excellent motor-cyclist messenger, would collect the prints from Euston station, despatched from a faraway Scots agency, and I would sometimes copy these shots. And later do a run for the nationals.

Off the Thames Embankment was an office of the Cable and Wireless organisation. Periodically we would be sent down to collect a lined cable photographic print, directly transmitted from across the world–from Australia, Canada, or other distanced sources. Its subject might have been a test match current in India or Australia. Or of a member of the royal family then on a formal tour overseas. In May 1954 I accompanied a staff photographer to the Thames side to meet the Queen and Duke of Edinburgh on their return from a tour. During my two years at Central Press I would frequently see members of royalty from close quarters, and remember Princess Anne with her fair curly top hair looking like Shirley Temple. And Prince Charles, though small, still as her guardian big brother by her side in a carriage. On another occasion it was meeting Sir Winston Churchill and his wife at Euston Station. As a boy there were fairly frequent notable excursions out of Central Press.

A regular feature of the job as messenger, or darkroom assistant, was to accompany the staff photographers on their assignments, and if Johnny was not due to collect a rush, then there was a certainty that I would return early from the job by taxi (or other transport), or bus, with a rush. Attending a Saturday afternoon football match–and leaving when a goal was scored–or mid-way through a match at Wimbledon or the Oval test cricket game, or a boxing match at a London hall – I never saw a completed game of any description. From my personal acquaintance I enjoyed the more unorthodox visits–the most unorthodox for me, that is. An early visit to a London West End theatre performing Shakespeare, and I was amazed at the visibly thick layers of theatrical make-up discerned, as the staff photographer manoeuvred his shots–and I held a flashlight close in to the actor combatants. This contrasted with fleeting, very boring visits to ladies' fashion houses where as a sixteen and seventeen year old boy I saw them not as erotica ladies, only acres of cold modelled folded clothes. And several visits to a Covent Garden boxing training weigh-in, to watch a number of naked hirsute boxers weigh in, and then pose, in shorts, for our press photographers.

Roman Mithras

Many of the City of London bombed ruin sites in 1954 were being excavated for re-building projects. And on one particular site off Victoria Street, close by the Mansion House and Bank, a group of building workmen had unearthed a wealth of Roman remains amongst which one identified as an ancient Roman temple. I was fortunate in accompanying one of our staff photographers to the site very shortly after discovery of the head of a statue, clearly an indication that the Temple was of Mithras, a sun worship faith akin to the ancient Zoroastrian eastern religion, and to be one of the Men of Books para-christian religions. It was thrilling to step under a rope line–keeping the general public off the Temple site–and stepping down into so different ruins (from World War II remains) wherein various so-then-recent just unearthed objects had been left uncovered, newly discovered, to be photographed and recorded for posterity.

As I held the electronic flash bulb apparatus and carried the photographer's equipment, I drank in this sunken atmosphere, a time capsule oasis on a large otherwise then barren site, in the midst of our modern City of London–and central in that ancient Roman (and Celtic) City of London. The Roman site was soon to be heavily built over, the artefacts removed and Roman walls either removed–or buried. To the credit of the City firm that used the ancient site, they saved some of this valuable Temple of Mithras. A section of it was later reconstructed and placed for permanent public view outside the twentieth century glass and concrete city building which replaced the temple.

And I would, as tourist, visit numerous home archaeological sites and, read many armchair travel books – and learn of faraway excavated ruins : Moche, Chimu, Inca and Mayan remains; of ancient Greek and Egyptian; of Australian and Indian Aborigines, Chinese dynasties; Frank, Tartary and Spaniard, Brahmin and Parsee, Eskimo and Indian. But for me, as a naive young teenage boy, there were to be few more thrilling, so brief moments, as among those few minutes in a London lunchtime in the mid 1950s. Me, on an ancient pulse – in the centre of the ancient Roman City of London in the 1950s.

Two years running I accompanied a photographer to the annual Farnborough Air Show. The first year I looked up, an listened, in amazement, at the still recent public phenomenon of breaking the sound barrier. A British film celebrated the research event. As I entered the press refreshment tent to collect some goodies for my mates back in the Central Press darkroom, (we always kept a bag, later learnt as a 'doggy bag') – we relished the minute taste of what our senior colleagues expected as hallowed right from hosting agencies. But we were bottom of the ladder rungs. As I entered the press tent, an aircraft zoomed overhead and, out to the horizon. Not a sound; then came the sonic boom; demonstrated several times. Breaking the sound barrier was the essential physical watershed before supersonic aircraft became commonplace–sometimes over the speed of sound. Jet aircraft had increased in numbers since the end of the last World War, and escalated during the Korean War.

At those exhibitions I particularly remember beautiful swept back wings of the Avro Vulcans. Also on exhibition were wartime Hurricanes, Spitfires and other historic aircraft. Massive twin-propellered, and single-seater propellered helicopters were alongside small commercial aircraft–propellered, and jet engined. The famous Red Arrow, Royal Air Force jet flying exhibition team was already a firm favourite. I remember the extraordinary looking flying bedstead of the 1950s, which would be developed into jump-jets, those incredible jet aircraft that–like helicopters–could take off vertically, and be so great on aircraft carriers or patches in deep jungle. And of course complement Sci-fact rocket ships, of the near future.

All went fine during my visits to Farnborough, but the year before my first visit a tragic accident had occurred when a machine crashed onto the field, and many of the watching crowd were injured. My knowledge of science was next to zero, but my imagination frequently fired by visiting influences, and I was reasonably observant at times. Less than two years before I visited Farnborough, I had accidentally become acquainted with the science fiction fantasies of H.G.

Wells, and through his genius I had in fantasy not only broken the sound barrier, but ultimately the speed of light and dimensional time wave-ratio barrier. Our lodger, Arnold, as well as enjoying jazz music, collected science fiction journals, and had given my brother and me a number of sci-fi magazines. I developed an appetite for science-fiction reading.

In my fertile imagination, to perceive just an idea a concept, was to believe it inevitably to become a real construct. Thus on my adolescent journey to the Farnborough Air Show, watching and listening to the breaking of the sound barrier was a marvellous reminder of it being but a present stepping-stone to other worlds. I even anticipated cruising beyond the speed of light with mortal quantum, matter in safe containment, and, through a knowledge of co-existent forces, ultimate make contact with parallel worlds of life already existent on earth. The phenomenal amount of research and human resources, plus use of immense natural physical materials, all needed to produce minute product proof of a new idea, just did not occur to my immature seventeen-years-old brain–so lacking in its worldly experience. And as for the social implications.

Girls

An ardent film fan 'The Picture Show' weekly, displayed a pen-pals column (as innumerable other magazines aimed at teenage readers), of which I made liberal use in 1954 and 1955, at seventeen and eighteen years of age. Initially I used the pen-pals column to bridge my shyness with the fair sex and briefly expand my horizons abroad. At sixteen I had not been out with a female since I was twelve years old. At seventeen, occasionally visiting Barrie's Dance Studio in Hackney, I was close to arranging my first date–and others. Egged on my colleagues at Central Press, I put my name in a week's edition of 'The Picture Show'; I cannot recall which date–early 1954. One reader who answered, was Edna who lived up in Shepshed, near Leicester. Eager to meet each other, she came down and spent a weekend with us in Stoke Newington. God, it was such an innocent romance.

From hard earned income, three paper rounds a day, each school-day, two in the morning from 4-6am, and one evening round after school, I obtained my first brand new drop handled bicycle. I can still recollect with pride the purchase of a brand new blue Claude Butler, with lightweight 531 tubing (as it was called). Its cost was just under £30, and I paid monthly credit – written down in a small book from the local shop. I loved that bike (still have a picture of it

– somewhere) in the 1950s, and was able to take it to my army unit in 1956 – before embarking abroad: after return from overseas I found it had, erm, just disappeared from home, along with other teenage artifacts, just disposed of by my mother.

Reciprocating, I later bicycled all the way up to Edna, in Shepshed, Leicester, and back. On arrival up north I asked her what she wanted to do – apart from a visit to the pictures. But she was adamant – she wanted to go cycling. And cycling back to London, after completing nearly four-hundred miles over that weekend, it started to rain about a mile from home. Down Green Lanes, close by Clissold Park, the road still had old tram rails intact and, after cycling all that distance–just over half a mile from home–I skidded and fell off my bike. Only a little bruised I had to laugh at myself, and completed the journey home. In retrospect I realised it was a very innocent beginning and highlighted when Edna attractive and petite, suggested we walk down Love Lane, and laid down under a full moon. Apart from a few kisses I recollect all we did was talk about space, the moon and the visible stars above us. Did she guess she was my first real date other than those ladies from Barrie's Dance Academy in Hackney.?

When not working on Saturday night, my brother and I would continue to go to the pictures, a music hall empire, or a local town hall for a dance – still ballroom dancing at this time. Girlfriends then began to come and go. My first, Pat, (I met a number of Patricias), lived up at Stamford Hill. Together we frequented the Finsbury Park Astoria–and attended Barrie's dancing. With fondness, I remember leaving Pat at home one spring, with pink blossoms in the tree lined route to her house, and feeling so happy with the elevation of courtship, running down that road.

Rita lived at Clapton, in an asbestos prefab; she was a raver I had also met at Barrie's. Out to court, Rita and I wandered out of the dance-hall into a graveyard at the rear of Mare Street, and rather innocently (no mischief intended, mere bravado) we danced, lit by a full moon, on a gravestone. It was Rita who, at sweet seventeen, let me have the first thrilling outside-garment caress of female breasts–marvellous an emotion. Anything further truly remained in my mind. Once, arriving at Barrie's at the top of the stairs, I spotted Pat, sat opposite the entrance, and so spluttering some suggestion about getting a drink first, Rita and I retreated down the stairs to the nearby pub–Pat had gone on our return to the studio. I thought twice about dating two girls at the same time in the future–least ways, from the same area.

At work I continued to do a large amount of overtime and assist in producing thousands of coronation private prints to be churned out. On that day of Queen Elizabeth's coronation, it rained heavily, and though I had followed with distant interest the mounting national excitement and prolific amount of bunting in the streets – with numerous snapshots which marked these events; as youth of sixteen I was *not* really impressed by all the pomp and ceremonial display of money, power and inheritance. There was no animosity – it was just another human-world within other worlds – outside my realm of recognised experience. And so I went to pictures, instead of visiting the west end with my stepfather and brother, to stand in the pouring rain and watch the coronation procession. And although we contributed to the Dynevor Road street party collection, my brother and I agreed that we were too old to attend such childish parties. And collected our coronation mugs from the organisers to gather dust in a family cupboard.

I admired the peak achievements of Edmund Hillary and Tensing mountain climbers and their team, in May 1953, in reaching the summit of the Himalayas – the highest known mountain in the world. And likewise, I admired other superfit supermen, athletic achievers like Roger Bannister and Chris Chataway – breaking the first British recorded four-minute mile the following year. Our Central Press's darkrooms kept very busy with its staff photographers' record of that peak event.

But, working in the press photographic agency not only highlighted national events, domestic changes and various happy occasions C.P. also documented national and international (via Reuters and other rota agencies) infamous events. I recall the ghastly Christie murders trial–from his abode in Notting Hill. And the death of Stalin, known as Father Joe, and the subsequent world address on the Cult of Personality–referring to Stalin's past record of genocide and totalitarian rule. The world breathed more easily for a while with Mother Russia under the more possible, paternal real considerations of his replacement, Khrushchev. This was before the Cuban confrontation of J.F. Kennedy and Khrushchev–but the latter was not a Stalin.

Politics was a subject not so much boring as wholly beyond my comprehension as a youth. It would mean much, much more, after I entered (and left) the armed forces. As the standard cliché piqued, ' I'm old enough to die for my country. And to be married. And have children. But *not* to vote in it. ' At eighteen years of age. In previous generations, most adults had few prerogative rights throughout their lives and, could be either willingly or wantonly, cannon-fodder to die for others. A knowledge of social inequalities and common injustices was still much beyond my awareness. Practically everything that happened, happened to me, or with me, or for me, and except for a brief social dressing, I did not question my uneducated lowly status in life. I believed myself to be free within set limitations, and bound in by the numerous laws and social conventions I was growing up within.

Christmas 1953

First Christmas of 1953 at the C.P. firm emphasised how socially gauche I was in teenage ignorance. Central Press enjoyed an annual dinner and dance held over an inn in the City, I think in Mincing Lane or Pudding Lane? It was a formal sit-down occasion, such a gathering as I had never attended before, but unworried in my ignorance and lack of evening attire, I sat with several of the other lads in a similar position. The main meal was served and enjoyed with a liberal amount of wine. The speeches and general festivities passed over my head and I remained closeted with my peers; only Sid and Alf gave us a passing aside punch, and Mr. Pope ensured we were not too neglected on the end of our long table. It was the one time we saw all the staff photographers together, and the senior executives and their respective wives and girl friends.

It didn't matter. We messenger boys were new to such esteemed a gathering. One had to begin somewhere–somehow. As the dinner plates were removed the waitresses came round for the next orders. " And you, sir? What would you like?... Do you want fruit salad ... or ice cream? "... What me?–Sir? And smiling too! God. It seemed banal in retrospect. But I did *not* know what a fruit salad was..I had a vision of fruit–with lettuce and tomatoes. And so I played safe and asked for ice cream. And, to cap the episode, came the ridiculous tiny coffee cups, in etiquette, presented as the last formal item–with liqueurs for the adults. Again the clean pressed waitresses in their equally formal attire of black dress and white starched frilled aprons and white crown caps.

" Coffee, sir? Do you want white or black? ". There is always a first time. And this was more new language to me. I mean–coffee is coffee–what's the difference? " Eh? " ... without knowing I quickly replied – " Oh! Black, please", and, came the delivery, I looked askance at my coffee and, dismayed, looked up at her and enquired : " Where's the milk? ". So naive – that in formal parlance, black is without milk, white is with milk. At sixteen years old, it was part of new language to be learnt in growing up.

After the dinner dances conclusion, several of us lads were treated to an illegal small draft of beer; brown ale. I recollect it was only a small dose. But on top of the wine, and the new excitement, three of us boys were affected. Rather happy and singing with the spirit of Christmas inside us. We had missed our last buses and I could not afford the price of a taxi. And so began a long affected walk home, singing as we inoffensively wended our way. Only months before I had enjoyed seeing for the first time that wonderful happy 1952 film, "*Singin' in the Rain*". And as the others split off for their respective destinations – I took off on my own for the long walk back home.

About Dalston Junction, with puddles visible after a recent rain fall, still heavy in the gutters, I took to imitating Gene Kelly, and swinging around some lamp-posts, and dancing up and down the kerbs, kicking the puddles–I was, sure enough, stopped by a policeman (Yes, really.) And the constable affably interrupted my loud happy rendering of the title song. It was clear that I had no ill intentions, and after being reassured that I could make it safely home, the constable smiled broadly and, after wishing me a *'Happy Christmas'* passed me by, on the pavement, going in the opposite direction.

It was sad but ironic that many years later I would see a film of Anthony Burgess's novel, '*Clockwork Orange*', which used the song *'Singin' in the Rain'* with a very different fictional effect. But my own happening, though sounding fiction, was a true sequel to a memorable evening. Christmas in 1953. And also began a brief series of *family* Christmases I shall always treasure. My maternal Nan, and Granddad Manton (veteran of the trenches) and, numbers of aunts and uncles and cousins, gathered in my mother's and stepfather's small terraced house in 139 Dynevor Road Stoke Newington. Our front room had a pull-back doors-divider that allowed two rooms into one, easily filled with my new found extended family. An acquired stand-up piano was played, and the sing-songs and prancing antics of two of my uncles, Jim and Nab, binded for a while all our London relatives. Together they sang raucous renditions of past music hall ditties, and current pop song hits of the time, of Johnny Ray, Frankie Laine, Jo Stafford, Kay Starr, and other American artistes.

Looking back it seems amusing that the BBC. had banned as too sexually offensive Johnny Ray's hit, *It was a Night*; perhaps compared in substance with a decade later Rolling Stones' *Ain't Got No Satisfaction*. To most adults and parents, these outrageous performers were initially a threat and offensive to Auntie BBC, but with the shock valve muted they became, for a while, stock numbers for party dance festivities. These popular song numbers competed with the firm old time music hall numbers and occasional Cockney rhyming-slang interjections in our family Christmas communications.

Cockney Language

Leaving the protective mantle of parents and school institution for the world at large, in that first full-time job, brought new means of communications. Almost daily for months the newness of it all constantly introduced new words– not just the relevant 'technical' terms needed to be able to function at work; but the day-to-day dialect and slang words of so many cosmopolitan Londoners in my expanding world. And, in visiting other areas, persons encountered would confront me with numerous new words–and expect me, as matter-of-fact, to understand. The new words might be in 'their' work, job or professional jargon, or be found in the lyrics of newly heard pop songs or ballads. It meant I was listening more, and not just letting the words flow over, above or around me, in a dumb acknowledgement. I wanted to reply. And if I wanted to reply, I had to learn.

Classic London dialect was often referred to as Cockney, and it was generally broadcast that the only true Cockneys were individuals who were, literally, townsmen born and living within the sound of Bow Bells. When I first heard of Bow Bells, I assumed they were of the East End church at Bow, E.3. (Traditionally, the saying refers to the Church of St. Mary-le-Bow at Cheapside in the City of London, a Church certainly constructed in early Norman times, and a site believed to pre-date Saxons – a Roman temple might have existed on the site, but I knew of no evidence on this suggestion.) Bow Church was certainly mentioned in the reign of William the Conqueror. The ruling Normans rang the Bow bell every night[25] as a curfew signal for extinguishing rush-lights of Londoners at home, within the City of London perimeter. Since its origin, as a saying, dates back to the sixteenth century and even earlier – anyone born in the town (to be city) of London would have been able to hear that mellow toned bell.

By this easily traceable origin one inferred that any person *born* in the inner and greater London area (*whatever* the colour and language nationality, of their foreign–not alienated–forebears) could rightly claim, as a Londoner, to be a Cockney. Purists would contest this analogy and insist that only persons born in the inner city of London, only close by the Thames, could adopt the Cockney term of self-reference; but this contests the other historical facts. Whatever the true origin of 'cockney' I certainly identified the bulk of my relatives and myself as Londoners. And, with spontaneous speech often dropping our aitches; a vocabulary including a good many rhyming slang words–most of us would accept ourselves as London Cockneys.

At work all my colleagues were Londoners, and frequently punctuated their speech with cut rhyming slang. *"Clean up the rodeo"* was confusing until I learnt it was abbreviated from 'rodeo more', rhyming with floor. *"Nip down the frog and get a cream slice"*; frog and toad rhymed with road; and for alley– was *sally*. And numerous other entertaining words were soon to be taken up, and for a few years would punctuate my own speech; until moving further south into Sussex when the aitches were restored, and in rural Sussex where they retained a residue of a different dialect.

Interesting that the *Reader's Digest* compiled a list in which I recognised many of the Cockney terms I was familiar with. There were quite a few slang words, I recollect, *not* to be found in that excellent book. The absence of some words was quite understandable. How many times as teenager in the 50s did I blush and reply "Not yet", to teasing peers on asking, me: *"Had any grumble and grunt lately?"* Or, *"Any grumble over the weekend?"* (Grunt rhyming with cunt for the female vagina, equalled 'Had any sex?' Other ribalds included–*"Struggle and strife"*–as wife; and *"Threepenny bits"* and *"Tom tit"* for tits–or rather breasts. No offence whatever was intended in the use of slang words. These terms were typical of regular tongue-in-cheek words used on the home front. And there were many others. No connection whatever. ... Doctor Samuel Johnson had compiled his lexicon, a very famous English *Dictionary* at Gough Square only two hundred years before, in the 1750s, as his ghostly neighbour. I arrived at Central Press Photos in 1953.

James Cameron

James Cameron (1911–1985), was a British, Scots born, journalist and foreign correspondent – and very talented.

As a teenage reader I regularly followed Cameron's newspaper articles and war correspondent reports; with Bert Hardy photos et al – great pictures and captions that accompanied gripping (often whimsical) text.

On entering, and leaving, one of the London metropolitan railway stations during the late 1940s and 1950s I, inevitably, brushed against the usual shouting, amiable newspaper vendors, with their engaging London based '*Star, News Standard*' evening papers.

And, of course, the national dailies and feature journals. I followed the often dire daily 'crisis' reports – from Korea, Indo-China, Vietnam and, later, Cameron's own personal accounts of witnessing the awesome '*atomic bomb*' explosions, in the South Pacific in 1946, and the Australian continent... in the 1940s and 1950s. The first US post-Nagasaki bomb was named *Able*, a ground zero test, and the next was *Baker*, three week later underwater test, part of *Operation Crossroads* (the US code for their first series of A Bomb tests) with military success – but, thousands of US personnel and indigenous, military and civilian casualties... yet to be recorded and, from the outset, remaining top secret.

The Bomb

Friday, April 2nd 1954, introduced a most cruel spring. Our *Daily Mirror* on its front page, centrefold and back page, disclosed four 'horrifying pictures' of an H-bomb explosion from fifty miles away. It was recorded least powerful of three H-bombs that America had exploded. Mushroom cloud eight miles high from ground level, fireball three miles in width, its core temperature approaching that of our sun, and initial recorded devastation straight out of one of our lodger's science fantasy magazines.

For the first time *pictures* were released to a stunned world public of two years past (details kept secret), one of two series of American Atomic Bomb Tests, called Operation Ivy, 1952, H-bomb explosions in the Marshall Islands, in the Western Pacific. The coral island of Elugelab (sounded Swiftian) , half-a-mile long and quarter-mile wide, had simply disappeared. The *Daily Mirror* reported that in Elugelab's place was left a crater three-and-a-half-miles across, and one-hundred-and-seventy-five feet deep–big enough to hold a seventeen storey building. The cloud rose to twenty-five miles high, expanded to one-hundred-miles across. It added that whilst the bomb was exploded at ground level, a bomb detonated ... only two thousand feet–*above* a city–would create a *much* greater area of total damage. Some mitigation.

The *Mirror's* back page was most impressive; it showed a huge bubble a blinding ball of fire measuring three-and-a-quarter miles wide, taken from fifty miles away. The graphic caption likened this hideous real apparition to 'a crouching obscene beast' which truly 'threatens the world'. The U.S.A. had been treated to a fireside 'official' television documentary film of that 1952 Marshall Islands H-bomb explosion. Aneurin Bevan on page seven began: *"At least the morality of mass murder is being seriously questioned. The hydrogen bomb is doing what imaginative pity up to now has failed to do . . . ."* The well written article that followed appears to have reinforced an article, *"Dearly Beloved Bomb"*, by Cassandra, of a few days earlier. Both plaintive works of prose deserved to be front page news again, again and again, but all this insistence is easy in retrospect.

The sensational exposures of *The Bomb* sounded like pure science-fiction and became blunted and so unreal to me–and passed me by. As a seventeen year old, the Mirror's letters on 'jiving' and comments on pop star Frankie Laine were much easier to relate to in substance. Older dancers had been trying to get jiving officially banned in dance halls – the *Mirror* had stood up to be counted in this vital matter, and advocated more tolerance of youngsters and their love of jive.

The Monster

Daily Mirror front page, from Friday April 2nd, 1954.

Jive

To dance inferred orthodox ballroom dancing, versus jazz–and to become rock-'n-roll jivers. Patrick Doncaster – On the *Record*–reported the partial banning of Frankie Laine's latest record '*The Kid's Last Fight*'–on Phillips' Blue Label 78 r.p.m. The record storyline was about The Kid winning his last fight–but later dying. The B.B.C. objected to Frankie singing of The Kid "climbing through the golden ropes of that Big Ring way up high"–objecting in the belief that this last verse might offend listeners. The B.B.C. had become renowned as self-elected censors of good taste. I bought the record, and we discussed what we considered the absurdity and narrow-mindedness on the part of the BBC at work in the morning.

The Mirror's inside leader reported the Queen homeward bound from Australia. And a one liner on page three: "Last R.A.F. Spitfire made its LAST operational flight – in Malaya". Rockfist Rogan and Biggles out, not with a bang, barely a whimper – end of an era. In that summer of 1954, Central Press lads and I emerged from the darkrooms into Gough Square above, and noticed an unusual crowd of people, with very large searchlights pointed at Dr. Johnson's house and steps. A film company was making a documentary on Dr. Johnson, and a member of the crew asking for a few volunteers to appear as extras. I volunteered; and for twenty minutes or so as directed, I walked to and fro in front of Johnson's house in Gough Square, and sweated awhile, under those so powerful white arc lights. I was given the incredible sum of a One Pound Note. I never did learn who made the film and whether it was ever shown. Probably, as an extra, like my mother back in 1935. I had ended up on the cuttings floor?

A couple of months before my call-up there was a month-long newspaper strike. One spin off from that strike was a dearth supply of old newspapers for wrapping purposes in the fish and chip shops. On the way home from a social night out, my brother and I were walking home up the Stoke Newington High Street. In one hand I brandished a somehow acquired old top hat, one of the collapsible type. On entering a chip shop, the gentleman behind the counter apologised that there must be an extra charge for the paper, so with humour I stuck the inverted hat across the counter, and grinning, he placed our fatty chips therein we weren't paying for any wrapping paper, and, strolling down the pavement, we ate in style to the wry amusement of passers-by. As we passed the local police station we threw several long chips down into their basement as a cheeky bravado finale... Such casual days were numbered.

Squaddie

Chapter Three - Squaddie

The author, a sapper in 1958, at Upnor Hard, on the river bank of the Medway; sited across the water from Chatham naval barracks, and HQ of the Royal Engineers, in Kent. ('Squaddie n. pl -dies. Brit slang, a private soldier: compare squaddy (c20 from squad.)' (*from Collins Dictionary of the English Language, publ. Collins, Lincoln and Glasgow, 1st Edn. 1979, p.1481*)

Call–up 1955

Employment at Central Press was drawing to a close. Now past my eighteenth birthday, I had already visited the recruiting office at Holborn and formally registered myself as National Service fodder. Waiting for 'the interview' I passed a bloke coming out of his interview who quipped in passing: "Bloody waste of time saying what you want to join. They ignore you and put you in summat else". And so, foolishly, when asked that inevitable question, I replied "Armoured Corps. But it's a waste of time isn't it, saying so?". I was piqued in my anxiety. Asked if I had any close relatives still serving in the armed forces, or recently done so, I said "Yes, an Uncle was in The Royal Engineers". And several months later–sure enough–my call-up papers for the Royal Engineers arrived, for entrance as a sapper, on the 4th August 1955 at a training camp at Malvern, in the West Country.

Just one year later my younger brother would also join the Royal Engineers as a sapper. A few months before call-up I had met a very pretty girl of sixteen years called Hilda, who lived with her family in Boot Street, in Hoxton. Taking a photograph of her into the service it recorded the voluminous skirts of the mid-fifties, of taffeta underskirts and a bolero over-jacket. We later agreed we felt too young to get serious and on a Christmas return to camp the brief romance concluded.

It was an innocent affair and unbeknown to me going into the army would, quite soon, prove the end of my cherry guarded innocence. One of my colleagues, or rather ex-colleagues, had been called up eighteen months before, and on visiting us at work, dressed in his Royal Fusiliers' uniform, mentioned how much he was looking forward to being demobbed and returning to the firm. Sid's wife was expecting her first child, I believe. And he had been giving me back punches in the darkroom with more than usual gusto.

Emmett (like my own an unusual name) a colleague near to my own age – I think a bit younger – sported a magnificent d.a. and owned one of the popular Teddy-boy outfits. Although he talked quite boldly, he was always a good friend to me at work. I retained my Boston haircut, but didn't fancy the Edwardian outfit. The prohibitive cost and parental attitudes were influential, but mostly the media image of razor toting thugs in Edwardian clothes was something I did not wish to associate with. But even as I went into the army I envied the Teddy boys and girls their abilities to jive to the alto-saxophone of Earl Bostic, jazz and popular numbers. National Service provided a constant supply of items for the public media. Shortly before I departed for the west country where I was to join my training establishment at Malvern, several of the national dailies published pictures displaying the ritual display of an army barber removing thick black hair locks off a Teddy-boy's duck's arse (aka d.a) haircut–with several other young men waiting the army barber's guillotine.

In the *Daily Mirror* (still one-penny-halfpenny) on Wednesday August 3rd, 1955, *the day before* I entered National Service, Garth–a fallible superhero cartoon strip character–learnt from an all-knowing Arab mystic that the alchemist Stone of King Solomon had been found, its unspeakable powers in the hands of evil men, and his people in danger of total destruction. The philosopher's Stone of medieval alchemy was still the realm of fantasy. But front page news: *"Space Race. The Russians Plan to Get There First"*. An account read that the Americans and Russians were–sportsmanlike–racing to get the first football-size satellite into upper space. The Russians won, with the unmanned, iconic *Sputnik* Satellite launched in 1957. Professor Sedor, speaking at Copenhagen, stressed that here was a demonstration of the non-military potentialities of the rocket and asked for 'peaceful aims' Sedor stated: *"I think our united efforts will greatly contribute to the cause of peace and to ending the Cold War"*.

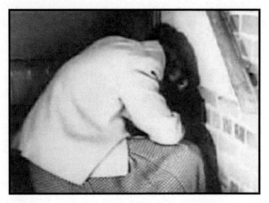

Practical advice on how to survive a sneak nuclear attack? Duck into the nearest doorway, close your eyes very tightly and try to cover any exposed parts of the body. Four minute warning of an incoming bomb – what the eyes can't see, the heart can't grieve... 1951 (Photo from *Duck and Cover* documentary)

Air Raid Precautions, 1938

Published in 1938, by WD & HO Wills, England. (2 of 50 pictures.)

LEFT: A Garden Dug-Out. The picture shows a dug-out, which is gas proof and will give protection from blast and splinters from high explosive bombs. The excavation is in the form of a trench 7ft deep and 6ft wide at the top, and 4ft wide at the bottom. The earth sides are supported by corrugated iron sheets held in place by uprights as shown in the picture. The roof consists of corrugated iron sheets resting on wooden joists laid across the excavation. Inside the entrance is an air lock formed by 2 gas curtains. Outside the dug-out, steps lead down from one side to the entrance.

RIGHT: How to cool down an incendiary bomb (preliminary fire extinguishing with jet from Stirrup Hand Pump). Much damage may be caused in an air-raid by light incendiary bombs. The intense heat and smoke from such a bomb and the fire which it will have started make close approach impossible until the atmosphere has been cooled down and the fire partly extinguished. This is done with a jet of water from a hose not less than 30ft long. The stirrup hand pump (...) is recommended for this purpose. The girl in the picture is kneeling, as smoke is not so thick nearer the ground. Note Redhill container in foreground (...).

(Source, British *Air Raid Precautions* cigarette cards and album, WD and HO Wills, c. 1938)

Duck and Cover USA

To recap. Earliest childhood memories were of the London Blitz, of September 1940. The house my mother, bro and I lived in demolished by a German incendiary bomb.

As an infant, I only had background memories of noise, smells, and considerable rubble, from the ongoing enemy actions. And, as an evacuee in 1942 (at five years of age) I retained no 'living' memories of my mother, bro and me (no father) entering brick built bomb shelters; or trips down into a nearest underground station, or whatever, taking cover from the expected bombs which we certainly experienced.

And after regularly using routine at four, five and six years of age hiding under a bed (time to move) to moving downstairs, as precaution, under a solid Morrison shelter in the front room. And, in 1944 – in the orphanage (fatherless and homeless), following instructions, as a young lad, to lay down prone – wherever I was at the time – and, on hearing aircraft noises, to place my hands over my head... and wait.

I had no fear whatever – unlike our distant cousins, in wartime Europe. The use of holes, trenches, and solid walls as obstacles to bombing was basic in British towns and cities, as advised in *Civil Defense*. I do recall hiding under our wooden desks in our primary school, over at St David's, in 1944, when the warning air raid sirens sang out their warning melody.

Time diminished childlike memories, as I entered adolescence and began work, in the early and mid 1950s. The massive plain of London's broken bomb ruins was still extensive; and I was reminded (a matter of fact – no problem) when each day passing St. Paul's Cathedral, by bus on my way to work off Fleet Street.

Among childhood artefacts, I played like many children of my blitz babies' generation (the boom babies born 'after the formal end of WW2'). We played coloured marbles; autumn conkers, by surviving oak trees. And, then, were the delightful, collectable cigarette card sets. These cigarette cards like our literary comics (*Champion, Hotspur* and *Wizard*) generally introduced us kids to world information – including then, from 1939-1940s, relevant wartime information; data from the Central Office of Information, from booklets (price, one penny – later, one shilling), which included *Air Raid Precautions* (ARP) (50 to a set), with excellent, full captions. As young children, we could all read – and enjoy; playing games and bartering with the multiple sets of cards and marbles, and khaki *Dinky* toys.

You played (like marbles) with your cards against another kid's collection – up against a wall, in turns, you flicked them up towards the wall surface on the ground, and if your card landed on one of your opponent's cards – you won all the cards laid on the ground before you. Thus aimed for 'sets' which had great bargain, commercial value, to a boy (Did girls play with them? I never learnt of this fact.) and, a bonus, you had an extra-mural education.

August 1955 (ten years since Hiroshima and Nagasaki), I was called up in the midst of the Cold War, an extension of WW2 we accepted as norm; called up for National Service. In the USA and France, and Europe, and USSR, et. al. they, too enrolled thousands of new recruits. The usual nations' expendable fodder in times of war.

In British media, reports came of (to me) extremely black politics of anti-communism, and McCarthyism, over the water in America – but, most, of USA *Duck and Cover* Civil Defence information; in event of expected atomic war invasion. It was completely beyond my own, and other British squaddie' colleagues, comprehension, us Brits, limeys, already living, surviving in threadbare postwar Europe. We had been really threatened by invasion, back in 1940.

A '*Duck and Cover*' movie poster, 1951 (from an American Federal Civil Defense Administration Pamphlet, *Bert the Turtle says Duck and Cover*, page 3).

Whilst the USA lost thousands of troops, especially in the Pacific wars with the Japanese; their mainland of North America never experienced an hostile invasion or the massive destruction, as our Europe and other theatres of wartime operations. Due to the awesome end of the second world war, Allies versus Axis; Stalinist Russia attacked, and succeeded in occupying most of the European states and ethnic groups in the west; one dictatorship exchanged for another...

In the far east, the seaboard of the Mongolian and Chinese ports, adjacent to the Pacific Ocean – and of the distant American coastline was substantially threatened, as the USSR Stalin military prepared to invade, and occupy, the islands of Japan. And, perhaps, as in Europe, threats to re-occupy much, if not most, of the islands in the Pacific, previously occupied by the brief (but deadly) Japanese empire.

However, victorious America, and Russia, from the outset, after conclusion of the open military campaigns of the second world war, were at loggerheads; In Orwellian speak, two of the three biggest civilizations (so called), the other, third, identified as the Third World countries, and their indigenous peoples...

Unlike recovering Europe – and occupied Japan – the USA, in and from 1945, lived in day to day fear of a nuclear bomb invasion, and adopted the 1939-1945 air raid precautions facilities, of non-nuclear war – from the late WW2 scenario.

Whatever our masters in government of the time decreed, most of (the squaddie) British indigenous people never took these new threats seriously, 'boots on ground'; military invasion by the severely stretched (though massive) armed forces of Stalinist Russia. But, the nuclear threats, Tweedle Dum and Tweedle Dee – growing stockpiles of previously unbelievable, but growing real, of atomic bombs and missiles were, indeed, real enough.

And, immediately following the surrendering of Japan, America started to dig in, in the belief of a Stalinist lead using the nuclear weapons. They had yet to learn of the to-be ugly gross results of early atomic bombs – toxic fallouts, manifest for up to thirty years suffering, for previous survivors. And several generations experienced – at least, in the USA – the believed real threat of a nuclear war, as did the USSR.

For upwards of twenty years, and more, Americans dug in, and sold materials for self preservation – exactly based on our WW2 European (nee Blitz) war conditions: the Atomic Age had yet to emerge...

Erlestoke Camp

Cartoonist Vicky, on page 3 of the *Daily Mirror*, August 3rd, 1955, recommended
an advance party to Mars to warn them of the forthcoming satellites heralding
from earth–and that *"There ain't gonna be any war–says Earthman"*. Dear
Marjorie Proops, on page 7, declared from Paris that "You won't catch me in
the–TUBE–", a pencil-like mode of fashion that, whilst indicating how slim a
lady was, also wholly denied the female bust and hips–sterile a mode. I preferred
my sixteen year old girlfriend Hoxton Hilda's taffeta skirts and fluffy blouse–
reminding me of her sex, even if it was for looking only. As I joined the long
waiting train at Paddington station, it was clear that large numbers of other
youths were also embarking for the same journey to Erlestoke Camp. There
were dozens of young men with cases, bags and personal belongings, some of
them were being seen off by relatives, but the majority of the new recruits were,
along with myself, unaccompanied. I settled in a carriage and chatted with a
small ginger-haired Cockney youth who, sure enough, was destined for the
same camp at Malvern in Worcestershire as myself.

On our arrival at the railway station, a line of army lorries was waiting for us,
a bored sergeant checking the names. A number of other intakes at the camp
were already at different stages of their training, the initial basic course taking
six weeks before going on to selected army trade training. As members of the
Corps of Royal Engineers all sappers were expected to complete a basic standard
of field engineering, which followed that army training common to all other
armed forces–drill, weapon training (rifle and bren), and some tactical exercises.
We strode into the ghost boots of thousands of soldiers who had preceded us,
either at this lone windy site close to broad western plains and hills, or based
at one of the hundreds of other training camps throughout the British Isles. We
were directed to one of the long barrack-room huts easily lost in anonymity as
they looked equally alike.

    Just inside the hut was a singular room for one of the training NCO's, and
opposite his kennel were the ablutions. Our long dormitory was again a duplicate
of those thousands settled in other camps. Two rows of narrow beds presented
each with a tall locker by its side. A wooden table with several chairs marked
the centre of the room. Red fire buckets hung on black painted brackets, adorning
the wall outside the ablutions. And additional two red painted buckets, neatly
filled with clean (no debris) yellow sand, were placed to the side of the passage,

on a white painted marked-out spot. As to the floor, it was of red asphalt and was highly polished; was it red from the blood of the hundreds, thousands, of our peers who had previously trained out of this human stable? I had a distinct foreboding that I had been somehow in this place already in my lifetime. It all seemed so familiar.

Arbitrarily kitted out and, like a movie script, much of the clothing included sizes far too big–or too small–the *nearest* in size was the correct. As we congregated about our allocated sergeant, corporal and lance-corporal, we laid our stuff on the ground–outside the stores–to check we had all our kit. We joked at the appearance of the long sleeved vest with buttons at the V-neck, and the long-johns underpants that narrowed at the ankle. They were either very baggy at the crutch or were much too –'ouch' – at that point. A full marching pack was issued with belt, twin ammunition pouches, front and rear box-like packs, groundsheet, mess-tins, and linked knife, fork and spoon, white pint mugs, army jack-knife, greatcoat, two pairs of new boots– shirts, socks, denims, two battle-dress khaki, two berets, one cap badge, and bedding and large kitbag. It took some juggling to carry it all back.

Issued with the proper paperwork was formal Identification–I.D. cards for which our photos had to be taken. And the bible piece of our kit, the brown papered cover of the service version of AB 64, the record of data which had to be kept at all times in peace and wartime in our left-side top pocket. And we were escorted to a training hut and introduced to our commanding officer, a colonel, who swore us in on the Queen's oath and (hush!) introduced us to The Queen's Regulations. And to standing orders, guard duty, fire picket, and jankers – or other duties for which work denims would be most essential, as cook-house duties. The introductory talk-down briefed us to what to expect from our training and how fortunate we were to enter the corps of sappers. At my original selection at Holborn in London, I had undergone a brief medical. How do you feel? What illnesses have you had? Step on this, Under here. Chest X-ray. Cough! and Into that room please and give a specimen. The sound of running tap water close by to prompt the organ.

There was a further medical of sorts at the introductory unit which culminated in having our hair cut to army model, and vaccinations on our left arms. At one point an R.A.M.C. member of staff said to me, somewhat quizzically: "Do you know you have one leg over half-an-inch shorter than the other?" I replied that it was the first I knew of it, for this fact had not affected me to my knowledge.

He suggested that my spine had adjusted and compensated. He also added I was rather thin and underweight. It didn't bother me as it obviously seemed to concern him. A passing remark on the evidence of bruising on my arms also gave cause for some brief comment.

After being fully kitted out, our N.C.O's informed us, back in the barrack room, what residue of national service pay we could expect. Cost of army grey blanco cake and other items was deducted at source, and we each could expect well under a pound per week. On completion of trade training – A or B, 1, 2 or 3, all grades qualified for extra money, although much was contributed by what formal qualifications as individuals we brought with us into the National Service ranks. There were about thirty-five of us in our intake between the ages of eighteen and twenty-five years old. A good number of the young men had had their service deferred to allow them to complete university training for a degree, or had been engaged on essential work – farming, forestry, etc.

We were a motley group – as all intakes. At the final conclusion of training a number of those educated men would qualify for the officers' training course – another group for immediate N.C.O's training, to be then used to help train others, etc. – but the residue in which I would remain would be eventually sent off to other camps for further training and despatched to units at home or overseas. And make up numbers. The press often discussed individuals who, through reasons of inner conscience, refused to enter the armed forces with a potential of having to kill or injure other human beings–whatever the reason.

As a teenage cinema devotee I had several times seen the classic antiwar 1930 film on the First World War, *All Quiet on the Western Front* based on the 1929 German novel by Erich Maria Remarque. [1] One of its famous 1930 film-star actors was Lew Ayres. Mr. Ayres adhered in real life to the philosophy of anti-war, and in early 1942 had been escorted into internment to a conchies 'conscientious objectors camp'. A gentle man as well as a fine actor, it was reported : '*He won't kill or help to kill.*' [2]

I never forgot that final scene of the young German soldier reaching out of the trench to a settling butterfly–and finding death through an opposing side's sniper's bullet. Lew Ayres played that role in the film. In contrast and closer to home, I knew of one of my uncles (my mother's older half-brother Len–one of two) who bore the same surname (no relation) as Len Ayres, who near the end of the second World War was a chauffeur to a high ranking army officer, *and* opened one of the gates for the vehicle to enter in a concentration camp in Germany to the allies – and witnessed an awesome scene of death disease destruction and human wantonness. ... Our family reported that his dark hair went white overnight in reaction to the graphic experience, despite being a very experienced veteran soldier. War as hell. Chauffeur Uncle Len Ayres would never talk about what he experienced in entering that infamous concentration camp.

There had been gentle men (and women) serving in the forces known as conscientious objectors in and out of the service – and the law in 1955 demanded that C.O.s (conchies) be dealt with as at least nominal, criminal offenders. [3] Those labeled conscientious objectors in recent wartime may have been incarcerated, but in the main, in peace and war, they were sent to one of the special occupations – coal mining, fisheries, agriculture, forestry, nursing et cetera.. And then there were a surprisingly large amount of men who did not experience any training for National Service, for being deemed unfit. But clearly neither I nor the thirty-four or so others in our intake complied with these criteria.

With the prospect of square bashing beginning the following day, the kit reasonably sorted – and having made the acquaintance of one or two of the lads, lights were ordered to be turned out. But shortly before the darkness, by order, descended, we listened awhile to the tannoy radio extension slung overhead in our dormitory hut, and its pop music very much reminded us of so recently left home life. Glenn Miller's "Don't sit under the apple tree with anyone else but me', led by association into my inner world of recent romantic associations. A few months earlier I had stepped up my teenage record buying from one to two 78 r.p.m. records per week. The price per record had gone up from four-shillings-and-sixpence to five-shillings-and-fourpence, and might have been a little more–whilst in the army they would soon climb to over seven-shillings each copy.

Head back on bare issued pillow less pillow-case, under two thin regulation grey blankets, laundered sheets. (How many before lay under these very items?) Night thoughts drew up the image of a cheap wooden record cabinet which I'd patiently labelled Pop Music, Male Vocal, Female Vocal, Jazz and Instrumental. And already record labels were of past associations–about people and events– already well tied to fixed dates and recent life experiences. In that aggregate of records: Steve Conway and *'Too Young'*; Jimmy Young and *'Unchained Melody'*; Dicky Valentine and *'Mr. Snowman'*, and The Crewcuts and *'Earth Angel'*–all reminded me of that dim-lit dance studio of Barrie's in Mare Street,

Hackney. And of girl friends Pat and Rita, and recently, now an ex-girlfriend Hilda of Hoxton. And there was Kitty Kallen's *Little Things Mean A Lot* and 'I don't think you love me anymore', a very romantic pop number – and I lay and thought of Shepshed Edna, a romance already well folded into my past, all coiled within as snug adolescent innocent stored memories.

Ruby Murray, a lovely Irish singer, was then frequently on the radio, and she too joined my teenage fantasy stable marked for time and specific associations. Kay Starr and Jo Stafford were more associated with my last school days–and contact with friends of our mother's London Transport days. Johnny Ray and Frankie Laine – especially *'Jezebel'* and 'Rain Rain Rain' – were typical of being merely a teenager and identified as slightly anti-adult pop music 'for teenagers only' (though in reality they were not), but such artistes were not for my purely romantic associations.

Head laid back on the pillow, arms folded under my head, the lights out and moonlight filtering through the un-curtained barrack-room window behind me the music was left on for a while, courtesy of the hut N.C.O. And the record memories persisted. On this, my *very* first night in the British Royal Engineers as a national serviceman.

I chuckled as a Jerry Colonna comic number was played: *Let Me Go Lover*, and *Ebb Tide*. Some-time or other I had heard a radio critic declare that it was often a sign of fame if a public figure was imitated or satirised. But that if an individual or group spoofed until then, a popular number, it signalled the end of its present economic run of prosperity. But to me it just added another variation or arrangement of (pop music) a topical musical number. Spike Jones and His City Slickers were hilarious in *Lulu Had a Baby*, and *I Went To Your Wedding*; this 78rpm disc I had bought down Petticoat Lane. The 78s Rhythm and Blues records I placed under the subheading Jazz for I knew very little about them as speciality, only that examples truly stirred up my insides (soul), and an urge to move my feet *far more* than to Victor Sylvester or Joe Loss– although I moved in attempt to time, to both moods.

The light music finally stopped and from somewhere outside the Last Post was sounded by a bugler, truly like the movies, even as I went off to sleep–like John Wayne? A few echoed tears were being shed by one or two neighbours in their beds, but mostly it remained very quiet as too, undoubtedly, all my new associates had their inner worlds of recent and past memories graphically accented on their first night in the army.

We were politely awoken at 5.15 a.m., and after ablutions, breakfast and dressing for our first formal barrack parade, experienced the fact that sergeant training N.C.O's were not just foul-mouthed threatening in fiction, but in real life. But first our appearance had to be very severely castigated, letting us know what to experience in the future. *"Get your hair cut"* and *"Did you shave this morning?"* and *"What do you call THAT?"*– at some aspect of dress. I still only shaved on an occasional basis at eighteen years of age, and thus had very little practical experience of wet shaving. And when I did, as on that morning, well, in scraping off the fair fluff it had almost massacred my face, and inevitably I gained a foul blast from our platoon sergeant.

On Parade

Dressed in B.D.–battle dress–for my first parade (as millions before us) we soon learnt the daunting importance of properly blancoing our belts, polishing our brass fittings, and having correctly ironed creases in our trousers and khaki blouse. Within days I again came under the vocal whip of our drill sergeant, as the cap badge was removed from my black beret and I was castigated for the white Duraglit cleaner evidenced in the mould creases behind the badge. Queen Elizabeth II had only been on the throne two years since her father, King George VI's demise in 1952.

Most veterans still had highly polished George VI cap badges–or very dulled old badges, as I had been given, and not yet properly buffed. The new badges of the Queen were beautiful to obtain, if you could be issued with one of those coveted emblems. Why? Because they were called Staybrights, made from a metal–which required no polishing. One or two of the lads had been lucky enough to have been issued with these badges. Similarly the all purpose jack-knives, experienced in the boy scouts and school army cadets.

It was luck whether you were issued with a Staybright – viz. needing little cleaning – or a black sided and chromium bladed knife needing much cleaning and many crevices for metal polish to languish within. I received the latter type, and with some mortification began to polish the blades. Much easier to clean was the long barrelled round rifle bayonet, although it too was of polished metal, but easier to clean. I was fortunate in that my bayonet never experienced a need to be cleaned of human blood, as millions of my fellows had done in years past, with their bayonet or spear variations. But on entry to the service I could not have forecast this optimistic outcome, and was but raw material for whatever the country called upon as a national service contribution, and whatever fate had in store.

Our NCO's dutifully introduced us to the mandatory right-angled elbow palm-to-above-right-eye hand salute – to our superior elite officers – whoever or whatever they were. We did not salute the human being, but the uniform-and-rank, it was heavily instilled into us. In training, we very soon memorised all the insignia of the H.M. Forces ranks – and R.A.F. and Navy equivalents. And likewise, we memorised all the other ranks and N.C.O's badges of merit and authority – including some trade identification badges. We were but the lowest of the low, it was insisted, the low scum of the services – viz. the lowest and bottom grade; raw recruits. S'funny, I thought, doesn't Brownian scum collect to float idly on the top surface? But kept such thoughts mostly to myself.

Unfortunately. I did *not* always keep my thoughts to myself (keeping my own counsel) and critical observations under my beret, as was frequently forced into us. And my rank immaturity, physical and emotional, at times remained self-evident. Mostly I shared with many of my peers an ignorance more real than crass. It was supposed to be peace time, not wartime, although various troubled spots were still very much in evidence since Korea and even more recently the Mau-Mau in Kenya had been come to terms with. And there was Cyprus. And so, as a recruit, I submitted in part rather than whole a subordination to my superiors.

For the first six weeks we were not allowed out on any weekend passes or home leave. In compromise, after the first week or so, we were allowed out after duties into the local community, if we could obtain a pass past the guardroom and barracks' gateway. These six weeks would complete our basic military training common to all armed forces basic training. We could then have a seventy-two hour pass, and on our return begin our eight to twelve weeks' field engineering training. But first we had to pass-out at the six-weeks' course. There was much to learn during our process as recruits. The rudiments and ultimate purpose of drill and instant discipline. Ability to fire with some modicum of success the Lee Enfield .303 barrel rifles dating back to the first World War conflagration. I learnt to fire sufficiently to gain the label of first class shot, for my eyesight was excellent, but each shot always bruised my bony shoulder hollow which literally hurt as I had no fat to cushion the wooden base in its recoil. Obviously I didn't hold it properly. The Bren gun on tripod was much easier to fire and again I gained first class performance.

We learnt some finer points in battle; to *not* allow the Bren gun barrels to overheat, but piss on them rather than allow this to happen. As I never experienced the weapon in warfare, I often wondered whether a soldier would literally stop his firing in battle, and stand or kneel to pee on his overheated weapon. Such fine detail was never given in movie reports of war, or in any books or press accounts of war that I had then read. Indeed, it was the 'fine' points of reality we were supposed to learn, though in truth only actual experience would dictate the reality of such stress on details in action.

There was a phenomenal amount of kit, each item of which was explained to us–and how to clean, preserve and present it at a formal kit inspection. The uniforms denims and other clothing were reasonably simple to understand and maintain. The cloth packs and other webbing items with their multitude of brass clips and fittings took a little time to comprehend and a good deal of cleaning and blancoing, with that awful messy clay-like substance not called blanco cake for nothing. And equally demanding, the metal cleaning polish – we used Duraglit, a cottonwool-like material soaked in an oily substance, to polish the brassware, quite effective. The web anklets, gaiters which had formally replaced the brown roll cloth puttees seemed strange garb, but soon became familiar items. It was the black boots below the gaiters which in breaking in caused me and other recruits acute discomfort.

The army black leather boots with their leather soles and heels were issued brand new. We were given two pairs–one for daily use, the other pair as best boots for formal drills and special occasions. A pair of plimsolls, called pumps, were also issued for use in physical instruction and casual occasions. All of us, as recruits, were given no time to break them in, and soon the daily drills. We soon experienced fifteen-mile and more route marches, in full kit, which drew blood from our well abraded feet. This was normal intake experience and although various homespun methods to soften the leather were spoken about, there seemed no easy way to christen them. Ankles bled considerably, and toes and insteps showed open sores. Though we grumbled a little about this necessary ritual to 'harden' us up, it was the polishing of the boots which often proved greater time-consuming irritation. The underside of the boots had a regular number of metal studs in a specific pattern; till lately, our N.C.Os insisted that these studs had to be highly polished with the rest of the boots and laces, but now it was easy, you only had to bull the leather surfaces.

The front toe caps were expected to be polished like mirrors–literally. And that it could be achieved was evidenced by the boots of the N.C.O's themselves, and the brown boots of the officers. In training camp some N.C.Os and most officers had batmen doing their cleaning and dirty duties – part of the status quo. These batmen were sappers – privates and lower ranks like myself. And me–initially I experienced some effort in bulling and buffing my boots. Formally not allowed, it was accepted practice that boot toes could be bulled in the following manner – though some detail escapes me after nearly thirty years on. A spoon or knife handle would be heated over a candle flame, and the hot metal methodically pressed in small circles against the toe cap. On new boots the leather toes, alike the rest of the mould, showed a multi-cellular structure, but after bulling the many cells would be fused into one glazed mirror surface. After bulling it was patient spit-boot-polish and a forefinger-in-rag polishing minute circles that insidiously brought the surface to a high mirrored gloss. Once broken in, a decently fitted pair of boots coupled with a decent pair of army grey socks proved invaluable comfort, and I learnt the truth of the maxim that the army marches on its feet and on its stomach – look after both facets and the men will do anything.

I would add the imperative cup of cha, available if possible, any time of day or night; the tea received as nectar vital as the red iron content of the blood itself. Comfortable feet, a full stomach – and for a British serviceman, a cuppa-tea, and... look-out-world! It was over the breaks and the cups of tea that we became acquainted with each other. As a corps, the unit gathered in recruits from over all parts of the United Kingdom. And within a short time, I befriended a broad backed amiable Londoner named Frank who had until recently been a bouncer at the Queensway Ice Rink in West London. Following an in-camp held dance at the N.A.A.F.I. hall with an excellent Royal Engineers band attracting young ladies from the locality. Frank and I had chatted up one or two friendlies and made dates with them in the local town. After a successful night out, courting and making the ladies' acquaintance in the local cinema, Frank and I remained friends through the duration of our stay in training camp.

Our training officer was a lieutenant, but I recall no details of him. The sergeant was small in stature, broad in shoulders, and, loud and threatening in big mouth. Jankers – extra dirty duties during out of normal training work hours – was frequently given out as a medicine, with which to kerb any of us in anyway subordinate or failing to achieve the standard of good dress, hygiene, and especially precise time keeping. But sometimes we had offenders in our own barracks who were summarily dealt with by consensus. One young man refused to daily wash himself or his clothes properly, and out on parade frequently let us all down. Often the N.C.Os would punish us all for the offence of one in our ranks. And so, fed up to the teeth with the so-constant smelly man in our hut, we suddenly grasped him, cast him – clothes and all – into the ablution showers, and using the fire hose, gave him a cleaning it is doubtful he ever forgot. There was no trouble thereafter in this offence. But it was a one-off incident.

Training continued, and we did our token charge with bayonets: pretend screaming and killing, that which in fantasy we loathed most in life, and cast our token hand grenades under the watchful guidance of our training N.C.Os. As sappers, and not rank infantry, we did not further develop those hand-to-hand battle skill of survival, and did them but once – so we knew how and what for – in numerous military exercises. Only the rifle practice at the ranges proved consistent in basic training. And we laboured on the assault course in denims and in full kit. Our greater training followed after that six weeks square-bashing. This basic bashing was soon completed and, on return from a brief weekend leave, we began our field engineer training.

Every sapper must learn the rudiments of trenching, mine warfare, bridging, explosives, and relevant ground and academic engineering principles. Many of the recruits like myself hadn't a clue what this field of study was about. My photo snapshots soon covered basic training and, various scenes of barbed wire constructions, trench digging, bailey bridging and booby trap exposures. We learned about anti-tank mines, anti-personnel mines, and the variant types of pressures and materials involved. And made notes.

I recollect exercises in fields, in locating and, marking with cones, identifying different mines, searching gently by hand and bayonet probe. We took turns in becoming 'ghostman' up front, and very, very gingerly felt the earth in front of us and marking out, found flat anti-tank mines, with those small cone pyramids. I learnt especially to fear anti-personnel mines as they only needed but a breath of touch to detonate. If we encountered a trip-wire then, basically, if it was taut we cut it. If it was slack we traced it slowly to source, I think? Ouch! Booby traps. Nothing about different colours and thick or thin entwined wires – that would be the actual defusing etcetera – which I was spared. (Though of course in the future...) It was an elementary field engineer training that introduced us only too well to the elements of death. (Nothing nuclear at this elementary stage.) And I subsequently looked with fervent *great* respect on the R.E. bomb disposal squads who defused explosives on a daily basis – all those deadly static weapons.

Taking an easier safer interest. I found the elements of Bailey and later light assault floating bridging, aka LAFB bridging, quite fascinating, and quickly memorised all the major components of the bailey bridge.

About half-way through the field engineering training, my cockney mate Frank and I visited the N.A.A.F.I. after a wet day's heavy excursion in digging, sapping, trenches – for liquid refreshment. Rummaging our pockets, we collected the princely sum of two pennies – just enough for one cup of tea – only. In jest, but also practical solution, we collected two straws and shared the cuppa. It was this singular event which decided me to 'sign on' as a regular, actually for only one extra year but with a get out option.

Our training sergeant and lance-corporal (a bumptious, slightly built fellow) were regular soldiers. Our intake officer and full corporal were competent national servicemen. I believe the regular N.C.Os were given a cash bounty for every national serviceman recruit who signed on whilst in training. The government were offering contracts to sign on for twenty-two years with three, six and nine year options. This meant that a on completing three year intervals, if one wanted out, then all one had to do was to notify such in writing to the commanding officer and opt out..

And for even one year extra service there were seemingly considerable spin-offs, not least a doubling of one's weekly rate of pay. Instead of only one pound or so a week, I would receive in excess of three pounds per week. I agreed to sign on, but reference to the follow-up medical I had had shortly after entering camp during a day's excursion of field engineering training, I was quite unexpectedly informed that I had to interrupt my F.E. course and transfer to a camp in Cheshire.

It was explained that due to the fact that I was grossly underweight, and had one leg shorter than the other (?), I would be transferred to Saighton (pronounced Satan) Camp in Chester, for a few weeks' extra basic training. Presumably to, erm, straighten me out! And for a few weeks I joined other men also sent to be toughened up, posted to this temporary unit, for similar reasons. The units of Satan (as we called it) accommodation were large black, single-tiered wooden spider buildings. And out of these facilities we practised a great deal of physical training. And always at standard, walkabout, fast *infantry* pace marching practice.

Saighton

At Saighton Camp I was duly given my first fire piquet. It was a time when the I.R.A. were raiding various army camps in Britain, to steal arms supplies, and there had been a raid quite recently in Chester's vicinity. The purpose of the piquet duty was to wear denims and merely follow a laid down pathway in the camp, and alert against fire and general intruders. On fire piquet we were issued with pick-axe staves and a metal whistle to blow an alarm if help were required. That first duty was funny, though it could have been troublesome. Problem was the whistle I was issued with had no pea inside it, and however much I might blow my lungs out, it wouldn't make a sound. The large camp also had an W.R.A.C. contingent and petting, courting was inevitably found on our doorstep.

The duty sergeant (or warrant officer) detailed the route to be checked, to include the heavy transport area, and especially the various weapon stores. One of the weapon stores was located in the leg of a spider building. There were many nooks and crannies to which our searching torches had to excavate in the dark of the night. And to my horror, on exposing a dark nook, my torch found one of the senior N.C.Os in an indecent state of undress, and an almost naked female engaged in a close tackle with him. I spluttered apologies and back-tracked to the concrete path around the camp perimeter. During one of those fire piquets, I spent several of the four hours off duty (you patrolled out for two hours, and then rested in the guard house for four hours–covering two stage duties), talking about the stars and planets with other rankers.

There was a great deal of horseplay, and I extricated myself from innumerable tussles like a well greased spring – with humour. The occasional elements of bullying fortunately didn't come my way within those ranks. Next to the N.A.A.F.I. and the guard room, the most hallowed spot in any army camp is the concrete barrack square. Whilst one's commanding officer and his adjutant were recognised as the most senior godheads on the post, there was never any doubt as to who always remained the backbone behind their padded throne–this was the singular regimental sergeant major.

From a very early time I had experienced the R.S.M's (or Rassam's) power as I traversed the square chatting with another recruit when, from somewhere up in the mountains of Valhalla it appeared – that is, many hundreds of yards away – a voice bellowed '*You there*'... His direction was very clever – I knew he meant me. We both halted in our tracks and then turned and saw this figure across the other side of the square, inviting us over to his presence. On arrival, he pointed out never, *never*, did one put your 'hands in your pockets' or next time seen committing this heinous crime, you will be 'put on a charge'. (Which brought back childhood orphanage memories – where the same duty of *caring* rule had applied.) But this fairly common acquaintance on the square and the R.S.M. became a secondary image after an amusing experience at Saighton Camp.

Inspections on parade were an everyday experience, but one day we were briefed a visiting dignitary would be inspecting us in our best B.D. on the barrack square the following morning. It was a bright, late autumn day. There I was, placed somewhere in the third rank – we were the only troop on parade at this time. It was a massive square, bordered by the guard room, a gym, the N.A.A.F.I., living quarters and the motor pool. Stiff as a ramrod, head held high, looking forward into nowhere as expected, I was aware of the slow approach of the inspecting crocodile of officers and N.C.Os.

From far across the square a radio tannoy was heard blaring from the vicinity of the N.A.A.F.I., its musical numbers indicating '*Music While You Work*'. I heard the snap crack of attention as each man came to attention, and presented his rifle for inspection. And, just as the leading gentleman drew up on my left, I couldn't possibly miss hearing – and pretending not to hear, as the whole of the gathering – the very loud voice of Gordon Macrae singing "*Everything's coming my way*" .. the popular musical '*Oklahoma*' (Rodgers) recently released as a film, in 1955. (I also knew of a *Glenn Miller* number of that name, back from 1939-44... US Army Recordings.) Blissfully loud came across that square:

> *Oh Wotta Beautiful Morning,*
> *Oh Wotta Beautiful Day*
> *I gotta Wonderful Feeling*
> *Everything's Coming My Way.*

It was a sunny autumn day and, taut with suspense, in that expected, exaggerated pastime. I found it very hard indeed not to burst out laughing, directly in the faces of our superiors oncoming military inspectorate. I know I grinned as close as I dared. The unexpected commentary on that parade for me forever took the deadly sting out of all subsequent parade inspections, as inevitably I would catch myself becoming too serious and recollect that barrack square parody. I wonder if that Saighton Camp N.A.A.F.I. staff knew what they were doing. It was a social equivalent of King Lear (or was it Poor Tom?) defying the elements.

My stay in ancient Chester was soon over, and returned to my original training camp near Moreton-in-Marsh in Malvern, Worcestershire, to conclude my field engineering basic training. My cockney mate Frank had inevitably moved on, along with Ginger and the rest of my original intake. And with but a short time to complete the training, I moved in temporarily with another loner to a small room adjacent to a hut N.C.O. I had missed a deal of the actual Field engineering course, but took the examination just the same, and was awarded the 'passed' minimum of a B3 F.E. Trade.

One of the guttiest chores in the dormitory hut was ˉthe occasional full kit-on-bed turnout, but next to this perhaps was inspection of the highly polished red asphalt floor. A few huts up from us an intake had just passed out, and celebrated by closing all their doors and windows of the brick-walled barrack room hut and, taking a fire hose from across an adjacent hut only yards away, they (hoping to be departed that day) shoved it into their room through a window, and turned the water tap on. It was a flood. But before they departed that group was rounded up, and they were not allowed to go on leave until the hut was cleaned up ... and re-polished. You got away with little.

Oh fickle man! How little we learn from others or from our own mistakes. Delighted with having just passed out, a number of our intake lads insisted on skating down the dormitory in their studded boots. And, sure enough, we too were not allowed to depart until the floor was wholly re-polished and passed inspection. December 1955, and I finished formally being a national serviceman on the 6th December, having joined at Malvern on the 4th August. The field engineer training concluded on the 16th December, and I departed home to London on Christmas leave, now a regular sapper of the Royal Engineers. But although I was no longer a sprog, a recruit, it is certain I remained an often naive, very-young eighteen year old.

In retrospect, passing time diminishes or disguises the harsher aspect: of life, even traumas; and certainly I recall with ease and some pleasure those more humorous anecdotes, but being a raw recruit had its harsher aspects, and private tragedies went on around us amongst the more comrade sharing endeavours. Put on jankers for some minor misdemeanour, I joined several others in using a minute scrubbing brush (not a toothbrush) and cleaning the barrack kitchens in the cook-house from 5 a.m. to 6 a.m. one cold morning.

Not long after this event, a not unusual chore, we returned to our barracks to prepare for our next parade. And with some surprise one of our group who had just completed a tour of guard duty reported excitedly that, whilst inspecting behind the cook-house, he found some poor devil from a very recent intake who had hung himself. It was suspected that the cause was an unhappy domestic pressure, but we never did learn what brought about this dreadful waste of life. And so soon to conclude my basic training, it proved a very sobering event whilst being a recruit.

I counted myself very, very fortunate in not having to face the vicissitudes of war – as all too recently innumerable of my predecessors had. And as cockney mates Frank and Ginger had already disappeared to postings overseas, and other intake peers were scattered about our colonial residue, or transferred for a final bout of specific training, I was cast in the latter group and was posted to the No. 1. Engineer Stores Depot near Stratford-upon-Avon, for training as a storeman technical, and also as a clerk technical R.E. – mundane, but it made useful chaff.

Home on leave showing off my sapper's uniform. Relieved basic square bashing was over. I formally parted the ways with Hilda of Hoxton, and distanced from pre-service days. On leave l met up with a mate from the training camp and we met up west to see the new Walt Disney film *'Davy Crockett'* (1955). And ever the John Wayne fan, I visited Marble Arch and saw Howard Hughes's 1952 production of *'The Conquerors'*. (Unaware of the cancerous nuclear threads, which downwind radioactive fallout, later, linked up in the making of this film.)[4]

I visited my old firm of Central Press Photos, a must, and we christened a pint or two with a few jars. My brother was to be eighteen the following year, and was already anticipating his own excursion into the army. (He too to join the R.Es.) It was a memorable leave. But I soon gathered my kit bag and full kit, and left for Paddington Station and on to the No.1 E.S.D (Engineer Stores Depot) at Stratford-upon-Avon in Warwickshire for further army trade training.

Stratford-upon-Avon

It was a massive engineer stores depot, sited in the Cotswold country at the foot of hills, surrounded by woodland and fields, and minute villages; about five miles away from Stratford-upon-Avon. The Second World War had not been long over, and this huge site was obviously a collecting and sorting point of Royal Engineers' materials used in bridging, ferrying, and shipping generally; road materials, cranes and transport of all varieties; railway rolling stock, and seemingly many square acres of enclosed long hangers and sheds.

The camp itself contained numerous services' contingents posted to running of the huge depot. Royal Army Service Corps, to manage transport; Royal Electrical and Mechanical Engineers; the Royal Army Pay Corps; and a large contingent of the Royal Pioneer Corps who were expected to do much of the heavy routine fetching and carrying in the camp. The essential and much voided, where possible, Red-caps, Royal Military Police, had many vigilant duties on such massive a location. And, last but not least, the sapper troops themselves, a firm mixture of regulars and national servicemen, including men like myself here on training courses, and permanent staff. I recall that the Women's Royal Army Corps had some personnel in the camp perimeter – somewhere – but far removed from our squatting arena. A group of specialist sappers managed a guard dog unit which we were strongly advised to avoid, as it was also a training ground for them.

For our entry into the camp, we were collected by a duty lorry from the station. The notable presence of numerous civilians on site became the first mild element of surprise. When I first approached one of the civvies to ask the way to somewhere or other, it was clear that he knew very little English and spoke with a very thick foreign accent. We new arrivals soon learned that there were numerous Polish refugees and other displaced persons – unfortunate men and women for whom the war had proved total desolation, devastating their homes and families; their country experiencing occupation even after the war was over. These were refugees from numerous countries. But there were no loafers, and everyone worked hard within the camp.

And to our accommodation. It was mid-winter time and very very cold as we were directed to our thin hollow Nissen huts. At Malvern basic training camp we had had luxuriously brick-wall single tiered living quarters, but at Stratford, there were too many people for far too little accommodation, a much truer reading of the real national housing shortage. We were directed to a scruffy collection of corrugated iron Nissen huts with holed battered doors, one to each end – no windows, for they were not very large – chipped white concrete floors and the singular cheery addition, each with the black lead polished pot-boiler metal stove fire, with a coke loaded scuttle alongside. There were two electric overhead lights and about eight single beds and lockers to a hut.

The ablutions were housed nearby in an equally inhospitable prefabricated hut, and from the following morning we learnt how to regularly shave, or scrape, with cold water, often frozen solid in the pipes. In truth, the circumstances were that common to many many troops in the field, such accommodation was, of course, pure luxury, but most of us had not experienced that set of circumstances. After we collected our bedding and straw-filled palliases, we made our beds up and explored our to-be yet-again temporary camp domain.

It was so freezing in the Nissen huts that, despite the pot-boiler fires, and our bedding, we had to supplement our blankets by using our pressed army greatcoats and other clothing to be used as eiderdowns. Several of the lads had moved with me from the Malvern camp, but there were numerous others from other U.K. units. A few days later I even bumped into a boy I knew a little from my orphanage days of only five years before. But in the main we were mostly strangers to each other on arrival.

In our Nissen hut was a Jock from just outside Glasgow, a small stocky lad who mostly kept himself very much to himself; a Geordie from Newcastle-on-Tyne, an outgoing more experienced man; and a tall burly Scouse from Liverpool. To me, from the outset, this scowling bully, made it clear he did not like Londoners and said so. (I hadn't met any Liverpuddlians before, it was an unfortunate first). A couple of Brummies, with heavy Birmingham broom brooms–one a small lad was very difficult to understand–especially when he spoke fast. I proved to be the only Londoner in the hut. Noticeably in those days I sustained a fairly obvious twang and punctuated speech with words I had acquired from local Cockney rhyming slang.

At Malvern training camp, groups were large but southern accents (or a lack of accents) had predominated. But here at Stratford I noticed that Londoners were most often outnumbered by gentlemen from the Shires, Scots, Irish and Welshmen. In basic training, foul language (yes, I was at first *that* naive) seemed to come more from the N.C.Os – deliberately. And only occasional individuals used 'fuck this' or 'fuck that' in all their communication. Thereafter in the army I experienced f--ing as its common, currency in almost *every* other word in expression.

I also heard new totally unfamiliar words in a lexicon of dialects. With each new course of study was being introduced a salvo of technical terms, a glossary in support. And I soon steam-rolled into acknowledging others' ways of life; from villages, towns and cities, tens to hundreds of miles away, came these soldiers or civilians. The intense pace of training, sanctions of hut N.C.Os–

and brief friendship with Frank and other southerners, had until that time eclipsed my newer experiences in listening and talking with others from afar.

The morning after our new arrival, we were directed from the main office to our training course huts. On the way, following signposts as we meandered along the sides of the internal roads, I observed upside down collapsed canvas boats stacked in hundreds. And there were many thousands of heavy bailey-bridge panels, a number in a respectable W.D. army green–but most sorely in need of a coat of paint. Perhaps initially most noticeable were the seemingly hundreds of thousands of upside down pontoon sections, used on rivers and lakes to support the bailey bridges, transoms and panels. The pontoons came in three sections, two ends and a centre piece. Attached were the steel hook-shaped hinges that linked the parts together. How many tales those sections could tell! Many were holed, the thin plywood exposed, and ribs – many left naked. At first I thought a painted-on 'US' meant American until it was realised that it was an abbreviation for useless – and awaiting disposal.

There was a great deal of heavy plant lining the roads; KCB cranes, graders, several steam-rollers, and lorries by the gross. It was all very impressive, if not a little daunting. But remembering why we were present – to learn, to identify and account for all 'parts' in use by the Royal Engineer sappers – and for construction, or tools of destruction. We became acquainted, as it were, with the tools of our humble trade. The new learning programme soon got under way, and we began to learn not only how to identify, log and account for the parts, whatever their size, but of desiccants and how to guard the stores against the elements of flood, fire and rot. And how to transport the stores and a multitude of other relevant factors. Very basic and undoubtedly very simple, but as the cliché insists – someone needed to do it.

Inevitably I became acquainted with lads billeted in other corrugated huts. The N.C.Os were housed some distance away from us, as were the distanced officers–well, we very seldom experienced them at all except in formal gatherings. Hut duties included minding the pot-boiler fire, collecting fuel, and, especially for barrack room inspectorates, blackening, with black lead, the metal parts and fireplace surrounds. The bed spaces were easy enough to keep clean–no polish. And kit inspections and uniform inspections, relatively few and far between, compared to recent training. Naturally, the beds came frequently under the scrutiny of the passing through routine daily inspections. But nothing new or unexpected.

When the day's studies, and homework – afterwork – was completed, and if we were not on fire piquet or guard duty, then we could go out into the community without a pass. Weekend forty-eight hour passes were issued fairly frequently. And so I joined several lads from another hut and journeyed into town. After all, Shakespeare was born in this vicinity, and there were a number of tourist attractions and a large cinema in town. The River Arden wound through this county, lined with numerous willow trees, and punts and motor boats on its gently flowing surface. Army lorries went regularly into town, and there was a singular pick-up point, and one time, close-by the 'bus station in the town–if you wanted a lift back.

It was customary to attend one's allocated Nissen chores *before* going out for the evening or weekend. And I always did my allocated chore. Thus, if it was my turn to black the stove, I would ensure doing this and then go out for the evening. It was Scouse, the foul-mouthed bully, who dominated our hut, and several times I attempted to defend my absent Londoner friends in crossing his path in debate over background. He was married and had been earning a good wage of nearly nine pounds per week, a princely if seemed exaggerated figure to me. When I volunteered that I only earned a maximum of four pounds a week in London, he called me a liar, and took umbrage, refusing to believe the figure. I wasn't Dick Whittington and all those broken bomb ruins and crushed paving-stones in my home town were certainly not made of gold. It appeared Scouse thought the London Streets (he's never been there) were *all* paved with gold, and we, the inhabitants, all lived in a state of opulence, austerity amongst Londoners he couldn't believe. And we rowed *almost* to the point of coming to blows.

The other hut lads remained subdued, not sharing his viewpoint. But it was to come to a head a few weeks later. I had taken to regularly going out into town and the surrounds with a newly acquired couple of mates, one in particular who came from one of the northern cities, Mike. On a routine trip to the cinema in Stratford-upon-Avon we went to see *The Lady and The Tramp*, a recently released full-length Walt Disney cartoon with the singing vibes of Peggy Lee giving human voice to the spaniel dog Lady.

Irma

There were three of us dressed in B.D. uniform sat in the cinema. Sat in front of us were three young girls, leaning back in their seats, laughing and joking, several times looking behind them and smiling at us, we thought invitingly. The lass in front of me had long auburn hair which trailed, overflowing the back of the seat. After communication was accepted between us, I began playfully to stroke and plait her hair, which she clearly enjoyed – to the gathering's amusement. After the performance we all met outside the cinema and, echoing a current pop tune *Cherry Pink and Apple Blossom White* – a Latin instrumental number at that time playing out in the foyer. And we arranged a firm date ahead.

A date and time was made.

Irma lived a few miles north out of Stratford, at Henley-in-Arden, near Birmingham, with her father, an ex-sergeant major, and her two older sisters. Although they spoke with the local Brummie brogue it was not so strong as our Birmingham City lad, and so there were no problems in any potential closer communication. Jokingly we would echo each other's accent–Irma mock my Cockney, and I her Brum–but it remained in good part at all times. She was a couple of years older than me and certainly more experienced in the more intimate side of courting relationships. Irma and her sisters were great fun. And soon the relationship began to get 'serious', and I was invited up to their house.

The first night I visited their Henley-in-arden home coincided with meeting another chap – from another regiment, the Armoured Corps as I recollect – who was courting one of the sisters.

It was still wintertime, thick hoary frost laid on the ground, as we kissed our girlfriends goodnight. We made for the last train south, back to our respective units. We found ourselves alone in the small local station waiting room. The last train had gone. And, fed up with the cold bare wooden forms, and loud wall station clock ominously reminding us of the very late hour, and the long dead fire in the grate, the two of us agreed to find somewhere else to lay our heads until the first trains arrived, a few hours later in the morning. There were a number of train carriages in nearby sidings. The cold so intense we agreed to climb up into one of the empty carriages and grab a few hours comfortable slumber. Suddenly, we felt the earth shake and awoke in aching postures, scraping the white glaze off a window – the train was moving...

Quick as a flash we fled the carriage as it began to pick up speed. Years later I would be more aware that such an innocent escapade could have been construed as a crime of vandalism. At the next date, Irma and I laughed at the previous event, but after a chat with her Dad it was agreed that in future either I would leave a bit earlier and make way back to camp, or stay overnight to share the bed with her father (once was enough, for it was a lumpy bed, he a big fellow, but always kindness itself), or I lay on the thin front room sofa. Most times I made it back to camp, making it at a very late hour. But the becoming regular, and frequent excursions into Stratford–and the reasons why–got up jealous Scouse's nose ... and nasty things began to occur.

Arriving back at camp at one o'clock in the morning, one night, I tiptoed in through a door and groped my way to bed. And, as I touched the end part of the bedstead, it collapsed, and laughter echoed around the hut. I thought it was a joke and laughed with them – the first couple of times. But it grew beyond a joke, and laughter was later stilled. Only a frigid silence ensued as it occurred night after night, and I found a collapsed bed. No-one would volunteer to state why. Several of the lads looked sheepish but it was the defiant sneer of Scouse's face that strongly hinted the root cause. Asking him "Why?" he just cast back "Just a joke."

The final straw came one night when the bed itself was not only broken up but the bedding and kit spread around. Some effects even outside. It was still very cold weather, snowing earlier that week. Reaching for the light switch – determined not to be riled into losing my temper – I found the total dark remained. The light bulbs had been removed. "Okay! Okay!" I screeched. "I get the message ...." and, after dossing on the floor for a couple of hours, I contemptuously cast a look at Scouse and sneered at the willing sheep, gathered my belongings, and at Mike's and his hut's suggestion, I moved in with them, about twenty-five yards away.

Scouse was mortified that I was moving out of his malicious grasp. I felt a bit of a coward in one respect, that I didn't pick the fight he was burning for–he'd have splattered the floor with me, but that didn't seem the point. Yet he refused to the end to admit responsibility for the malicious acts. To me that was even more cowardly. One man in the hut had been with me back at Malvern, and muttered in subdued tones, "I'm-sorry-but-there-was-nothing-I-could¯have¯ done ". Friend? No! But *he* was no bully either.

Life at times has a strange way of redressing balances, and less than five days after my moving hut, retribution was at hand. A personal expiation. Mike and I visited Stratford-upon-Avon for an evening out, and made our way back to the 'bus station, intent on picking up the lorry back to camp. As we passed the low brick wall which marked the borders of the station – only two or so single-decker buses lay idly by – we noted a scuffle going on beside the exit gap of the station. Mike and I were dressed in full B.D. with our Royal Engineers insignia clearly noticeable. Suddenly a girl's scream came from out of the scuffle, and a young woman fled from two soldiers dressed in the motif of the Royal Pioneer Corps. To our surprise she came straight over to us and screamed "Help me. Help me, please".

We looked up and noticed the two other soldiers slagging their way over to us. One of them had a quart bottle of beer in his fist; they were clearly drunk, feeling offensive and aggressive. The bus station had a large number of other Royal Pioneer Corps personnel also waiting for transport. Mike and I were broke and hadn't the 'bus fare back to camp between us. Quickly we looked at each other for instant decision. There was no time for debate, or time to grow scared. Mike had a while back talked of some acquired skill in judo, whereas on my own it was pure folly. Although, had I been approached on my own with such a plea, the answer would have foolishly likely been the same. We nodded our heads in agreement, looked to the girl and started to ask "What's the matter ... ?". Then the two drunk offenders felled into us. The problem was that, almost immediately after this affray began, groups of their comrades decided to join in the fun, likely unaware of the origin of the fracas. And within seconds, Mike and I were at the centre of a threshing, bashing, kicking and at least two bottle-hitting men.

It was difficult to aim at anyone in particular, as they milled too close and too many arms and legs were attempting to injure us. But Mike had managed to grab the arm of one of the bottle-maniacs, and twisted it with great effect. From somewhere I almost fell to the ground as a studded boot hit my chest, removing several shirt buttons in the process. My arms simply flailed, fists clenched with a few pounds of hope to connect. In the background we could see a bus just drawn up, and in it a large contingent of fellow sappers gazing fixedly out at the medley – with screams and curses echoing everywhere. The girl had long disappeared. And no-one had come to our assistance. As the man with the afflicted arm from Mike reeled back for a moment and, I recoiled from a blow on the face, together we fled through a gap in the group and made for the bus as it began to move away. Fares or no fares. It was clear that we two R.E's had been very heavily outnumbered. Someone paid our fares back to camp. My nose bled profusely, and both of us sported numerous bruises and abrasions on battledress, chest and legs.

The following morning at the breakfast queue the escapade had already spread amongst a number of our peers. And it was with a considerable inner sense of satisfaction that I had *not* opted out. It had cleansed the other event. Was it a question of loyalty? A military police patrol was on duty very close to Mike and me under attack. They were clearly 'Royal Pioneers', with their customary M.P. armbands to mark out their roles for the evening. And *they* had not only *not* made any attempt to split the group, but Mike swore they joined in the eager melee. Soon the bus station event seemed forgotten. I experienced no more aggro from Scouse of the other hut group.

The course was nearing its end, the technical storeman R.E. programme completed, and we had moved on into the clerk technical. Amazed, I had been expected to master how to type, in a matter of days (without a typewriter). My own allocated typewriter had several broken keys, so I learnt the principles only on how to type (no practice) off a neighbour. I never did learn to type, except in a one-finger boogie.

Our posting was made interesting by another incident, a few of us deciding to investigate a local legend. One of the nearby villages had experienced a scandal a few years before our arrival. A murder had been discovered on the adjacent hills overlooking the camp perimeter. The victim had been staked out, the local legend went, with a pitchfork through his (her?) heart – the corpse pinned to the centre of an inverted satanic marked circle.

An air of secrecy pervaded with the local (frightened, cross, alienated?) villagers. Any enquirer received short shrift. Mike and I made a couple of attempts to get someone to say something about this infamous witchcraft murder, but no-one knew anything. For our pains as we descended the hill and cut across a farmyard, we were set upon by an outraged sow – guarding her piglets, and just leapt over the opposite wall in time. Talking to a number of the resident regulars on the camp, we were told that there had certainly been a murder; and the London CID had been called in, (hearsay?), but nothing was concluded. At one time one of the Poles in the camp came under suspicion, but there was no justified cause for this accusation. The murder, with or without witchcraft, remained unsolved.

If I was not out with Irma, or Mike and friends, then I hitch-hiked home to London in uniform. At one time Irma came home with me to London, and my mother obtained tickets for one of the London Transport beano bus outings to the seaside, and we enjoyed one hectic weekend. This time was very close to my then leaving the country. And I recall one chorus we sang 'While I'm away oh please remember me,' with immediate relevance, on the transport home.

We regularly took our share of statutory duties, so I performed uneventful guard duties. But one fire piquet had an intriguing interlude. It was early in the morning, about one a.m., as I recall, and gazing up at a clear night sky. I followed the paths of several shooting stars, and occasional lit aircraft. And then, curiouser and curiouser, a number of coloured lights, red and green, were literally *hovering* in the sky only a few miles away. Quite naturally I supposed them to be the landing lights of a lone aircraft, or, even though unlikely, more than one aircraft from out of an aerodrome. But there was no noise, which made it a little more odd. Were they balloons (wind driven party, weather or candle lit, or Jules Verne balloons)? The hovering lights lingered for a long time—until I realised I had to continue my piquet round. And when I again looked up some minutes later they had disappeared. Out of curiosity, I asked a number of other men if they had witnessed the sight, and at least two confirmed their own puzzlement. It was a one-off and I never saw the lights again.

Without doubt, the most important aspect of my stay at Stratford-upon-Avon (never mind my army life) was adding 'the' notch to my growing up. Irma and I had got quite serious. And encouraged by the new grass of spring, we took to walks on the hills behind her village. It was a warm afternoon. I was dressed in full B.D. complete with gaiters and boots, and Irma dressed in a large flowery skirt, loose white blouse and sandals. We were accompanied by her sister, Kate, and, Bill her Armoured Corps boy friend—also in uniform. After some walking, we agreed to go separate for a little while and be on our own, and sat courting on sloping, but soft springy turf. Talk was not enough. And it finally happened. Although we had built up some pretty heady petting sessions, they had never been more than that, but at our found hidden spot situated on that spring hillside, a number of bushes clumped in camouflage about us – we got carried away by our passions. I was unprepared for that beautiful, yet amusing, first event, and finally lost my cherry.

Never will I forget that first (but so-o lovely) clumsy attempt at our (my first) sexual intercourse on that tricky angled grass slope. How did it look with my army blouse off–but army boots and gaiters still on, and the thick B.D. trousers hauled below half-mast, shackling my legs, for the, erm, task in hand? For Irma it was easy with her most co-operative skirt and easily vacated undergarment. We had no condoms and so it was the agonising sweet pain of the last moment withdrawal and ejaculation method of arrest and, following, a period of worry whether or not she became pregnant. I was now, then, *just* past nineteen years of age. Thereafter for those last couple of months we took precautions. The ghastly but essential condoms purchased from the local men's barbers. There was one very close embarrassing moment during a visit home to London. My mother asked for my B.D. trousers to press, and discovered a sheath accidentally left in my back pocket. Ma looked with horror, and said "What is this?" most indignantly, and I made sure such an error of oversight never occurred again.

The course finally came to an end, and one of our senior N.C.O. instructors brought the results of our tests. I added two more B.3 trades to my training list–making no difference to my income, but useful to the service. Most important was the new list of postings. I was listed as posted to some place called Christmas Island, 28 F.E.R (Field Engineer Regiment). So were Mike and a couple of the other men. We were not given any information about the posting. Scouse was not for this journey – I never saw or heard of him again. Thankfully. Our picking up point was at Erlstoke Camp, near Devizes, Wiltshire. And with several other lads we travelled down by two trains, changing at the old port of Bristol where I saw Brunel's famous bridge for the first time and compared it to the finest bailey bridge I could envision.

Two cousins from Dorking were serving in the forces at that time. Paddy Creagh (whose father had died in the war), the eldest, was in Malaya in the Army–in the Queen's. And his brother, Mickey, was in the R.A.F., in Cyprus. One of my uncles, Arthur Manton, also in the Royal Engineers, had left the Malayan affray, based at Kuala Lumpur, several years before, in 1952 or so. Cousin Paddy Creagh, three years older than me, was in the 1st Battalion of the Queen's Royal Regiment and, back on 18th November 1953, proudly marched through Guildford in Surrey. The Queen's entire regiment marched through the city streets with bayonets fixed, bands playing, and colours flying, for the first time in twenty-six years. I knew that their local council had granted permission for such a march nine years before, and that it was the first time for this specific battalion. The Queen's had been raised over 292 years before this event – connected with Guildford since 1756.

This was the first time my cousin's battalion had exercised their privilege. The city's mayor, Alderman Donald Wilkinson, J.P., took their salute as they proudly marched past the guildhall: gleaned in a photograph and back caption information, whilst I was working for Central Press Photos in Fleet Street. After the celebration Paddy and his regiment departed for duties out in Malaya. He went out a hulking confident fellow, and not surprising, underwent numerous hair-raising traumas on frequent excursions into the jungle against insurgents.

On his return and shortly before I joined up in 1955, I met up with my Dorking cousin. Paddy described to me several detailed grim memories of his National Service in Malaya – against invading insurgents; and spoke of friendly tall Fijian allies, one of the colonial troops' contingents. How in one particular grizzly chore, after a successful battle, the natives collected decapitated heads of captured rebels and like American Indians taking scalps, or Japanese troops and Chinese warlords, cutting heads off and presenting them as a tally body-count score.

In the 1950s I was quite naive and unaware that such practices as human decapitation were still all too common in many parts of the world. Paddy and his National Service contingent of squaddies had experienced this as witness of guerilla warfare on numerous occasions. He returned rather thin wan and for a while, as his mother, Dilly, too well remembered, quite nervy–experiencing terrific 'mood changes'. But fortunately, back in blighty, he soon recovered and regained his normal sense of humour and dignity.

Guinea Pigs

1955. Not long after training in the Royal Engineers. And, before I completed another six weeks trade-training I, along with other squaddie sappers, was informally approached by an officer – would I like to join an UXB (Unexploded Bombs, Bomb Disposal Unit)? I politely declined.

And shortly afterwards, wintertime, we were asked would any of us fancy earning a few extra pounds 'volunteering' for a course of several weeks – to help experiments in discovering a cure for common colds? It was at Porton Down. It certainly wasn't presented as being guinea pigs for toxic gases, new drugs, etc.

Fortunately, I didn't fancy going to Porton Down as a guinea pig, though it would be some years before we learnt of this awful (sounded like a hospital of Dr Mengele in a concentration camp) classified piece of information.

But, another (routine it seemed) approach for a few of us – did any of us fancy joining a parachute (wings) battalion? Tempted, but I didn't feel that brave.

However, after completing my trades training in early 1956, and acquiring three field engineer grades, a list was posted up; and I was formally detailed overseas, to a place called Christmas Island, to help build an airfield. I was selected to join a stores troop, in 28FER. This was an official posting, and certainly *not* another offer in 'volunteering' to this place (what for?). Certainly, none of my 'squaddie' peers with me in early 1956, were asked to volunteer.

It would be many years before we learnt that we were a few, of thousands, of Guinea Pigs. Not on Porton Down, but as a troop, taking part in nuclear tests. Of course, none of us had a clue; no details, of this transfer, other than leaving (as usual) being military – we were already sworn (for what?) under the Official Secrets Act...

28 Field Engineer Regiment

As we journeyed down to the 28 Field Engineer Regiment I was very much aware of Paddy's experiences in Malaya – much closer to home – and the immense wealth of horrors endured by numerous menfolk of the family during World Wars One and Two, the Boer War and Second Afghan War before it. At this stage I hadn't a clue what or where this latest posting was at – just followed my orders, what else? This Regiment, the 28th F.E.R., had been raised in Benghazi, North Africa, in April 1951, and recently withdrawn from the divisional engineers of the 1st Infantry Division on active service in Korea; presently we retained their white-triangle sown on our B.Ds. The Corps of Royal Engineers traced its formation back to the Corps of Sappers and Miners of 1772, specifically trained in siege work (as basic training in Field engineering). R.E. Staff Officers acting as technical advisers to commanders in 1797.

The Royal Engineers Corps had no colours, but wore on its collar badge, a bursting grenade with inscribed motto 'Ubique' . The sappers cap badge recorded the reigning monarch's initials as its centre piece, '*Honi soit qui mal y pense*', translated appropriately as 'Evil be to him who evil thinks' and captioned Royal Engineers beneath, laurel leaves on the left and right sides.

The 28 Field Engineer Regiment was comprised of the regimental headquarters, 12 Field Squadron and the 64 Field Park Squadron. The HQ 12 was one of the original Royal Engineer companies dating back to 1784. On their arrival in Korea, 55 Field Squadron and 57 Canadian Field Squadron, who were already in that country serving with 29 British and 25 Canadian Infantry Brigades, were also placed under the command of 23 F.E.R. At this time, the regiment became the Divisional Engineer Regiment of the 1st British Commonwealth Division in June 1951. And remained in Korea throughout the conflict and difficult truce afterwards – a New Zealand section and several Australian officers had been integrated into the regiment.

After Korea, at the end of 1954, the 1st Commonwealth Division was re-organised, and 28 F.E.R. came home to the United Kingdom to Erlstoke Park, near Devizes in Wiltshire: 55 Field Squadron (aka FiveFive) had remained behind in Korea as an independent squadron. The Canadian Squadron returned to Canada and in February 1956, when 71 Field Squadron joined the regiment at Erlstoke. They were still settling as we joined up with 64 Field Park Squadron at the end of March 1956, and I sewed on B.D. sleeves the 1st Division white triangle. After a while out on the island I would, later, transfer from 64 to 71 Field (Transport) Squadron. A substantial amount of the men in 28 F.E.R. appeared to have recently served in East Africa, Kenya, combating Mau Mau jungle activities and protests: a statesman, Kenyatta, emerging from that state of emergency.

On arrival at Erlstoke Camp in Devizes, we were briefed, as to what duties to expect in the coming months. Our task, to support something called '*Operation Grapple*' – the name of the assignment in building an air-base, seaport and several small townships on Christmas island in the middle of the Pacific Ocean. All to provide a Headquarters base for boffins on an R.A.F. experimental 'H' bomb drop *(just the one H bomb as we were then told)* – in the mid-Pacific. Details were supposed to be hush-hush, but the daily press were already leaking out information relating to the nuclear bomb project.

It was imperative, of course, that on arrival, we new sappers explored the local terrain in Wiltshire, while at Devizes. And this meant the local pubs, its 'scrumpy' (raw apple cider) and introduced ourselves, where possible, to the dances at local dance hops in church halls and thus helpfully subscribe to town hall fund-raising activities. Girlfriend Irma's father had been an excellent pub darts player, and I had realised that for some strange reason I too played a reasonable game of darts, and better, whilst under the influence of a pint of scrumpy, although my stomach suffered dreadfully after making a hard won score. And on a return from one pub excursion with the lads, I stupidly nearly lost my life as I walked in front of a bus and held my hand up to stop it, a passing indulgence of local scrumpy of course. I only hitched home once from Devizes to London before our stores troop, 64 Field Park Squadron, was sent off to another camp near Liphook, in Hampshire, to assist in preparing and despatching many stores off to Christmas Island.

The Hampshire camp was a specialist R.E. Railway's Unit at Longmoor, near Liss, Liphook. The unit had its own railway called 'The Bullet', which linked with the British Railways stock, linking up at Liss, Hampshire. A huge amount of the unit's rolling stock marked the industry of its sappers, and had attached R.E.M.E. and other corps' detachments that (like the R.Es themselves) were to be found at each field posting.

Apart from the hundreds of large wooden crates we checked, sealed (ouch, those metal staplers!) and stencilled, we spent a surprising amount of time helping the locals to beat out local heath fires about Lyndhurst. One large heath fire proved rather dodgy, it must have been on a one-time firing range, as numerous live rounds cracked off amongst the burning bracken. It was during one of these firefights that Mike and I met a new set of mates, Yorky, Swede, Edge, and another, and a more friendly Scouce than the bully back at Stratford. There were also several Londoners and southerners. No problems, we slowly came together and gelled as a congenial working troop and looked forward to our embarkation overseas.

One Sunday morning just before embarkation, I finished ironing a few B.Ds. and earned a few shillings from my mates. And after the obligatory church parade, we visited a large marquee tent for dinner, which served as a dining room for one section of the troops. We had completed an enthusiastic debate on the size of rats seen at night-time in the camp area, specifically in this tent. And took up what, we thought, a lightweight discussion on something or other with some other soldiers sat eating on the same table. I addressed a bloke, jokingly, as bastard (no offence intended–just parlance). And to my amazement he almost went berserk, reaching across the table and grabbing me by the throat; "Who are you calling a bastard. I'll have you know my mother was . . . " His mates pulled him off me–and one of his mates said that this bloke was particularly sensitive about this term. My own mates grinned broadly as we walked away, and pulled my leg unmercifully. I was very careful who I called bastard from then on. It was to be twenty years on before I learnt of *King Lear*, and Edmund's deep feelings reciprocating, 'Now God stand up for bastards!'. It never occurred to me at that time I had never, ever, met my father (but then he married mother): I could have been a bastard, too.

Determined to keep local travelling costs low, I had brought my bicycle across from home to camp; and with insufficient funds I arranged to go up and see Irma for one last time prior to our departure. I bicycled up to the village near Birmingham, via Oxford and Newbury and, after a fond weekend, travelled back overnight – well, almost. The return journey was interrupted. Six miles south of Oxford the chain on my bicycle broke, and proved irreparable. It was then past midnight and raining hard, but no occasional passing lorries would stop and give a lift, though I tried. About 4 a.m.

Pushing my bicycle along the night-time darkened pavement, I noticed (it was eerie – no-one about and a little foggy) with considerable surprise, a village, named Harwell, and passing a thick perimeter of wire, a complex of buildings. It was the Atomic Weapons Research Establishment (A.W.R.E.). I walked on through the night and finally arrived at Newbury railway station. At 7 a.m. I telephoned the army camp and spoke with the duty officer. I left the bicycle in the luggage room and caught a train back to camp. Our helpful officer, a captain, later allowed a driver with his Austin Champ (Rolls Royce engines) to take me up to collect the bike, none the worse for wear. And that wet early morning light view of the Harwell atomic site was an ironic association with one of our U.K. masters' nuclear exploratory projects. But *how much so* I could not have (thankfully) possibly imagined.

Embarkation

At nineteen I had never been further than the Isle of Wight, and the oncoming trip overseas to a tropical, isle of paradise was considered a welcome adventure. Having our jabs and collecting our tropical kit packed into a smaller white kit bag, with stencilled details. And in turn our group was packed off into a specially selected troop train for Southampton at the end of June,1956. After marching through Southampton as a regiment, we passed awhile at a marshalling transit camp–and on again to Southampton Docks. My small camera recorded the huge ship, *The Queen Elizabeth*, close-by, and seen towering over our specially chartered old and battered troopship, the *T.T. Charlton Star*. As we waited by our boat, a questioning rumour circulated that the ship was medically unfit for our embarkation. It became clear that the ship was saturated with vermin. However, after a delay of twenty-four hours at the transit camp, we finally boarded the vessel, after being cautioned that all the cabins had just been thoroughly fumigated.

LEFT: Southampton, departure. *HMS Queen Elizabeth*, a picture of luxury was, ironically, sited adjacent to the *Charlton Star*, our hired, cockroach infested troopship; so polluted, our departure delayed 24 hours... **RIGHT:** The Greek *Charlton Star* at Honolulu, Oahu, in the centre of the Pacific Ocean, en-route for Christmas Island. 1956. Source, photos by author.

From the outset of the voyage I maintained a laconic log, a diary of the day-to-day mediocre events. It opened on '*Thursday, 21st June 1956–sailed from Southampton at 2210 hours ...*' It was a warm summer and got hotter and hotter as we moved further south. Two days out and we awoke to find the ship stationary, one propeller shaft was bent, which meant we ran awhile on one shaft. After a day at half speed, normal pace was resumed as we headed for the Portuguese Azores island of San Miguel.

One morning our duty officer ordered several of us from the stores troop on an errand down into the bowels of the ship to the stores section. At one point we opened a steel door, and to our astonishment found the whole room was padded with a thick green rubber that smelt appalling. The door too was thickly padded. Only the small porthole gave light, and this had small iron bars in place behind the thick glass – as did the small peep-hole in the door. We asked our guide to the portals below, who informed us that 'that room' was reserved for persons who went berserk, mad, whilst on board ship. It was a chilling thought whilst down in this darkness below decks.

Exposure to too much sun soon led to a collection of sun-blisters along my shoulders, the resultant scars from the painful bubbles to remain visible for many years. Ironically, orders were given for compulsory sun-bathing – at fixed times–to acclimatise ourselves. Unfortunately I acquired toothache as well as sunburn, but it didn't deter my growing enjoyment on the voyage. On the sixth day, we arrived at San Miguel, and were allowed ashore at 1600 hours. That first overseas view was captivating, a green island patched with white and red roofs, girdled with a low white cloud. I took one hundred and twenty pesos (escudos), about thirty shillings, for my six hour excursion on the island. I remained with a group of six lads. Dressed in short-sleeved B.D. order, we explored the very Portuguese Ponta Delgada. A beautiful three-masted schooner provided a worthy snapshot as we departed ashore. The poorer streets had shoeless urchins begging for change and cigarettes; (they were one-shilling-and-ninepence for forty–but I didn't smoke), crowding several donkey drawn water carts and millions of flies along the mostly un-metalled roads, the better routes with cobbled stones aground.

There was little to no overt entertainment until we found an excellent cafe where a man with a violin played for us as we slowly got drunk on the unfamiliar red wine. Vaguely I remember touring several other cafés and acquiring a small pack of badly photographed naked ladies. As we staggered happily back to ship, I recalled a man smelling strongly of oil trying to pick my pocket whilst pretending to assist me in transit to the ship, but, swinging round to thump him (most unlike me), he scuttled off, fast. And as I approached the gangplank I must have passed out, as the next thing I recollected was someone helping me onto my bunk. So much for my initiation on foreign soil.

Before we went ashore at San Miguel, an issue of army threes (Durex sheaths) was made to most O.R. troops–correct prophylaxis. On our return to ship I met no-one who had been able to boast proper usage of their rubber garment But a use was found for a dozen or so army johnnies. As the *Charlton Star* slowly left the harbour, I was amongst a small group of amused soldiers who blew the condoms up into long balloons and, tying them together, released them into the wind whilst still in the harbour. I had seen this act done once before; whilst as a boy at Reigate Grammar School one of my classmates blew up several Durex balloons and gleefully released them into a wind as we passed the girls' school and girls playing hockey–we boys on the way to our games afternoon. This event took place six years before. One or two men on board ship contributed to a rumour that a brothel had been located in the port, but I did not believe this as fact.

Life aboard ship was punctuated with the marks of progress–fishing smacks visible, first sights of flying fish on day nine, the day we commenced wearing our tropical kit and travelled on a south-west course. As I sat pensively on the head up forward, a flying fish came up and in through the low porthole to my amused consternation, and I scooped it up from my feet and threw it back to sea. There was plenty of P.T., and regular film features, though the compulsory watching of the films on malaria and V.D. were boring. On day twelve, my offending tooth was finally seen to, though the ache continued awhile. Individuals suffered a variety of symptoms – or none, if they were particularly fortunate. Some, like myself, experienced blistered sunburn and toothache. Others, a few, endured sea-sickness, though there were few whom I recollect suffered from this malady – soldiers or not. One or two indicated home-sickness, newly married, or with children at home. Some of us for a while endured – at least the O.Rs. (I could not speak for the officers and senior N.C.Os. who were far removed from our berths) the effect of the awful pervading smells of various ship oils – fusing with the stink from the laskar's galleys.

Worst of all, that stink of the crew laskars' curries! We had several tastes of those curries, and for five years afterwards I loathed the sight of curry. Perhaps my view was jaundiced by a daily sight of streams, seeming thousands of large black cockroaches enjoying their feeds in the vicinity of the galley, which I passed several times each day, close to my berth. Men walked about with a patchwork of whites and reds, Nivea sun cream cooling surviving islets of skin. Eyebrows, lips' crevices, and shoulder blades oozed their tell-tale blobs of white eruptions. The intense heat insisted on rusty brown water showers–sea water through scarred piping, and that to-become-familiar, hard block of 'sea soap'. Keeping heat rashes (and worse) at bay, feet, crutch and underarms deftly experienced preventative white powder. Prophylactic measures became a new norm, regularly encouraged by talks and films – and most, mother experience. We commenced taking small yellow Paludrine tablets to counter exposure to offensive malaria laid mosquitoes, as we drew closer to Panama and the tropic. Some quack had said that we too would become yellow as we regularly took the tabs–though this would be masked by our frying under the tropical sun?

Deck games; prolific letter writing–to parents, my brother, Irma, grandparents, and Great Aunt Lil; card games and occasional games of chess, all were a normal diet of time filling; if one wasn't on fire piquet or guard or lifeboat drill.

Meeting up the foreward deck with one chap, we chatted – about friends we knew from training, and to my surprise he knew of Ginger – whom I had last seen at Malvern. This chap had several friends who accompanied Ginger to Cyprus, and corresponded regularly with one of them. He informed me, unhappily, that Ginger had been killed during his first week on that then unhappy island. Ginger had been shot in the back whilst on duty on the known infamous murder mile. For that shocked moment I was coldly reminded that, whilst for most of us living or serving in peacetime, close others still died in its cause – in war (aka conflict).

On the fifteenth day we entered the Caribbean. It seemed noticeably rougher than the Atlantic we left behind. During the afternoon of the seventeenth day we arrived at Cristobal in the Canal Zone. Loaded with the princely sum of five dollars, I finally went ashore at a late hour, its open to the street bazaars open through much of the night. Leaving Cristobal at 0815 hours, we were through the canal by 1630. It rained very heavily throughout the day as we listened to the billions of echoing crickets out of the jungle on either side of that narrow cutting.

The Galliard Plaque, commemorating the head engineer on the Panama Canal project between 1908 and 1913, David DuBose Galliard. (Source: Photo, by author.)

After Cristobal, we entered the Gatun Locks, passing through (often, it seemed, so tight). We realised that we could have stepped off the ship and, minutes in, entered the soaking heat of the Panama jungle, to the background screaming concert of trillions of insects, mosquitoes and monkeys, constantly chattering but out of sight. We knew we were in the constant climate of yellow fever and other tropical diseases. As we travelled west towards the Pacific ocean, we observed on our left (south-side) a rocky face, with a dug out platform, and a plaque, in memory of the thousands of navvies who died of the yellow fever during those years. From that time, we were issued with anti-malarial Paludrine tablets to ward off the yellow peril – skin might, for a while, appear a little yellow but it wouldn't last, we were informed. And, do I recall the suggestion of possible iodine tablets too – I'm not sure of that detail.

As we cruised, the ship's tannoy tempered our vicissitudes with either a plugged in radio contact; or more often, a disc jockey, operated turntable with a variety of popular music dissipated into the vast sea air. Shortly before departure, I had seen the film 'Picnic' with my girl friend, Irma, the romantic story starring luscious Kim Novak and lean William Holden. Over the tannoy was overheard the beautiful theme music from that film, and its equally romantic other-side, '*Moonglow*'. Also heard, a recently known American singer, Elvis Presley's '*Keep off my Blue Suede Shoes*' – played loudly, defying the sea elements, and other music already reminding us of home.

Travelling northwards along the coast of Mexico and North America, we went sixty miles off course to avoid a hurricane, but, undeterred, a genital inspection (cough!) was performed on an upper exposed deck as it rained heavily. It seemed very funny, as the T.T. *Charlton Star* dipped and rolled into the stormy seas, with lightning spotlighting the privileged under inspection. O.R. troops lined the sloping deck passage, in a slim crocodile, dressed only in shorts and plimsolls and, keeping balance if possible. One by one the shorts were dropped ahead. As it rained and rained and rained – and we spluttered, coughed, and chuckled.

As our ship crawled across the Pacific's turbulent surface, the weather became colder as we approached the islands of Hawaii. I was not pleased to learn that I was on guard duty when we docked at Honolulu, and grumbled as belt and gaiters were scrubbed. Fifteen days out of Cristobal we docked at Honolulu. The local newspaper, the *Honolulu Star-Bulletin* dated Monday, July 23rd, 1956, published a dockside picture of our vessel with six short caption paragraphs:

> '*At Pier 8 today, British Trooper for Christmas. British Troopship Stops En Route to Christmas Isle. The British troop transport Charlton Star was at the foot of Bishop Street today with four hundred and sixty five troops for Britain's growing H-bomb test base at Christmas Island.* '

There was no secret, at home or abroad, surrounding our task in Operation Grapple. The newspaper reported our troops being assisted by local U.S.A. army lorry, shuttling us into downtown Honolulu and into Waikiki. Chardris, the ship's owners, had trouble obtaining a round-up of fourteen tons of coal and expensive blacksmith's coal was eventually found at a cost of fifty-eight dollars a ton.

My guard duty finished at 12.15 and I went ashore with two other lads, for six hours of this millionaire's paradise. I had a lot of money to spend–all of four dollars. After a lorry lift to Waikiki beach, we undressed for the fabulous beach–and I discovered why so many people surf-boarded, rather than swam in the not private U.S.A. troops sector of beach. Diving into the lower surf, I hit my head, then grazed my feet on one inhospitable rock after another. And so we stayed awhile on the Waikiki sands, taking our tourist snapshots with the Diamond Head volcano husk as our backcloth.

I had never personally met a native American citizen, let alone a Hawaiian– despite my dedication to Hollywood films and John Wayne in particular. And at that time in 1956 racist issues (over any colour claiming natal superiority over any other ethnic group–which politics privately appalled me.) black and white and yellow ethnic skin colours, were issues, as such, viewed by me as naive and sad arrogant fantasy. As the recent war had well demonstrated. So I believed.

Whilst we enjoyed a coke in a Waikiki beach-side bar, I spoke briefly with a young Hawaiian boy who quizzically looked at our group of British squaddies, and asked me if I spoke American? I grinned a reply and said–"Well, yes–but actually the citizens of U.S.A. speak English '. To which the youngster answered with considerable indignation–"No, I do *not* speak English–but American"'.

In 1898, the Sandwich Islands of Hawaii became US territory. Shortly, in 1959, unknown then by my young Hawaiian friend and me, the people of Hawaii became citizens of the US 50th State – an extra star on its national flag... stars and stripes... Original 18th Century thirteen Stars. Throughout the *Cold War*, the Hawaiian Islands remained a base for the US Pacific proving grounds' nuclear test' operations.

Oahu, Hawaii

4000 feet high Kilauea, volcano eruption. Picture shows bubbling, flowing lava, as seen in this night picture. The volcano is in Hawaii National Park, on the Island of Hawaii. Kilauea, Island of Hawaii (Owh y hee). Maw of an active volcano. On one of 'The Sandwich Islands'.
From its mid Pacific vantage, Hawaii witnessed USA Nuclear Tests. The small *Johnson Island*, to the south west, was used to fire two megaton range nuclear rockets, called *Teak* on 01/08/58 and *Orange* on 12/08/58. High bursts seen, photographed, from 780 miles away. From Hawaii, for seconds, showed the fireball, and red luminous spherical burst, waves of *Teak* and *Fishbowl* tests. (Source, Hawaii Colour Postcard... Honolulu, Oahu, early 1950s. Purchased in downtown Woolworths, Honolulu, 1957.)

Fireball and red luminous spherical wave formed after the TEAK high-altitude shot. The photograph was taken from Hawaii, 780 miles from the explosion. (Source, 1962 USAEC report *Effects of Nuclear Weapons*)

One of the later American Dominic nuclear test series, *Starfish Prime*, exploded on July 9th, 1962, 250 miles above the earth, over nearby Johnson Island, a small coral atoll, with awesome results; its flash seen on the Hawaiian Oahu – briefly cutting off electricity. But this event was later in the cold war.

LEFT: Afternoon lunch, at downtown Honolulu Woolworths, March 1957. (Source, Author.)
RIGHT: Waikiki beach – 'extinct' volcano 'DiamondHead' in background. Picture taken in March 1957. (Source, Author.)

LEFT: *Honolulu Star Bulletin*, Sunday December 7th, 1941. (Source: Google, Public Domain.)
RIGHT: The author in Hawaii, adjacent to dock, close to the Aloha clock tower, with the *Charlton Star* in background, Monday July 23rd, 1956. (Source, Author.)

Captain Cook RN

British explorer, Captain Cook of the Royal Navy discovered the islands of Hawaii in 1778. One year later, he was killed by indigenous natives, in February 1779, on the shore of Kealakua Bay, on the east coast of the island of Hawaii.

Hawaii is situated about midway between America and Japan, in the Pacific Ocean; some 2,387 miles (3,841.5 km) from the nearest part of the west coast of America.

Hawaii was never a British Colony, and retained its sovereignty (with its own royal family). It became a British protectorate from 1794 to 1843, exchanging good relations and expanding two-way trade benefits. In 1816, a National flag was agreed with the reigning monarch – which included a prominent Union Jack. The United States of America took over much of the administration in the 19th and early 20th century, with its English language intact.

Pearl Harbour bay, off the island of Oahu, north of the island of Hawaii, began its first deep harbour in 1909 when, too, the Schofield Barracks also commenced construction. I would spend several nights in Schofield Barracks, whilst on corporate leave in early 1957.

Oahu's Hickam Airfield, is one of several airfields; Hickam, from the outset, became a main stopover base between Christmas Island and Hawaii.

Cook had visited Christmas Island just before his fate, due north, ended his voyages. Not until 1959 (well after my last visit) would the Hawaiian Islands become the 50th US State, marked on their American flag of stars and stripes – exit the British Union Jack.

On our visit in 1956 I first saw, from the above hills, the still seen wrecks of the destroyed battleships, in Pearl Harbour below; thanks to the goodwill of one of the islands residents. But, as a teenage squaddie, I more recalled a memory of a pineapple factory with a public drinking fountain outside – which flowed surplus, thick pineapple juice. Delicious. On Christmas Island, I would only find coconuts – fruit of the palm.

A middle-aged local American lady (Eugenie, pleasant most proper) at some point picked us up and gave us a brief tour on part of the Island of Oahu in her automobile, a Plymouth. We travelled along the coast to Kaimuki, up to Diamond Head and back to Honolulu. Whereas on the Azores we English troops were relatively well off, on Hawaii we were certainly seen as poor Tommies. Five days travelling south after leaving Honolulu, the T.T. *Charlton Star* – 1,335 miles (2,148.5 km) from Oahu and, after an overall thirty-eight day voyage, arrived just above the equator line, at a white ribbon of coral sand and palm trees, surrounded by coral reefs, and the deep of the Pacific Ocean. It was Christmas Island. Saturday, July 29th,1956.

Christmas Island

We first sighted Christmas island about 0800, a thin line on the bright cloudless horizon, on which a patch of coconut palm trees indicated its maximum height. The average height of land surface was only ten feet above sea level, rising to a maximum of forty feet, with barren sand dunes on the other side of the island. Christmas Island had been discovered by Europeans on Christmas Eve, 1777, by Captain James Cook, R.N. with his ships *Resolution* and *Discovery*. The ships' crews had replenished some of their ships supplies and themselves planted some coconut palms and yams on the island. [5]

(Years later on, I would read of Scot's journalist James Cameron's witness accounts of Operation Crossroads, two USA atomic tests in August 1946, as reprinted in his book, *Point of Departure*, 1967 – c.3 p.60-61 – where he had described Pacific, Bikini, as a *'typical coral atoll, several tiny islands surrounding a lagoon twenty miles long by ten miles wide... the highest point of Bikini'* (in 1946) *'– ten feet above sea level.'* Those events he had witnessed only 10 years before out arrival on Christmas Island: of course, such geographic details were top secret, and remained so for many years to come... But, our island's similarity is quite striking.)

One of a number of coral islands, it was one of the designated Line Islands (Christmas Island, later called *Kiribati*) in the middle of the Pacific Ocean; found only two degrees above the equator, or 1 degree 57 minutes North latitude, and 157 degrees 27 minutes West longitude. A map shows it to resemble a large lobster claw, the jaws of which, opening to the north-west, contained a spacious and almost semi-circular lagoon. Fresh water lagoons (not so – they were full of poisonous red algae and other toxins, we were warned) were spaced at intervals inland, and took up a considerable amount of the two-hundred-and-thirty-four recorded square miles marked it the largest coral atoll in the Pacific.

So-called still local 'fresh water lagoons', drinking water collected from non-tainted rainfall; holes in sand, always filled, collected salted water from the adjacent seas: (springs did not exist on this desert island) indeed, turned out to be a deception, short of salt they may have been, but – drinkable? – not at all. Neither could one bathe in these waters unless prepared to disturb the rich variety of toxic multi-coloured algae, or worse, with still smaller lakes lurking minute monsters under its foetid surface. There was also evidence of recently dried up inland lakes, also called lagoons. Around the central island a deep fringing live coral reef of several hundred yards in width marked the outer boundaries of the relative mainland. Beyond the reef was very deep Pacific Ocean depths, which, whilst pacific by name, were decidedly inhospitable to man, filled as they were with flesh-eating sharks and poisonous fish of many varieties, and a very strong circle of turbulent tides and undercurrents.

The island's vegetation was sparse. The coconut plantation to the west of the island was farmed by Gilbert and Ellice Islanders, natives contracted to yield a supply of copra , and collected by visiting trading vessels. There was also a sparse covering of tough toxic prickly grass and shrubbery, on which no cattle or sheep could be maintained. The low ranges of shrubs partially concealed a wide variety of bird life–frigate and bosun birds with their broad wingspans and long shapely heads.

The frigate bird had been chosen as insignia for the combined armed forces and boffin 'H' bomb island operation–the bird in flight with wings spread, carrying in its two claws a four-pronged grapple–hence Operation Grapple. Other bird life included gannets, petrels, terns, red-tailed tropic birds, golden plovers, bristle-thighed curlews, wandering tattlers and the curious booby birds. Booby birds were so named because, though attractive in appearance with their lean white bodies and swanlike necks, wings fringed in black, they were very noisy frequently pushing their necks up into the sky, but they couldn't (or wouldn't?) fly one yard, and reminded me of a live dodo.

Before disembarkation, we had been given a general description of the island and what to expect, what we could do and could not do. Mostly what we were not allowed to do on the island: keep away from the one native islanders' village located at the north end of the island known as London Port Camp; where we disembarked by LCMs. And especially to keep away from any official secret installations which were marked Out of Bounds. We received warnings of the dangerous coral reefs, and other tropical phenomena, and of the deep, deep waters of the Pacific Ocean which surrounded the island. How dangerous the reefs and tides and sharks were I would find out during my thirteen or so months or so stay on the desert, sorry, coral island.

Our *Charlton Star* party had composed the main body, the second group to arrive on the island. A small advance party, the 55 Field Squadron, had been included in the first body of troops, transferred from Singapore, and had arrived a month before us, on the 24th June 1956, on the troopship H.T. *Devonshire*. Vehicles and heavy plant arrived with 55 Field Squadron on the S.S. *Regional Kerr*; accompanied by other advance party groups cut of the task force. Five-Five – the veteran group from Korea, forthwith colloquially referred to by the rest of our regiment – had been very busy indeed. Since Five-Five's inception (they were the first advance party – we were the second) they had already put up a base tented camp at our point of arrival – dubbed Port London, and had just completed sufficient tentage for our followup group at the main camp. Cape Manning was located some ten miles distance from the Port Camp.

Facilities were understandably primitive on our arrival. The cooking facilities under an erected shelter tent–washing of selves end crockery temporarily down at the beach, in the sea. We scooped holes in the white sand for our bedding. First night in the tent I spent a lot of time trying to track down a singular cricket castanet whose loud clacking feet echoed so loudly that we were kept awake, the offending cricket located around my tropical white kitbag, behind the top of my bed area. Initial camp activity much resembled boy scout or army cadet arrival at a fields camp. The underlying sinister import of our tented camp would be some time in being realised. Meanwhile domestic settlement continued.

Wooden duckboards were laid down and we constructed wooden supports for our thin canvas camp beds. Technicolor film desert islands, presented fantasies of soft sands, beautiful willing girls, and all nurture under the sun as tropical paradise. Christmas Island sands – coral sands – white fine and deceptive a surface. Throughout much of the island, as you stepped forward onto the firm sand, your foot caved into one cavity after another. The island was honeycombed with crab's dwellings which lived just under the surface. Jumping crabs, hermit crabs (like snails they carried their shell houses about them), and the occasional rat were to be found in large numbers. The large two-pronged crabs were evidenced in their thousands throughout the island. Their orange centres were frequently crushed under the wheels of ten ton lorries and other island transport, the internal gooey substance a common sight – evidence of their demise.

The Land Crab Race

There were no beautiful willing girls to court on the island, in the Hollywood film company sense. The native village and its inhabitants living by Port Camp were formally out-of-bounds. The open air camp cinemas, one at Port Camp, the other at the Main Camp, continued to remind us of our ladies at home–and our dreams. But there was recreation. I recall one early recreational game, someone's inspired innovation, we called *The Land Crab Race*. A Main Camp cook-house concrete foundation had recently dried, and was marked off for a later overhead marquee tent to be erected, but first another use was to be made of this site.

With the commanding officer's sanction (it must have been?) a group of our army personnel challenged the airfield R.A.F. to a land-crab race – these specimens to be found in their millions about the island. The concrete platform was temporarily marked out with string race courses. A race card and betting station were organised, and soon the event got under way. 'To have crabs' was normally a euphemism for having a rather obnoxious dose of VD – clap. But most of us attending the race bet on a crab or two. The crab runner – or sideways mover – was gingerly tied by string to the wrist of its assumed owner – backer. I cannot remember who won the race, but it was a good-natured event, accompanied by much shouting and liberal use of drink to reduce the effects of the tropical sun.

And after two months the third and final main body of Grapple troops arrived on the H.T. *Cheshire* in early September 1956. One cook-house building had been completed by their arrival. But two cook-houses had to be completed, the largest at the Main Camp, a smaller facility at the Port Camp. Airfield workers to be serviced at the Main Camp.

The Cassidy Airfield was only five miles away from our Main Camp and had previously been the island's only concrete airstrip. This one old strip had also been used by an American armed force of ten thousand men occupying the island in 1942, in situ, against the Japanese occupying other islands in the Pacific. American troops remained on the island until the U.S. Government vacated it in 1948. And there was plenty of evidence of the Yanks' occupation on the island upon our arrival – they had left only eight years ago. Yanks during the war had constructed airstrips for bombers and fighter aircraft, and installed various concrete and wooden sentinel buildings throughout the island–most had long since been destroyed or decayed in the tropical heat and especially salt laden air, which escalated canvas – rot and metal-corrosion.

Evidence of the Yanks' wartime occupation was broadly advertised about the island. Outside our main camp, off its adjacent beach, a substantial line of wrecked American vehicles led out to sea, along the reef. We appropriately dubbed these fast oxidising remains the Wreck and used their rusted, crusty chassis, remains to dive from into the oncoming surf waves–though it paid to retain one's pumps, as the rugged decaying metal would otherwise soon tear open exposed limbs. Amongst the palm trees wooden structures survived, albeit dangerously, the nailed on white sun-bleached wood becoming very brittle after fifteen years or so construction. Nailed to the tallest coconut palms, these steps and narrow platforms were undoubtedly used as sighting posts against invading enemy aircraft. I climbed several of these relics before accepting their danger wasn't worth the risk. A long disused wooden shed with 'DANGEROUS KEEP OUT EXPLOSIVES' painted in red, was recorded by my snapshot camera.

Our regiment the 28 F.E.R. when completed, had comprised four Task Force squadrons (12, 55, 64 and 71), 'with a total strength of forty officers and nine-hundred-and-thirty-one men', I was the odd one. This made up as follows: 12 Field Squadron and 55 Field. Squadron, both 'streamlined' units of only one-hundred-and-forty-nine all ranks. 71 Field Squadron was a specialist Squadron comprising Transport and Plant Troop with over one-hundred-and-ninety-five pieces of engineer plant. And an electrical and mechanical R.E.M.E. troop unit to build and maintain the island's electricity supply, piped water supply and refrigeration; and a tank farm of twelve large tanks for storing bulk petrol and other fuels. Our 64 Field Park Squadron was made up of a workshop's troop with its stores containing many items for engineer construction work like the cook-house buildings, office accommodation et cetera. For a while I worked in the tented office of the stores troop controlling stores which issued much of the Grapple's island 1956 buildings and engineer stores.[6]

Other task force army personnel included: 51 Port Detachment, Royal Engineers, a detachment brought out from Marchwood , specially formed in early 1956 to comprise two officers and forty-five men–all ranks specially selected for having at least three trades, allowing major flexibility in their manpower. The R.E. 504 Postal Unit was split into two sections – one unit remained at Hickham Air Force Base at Honolulu to work with an R.A.F. detachment organising a shuttle mail service, passing our mail via the U.S.A. post office to Christmas Island and return. Christmas Island was given the postal identification of B.F.P.O. 170.

There was also an No. 2 Special Air Formation Signal Troop, of the Royal Signals, with two officers and forty-eight men. This specialist group was formed on the 1st April 1956, by the 1st Infantry Division Signal Regiment from a nucleus of twelve volunteers from 2nd Tactical Air Force Air Formation Signals; the remaining thirty-seven members of the troop (many of whom were also volunteers) joined from 1st Infantry Division Signal Regiment and other Royal Signals' units in England. To my knowledge, I certainly did not 'volunteer' and I recall no other sappers that I knew who had 'volunteered' as later records appeared to inform the public – we were all volunteers. We were just ordered and transferred to Operation Grapple with no real idea what it was about – except the obvious description, being a posting to assist boffins in preparation for military nuclear tests. And we had had no problem with this posting. After all, we were in the Army.

Apart from maintaining all communications between the Port, Main Camp, airfield and administration and boffin sites, this Signals Group had laid an incredible over three-hundred-and-sixty miles of cable including ninety-five high quality circuits, installed four telephone exchanges, and fixed over three-hundred-and-fifty G.P.O. telephones in the first six months on the island in 1956.[7]

To gain an idea of the immensity of the island construction side of *Operation Grapple,* it's worth projecting the utopian suggestions of the B.B.Cs affable Desert Island Discs – and being alone. And being set down on an almost (there were of course coconut palm trees and a few yams, but no fresh water source) barren hostile, desert island environment, and expected to provide all living facilities, albeit suddenly, for upwards of over 2000 men. One must presume that for the Yanks to provide for *five times* that number, their relative close proximity to Hawaii and the States was of great advantage, whereas the British (true, it was in peacetime), had to maintain its task force from a distance of 9000 miles, and govern a highly sensitive nuclear project.

For the first few months I remained with Stores Troop of 64 Field Park Squadron, under the direction of the excellent Captain S. (a national serviceman I recall) and two senior N.C.Os. who were regulars. These officers were always most supportive throughout their stay with us. Several junior N.C.O. appointments with 64 (Yorky one of my tent mates was one of them) took place on the island. Our troop controlled all 28 F.E.R. army stores sited on the island, and on its books were collated objects from thousands of minute washers to large numbers of heavy plant–graders, cranes, bulldozers, earth augers, etcetera. Inevitably a mammoth amount of prefabricated building materials for the cook-houses and other essential administration buildings throughout the island was deposited close by our site. And, to complete all buildings, our unit held the electrical, plumbing and other materials in great quantities.

Stores Troop Clerk

My own minute designated role was to make up and maintain ledgers. I had never experienced 'ledgers' or accounting of any sort before and honestly found it quite boring. The improvised ledgers I made up from W.D.S.O exercise books included all building huts materials, and necessary fittings, electrical, plumbing, et cetera. I worked in the same open office tent as our Captain in-charge, a singular stores troop officer and a very pleasant national serviceman, and two other squaddies.

Also working with our stores troop we had a small group of daily attached Gilbertese natives, men brought up from the Port Camp village every morning by lorry. Our natives' help worked mostly only in the mornings and retired for 'siesta' in the too-hot afternoons. They were large husky, fun loving, friendly, dark brown fellows, wearing only brief sarongs around their loins, with black curly hair thickly greased in coconut oil, also oil daily greased into their supple skin. I wondered how many, if not all of them, had known the Japanese occupation and subsequent American liberation of their home islands back in the Gilbert and Ellice Islands, not so long ago.

Gilbert and Ellice Islanders

Our Gilbertese natives were very likeable blokes, full of humour and often prone to playing jokes on each other – and upon us. They enjoyed playing cricket–and played a mean game of football in their bare feet–for they never wore shoes, their under-soles skin grown thick and calloused for protection.[8] At no time would any of our daily allocated natives work, unless one of us too was actively working alongside them: to give directions alone seemed to be not on. But come a legitimate break and daily one of them would disappear into the adjacent plantation and return with a number of very freshly picked green coconuts which would be shared with us.

The unripe coconut's milk was a unique taste – fresh off the tree. Topping the unripe nut, as one cuts the top off a chicken egg, the fresh cool milk inside was most refreshing. But the white soft interior of the green coconut proved so tempting that it was responsible for many a nasty stomach-ache. The natives also told us of an intoxicating strong liquor that could be made from the saplings off the top of the tree where coconut fruit was not yet matured. And, as they sapped off a liquid from the growing shoots, the amber product was used to make an intoxicating beverage. Sadly I never experienced that pleasure though, true, I did use the white coconut oil dressing which was available on a commercial basis. And, together, the Gilbertese and our team worked moderately hard, under our common tropical sun.

I befriended several of the natives for the duration of my stay on the island. And later, regularly going down to the Port Camp to the Copra Jetty, fishing with crab bait, I was seldom without an acquired Gilbertese native acquaintance to aid me with his expertise. Favourite photograph was of one of these friends sitting at the end of the jetty, pipe in mouth, whilst down on the beach his village community were turned out to launch their latest newly-built outrigger canoe (not one iron-nail present). This photo was one of five later published by the *Illustrated London News* magazine only days before the first H bomb explosion – but a few miles away.[9] Before the first explosion I'd sent a batch of otherwise mediocre domestic Christmas Island snapshots off to my old firm of Central Press Photos in Fleet Street. The island's censor had forbidden anything but 'domestic' photos for publication, which under the circumstances was understandable.

Before departing the island the following year, I purchased two model outrigger canoes, from the all purpose village shop (also the post office) down at Port Camp and, had two of my then Gilbertese friends' names painted onto the wood of the models. Their names were *Taaker* and *Itaia* . Taaker introduced me to local tuber plant roots they then cooked, equivalent to our potatoes; and tit-bits of information related to their family lives at home. I took a few snaps of their family cooking a meal by wrapping fish in palm leaves and, burying the bundle in a small hole in the sand, lighting a fire constructed over the tempting offering.

Quarters

Our domestic life soon settled, with a daily task of despatch and control of army stores items. Grapple forces progressed in construction of the extended for jets airfield, and the numerous buildings and fittings. And there were intervals of rest during periods of formal 'off work' hours. At the main army camp – I cannot comment on the other forces – we other ranks nested four, five or six to a tent. The tents plotted in customary straight rows, their boundaries marked by planted rows of painted white coral beach stones. Each tent's occupants were made responsible for the upkeep and cleanliness about their patch.

I had five comrades in our tent. We slept three to a side. An entrance each side of the tent opened onto a pathway between other tents. The tent was lit by a singular light bulb, the electricity fed by a generator, not many hundreds of yards away, whose loud sounds echoed throughout the night, every night, its grating civilised sound competing with the relentless crashing crescendos of the surf breaking on the nearby coral reefs–and night-time bands chorus of overhead screeching sea-birds.

Our tent boasted two wooden slatted duckboards, placed lengthways in the centre over the white coral sand. We built in each bedspace a sideways-on wooden box–an orange carton from the cook-house, or other innovation. Our B.Ds hung over our bedspace and were vulnerable to the rotting (as tent guys) instigated by the high salivated sea air. All clothes remained in our kitbags or cases–no room for unpacking, or necessity for doing so. A folding table and four folding chairs in the centre of the tent completed its furnishings.

I doubted this tent and layout model had changed much for our armed forces in a thousand years or more. My 64 Field Squadron tent mates were Yorky, Edge and Mick from up north. Yorky was from Hull; Boots from Brum; Swede from the west country; and myself from London. Yorky as I recollect was the most capable of our group, and accordingly was later promoted to corporal. Apart from occasional petty wrangling, we got on well with one another. And if we weren't playing cards at night, writing letters, reading books, or attending the camp cinema, the chances were we were out exploring the island lagoons – swimming, fishing, or even dinghy sailing down at the Port Camp lagoon, close by the Cook Island. This small isle, nearby the Port entrance, was a haven for settled bird life, and one-time centre of guano deposits from the multiple acres of bird droppings.

On one of my lone excursions to Port Camp, with the help of a native friend, I caught a large fish off the Copra jetty and slung it over my shoulder, intent to walk all the way back home to our Main Camp, but hoping get a lift at some point. Unfortunately I walked at least five miles under the blazing tropical sun–passing through several mirages cast onto the dried mud road ahead. I observed an *upside-down* island with several palm trees on it – most bewildering a vision. But most mirages were of flowing shimmering waves of water across the actual very dry compacted coral sand roads.

The fish overhanging my back, apart from proving heavy, and chaffing the skin, attracted numerous unwelcome flies and when I finally received a lift in a truck, one of the eyes had gone from my now-smelling carcass. But I was determined to get it back to camp and show my mates – it was a large fish with huge teeth. I wore grey army socks that day inside my plimsolls and they too began to hum a bit. Very large holes had arisen in the heels of the socks.

Phew! My tent mates were *not* very full of admiration for my fish catch – and certainly had no desire for a cook-up with the now pathetic dried smelling fossil before them; we, fish and I, both smelt. Back home at training and base camps I had grown accustomed to darning my winter socks in a criss-cross armour plate fashion, but no way was I going to repair those smelly socks, or dream, of taking them to the Q.M.'s for a replacement. But I had a brainwave – I'd bury them both, socks and fish, down on the beach–together. Ceremoniously I dug a hole into the sand, trapping a fly or two in the process, and buried my old socks and the fish together. We laughed at the antic, but the following day we could see graphic evidence of my burial plot; flies in abundance hovering over the area. My dirty laundry again begged to be aired – but a solution was at hand.

Shark bait

A friend in another tent asked if I fancied a night shark fishing, down at the sewage farm, a mile or so down the beach. At this point the Elsan night soil, toilet closets were emptied out to sea, and, other sewage was pumped out via a recently placed pipe, out near the reef – it was the closest that the administration could arrange with health and hygiene in mind. At times of high tide the effluence attracted numerous large fish of all types, particularly the large tiger and hammerhead sharks, and huge mantra rays. It was an eerie night. With the meagre beam of our two small hand torches we baited our thick hooks and heard, rather than saw, a great deal of wild threshing, contrasting with the incoming tide waves upon the beach. The screeching of loud, sea-birds overhead– and in the distance a pin-point of lights and distant generators. Their throbbing engines, just discerned, marked our home Main Camp.

Most it was Stephen ink black darkness, and, well, I deliberately dug up my smelly fish-and-sock concoction and, after tying it up with string, not wishing to touch it more than I had to, we departed with a mixture of humour and a little tension, recognising the sewer site as a potentially dangerous one. Depending on the tide. Fortunately it was a Friday night and we had this Saturday off. Eventually I linked the heavy bait onto my hook and, circling it into the air (it was a thick line, not a rod), I cast it out into the blackness and heard it splash into the water. After a few moments I felt an *enormous* tug, pulling me fast towards the waterline – then my line suddenly broke and I fell backwards onto the beach. It had snapped. All we could hear was a lot of loud splashes, but saw nothing. And that was that.

Fishy Tales

A couple of married lads received regular mail from the U.K.–the rest of us depended on friendly mail from relatives and girl friends, and as thousands of soldiers before us, shared much of the good and bad features referred to in our mail. One forces' custom was the pinning up on a centre tent post any '*Dear John*' letters; those unhappy missives terminating a believed close relationship with wife or girl friend back home. One chap in our tent for a while received vindictive mail from a '*well wisher*', an un-named neighbour who reported regularly that our friend's wife was regularly going out with another man. He pinned a letter up to one of our two main wooden tent posts. I too proved unlucky, though to a lesser degree (though not to me). After receipt of several letters from Irma, they suddenly ceased, and I too felt, for a while, rejected – pinning up the last of my received letters. I never heard from Irma again.

I was fond of tropical fishing (fine-weather sport), and for some months a group, my mates of 71 went fishing out of several large inward tidal lagoons, waters fed regularly by underground tide channels and through narrow bottleneck inlets direct from the ocean. I don't recall from where we had obtained our flat crude bottomed boat, but we left it hidden in bracken after each excursion and walked back via one of the narrow channels. It was imperative that we returned before high tide, else we would have been marooned on a narrow island–which too might later flood. I recall one trip, after fishing for tuna, a large shark (we could see it) seizing, biting my line and wire and large hook clean off – to our horror.

Returning home, we found the seas had almost filled our narrow isthmus, with its treacherous undercurrent and unseen monsters of the deep – rays, sharks or other unfriendly fish. Using rods and stick, we held a human line, the four of us then gingerly fighting the undercurrent, darkness descending en route as it does in the tropics, like a shutter. The flooding water with considerable noisy signs of marine life, came up almost to our necks. But fortunately we made it to safe land without casualty. Never to be forgotten.

There were more formal – informal, troop outings, organised by our officer and N.C.Os., and together we, then in 64 stores troop, enjoyed taking a Bedford three-tonner truck across the island on various picnics and swimming parties, playing water polo with coconut husks. (Several of these troop outings pics were published on May 10th back home.) At three months or so intervals, a chosen number of troops were selected to attend the S.P.A.L. Rest Camp at the other end of the island, near Benson Point. This centre was a shed accommodation alongside an old American war-time narrow jetty. From this rest unit I finally caught and landed my first shark. First using a green-stick rod I caught a small fish using crab bait, and then, placing that whole fish on my thick line with wire and hook (in retrospect I shudder at those youthful tactics), I walked out near the reef edge at low tide, placed the baited hook in the low water, and walked back a hundred yards to await high tide. With the tide water came in numerous large and small fish, sharks and twin-finned ray fish swam around my standing body.

Eventually I felt the thick line tauten and instantly it took off, with me in ragged watery pursuit. Running up and down in the water I slowly drew it in until, up on the sandy beach I continued running, eventually landing the poor four-foot-six-inch shark. With absolute horror I recollect how difficult I found killing the threshing shark with club and large nail. (I look back with horror at my action.) And the walk back to rest camp with the shark awhile over my back, its tough sandpaper-like skin removing areas of skin, before I changed position, just as I had journeyed some weeks before in travelling from Port Camp.

Thereafter, I changed the nature of my fishing tactics and never again butchered a kill, although I had fully exposed myself to risk within the turbulent waters. Indeed my mates and I after a few fish catches had them cooked for us in the cook-house, or by ourselves on location. But one fish had to be thrown back when inadvertently caught – blowfish. This strange uneatable fish had no separate teeth but a singular bone at its mouth which would prove difficult to extricate. It was not normally inflated, swollen like a balloon; but became so in alarm at any unwanted contact. Clearly a defensive action. The blowfish was poisonous.

Walkabout

Work completed, unless on special duties, we enjoyed most of the island activities, but over the months there were times when I could and, preferred to wander off to explore on my own. Filling my water bottle at the cook-house, and wrapping a sandwich or two, I explored vast areas of the Plantation and relatively distant terrain–several times ending up at the Bay of Wrecks – aptly named for the wreckage of vessels strewn upon its wasted beach. A large conch shell (still have it) with a minute fish therein (erm! not the fish) was collected as a souvenir, the shell returning to the U.K. with me some months later. On these lone outings away from all other humans, I stripped off my shorts and enjoyed walking naked across the stark white sands and broken corals, the hot sun completing the tan of my skin hide. Of course, no bombs had yet exploded near the island.

Officers and senior NCOs, sergeants and warrant officers, had their own tent camps and messes. The other ranks had N.A.A.F.I. premises close by the beach-side. All beer and spirits were especially imported, Tennants the name of one tinned beer. In the tropic sun, beer went off very quickly, and one consignment was buried as it went flat and too bad for even us O.Rs. to drink. A few months after our arrival, the relative free and easy attitude towards our dress, out of work, ceased. Swimming down at the beach or strolling down to the open showers, or easy abandon to the sun, in full nakedness, was ordered stopped.

Two W.V.S. ladies arrived from Blighty to work with the N.A.A.F.I. facilities, and although they remained distanced from us O.Rs., staying with the officers and senior NCOs., we were ordered not to walk about in the nude forthwith – costumes were to be worn in all swimming activities. This was, at first, felt to be an intrusion, considering the hundreds of other ranks representing the three armed services–army, navy, and air force. But the rule was enforced, and only when we knew ourselves to be well off the beaten track would we down shorts and into the water, as on lorry drives to and from Port Camp, when we would stop for five minute dips in the lagoon briny.

A dinghy sailing group met occasional Sundays down at Port London Village, and we would sail across the bay to Benson Point, to Paris. It was a sizeable sail that culminated in a picnic lunch at Paris. Imperative that the tide was watched as it was easy to become stranded on coral reefs. On one Sunday I left with two others across the bay – I manoeuvring the centreboard across the treacherous living coral beds and low level mud flats. Across, we were entertained by a school of porpoises that physically jostled our boat. We had a daunting moment when a *huge* mantra-ray rose from the lagoon and leapt up out of the water and, flew up over the boat, looking like a mammoth great butterfly (or black cloaked vampire bat) in momentarily blocking out the sun, and diving down and disappearing into the deep waters the other side of us. A scary moment – but worse was to follow on our return trip.

We almost missed ˉthe tide as we left Paris, with difficulty tacking up narrow channels out into the deeper parts of the lagoon. On one outing, halfway across the bay we encountered a large area of live coral that came close to the surface. Two of us had left our pumps off our feet – I was one of the two. Suddenly we realised the tide turning was leading us onto an island of coral – and we stuck. It was only at one point and we became aware that with the centreboard up we could push the dinghy from outside – over the side.

Without really thinking, I jumped out onto the ragged jagged sharp leafed live coral, collecting several small cuts and abrasions from the white and colourful polyps, (unaware it could be toxic), and braced myself with difficulty to shove the boat off. One of the chaps shouted "Watch Out, Shark!" Panicked for a moment, I shoved, and the boat moved off – leaving me alone on the submerged coral island in the middle of the bay. I saw twin fins moving parallel on the surface – sign of a ray fish swimming – but I didn't see the shark. Anxious minutes later one of the men – the skilled sailor – steered the vessel in my direction. I swam across and was hauled up over the side. And we returned safely.

Selkirk

Christmas Island was often referred to as a desert island which, though not strictly true, was not far off being a fact. The sand was mostly of dead coral origin. Such vegetation as existed on the island was scarce and much of it was toxic, with only a tenuous coating of air-born soil upon the coral-sand and fossilised- rock . The terrain could easily be rendered barren. Survival on the island, for food, water and ample shelter against the naked elements, much depended on natural resources, and proper philosophy and skills to make good use of those resources. As numerous settlers and visitors before us, the bulk provisions were delivered and depended to be from sources many miles away from the island. And the manpower, materials and skills were brought to the island – almost in toto. Inevitably, as but a dependent youth on numerous elementary excursions by myself, or with others, inland and across the almost barren island – I compared fairytale and folklore literary models of personages who experienced the need to survive on castaway islands, or otherwise human archipelagos, compared with facts and known fantasies.

The son of a Scots shoemaker, Alexander Selkirk (1676-1721) feeling adventurous, ran away to sea and joined up with an exploratory expedition in 1703. After quarrelling with the ship's captain, Selkirk asked to be put ashore at an uninhabited island called Juan Fernandez, in 1704. This island was found about four hundred miles off the south coast of Chile, South America, in the Pacific Ocean. Juan Fernandez, located at latitude 33 degrees 45 minutes south of the equator, and longitude 79 degrees 2 minutes west, it can be spotted on a map directly due south-east of Christmas Island. The island of Juan Fernandez is about twenty-five miles long, and only four miles in breadth; it contrasts well with Christmas Isle's lagoon locked thirty-five miles long east, and west by twenty-four miles – at its greatest width – and there any similarity ends when related to other obvious realities, but his island was much more hospitable.

Juan Fernandez island was a thick volcanic and mountainous island with one cloud crowned peak called Yunkque, rising to three-thousand-five-hundred feet above sea level – compared to our coral island's miserly forty sand ailed feet. Selkirk's isle had fertile valleys, good grass up to eight feet in height, figs, strawberries, peaches, cherries, and of course, coconuts; valleys and hillsides greatly wooded in their bearing edible fruits. The mountainous land honeycombed with deep caves, water cascading down from the cloud capped mountains. On the eastern side of the island, the off-shore water was twenty fathoms deep at the head of its bay, and in some places, nearby, as deep as seventy-five fathoms. The foregoing, geographical description of Selkirk's Isle, Juan Fernandez, I culled from an 1861 Beeton's *Dictionary of Universal Information* (p.704). And the specific natural history data based on a recorded visit by Captain Pendleton in 1859, in his ship *Golden Rocket*.

Juan island was formerly used as a base for buccaneers in their expeditions against American possessions, and one-time an unsuccessful human penal colony. Pendleton's crew found numerous wild goats inhabiting the island, fresh fruit provisions, ample drinkable water supplies, and an abundance of edible fish–proving the island a veritable haven for any shipwrecked mariners.

In 1719, the famous writer and pamphleteer dissenting Englishman, Daniel Defoe (1660 - 1731), published '*The Life and Strange Surprising Adventure of Robinson Crusoe'*. Defoe's invented hero was directly modelled on a knowledge of Selkirk's exploits, and has since become a basic literary model for human survival on an uninhabited island–extended in folklore to desert islands. *Robinson Crusoe* was written when Defoe was sixty years old, his hero–and co-hero, Man Friday–a novel, much abridged and re-written I believe for contemporary children's enjoyment (much like Swift's *Gulliver's Travels*). And so it was experienced by me as a boy. I suspect that *Robinson Crusoe* was a model for every lone explorer who had heard this tale of survival. Perhaps it will be so in future space history?

A second useful model was *The Swiss Family Robinson* or *The Adventure of A Shipwrecked Family on an Uninhabited Island near New Guinea*, written in German by a Swiss professor of philosophy, Johann Rudolf Wyss (1781-1830), and first published in 1813, almost one hundred years after Defoe's epic. This fictitious tale was originally a fantasy related to Wyss, his wife and their four children, but that version was never published (or intended to be). Whereas Defoe's original classic contained a good deal of social comment as well as a base of fact from Selkirk's exploit, Wyss's excellent family adventure appeared to be primarily a backcloth presenting flora and fauna of natural history.[10]

William Golding's fantasy novel, *Lord of the Flies*, was also such a tale, of how fragile civilisation can be. Golding's tale of schoolboys whose plane crashed on an uncharted tropical island, and the insidious disappearance of their civilised veneer when daily confronted by personal survival. The point well laboured. There were natural and superficial facets, implicit in living and surviving on a desert island. Facts woven into patterns of fantasy–and longer true facts exposed to real life on a desert island (or human archipelagos). There is flesh which is grass; *prickly* grass and edible grass–and areas with *no* grass. The island had no cows or sheep.

As described above, a small amount of fresh water was found on the island, this supply to be had at the Port Camp. But to maintain the thousands of men (and two women) and the Gilbert and Ellice Islanders, this meagre supply was wholly insufficient. Agents of the Merchant Navy – Royal Fleet Auxiliaries specially chartered to the Admiralty – were equipped with large refrigerated spaces enabling them to hold a fresh supply of food: *Fort Beauharnois* and *Fort Constantine* were two of these vessels.

Food and Water

The troopship *Messina* arrived a month *after* us, in August 1956; as well as then serving as the Headquarters' ship for the senior Naval Officer in the area, it delivered six L.C.Ms *(Landing Craft Mechanised)*. Each held one hundred tons of fresh water per day for consumption afloat and ashore. The *Messina* was especially fitted with extra evaporators which produced this limited precious daily fresh water contribution.

Constructed showers used a percentage of salt water from water holes on the island, and ordinary soap could be used under this water. The majority of main camp showers produced desalinated sea water from R.E. built distillation sites. With sophisticated filtration, it needed little imagination (for times of severe drought) to depict numbers of these commercial structures built along a long U.K. island shoreline, to ensure that we need never suffer from too severe an ecological drought. Water (more precious than oil) came out a bitter taste from our shower pipes, water often tinged with red from oxidation off the pipes themselves.

Fresh milk supplies were out of the question for O.Rs., and we became used to dried milk and mostly canned food supplies. The cook-house fried eggs were rubberised to perfection as the dozens of eggs at a time were printed out on the immense tins. All the cooking and distillation were done by using diesel oil. Fatty bacon, for me, was foul, apparently it was likely all tinned American supplies (that Yanks like Yorkshire men purported to love). The very thick and fatty sort of bacon that would suffocate my gut if I gorged upon it. I loathed fat. Preferred to stay hungry.

On our occasional picnics we were issued with old American. K.R. rations dating back to the early 1940s (the dates visibly stamped on the round containers) in many of the tinned supplies we took out on picnics. Fresh fruit came off the supply ships and might be supplemented by supplies flown in from Honolulu. Fresh potatoes became a dream, and even a legend, in line with looking forward to a glass of cool fresh milk, and a hot bath and clean sheets and a bed, and... and... other things, with only memories and imagination to feed upon, till the real thing could again become a reality. Dreams. Pom–dried potatoes, a flaky almost completely tasteless substitute for the real thing, was the major staple part of our daily diet on the island. Aided by our salt tablets. I have since those days remained loyal to real spuds and almost chips with everything.

Christmas 1956

Christmas-time on Christmas Island arrived, and it was a very hot day as usual, only tempered by a fifteen to twenty knots wind which blew throughout most of the year in the operational area. The lads and I remained in bed on Christmas morning, we had the day off and, following a boozy Christmas Eve at the N.A.A.F.I. with endless singsongs and dedications, I contributed my passionate rendition of 'Maybe it's because I'm a Londoner'. We were suddenly, loudly awakened as our two senior N.C.Os. entered our tent (a rare occurrence, even rarer if officers visited) and, one to each hand, they produced a pint mug of tea – but the smell almost overwhelming, there was an additive, liberal dose of strong rum. And so we finally arrived at the cook-house for breakfast almost drunk, and certainly as warmly glowing inside as the tropical sun boasted outside.

After a Christmas day dip, swimming and diving into the large incoming surf waves, and lounging about in the sun, we returned for Christmas lunch and a further surprise–we were actually waited on by our officers and warrant officers. I had heard of this Christmas military tradition, but never really believed it possible; that the gods could descend from distant Valhalla, down into our ragged marketplace. Highlight of the Christmas festivities on the island was the camp concert–of which I retained the programme printed by the Education Corps. 'The Elsanaires'–"Duff". By kind permission of Col. J.C. Woollett, O.B.E., M.C. Graphic title page with a round 'duff' plum pudding, and captioned 'Or what to do with Your Christmas Pud! Christmas Island.. Christmas 1956.' Producer, Major A.S.H. Telfer, R.A.P.C. Stage Manager, Capt. R.A. Quiton, R.E.'

Pantomime

Army, Navy and Air Force united forces grappled eagerly with that balmy 1956 Christmas Concert– a whimsical introduction on its printed programme: 'The show compered by DIANA. No Whistles, please–just oo-oo-ooh: And Eddie Fisher Gallagher (Spr.) Sends You for a few minutes with a song. But Where?' However. Work and play did *not* always go smoothly on the island. 55 Field Squadron had been away from Blighty a very long time (*this was peacetime*) and, many of them, were discontented that they were many months late in shipping home. Some representatives declared then should have returned from Korea (or Japan) (or Singapore) long ago–but came straight to this (for most of them) boring desert island. In truth, not everybody wanted to sail or swim all their spare time. And, since all forces were formally banned from direct liaison with the natives' village–and there were no women–well almost– and where could you go to on a small desert island hemmed in by treacherous coral reefs?

It was Christmas time and I joined several of my tent mates on the planted wooden forms at the *Komack San* Main Camp open air cinema. And as we waited, and troops collected in front of the large open air cinema screen, it rained. And how! In the tropics when it rains it falls very heavily. Anyway, we hoped it would be but a brief shower, and shivered awaiting its end. At this 1956 Christmas performance, suddenly several excited men stood up in front of the audience on one of the log wooden seats with raucous bursts of laughter interrupting their excitation.

"Look at this then", one of the 55 men, veterans of Korea, exclaimed and brandished in the air what was clearly a graphite 78rpm gramophone record. 'It's from some new pop star called Tommy Steele' (I'd only vaguely heard of him). The spokesman said he had made a record referring to Christmas Island *'How'd you like to spend Christmas on Christmas island.'* Christmas Island was, back home, it seemed, compared to Barbados or Jamaica in the West Indies. A tropical paradise. There was a roar of united voices as the point was made. And as if divine acknowledgement, the heavens opened as a sudden heavy rain fell down on him.

And so the small group of active dissenters (it was only a play, no real aggression) ceremoniously smashed the Tommy Steele record and trampled it into the then sodden ground. It was no reflection whatever on the vibes of the new upcoming rock star (and later still, superb Bermondsey all round entertainer). Some months later, when Tommy Steele was better known, one of the visiting merchant seamen insisted he had known Tommy by his real name on board ship when he used to practice his guitar. This seaman thought highly of the pop stars vibrant personality, but little, at that time, of Tommy Steele's performance on the guitar. There was no way of verifying anything the witness declared. Tommy Steele (Thomas Hicks) was a few months older than me, a Londoner: In the early chapters of his autobiography *Bermondsey Boy* (2006), he vividly described memories of living during the Blitz, and thus resonated with my own recollections of those noisy days, when we were but wartime infants... rock-and-roll. I never had the pleasure of meeting him – only through his films.

In retrospect, I learnt it wasn't Tommy Steele who made that October 1956 Decca vinyl record, *Christmas Island*, but English pop star Dickie Valentine – who we knew well in the early 1950s. But, Tommy Steele was a newcomer, then creating a British introduction to American rock-and-roll; Bill Hayley and his Comets. Dickie Valentine's record was of course not known by us, when the Korean Vets ceremoniously broke the disc – but we (the royal we) did not know that at the time. As teenagers we were out of touch with our British music culture. The memory of that event on Christmas Island in late 1956 was in no way aggressive, but illustrated how many of our 55 sappers felt at that time.

Crime

Crime of any description was little known on the island, though the odd punch-up or petty theft was known to occur. One day in early 1957 occurred an unusual event. Two men had broken into the cook-house and stolen some effects. They had been observed and chased across the island by several M.Ps., but escaped capture. Several days later, they had still not been caught, and were rumoured to be hiding somewhere in the Plantation. The irony hit us. Where could they run to on this desert island, with its formidable Pacific Ocean moat and coral rock formation ring? If they appeared at the airfield or Port Camp they would be conspicuous and be caught by watching MPs, and presumably they would soon get fed up with their self-imposed exile within the coral island perimeters. They did give themselves up, but I cannot recollect what punishment they received. I believe they were shipped back to a glasshouse in Blighty.

Thoughts of home were always constant in our midst, inevitably. And as there were no transistor radios in those days, we listened raptly to the high frequency radio in the N.A.A.F.I. tent. We listened in particular to the Honolulu Top 30, a pop chart selection of records. And occasionally we even tuned in to a radio station out of California. I eagerly wrote back to my mother and began to order regular records to await my return home to London. Johnny Ray's *Walking in the Rain*, Fats Domino and numbers of Bill Haley and his Rock 'n' Roll Comets, Elvis Presley records, ordered to keep me up with the pop music trends back home. All cash postal orders were sent through the N.A.A.F.I. mail order service. I ordered a modern refrigerator (a very first) to be sent to my parents out of my army savings. Milk at home had been, till then, kept cool by immersion in a kitchen filled sink or bowl of water. And meat contained under a white cotton mesh net, Till electric refrigeration.

And, apart from a fishing rod, only one other main article was purchased—a 120 roll film Agfa Isolette 1 Camera, which was to give me ten years of pleasure before being lost on the Isle of Wight. Many of the Christmas Isle snapshots recorded mundane domestic shots and sappers at work in building airstrips, roads, plant, lorries travelling on the beaten roads, of natives, crabs, birds, plantation life, coconut husks and my mates and self ad nauseam. At one point I sent a selection off to my old firm of Central Press Photos, after first having the selection heavily censored by the island J.O.C. staff, and had them published.

Leave in Honolulu

In March 1957, Sixty-four Field Park Squadron and a detachment of our regiment enjoyed some leave, and an unexpected sea trip on the flat-top aircraft carrier, 'Warrior' for a few days at Honolulu. *H.M.S. Warrior* launched in 1944, had served extensively in the Far East and Korean waters. We learnt it was to be the Operational Control Ship in the H Bomb nuclear drop target area. The ship carried the broad ‾pennant of Commodore P.W. Gretton, D.S.O., O.B.E and D.S.C., as commodore, Grapple Squadron. The huge Warrior's angled deck carried Avengers, Westland Whirlwind helicopters and other specific aircraft. Warrior had been specially fitted for meteorological reports and equipment related to the nuclear project. (God, I had no notion just how vital in nuclear experiments this precaution was to be.) The light fleet carrier of 14000 tons normally carried 120 officers, and 1100 ratings, but was believed to have less than this complement during its Operation Grapple involvement.

Sleeping accommodation was so tight on board that you took your folded bed and searched for a spot about 4 p.m. I settled in the canteen, and slept under one of the tables. Somebody lost his bed. Another had his stolen, and pinched someone else's – you guarded your pit with extra Egyptian P.T. With such an unguarded deck, it was dodgy on board upper deck if the weather was rough. An open air cinema show was given on the four day journey up to Oahu. It was reported that we just missed a cyclone, and at one time were riding a small tidal wave (reported in the Honolulu press). But the funniest event, and certainly most memorable, was our arrival on leave at Honolulu.

Naval crews are well used to lining up alongside top-deck on arrivals at port, but most of our troops were *not* used to this traditional exercise. All bulled up with scrubbed belt and gaiters, togged up in our tropical b.d., we were instructed, as customary, to line up alongside the naval crew at one end of the H.M.S. *Warrior*. As we approached the dock, we could see a military and civil reception committee, and an American Forces' band playing in our entry. And as we drew up to the dock we witnessed Hawaiian dancing girls with grass skirt regalia and aloha flower necklets being given to senior chiefs. We were delighted to see and hear their band playing *The Colonel Bogie March,* background music to the 1957 recently released film *The Bridge On The River Kwai.* I'll bet there were many older rank and file personnel with wartime memories who recalled London, Murgatroyd & Winterbottom's 1939 cheeky *Good Luck (And The Same To You).* High spirits taut, a number of military police fussed around behind us, keeping order.

Suddenly a rhythmic chant began from a few O.Rs. lining the ship's edge. It started with a whistling commentary, as depicted in *The Bridge On the River Kwai* film. Then words became clearly heard – a very ribald version of the Colonel Bogie March was being sung. Hand over mouth, laughter escaped as a number of the O.Rs. took up the friendly but defiant march song (viz. against the formal American forces' reception). Officers and M.Ps. dashed around to try and shut us all up, but they mostly accepted it was temporarily out of hand. I joined in with my mates alongside: '*Bollocks they Make a Lovely Stew. Bollocks. And the same to you ...*' (echoing Murgatroyd's original wartime version). It was so loud at one time that the Americans on the shore (despite the band) could hardly have missed our brief, but good humoured, loud, mischievous gesture. And no action was taken against us.

With our allocated five dollars currency we were driven to the Fort De Russy U.S.A. army barracks (scene of the film *From Here To Eternity* – aka by some of us as From 'er an' Maternity) where we were housed for three nights. The Camp was almost on top of Waikiki Beach itself. There was little basic difference from our open U.K. wooden spider barrack rooms and the Americans. But in the Yanks ablutions one notable feature was different–they only had open toilets. Privacy, even token barriers as the hessian net half curtains guarding our Elsan toilet cans back on Christmas Island, was a rank U.K. convention. But at the Yank De Russy O.R. quarters I was surprised to see that the seating arrangements in the toilet cubicles were all without doors, and the occupants were able to freely converse in sight of one another whilst engaged in all aspects of the triple S's (shower, shit and shave).

The American troops wash basins were lined up directly in front of all the standing naked porcelain toilet bowls. On the island we had every toilet – aka chemical Elsan – surrounded, draped, with a hessian net for privacy; and I was probably being naive, but I preferred my dug holes in the Plantation sands –to those American exposed civilised monuments in otherwise superb Waikiki barrack rooms. (I later realised that back in December 1941, these same Hawaiian barracks' inhabitants had experienced the infamous Pearl Harbour invasion.) Although I accepted that, with some familiarity, the conventions in ablution would likely have soon disappeared. In India, as I understood – it was just not mentioned – most persons had no choice but to relieve themselves, often, on the wayside – city or countryside in public view (the journalist James Cameron had written about it in one of his masterly essays).

I stayed awhile on Waikiki beach, with the dormant Diamond Head volcano in the background. There was a lot of surfing going on and I tried, unsuccessfully, to stay on the hired surfboard, and so decided to swim awhile in the sea; there were few bathers in the water. I dived into the shallow surf, and learnt why this part of the beach had few swimmers. Burt Lancaster, out of The Barracks, would not have brought Deborah Kerr here in the classic film *From Here To Eternity*. On the other hand, it's the beach scene. As I went under the water I hit my head on some submerged rocks. Apparently this section of the beach was littered with these underwater obstacles.

We asked a local about it. He grinned. 'You will have to find a private beach if you want to go swimming,' he said. 'Like The Aloha Hotel's private beach,' he concluded. So, sunbathing and swimming over on Waikiki Beach, we went downtown into Honolulu's Chinatown – where I purchased several long-playing jazz records from a shop in Beretonia Street. I noticed the huge piles of second hand.45 r.p.m. records, and regretted that there was no point in buying any, as in the U.K. one could only then play 78s or 33s.

There were four of us out and about in Oahu from 64 Field Park Squadron, and wistfully, but paupers really, we waited in vain to be titillated by some young female company. We were between twenty and twenty-one years old. Walking up one of the main streets in downtown Honolulu, we were attracted by a sign that invited Armed Forces Personnel to a real life sex show for only one dollar. Too good to be true. But ascending the steps we soon learnt – we were being conned. It was a plaster-cast collection of life-size naked female and male models – all depicting various graphically illustrated advanced stages of venereal diseases; clearly intended for American servicemen on leave. It was horrible, and certainly left a heavy taint on sex-starved young males, and obviously a success story for its proprietors.

Tattoo Parlour

Having a tattoo was not uncommon to sailors, and squaddies, most obtained serving abroad: a sort of souvenir, blue-woad of ancient Britons, with natural colours, produced from vegetables.

On our trip into Chinatown, we had in our company an old sweat, total war-time squaddie, nearing his long-term demob. We espied several young servicemen, entering a tattoo parlour. One or two of our group were thinking about this badge of travel: But our old soldier said; 'Don't, whatever you do – you'll regret it in later years, believe me,' and told us why not.

Sure enough, years later, I would be employed in a Sussex mental health clinic and, on several occasions, old vets appeared with numerous scars where awful attempts to remove, now flabby, creased, words and pictures – like fissures of skin, map of a mountain terrain; names, like old girlfriends – but, mostly, tokens of past ages. And, for me, I couldn't help remembering the awesome horrors of concentration camp victims – skinned alive, to use the part tattooed images to make lampshades and other adornments. Just an opinion.

Surprise, none of our group ventured within...

Christmas Island, 1957, shirt from Honolulu.

Showtime

We ended the day out at a theatre show, and I saw my only ever live American burlesque show. (To think my father had performed in the 1930s with American burlesque comedians Olsen & Johnson, in many such Vaudeville palaces – lucky man). It could hardly have been anything else, with the obvious obscene gestures of two golf players, and female companion, on stage. And then to eat. At midnight on the 13th March, 1957, five of us went into Calypso Joe's, a nightclub in downtown Alakea Street, where we had our picture taken by a resident photographer. It was also a humiliating unexpected experience. The price to us of *any* food was prohibitive. Behind us sat a number of middle-aged matrons in flowery dresses, enjoying a large luscious meal. And seated nearby were several young American marines on their way to Tokyo, with money to burn. We managed one iced bottled beer apiece, and the price of one photograph; a mute witness to the event, a smiling hostess joining the photo for display only.

The following day, after visiting various sights and gardens down Kuamoo Street and Kalakawa Avenue, we passed the Waikiki Lau Yee Chai Restaurant and nightclub (in which we now knew we could certainly not afford a visit inside). We spent the afternoon in a Waikiki cinema, showing *'Don't Knock the Rock'* starring Bill Haley and the Comets, the Platters, Little Richard and other rock 'n' roll artistes. Rock 'n' roll as Bill Hayley's previous film, *'Rock around the Clock'* had introduced, represented the new national phenomenon – causing Waikiki's cinema' manager acute anxiety at this sudden appearance of a group of English soldiers sat at the back of their very conventional cinema watching the film. Would they get up and jive in the aisles, and wreck the place? But we behaved ourselves.

Back home in England the media had reported a group of adolescents who had literally got up and rock 'n' rolled, jiving in the aisles to this new live exciting music. We were warned that if we made too much noise we would be expected to leave the cinema. We grinned broadly, and though we responded with our feet, sitting down, we otherwise behaved ourselves, to the relief of our sentinel host. In the evening we visited *The Sands Nightclub Restaurant,* on the beach-side at Waikiki. This was really special. For only a fifty cents cover charge, we could have stayed for as long as we wished to watch the fabulous cabaret – and buy neither food nor drink. But for only one-dollar-and-twenty-five cents we chose to fill our plates as many times as we could with numerous exotic foods; there was Poi and Lomi Hawaiian salmon, Chinese noodles, Japanese sushi, Korean and Filipino dishes – an excellent bargain at the Sands Cosmopolitan Food Bar.

The Sands' beach-side Waikiki Restaurant provided our one real taste of the much advertised Hawaiian dancing and high life. There danced 'Lovena', the native Hawaiian dancer; there was 'Leinaala', the drummer; 'Blossom', the hula instructor; 'Roti' from Tahiti; 'Kealoha', a hula specialist; 'Gene Roland', Island-born singer 'Leialoha', dancer end hostess; 'Faavila' amazing Samoan knife twirler and flaming sword dancer, accompanied by a drummer, (we sat only feet away in front of this performance on stage–the soothing waves on the sands behind us). And gazing up in wonder at 'Mona', another Samoan dancer.

At the and of this, our last leave evening, we went back to the De Russy barracks. But I decided I couldn't sleep, got up and dressed then walked out onto the then almost empty Waikiki beach. As I walked alone down the beach and enjoyed the cooling clear night sky. I thought later what a pity it was not to enjoy a female companion.

The following morning of our last day on this *real* tropical paradise, we agreed to split our group up to wander and spend our last few cents, before returning to The Warrior. I wandered back alone, into downtown Honolulu, and into its Woolworths. I noticed Elvis Presley's long-playing records piled in the record section, blazoned in his recent spiral to success. But I preferred Bill Hayley Rock 'n' roll, and New Orleans Dixieland jazz and gave Elvis a miss, and finally I sat up at the Woolworths' Aloha restaurant bar and had a full roast turkey dinner for only seventy cents, with apple pie fifteen cents, and an iced lemonade for ten cents. All under one dollar. The food was delivered in separate compartments, in a tray, just as on board ship, not all on one open plate as I was then accustomed. And so I returned to our ship, and returned to Christmas Island – latent horrors in the launch of an H bomb peacetime experiment. As advised, I hadn't breathed a word to anyone on Oahu about the island – but, then, I knew absolutely zero about the Boffins' installations anyway.

Church on the Main Camp beach

We resumed island domestic life as the detonation date in May 1957 drew closer. But, for myself, several unexpected traumas occurred. After Christmas 1956, volunteers were asked to assist in the construction of two churches on the beach side adjacent to our main camp. I volunteered. It was a pleasant exercise and my camera soon recorded the single-tiered churches built of cement-plaited coral rocks which we collected from the beach. Our Gilbertese natives assisted in providing palm-leaves thatching for the roofs. I made the acquaintance of a Catholic priest, Father Paul, for whom the church was to be an asset. A small blue and white statue of the Virgin Mary was placed in a recess in the wall. I had never experienced a Catholic priest before, and Father Paul was a gentleman with a great sense of humour, and certainly no strait-laced image of unreal Sainthood. It was in that almost completed Catholic church that I celebrated my twentieth birthday. I was registered a C. of E., but–rightly–it made not a shred of difference. Father Paul was kind enough to provide a whole crate of beer for us workers to celebrate my declared birthday. We drank its contents unashamedly inside the not yet consecrated, almost finished, church, and gave it a personal baptism.

Sepsis

Not long after working on the Catholic church, I went fishing by myself, off the beach, and, then decided, to go for a lone stroll across to the big Plantation. I took my plimsolls off, and walked (stalked) bare-footed across a largish area of prickly grass. Perhaps predictably, several of the sharp grass thorns pierced one foot, rather deeply, and several days later it turned quite septic and swollen, giving grief, and causing considerable pain and irritation. And in some *toxic* confusion, briefly, to my mind. Back at work the following day, in the stores troop office tent, I found myself unusually brittle, annoyed with the otherwise menial task of correlating rows of ledger Grapple stores' items. The combination of intense stabs of pain in my foot, and overheated feverish *shut-in* temperament – then, in frustration – I momentarily exploded in one sudden moment of explosive pique...

   Bewildered. I threw my chair back and became hysterical, throwing all the papers on my desk about and hobbling at a run out of the tent which I felt, closing in on me, much to the consternation of my colleagues. (In retrospect I could think of no reason whatever why I behaved that way. This loss of control, whatever its hidden toxic cause, and brief fever, would continue to baffle me, long after I was demobbed at the end of the following year in December 1958.)

   I was rushed down to the single tented hospital, close by the beach, and very painfully my foot was worked on by the medical staff. I was kept in hospital for a couple of days, while the wound healed, and returned to work—sore confused and most bemused – and suffering a gross loss of dignity. It was about this time I was one of a number of troops given a choice as to our mode of return to Blighty. Either one could leave earlier and go back on the *Warrior* in a goodwill tour, via Fiji and South America, arriving back some time after the other troops or embark on the troopship T.T. Empire Clyde and take a quicker return home. I chose the latter, foolishly wishing for a fast return home—and thus turning down a Pacific tour, care of H.M. Forces. Oh foolish youth.

Empty Diesel drums, 1957.

Transfer. P.O.L.

Attached to POL (petrol, oil, lubricants) depot, my allocated driver and I collected empties, and arranged delivery for filled replacements of petrol in jerry cans, and diesel drums. (Jerry cans were named after the excellent metal cans first used by the Germans (aka Jerries) in North Africa.) We used an all purpose workhorse, a Bedford three tonner. Contact with the diesel first gave me psoriasis, but that soon disappeared. The large empty diesel drums have since been used for many other purposes, and can be found marking many a road crossroads in the desert. But, the drums would soon be reused for a much more sinister purpose – refilling with atomic, nuclear waste; and leaking.

As a direct result of choice, I had been transferred to 71 Field Squadron, remaining good friends with former mates of 64 Field Park Squadron, all who shortly afterwards embarked for home. But I quickly found a new group of friends as I was introduced to 71, a transport and plant troop. In a tent, first in row, and close by the cook-house premises, I was introduced to Len, Derek and Nobby. Len, the eldest, a small but very fit wiry mature Londoner, with dark hair and a small over-lip moustache. Derek, the otherwise youngest (but two years or so older than I), from Hampshire, a confident fair-haired National serviceman. And Nobby Clark, a stocky well-built chap from Newcastle upon Tyne, a Geordie with a helluva sense of humour – and a dab hand at obtaining items by quick bartering. Cockney Len too, was adept at this foraging ability. I believed both Len and Nobby had recently served time out in Korea, and were regulars. Both Len and Nobby were 71, Ten Ton Lorry drivers. I would often accompany them to the airfield to collect *stuff* from Oahu Hickam air force base – and Blighty.

Tent mates of 64 had all been young men, and differently experienced from the 71 group – like Len and Nobby who had recently served in Korea and Kenya. For me, Len, the oldest of my new group served a role of a highly esteemed elder brother; and with Nobby and Derek, and their mates, accepting (rather than adopting?) me in their midst. A new job was allocated to me, serving the 71 squadron's P.O.L. site, based at its adjacent open tent, and tucked in to one side of the Plantation. The petrol-oils-lubricants site was a large, neatly stocked supply which included a large supply of horrible smelling drums of diesel. It was a pleasant, easy, store-keeping task. Allocated a No. 51 three-ton truck daily by the transport troop officer – and driver (for I couldn't drive), together we travelled about the island sites, replenishing P.O.L. supplies. And I became far more aware of the magnitude of the Grapple project facilities.

Once we travelled down to the Port Camp R.A.S.C. depot, delivering empties–and collected filled supplies. I was almost stung by a scorpion (with a new delivery) and the driver and I demolished a stack of cans in its pursuit, actually finding it near the bottom of the Port London stack. My new role enabled me daily to travel across the island and so I viewed (not closeup) the J.O.C. site (joint operations control. The refrigeration plant. The secret – hush hush – white corrugated steel sheds (not insides). The main transmitting site. Officers, boffins and N.C.Os' areas. The meteorological site, where huge tall masts were erected, and from whence daily a large orange coloured balloon was released. The massive Starmix site with its huge stone crushing machines.

The large water Distillation Sites. Cook-houses . Laundry sheds. The RAOC.
The RASC. REME. 51 RE Port Squadron. RAF, and various civilian scientists'
sites; anywhere, everywhere where fuel and or lubricants were needed. It was
71's task to not only supply heavy plant, but to service all the installations.

One exception to all the regular POL visits–and one area our Transport
Troop seldom visited, was the R.A.F. quarters and installations. The RAF and
RAF Regiment and MPs, had their own backup systems, and naturally proper
secrecy had to be guaranteed. And was. Len and Nobby drove ten-ton trucks,
sometimes with trailers. And on several of their trips up to the R.A.F. Cassidy
Airfield to collect incoming fresh food stocks for the cook-houses, I was able
to give a hand and record a few snapshots, depicting off-loading Hastings
aircraft linked to 71 heavy transport in from Honolulu.

On one humorous occasion, sat one evening outside the N.A.A.F.I. tent.
Whilst I was pleasantly inebriated with Tennent beer, in the company of Len
and Nobby, a lighted cigarette was placed between my sodden lips, and lit.
They knew I did not smoke, and never had. It was offered out of amusement
and not malice. In response I duly sucked in the whole offensive lighted object
within my mouth, and promptly ate it (rather than take up a first cigarette),
much to my mates' momentary laughter. They didn't try it again.

Mosquitoes were a nuisance and sometimes left weeping spots as evidence.
Sometimes I used my mosquito net, but mostly left it rolled up, over my bed.
Flies were attracted to the naked light bulb and many died for their habit. The
sound of an occasional bird trapped between the flysheet of the tent and the
inner roof was nothing compared to the now recognised scuttling of rats around
the tent area. One day I heard a scuffle going on under my bed, with considerable
squeaking, and quickly jumping off, I spotted with some surprise – a crab in
the process of eating a small rat; my camera and flash were handy, and I recorded
the incident for posterity. Most memorable was the morning we awoke and
found our bodies red with a rash of itching sores; we were invaded with bed
bugs, their eggs matted in the crack of our makeshift wooden bed-frames. Our
tents were closed up and fumigated; fortunately we never suffered a recurrence
from this nest.

Numerous snapshots recorded our domestic and work events. A shot of 28
FER's Cockney Len, southerner Derek, affable Newcastle (Geordie) Nobby,
and a lance-Jack friend, reading the Australian *Sunday Mail*, newspapers
periodically coming in from Australia where a communications link was
maintained with the operations team. And pics of numerous party antics. There

were several snapshots of Len and separately of myself (which Len took) on the beach examining crayfish, and one with a lifebelt with *Christmas Island* printed on its rim. A white straw hat appeared from somewhere. This event was in close correlation with a local tragedy whereby I very nearly lost my life, and one man drowned.

Land crab with a rat, under my bed!

Almost Drowned

Veterans of Christmas Island, well into spring of 1957, we residents were marked by our dark tanned skins (all over) and white sun-bleached hair. New arrivals to the island occasionally flew in – R.A.F. and Army personnel – and were easily recognised by their very white skin. Our newcomers were dubbed 'moonies' (night-time lack of sun equals white). Yanks called newcomers 'White meat'! It was a time of high tide, close by the wreck, at main camp. We had finished slightly earlier than usual; and so I went down to the Main Camp beach for a swim, the lads to follow later. On arrival I found I wasn't alone, there being several moonies about, but as I approached the waterline some shouting had broken out. Those servicemen personnel who had been around for sometime were well aware that a *very* strong undercurrent existed at high tide, this force dragged back and over the reef barrier itself, so we always kept close to the beach at high tides.

One moonie had swum out too far, and two others were in the act of swimming out to their friend's assistance. Too far for the lifebelt, two lads in the water who were recording their own distress. Several other new men arrived at the site. One moonie was sent off to give the alarm and get help fast. Without thinking, knowing I could swim, I plunged in, intent on helping one of the two in trouble but not yet at the reef; one man had already been swept out to sea. Inevitably I too fell victim to the immense power of the undercurrent, and felt it taking me out to sea when despite my flailing arms and legs and, weakening strength, I actually got in spitting distance of one chap, both of us attempting to return to the shore.

At one stage, as I emerged from under an incoming wave and, looking back, just saw a wavering thin ribbon of sand, I made out running matchstick figures collecting on the distant shoreline. God. I momentarily panicked and really did think of my past life, peak events, (not at all, all past life) and that second motivated me to find that extra strength for attempting to return to shore. I really thought 'This-is-it, but-not-if- I-can-help-it.' Someone on the beach was organising a human chain, as more and more troops came to the beach to offer their assistance (or out of curiosity). And quickly their leaders entered the gripping heavy waters. As I was becoming more and more exhausted, suddenly an arm grabbed me, and someone spluttered, 'Relax mate, you're all right now.' And my body was passed down the line. I believed one of the two moonies, too, was rescued in time.

Unhappily, despite urgent helicopter searches, the missing chap was not discovered until his body was washed up several days later, much affected by the watery delay. It was a sad tragedy, and one which reminded me never to attempt such a swimming venture again. But I had no regrets, having really tried to help in saving one of the chaps, though nearly losing my own life. To my limited knowledge that unfortunate death by drowning was *then* the only visible casualty, to me, of that whole nuclear explosion operation. It was also a minute prelude to the main event.

First H bomb Explosion

The day arrived. It was May 15th, 1957. All troops at the Main Camp who were not involved in the actual operation were ordered to be dressed up in best tropical dress b.d., and muster just outside the tented camp on the beaten coral-mud road. Under the control of our various troop officers we answered to roll call, likely a security routine as much as a safety organisational device. A number of ten-ton lorries were placed in a neat symmetrical line, each vehicle angled towards the direction of the Port, but off the road. A driver sat waiting in each truck.

The airfield was about five miles away: the bomb was to be exploded south of us, over the sea off Malden Island. I thought it was safe (for us on the island) as we believed it was to happen 400 miles away. But I had no real idea (or anyone else I knew) of what was happening, so vague was our information about the nuclear experiment in the ranks. And in absolute silence, despite the distance, we thought we could hear the Valiant jet's air-scream as the bomb was loaded up into its huge experimental H-bomb undercarriage. We watched it climb up into the clear blue sky as it took off.

As we were mustering in troop formation, lined up in front of our commanding officer, a padre was asked by the C.O. to offer up a prayer, accenting the wish that 'no accident' should occur on take-off with the bomb. And this was an H not an A bomb. One gentleman advised, over the tannoy, that drivers of our transport, should any accident occur, were to drive the troops down to the Port Camp, where we were to instantly go into the water and immerse ourselves as long as possible (an anti-nuclear deterrent?). This statement was made in all due seriousness.

So we were loaded up onto the trucks and watched for the timed minute of take-off. There was in the absolute silence a biting tension as we looked and waited for the moment to arrive, but one of the drivers panicked. We looked down the line and the tension broke as many of us burst out laughing. I'll not say whether it was an R.A.F. or Army vehicle, but I remember it well – and chuckle. He quickly braked, and silence resumed. And finally we all saw the Valiant jet leaving the Cassidy airstrip, its target the vicinity of Malden Island over the equator, south of our base.

If a nuclear accident (within what radius?) of any description in peace or war, had occurred, it would have been impossible for us to have been driven down to the Port Camp and into the water during that split micro-second before the H-bomb would likely vaporise us and much of the tropical island, into oblivion: much less, how long we could remained immersed in the Pacific waters whilst hoping to minimise after explosion side-effects? And what of airborne and sea tide water carrying irradiated debris as fallout?

I later (albeit years later) questioned whether in the immediate aftermath of the explosion, wouldn't the sea surface, below, and all 'life' bombasted by the blast, become irradiated by the so-called 'clean' bomb's fallout. And any shortly after subsequent rain and blast flowing winds, and tides, spread out, ionised materials.

What a calculating logistic nightmare, experiment, that must have proved.

Mid-pacific News

Our Grapple boffins and H.M. forces were stationed ten-thousand miles from home. And of course, it was not possible to acquire current U.K. home newspapers. We were able to obtain Hawaiian and Australian newspapers, which were flown in daily. And in addition a newspaper was printed on the island, by a news team supplied by the Royal Army Education Corps. The team published an excellent four page duplicated foolscap paper on the 1st August, 1956, its topical title the *Mid-Pacific News*. During its existence it produced 298 editions (a terrific effort) closing its final edition on Saturday, 3rd August, 1957, twelve months afterwards. I thought it most helpful.

The Mid-Pacific News kept us in tune with events back at home. A typical edition, included a page of foreign reports (News from Round the World), a sports page, cinema programmes for the *Kamak San* open air cinema at Main Camp and the *Blue Lagoon* at Port Camp, home news (U.K. events), meteorological reports and local island news. The newspaper also kept us abreast of the Suez Crisis of autumn 1956; the changing over of Prime Ministers; results of the Olympic Games; events in U.S.S.R, South Africa, Rhodesia, China, Algeria, and other winds of growing change. And of perhaps greatest topical importance – it published (anonymously) a *first hand account* of the H-Bomb explosion itself, of which residing servicemen and civvies formed part of its history.

As far back as June 1956, Prime Minister Sir Anthony Eden announced to the House of Commons that tests would take the form of 'nuclear explosions in the megaton range' and would be high air-bursts (high?) which would *not* involve heavy radio-active fall-out. Keesings official records[11] added that:

> *'A note has been sent by the British Government on January 7th, 1957, to all diplomatic missions in London, informing them that an area of the Pacific Ocean, nine-hundred miles north and south of Christmas Island, and seven-hundred-and-eighty miles east and West, would be declared dangerous to shipping and aircraft Between March 1st and August 1st, owing to the British nuclear weapon tests'.*

Not Really Dangerous

In 1977, a small non-fiction book was published, *The Christmas Island Story,* by author Eric Bailey of the British Colonial Service. He gave an excellent social history of the island, especially the 18th and 19th Century; and, more recently, the American WWII forces occupation from 1941 until 1949.

Bailey's account gave no reports from participants or witnesses of the 1950s and 1960s Atomic Tests, and said: '*Very little damage was reported by the H Bomb tests.*'

Even after November 1957 (viz Grapple X), and *dismissal* of Grapple Y, and Z bombs in 1958:

> *With the prevailing easterly winds, the dangers from radioactivity were said to be nil, and very minimal for 'blast'. Only the danger to eyes from 'flash' made it essential for people to be under cover.*

And, in one sentence to follow:

> *In April 1959, H.R.H. The Duke of Edinburgh visited the Base during a Pacific tour.*

The 1977 published history, gleaned as a journalist, from press handouts, reflected government propaganda as much as ignorance, but reflected the top secret, ugly realities of the times, and, certainly of the public media insistence during our occupation of the Grapple Tests and, indeed, of the Dominic US tests: all very safe – no problem – clean, healthy. (*The Christmas Island Story.* Eric Bailey. Stacey International. 1977.)

Really ? Dangerous within 780 miles? How many Megatons? (We were on top of it then.) Erm! There was '*no risk*' for us though as it was a 'clean' radiation bomb, we were informed. And any fallout could *not* be blown our way, due to the easterly winds, keeping any cloud and water debris from *infecting* the elements in and all about us. The *HMS Warrior's* met reports would ensure our safety. But we thought (if we really did think about it), this was *new* business and experimental. How do they really know? If this is *new* business?

For weeks we followed media accounts of protests – home and foreign – the world demonstrating against the British nuclear device explosions. A crop of rumours circulated of a fleet of Japanese fishing boats coming in to the danger area. And there was at least one definite lone protest vessel, even of a suspected submarine emerging in an island lagoon (*impossible a feat*). But of course, none of the rumours proved other than hearsay. Yet the international protests were real enough, and obviously made good copy for global media.

Russian Soviet tests[12] were already being well reported. And a U.S. series of nuclear tests continued in the Nevada desert in May 1956 and were still on-going when I was on Christmas Island, in post-war 50s and 60s. Knowledge of nuclear explosions were closely related to the war-time ground zero, '*dirty*' relatively, now, small A-bombs dropped on Hiroshima and Nagasaki in 1945.

But it always remained *unclear* whether a Government (*any* government) in power, or boffins, really took notice of an '*aftermath*'. Of radiation sickness and, worse, the potential internal, somatic, *genetic* malformations likely – and *not* just in science fiction – where there was already considerable literature.

Yes there was already a substantial body of available 'warning' credible, scientific forensic evidence, stemming from atomic destruction on after-effects found in Japan and elsewhere. But, so what! Critics appeared to be informed. There's-no-real-risk involved from any peacetime nuclear activity, and any fallout radiation. For example, our own U.K. government had published relevant literature on the subject back in 1950. But, as a squaddie, of course, I knew none of this information by experience. Just as well. Perhaps.

One British Home Office pamphlet[13] was produced by His Majesty's Stationery Office back in 1950, and sold at an affordable price for a general public's consumption at one shilling ànd three pence. This booklet's content was full of photographs of Hiroshima and Nagasaki.

And, although the awful fate of those Japanese cities was well known, *so was the even more publicised Nazi atrocities in the concentration camps*. And multiple death of six million and more persons. And the still, in the 1950s, extent pervading bombed ruins from two total world wars. Most people like me were unaware of what a looming threat world wide nuclear war could become. As too, *Atomic Warfare*. It was very much still the vogue of popular science fiction.

A positive dissonance, a distancing of realities was perhaps a net result amongst world leaders? (And dangerous, negative, observations kept hidden by compulsory Secret Service Acts.) On one conspicuous POL visit I made in 1957, adjacent to Cassidy Airfield, my driver and I saw through the wire fence a large, what looked like huge bomb-like object in a waiting cradle on wheels. (It had no real implications to us.) The object and the aircraft behind it was smothered in a covering of thick brown grease of some sort (or so it seemed). On duty about the island, it reminded me of one London bomb-site public exhibition, about 1945, where my bro and I, as young boys, and my mother saw a collection of *huge* bombs standing up-right on plinths. They were really massive.

What did our collective H-Bomb look like in May 1957? I don't know! I am dependent on others' descriptions, as any other curious individual might be, aware of an inevitable gross under-estimation. How had the A-bomb been described, its deadly predecessor? Back again to popular press media descriptions. The English weekly magazine *John Bull* [14], under a heading of '*Talking Points About Atoms*' said: 'The single atomic bomb dropped on Hiroshima of which the charge weighed about two hundred pounds produced the effect of twenty thousand tons of T.N.T. The whole bomb, because of lead shielding to protect the aircrew from radiation during transport, weighed around four tons. ...'

That was back in 1946. The run-up to Christmas Island's H-Bomb in 1957 had been christened in concept back is the 1930s. (How easy, in retrospect, to trace such facts.) *The Picture Post* weekly in 1950 [15] had published an *illustrated* article entitled : ' *Can Man Survive The Hydrogen Bomb?* '. In Picture Post's graphic report the author referred to the Austrian physicist, Hans Thirring's 1946 work "*The History of the Atom Bomb*" in which he stated–'*his fears of a super-bomb*'. And with hideous insight, in a subsequent work '*Atom Warfare and World Politics*', Thirring stressed '*the dangers of atomic warfare to mankind through lethal radio-active dusts.*'

The potential of hydrogen to helium change was discussed by Max Born in '*The Restless Universe*', published in 1935. And before British-born scientists Cockcroft and Wanton had demonstrated how to disintegrate the lithium atom nucleus. And earlier still, the intense work of the Curies on radium and beryllium particles–bombardment with alpha particles was executed in the early 1930s. And... and ... science fiction or scientific fact?

Culled retrospective research material is easily located from second-hand bookshops and junk shops. Small wonder that in later years reports would be forthcoming in the media of moderately intelligent individuals, able to construct (sans radioactive fuel) atomic weapons from already well published scientific data obtainable in most public libraries. But such horrendous realisations were a whole world apart from my nineteen year old reality in 1957. More fiction than fact. Atomic warfare was read as science fiction. But as to *living* reality and authenticity–what we, servicemen and civilians, stationed on Christmas Island learnt, was recorded in the island's newspaper *Mid-Pacific News.* [16]

The local nuclear H-bomb plus *tests* explosions were *now* proven fact.

The First Grapple H Bomb

To maintain a mantle of diary authenticity. I extracted an at-the-time account of the first U.K. 'Clean' H-Bomb air-drop, verbatim. Contributed by an un-named RAF man who flew in a Vulcan which dropped the first of the Grapple H-bombs off Malden Island. On May 15th 1957 it happened, he wrote:

'Bomb Gone!–H-Bomb Puts Britain On Level Terms. A flash, stark and blinding, high in the Pacific Sky, signalled to the world today Britain's emergence as a top-ranking power in this nuclear age. No one saw it! No human eye could survive the hellish glare of white-hot air brought to incandescence by the fantastic heat. But those who were present on this historic occasion, backs turned to the explosion nearly thirty miles away, could sense the brilliant intensity of the flash through closed eyelids. Even through thick clothing a flush of warmth penetrated to the body. Ten second after the burst, spectators turned to see the dying explosion still threshing with the mighty powers that had been unleashed. High above the sea, and rising rapidly, was an enormous ball of fire that changed swiftly into a bubbling cauldron of coppery-red streaked with grey. A feathery white cap spread over the top of the cloud., extending downwards to form a gigantic snowball poised on a white stem, that appeared in sections between cloud and sea. ...

The 24 hours prior to the release of the bomb were tense and dramatic. Long before dawn on the day before D-Day, the first aircraft roared off the runway on a met. flight aid as faint streaks of daylight showed, the ground crew of Valiant 818 and scientific teams began comprehensive preparations for bombing-up. One after another, aircraft were ordered off or their allotted duties. Shackletons of 206 and 240 Squadrons, and Canberra's of 76 and 100 Squadrons broke the still morning air with the thunder of their engines as they took off from Christmas Island on weather reconnaissance—with the added duty for the Shackletons of searching vital areas to ensure they were free from shipping.

From H.M. Ships Narvik and Warrior, HMNZ Ships Rotoiti and Pukaki, from neighbouring islands and stations farther afield, reports continued to arrive in a steady stream. Before noon, the Met. Office at Christmas Island had compiled its main forecast for the next 24 hours—and the Pre-Firing Phase had been declared. From this point, the tempo of work in the Met. ... By the time dawn had broken on D-Day, scientists on board ship and at the various instrument sites on Malden Island had checked and rechecked their recording apparatus designed to take photographic records and to measure the air blast pressures, and heat and nuclear radiations. Already in position were forward control ship Warrior ... and Scientific Base Ship Narvik, together with the observer frigate Alert, and the survey frigate Cook, in which scientific measurements were to be taken. Warrior's helicopters and Avenger aircraft were warming up. Health Physics teams were checking on their equipment.

Back at Christmas Island, vital traffic along the roads linking the Port, Airfield, and Operations Centre was watched anxiously by engineers of the Army Task Group. For months they had shouldered the near impossible task of maintaining road communications for this Day, overcoming topographical difficulties and ceaselessly striving to mend the ravages of tropical rain that washed away the surface quicker than it could be restored.

'ALL CLEAR'

The delicate task of stowing the bomb into the bomb-bay of the Valiant was completed. A steady stream of final reports began to flow in, and at 5 a.m. the Task Force Commander

... confirmed that the situation was favourable for D-Day, before taking off for Malden where he was to make a final decision from the Scientific Control Ship Narvik. Throughout the previous day, scientists and members of the three Services had been withdrawn from Malden Island and embarked in H.M. Ships Narvik, Warrior and Messina, until by dusk only a handful of scientists and R.E. personnel remained. The pressure on the Signals communications rose to a peak as messages flashed between the Task Force Commander in Narvik and the Operations Room at Christmas Island, culminating in the order to Valiant 818 to take off. Piloted by Wing Commander K.G. Hubbard., O.K., D.F.C., the gleaming white aircraft taxied out onto the runway. Only the knowledge of it, sinister load touched graceful take-off with suspense, so nonchalantly did she rise off the tarmac and climb into the morning sky.

Years of planning and months of heavy labour were now being put to the final test; and Wing Commander Hubbard, holding the plane on its arrow straight course, formed a triangle of heavy responsibility with the Task Force Commander and the Scientific Director watching; from below.

'BOMB GONE!'

The pilot had begun his running commentary, his voice coming through clear and unhurried. The trial run-in completed, the giant V-bomber turned north again to take position for the live approach run In the ships. Task Force personnel and official observers from Australia, Canada, New Zealand and the United States turned their backs to the point in the distant sky where the explosion was planned to take place. Then it was 'Bomb Gone!' followed by the count-down. Its bomb released, the Valiant made its carefully rehearsed evasive manoeuvre and swept away on all the power of its four jet engines. Shortly after, a Canberra carried out the first high-level sampling run. Other aircraft which had been orbiting in the area moved at speed to their appointed tasks. Warrior's helicopters flew towards the target area and took radiation readings from sea-level up to various heights. Ships sampled the sea at their locations. Among those who felt the greatest satisfaction at the success of the drop were the Garrison Commander, Colonel J.C. Woollett, O.B.E., D.F.C., and the Officers and men of the 28th Field Engineer Regiment R.E. who had laboured for so many months in the construction of the base and 71 Field Squadron R.E. who have been responsible for its maintenance.'[17]

Second Grapple Bomb

Which was us, the 71, of the 28th F.E.R. Royal Engineers. It was quickly publicised that *the first clean explosion* had been deemed a complete success, and so confident were the powers that be of duplicating that success, that when the second explosion was recorded sixteen days later, in our unit, it was business as usual. And to the best of my memory we would know of no subsequent details of any other H-bomb explosions, until *The Mid-Pacific News* published another excellent dramatic account: [18]

> *'... 6, 5, 4, 3 ... in the tense stillness every-one waited, poised., expectant. Only the harsh shrilling of a bell came to cut across the thoughts as eyes were closed and shielded from the searing, flash to come. The ringing stopped—and there was the fireball, surging and boiling with per up power, forcing its way upwards and outwards. It flared like the sun, rising quickly, and then it was white, suffused with red fire enclosed in vapour. The round, ragged ball, its top coated with a thinner vaporous layer, heaved its way up through the clouds to take or the now well-known shape of nuclear explosions.*
>
> *As the fireball rose, it drew after it a round, twisting column of grey white, tall and slender, wonderfully smooth at the lower half, wispy and ragged nearer the ball. Higher and higher it rose, flattening off at the top as the winds pulled and tugged at its shape. The stem leaned over in a westerly direction and its outline blurred as the minutes passed. ... A sigh escaped those who were watching. In many ways it*

looked so beautiful in the bright morning sun; only the knowledge of its lethal power gave the scene any added poignancy. And yet still it grew—a wide pink disc, which shielded the clouds below from the sun, like a gigantic cotton-wool umbrella. And as it grew, it became thinner and more tenuous, still surging in the centre, but losing its former angry force.

As it receded into the distance, all eyes remained steadfastly watching it, noting its slightest changes, fascinated, as it streamed out in the wind and merged slowly into the haze of the horizon. There it hung, majestic and strangely beautiful, high above, and dwarfing Nature's clouds, a monument to the genius of a few men, and a warning to all. ...

SECOND OF THE SERIES.

This, the second of Britain's nuclear tests in the Pacific, came but sixteen days after news was released that Britain had tested her first hydrogen bomb. The test was watched by representatives of the British Press and. Press Agencies, from H.M.S. Alert.' [19]

The Immediate Aftermath

Since *our* three bombs were demonstrated *clean bombs* (no risk) with a minimum of fall-out, what after results could there be. We squaddies hadn't a clue. Over twenty years afterwards I followed an unexpected U.K. television documentary from America, which referred to my boyhood Hollywood hero John Wayne possibly suffering cancer from *down-wind* fall-out after effects when working on a film in the Nevada desert in the early 1950s. How can weapons of mass destruction be clean?

Most media in the 1950s and 1960s seemed to be convinced that any suffering from nuclear fallout was only resulting from 'dirty' bombs, and gross immediate (aka collateral) damage. My colleagues and I at that time in May 1957 certainly accepted this as fact. An insightful 1962 *Sunday Times* supplement, printed five years after our event[20] recorded devastating comment on the retrospect, aftermath of the American H-Bomb explosions after the 1949 Bikini

Tests. Eight years before Christmas Island and Malden Island 'clean' air-bomb bursts. [21]

And any British serviceman injured through neglect, by Government and The Military, was *muted* by an extant 1947 act. [22] Government Policy *forbade* any citizens (especially military) the right to sue the government for a gross neglect of a duty of care; albeit a recognition and possible compensation; in *denial,* as *official policy* – crassly refusing appropriate treatment to servicemen and their families through this awful persistent denial of wilfully exposing certain personnel to radioactive pollution during nuclear tests.

Genetic mutation

The blast wave of nuclear weapons produced, later, after-effects, after even a *minimum* of exposure to infected matter. Genetic mutations in extent lifeforms, on animals definitely proven. But I had no idea that the effect of irradiation on botanical life, through atomic bombardment and general nuclear interference, has became a terribly proven reality. Evidence. A *Sunday Times Supplement* [23], published five years after our Grapple tests, recorded *devastating* comment on American Bikini Nuclear Tests eight years *before* Grapple. One of the Australian Monte Bello islands on Oct 3rd 1952 (the year U.K. begun production of Plutonium at Windscale in Cumbria), had been atomised, *vaporised* in a mushroom cloud.

The Sunday Times [24] reported damaged wildlife; turtles had mutated and no longer migrated to and from the waters of the sea, just lost their sense of direction and went on into the land and died, along with their eggs. Such surviving life on the island and adjoining sea life, were so saturated with radio-activity. Bikini Atoll nuclear explosions, had *mutated* most surviving, living species, into future generations, and local fishermen too were adversely affected by nuclear bomb radiation fall-out. *.The Sunday Times* 1962 article concluded :

'*The real tragedy of a nuclear war lies with the survivors, not with those which are killed by the first blast.*'

It was savage, the slow discovery, that never again could, in perpetuity, the myth of a blue lagoon be *safe* in a tropical island paradise (as I had one-time experienced it) : to become a Robinson Crusoe Alexander Selkirk – safe human haven. Fatuous to bander feckless words in retribution as to who was to blame – which nation was most guilty – and fight inter-nations like Tweedledee and Tweedledum. I am reminded of a long ago captioned illustration of H.G. Wells' book, *The War of the Worlds*, which commented optimistically (like a League of Nations) – the world's nations united to fight a common hostile ... other-world foe.

After conclusion of the second test, there was a general winding down, and a number of installations were dismantled. One of the regulars I spoke with said he had recently chatted with moonie 'Brylcream boys' (R.A.F.) who had been warned that they would likely be transferred to the island of Gan in the Indian Ocean in the near future, and that Christmas Island would be discontinued as an Armed Forces base. How very, very wrong they were! Gan did become for a while a base for U.K. forces.

There was, in fact, a *third* Grapple test whilst I was on the island; a 200 kiloton (kill-a-ton weight of a nuclear bomb) detonation, *only* 2400 metres above the sea off Malden Island. But there was no media fanfare and I have no memory of that third explosion and, as all our regiment, believed it was the final Grapple event. And since tropical rain and wind patterns were a normal experience, I have no memory of the rain-full days since the detonation on May 15th, and two following tests. Obviously the JOC and Met sites would have minute details of such post-explosion weather behaviour. And of any subsequent acid-rain – *if it was recorded and reported*: the big taboo of and if.

Voyage Home

Shortly afterwards, I left the island on the troopship *H.M.T. Empire Clyde* on Sunday, 25th August, 1957: I never learnt the fate of the Line Islands – Washington Fanning and Christmas Island – and south of the equator, Malden and Starbuck Island. I hoped that native islanders did not suffer any ill effects from the Grapple tests as in retrospect servicemen in the earlier Bikini nuclear tests. I look back and wonder how big *Taaker* and laughter-making *Itaia* and descendants had fared?

Our cabin on G-deck held four people, placed up forward. Again I wrote in my menial laconic log book for the voyage, and recorded domestic trivia as trying on-board beer, Black and Tans, most satisfying at the time. We were delayed several days till leaving, awaiting R.A.F. personnel. I started my new job, for the duration of the return trip – R.A.M.C. hospital ward orderly cleaner, the ship raising anchor on Tuesday, August 27th. 1957.

Once-more, we adapted to a mixture of fatigues and time filling card games, cinema shows and prolific reading. On the Wednesday alone I read the paperback novel *Road to Stalingrad*, and followed it with *Sugar Doll* and *The Prowler*, devouring the books at a literary speed acquired over the past couple of years.

On Friday August 30th we docked for a last time at Honolulu. Len, Nobby and I went ashore and settled awhile at a bar in Motel Street. We jawed awhile with some Yankee sailors on their way to Japan – one from Rhode Island, another from Texas. And walked a while up into the hills and, looked down into the bay of the American Naval base of Pearl Harbour and saw the still prominent remains in the bay, now symbolic of the tragic raid by the Japanese in December 1941.

After some final shopping, I acquired a palm tree motif shirt (which I kept and used for an incredible twenty years until ripped in play, off my back, as a social-worker at a children's camp in Sussex in the early 1970s a Waikiki purchase at only one dollar and ninety-nine cents). I arrived back on board half an hour after midnight Len and Nobby got back about three in the morning, and our randy Nobby Clark had a hilarious tale to tell us.

Nobby on his walkabout had finished up at a sleazy nightclub, half-hitched to the wind. Sat at a small table in a very low light, he called a gorgeous looking cigarette girl over to his table. As she stood by him, exchanging coin for cigarettes, he mischievously reached out to a stocking clad leg, 'An' she was gorgeous,' he repeatedly emphasised. To his surprise she smiled invitingly at him and, didn't move. Unable to believe his luck, Nobby slid his hand up, and up, till (and we imagined his anticipation) as he reached the stocking tops, and found' soft naked yielding flesh. And Nobby probed upwards and hotly fondling his way into her groin. And he froze, stopped in horror as he discovered she was a he – with real balls. We split ourselves laughing at his real enough indignation – he hadn't made it up. Several days later a couple of other chaps confirmed a similar discovery (though not so graphically); it was a club haunt for overt homosexuals.

We left for Panama the following afternoon, after a final brief visit ashore. My laconic voyage diary recorded: ' Enjoyed reading two American paperbacks, *Young Manhood of Studs Lonigan* by James T. Farrell and a blockbuster by Norman Mailer called *The Naked and the Dead*.' I read an enormous amount of paperback novels. The clock was put forward a little each day, four-and-a-half hours forward as we approached Balboa, fourteen days after leaving Honolulu.

Denver

As we cruised south, down the West Pacific Coast of the USA between Hawaii and Panama, on September 11th 1957, inland, a dreadful nuclear incident occurred; sixteen miles from Denver, in Colorado, USA. But I would not learn of it for over 65 years, due to the total secrecy of the American government. A cold war episode, in the heart of the *Rocky Flats Nuclear Plant*. A fierce conflagration in a factory owned by Dow Chemicals, later renamed Rockwell, which, from uranium, produced fatal plutonium 'triggers' for their piles of atomic bombs.

Obviously, we were unaware, as of Windscale in Great Britain, only days on, where an identical catastrophe would occur. But, as in the rest of the world – including the USA itself – the secrets held; and we then approached Panama, on our way home.

Panama

As we approached the entrance to the Panama Canal, we saw a large flat turtle, followed by a frolicking school of porpoises– numerous birds, pelicans, parakeets, and budgerigars–and chattering monkeys. We started threading through the Canal at 8 a.m, and through to the canal zone port of Colon by 4 p.m on Saturday 14th September, twenty-first day since leaving the island.

It was great watching wildlife emerging from the jungles; a large green chameleon was seen drinking at the waterside. In the lakes we passed through, leant over the rails eager watchers waited to catch a glimpse of alligators cruising along, or sunbathing on a shore.

At one point in the narrow cuttings we saw carved on to the stone a memorial plaque to the men who died building the Panama Canal–thousands died through malaria–and as we took our tiny Paladrine tablets once more we were momentarily very aware of one benefit of modern medicine. My Agfa Isolette camera continued to record numerous photographs in journeying through the Panama Canal–and I took in more than on my outgoing wet journey only thirteen months before.

Saturday 14th September 1957, at 5.30 p.m. we were allowed to go ashore at Colon, expected back on board ship by 11.00 p.m. Len, Nobby, Derek, Babs and I hired a taxi to take us to the local American branch of the YMCA for a subsidised snack before exploring the Colon canal zone. Occasionally crossing the paths of other servicemen and merchant seamen in bars and night clubs. At one point we sat drinking Tom Collins's (45 cents) and powerful Zombies (60 cents) at San Cristobal's hospitable minute all-night bar, *The Doghouse Bar*.

Much of the dockside Panamanian town was a pot-pourri of the American Wild West with local policemen openly carrying loaded side-arm pistols; numerous open-bars with wooden half-swing doors open to the ever busy pavement hawkers. Instead of enthusiastic piano-players, loud raucous juke boxes emanated into the humid streets a mixture of Latin-American and western pop music, firmly marking out each large public bar.

Roadside touts sold gaudy cheap cigarette lighters, pavement shoeless ragged boys offering to clean your boots and offering to take you to meet their sisters for sex. Plump brightly dressed dark-eyed ladies sat in open wooden kiosks plastered with advertisements–selling state lottery tickets like postage stamps to passing trade. And some half-naked ladies offering themselves.

Brothel

After some while drinking in the *Doghouse Bar,* relaxed with berets and belts off, jackets unbuttoned, we met up with two old salts, a couple of merchant seamen off our own ship, when we were approached by one of the local pimps. We had already passed numerous ladies sat in opened windows or stood in dark doorways who in a sing-song, tapped the palm of one hand into the other forearm, closing their arm up on to the tightened hand suggestively loudly, proclaiming 'Jig-a-jig?' One tout attempted to sell us a visit to a 'live show', a lady with a donkey, a lady with a bottle etc. and other diverse seedy sights. We declined. We had refused not out of outraged purity, but preferring an offer of wanting flesh. After all. None of us had any carnal experience since leaving blighty 13 months before.

Before leaving ship our CO had briefed us all over the tannoy, on the importance of not walking about alone; and not being seduced in isolation and subsequently beaten up and robbed – as several lads had in an earlier ship's visit to the port. Although laughter had followed the tannoy warning, we realised the gravity of its content. Thus four of us agreed to accompany the man in his taxi to the outskirts of the canal zone, accompanied by a bottle of beer apiece. After some while driven down numerous unlit roads we arrived at a small white terraced house.

Ushered in through a darkened doorway, as if we might change our minds, we entered–a front room. It was the most unlikely brothel I had ever imagined – a family affair? The first doorway we entered from, a large crucifix was secured, and a number of other religious objects adorned the room. I recollect 3 or 4 black haired ladies (the man departed for a while) playing host and, setting us down, we were each offered a further small bottle of beer, with manufactured grins and meaningless chatter before pursuing the reasons we were being entertained.

It was a small sitting room with a drab curtain over the doorway to the bedroom next door. My head already well muddied with drink and excitement for the occasion was further confused by the location of a child's occupied cot only a yard away from me. But soon, one by one, we were escorted next door by one of the ladies, and it came my turn. Meek in capture, I followed my lady in through the curtains. The room was small and only dimly lit. There were two beds, one to the left of the doorway as we entered and a slightly larger bed to the right almost against the wall. A singular chest of drawers and one bald chair, and few belongings, completed the brothel room furnishings. An open doorway led to a smaller annexe where its white light lit a low toilet, adjacent porcelain bidet and sink unit.

To the muted pantings of the other occupied bedspace cast in a shadowed outline I stepped to the side of the larger bed. The forced smile departed off my lady as she held out her hand and said, 'Twenty dollars!' I looked askance, frozen in my tracks, money had completely slipped my heated mind. All I had left was three dollars and one English pound. She looked back at me, paused, and then shrugged her shoulders, taking the money. And it was soon over. Removing her blouse – she had no drawers on – she went to lay back on the bed in bra and upturned skirt, when I felt too much tied into a machine, and blushing, asked her to at least remove her bra, which she did remaining thenceforth in complete silence. Now stripped, I laid upon her ample breasts and with no foreplay whatever was literally inserted, the action soon completed. Across the room I heard and partially saw someone leave and another enter – one man obviously recognised me, gestured and got on with it.

In retrospect, it was a miracle I'd gained an erection in the brothel, with the quantity of beer and liquor inside me, the human traffic, seedy family atmosphere, and cold treatment from the lady but I was twenty years of age, and it seemed very long time since my last union, biological urgency fed by months of desert island dreams and fantasy. The greater being of nature ensured my glands had no trouble in that all too brief mechanical act. As I dressed in sober silence the lady walked across the room and promptly sat on the bidet in front of me. And meanwhile, across the bedroom another serviceman was having his fiery loin thirst quenched, but not of beer. I found it all rather overwhelming and certainly very disappointing.

As the experiences of years ahead would repeatedly accent, reality is too often far less satisfying than dreams and illusions. Better at times to keep one's fantasies than blot a subject for life. Fortunately, I was too young and immature to grasp a fuller import of that bleak sexual experience and subsequently gained a greater enjoyment from the social adventure itself. On leaving the premises another taxi arrived and dropped its eager cargo to be milked and quickly put back to pasture. We returned to the American Servicemen's YMCA back in Colon.

Passions momentarily neutralised, and a degree of soberness upon us, I recognised that event as my first (to be last) encounter with a prostitute and proceeded to bolt the stable door ages after the mount had fled the scene. The numberless medical lectures on venereal diseases, numerous servicemen related anecdotes (all horrendous), and the American exhibition on Hawaii on sexually transmitted ailments, flooded my head with fears as I made for the toilets in the YMCA and proceeded to scrub my genitals, as if to remove any possibility of outward infection. Fortunately nothing was subsequently contracted but the experience was salutary.

On leaving the American YMCA we once more made for the dark bars and clubs of the Canal zone, borrowing a few dollars off one of the lads. Drink and the dark night again took its toll and only three of us remained together when hells-bells, we were picked up by our MPs on shore patrol and escorted back to ship, several hours after our due back time. As the bum-boats left the vicinity of the ship and we drew away from the dock in the bleak early morning, I cast my eyes for the last time in the direction of the famous Gatun Locks, which made up a substantial construction on the Panama Canal: I had numerous photographs to remind me of the event. And we sailed for our next port of call, Curacao in the Dutch West Indies.

After a good night's contented rest, I hastily downed breakfast and made for the ship's infirmary for my daily chores. It was hilarious. As I had previously dashed for the toilet sinks of the Colon YMCA, following our excursion to the small family brothel – surprise, surprise – there was a long winding queue outside on deck, all waiting to see the duty medical officer. A rumour had been received that a very substantial amount of servicemen and crew from the vessel which preceded us on the way home, about a third, was believed to have thought they had contracted some genital ailment. And despite the CO's warning for no serviceman to find himself alone, an RAF man had been surprised by an irate husband whilst enjoying his wife, and he was subsequently robbed of all his valuables–but, fortunately, not beaten up, as I recollect. Panama was an unforgettable experience.

The second day out of Panama we idly watched the coastline of Venezuela, and a number of could be islands, and observed a French destroyer passing us by the other way. During the early afternoon Babs, Nobby, Derek and I were informed we were not to be allowed ashore at Curacao for being late back on board at Panama but, instead, would be doing extra fatigues – we grinned openly and declared it worth the token punishment.

On Tuesday 17th September 1957, our 24th day on the voyage home, we awoke to find our ship anchored in the bay at Curacao. Looking out of the porthole I noticed an abundance of oil depot storage tanks and in the distance pretty coloured roofs of the Dutch colony houses. Remembering I was not allowed off ship I shrugged my shoulders and went to sleep again. The good lads were off at 10.00 a.m. and back at 15.45, and judging by their comments we hadn't missed much. The island had a high cost of living and the returning lads felt there was very poor hospitality towards them as British servicemen. I obtained a few purchase souvenirs off the inevitable bum boats, and we set sail at 17.30 hours for Liverpool and home. The ship's mail received at Panama included a letter for me from my old Fleet Street firm, CP., and it enclosed postal orders for just under ten pounds for my commission percentage for the five photos of Christmas Island published by the *Illustrated London News* back in May. And also for several provincial publications.

On Saturday 21st September the sea continued to be very rough and walking the decks was often like walking the plank on a see-saw. An extra heavy downfall of rain stopped a tug-o-war on board deck. The following day the sea returned to a relative calm but the ship's tannoy relayed some surprising sad news: a strong hurricane had been experienced 300 miles ahead and a German training vessel had sunk. We were asked to cast our eyes for any wreckage. Ironically we were one day late and if we had been on time we might have been caught in that hurricane. The next day, our thirtieth out of Christmas Island, the sea again became choppy and our ship dipped and rolled like a drunken giant.

The ship's tannoy informed us that some survivors had been found from the recent disaster. Day 31 and for the first time in over a year we were ordered to wear our thick B. D. which felt like hard sheets of cardboard. On Wednesday 25th September we were paid a week's ship wages of £2. Most of it went on tombola and beer. Cinema shows remained a regular draw but, in a dramatic flourish, two of us tore a pack of cards in two and cast them overboard in the ship's wake–once too often pontoon had claimed too many pounds–a parting gesture. Day 34, Friday 27th September, we sighted a liner which turned out to be the *Queen Mary* (odd: our TT *Charlton Star* had parked, as it were, almost alongside, the *Queen Elizabeth* at Southampton back in June 1956 on our way out), probably bound for New York.

From early morning on Saturday 28th September we followed the Irish coast in the south, and I stayed up all night watching changes of fire piquet, excited as we drew near Blighty. At one moment, in passing the coastline, one of our old hands, leaning over the side, said sadly, in a broad Irish accent: *'I'll never go back to Ireland, I remember the beatings we had from the priests...'* We deemed it right not to reply.

At last on Sunday 29th September 1957 at 0545 we were up and ready to hand in our bedding and by 0700 hours we were, very cold, approaching Liverpool. At 1215 we disembarked for our troop train, home for London with a number of large white £5 notes.

As we said our goodbyes, I parted from friends and acquaintances, made in the 71 Field Squadron and previously in the 64 Field Park Squadron of the 28 FER. Unknowingly, at the time of disembarkation at Liverpool I was never to see or hear from any of those men again – they were good company

It would be over 50 years on before I would learn that during that long-time past balmy 1957 voyage home, back on Christmas Island, a new and much more deadly (to personnel) set of Grapple X H-bomb tests had suddenly, and hastily, been made in preparation. The Vulcan bomber squadron based at Cassidy Airfield, had been suddenly notified about this new test, during September 1957; *'saving time and money'* with only four weeks of intense training, before dropping an 1.8 Megaton H-bomb–off (on) Christmas Island itself . ... on the *8th November 1957* .

Even as we left the island on August 25th 1957, in the (later) naive belief, that was that: Operation Grapple complete: the USA, and Britain in Australia, with incredible global secrecy, contrived to fire off hundreds of dirty atomic tests; from towers, balloons, and by plane, or ships, and underground. As 'the towers' were likely limited to 100–200 feet in height, it is reasonable to consider them as Ground Zero, since any fireball would quite clearly have reached terra firma – or aqua, as the case could be. Our last H bomb test at Grapple was detonated on the 19th June, 1957, as we sailed for Liverpool and blighty.

America, since 1951, had commenced a massive extension of its Pacific proving grounds from 1946 to 1960s, in the Nevada Desert, New Mexico. Its *Operation Plumbbob* series placed thousands of American servicemen, deliberately, in their line of fire; to test out different experiments on their own human beings: May 28th, June 2nd, June 18th, June 24th, July 5th, July 15th, July 18th, July 19th, July 24th and July 25th 1957 (bloody hell!); and there were more, much more experiments on their military and indigenous population.

And our (then) last H-bomb test was on June 19th: leaving Christmas Island, in the belief it was the last detonation of the Bomb.

Missed Horror

Troops (after my departure) on the 8th November 1957 were subsequently sat down on the beach, to *watch* a detonation's mushroom of Grapple X south of Port Camp, (where only a few weeks back, I'd enjoyed fishing and sailing on weekends off duty). But then our Grapple tests were out of sight out of mind, and were at least 'out-of-sight' and *safe* south off Malden Island. It was the first of *many* such tests to come – none of which I would know about till the awesome revelations *after* the repeal of the 1947 and 1983 Acts – Web and Google information-technology and IT gateways – and, for me, then first reading of the phenomenal, brave revelations of Sapper Ken McGinley's 1991 book: *No Risk Involved.*[25]

While I was enjoying disembarkation home leave from September 29th 1957, including Christmas home leave, Sapper McGinley and his R.E. colleagues, that Xmas, were preparing to go out to Christmas Island. He left New Year's eve 1957, arriving in February 1958, where he would, unknowingly, join a growing, ghost company of global nuclear veterans (McGinley founded the admirable *British Nuclear Test Veterans Association* in 1983). They found themselves in a Bosch and Dantean gateway to Hell, yet in a world I never knew. The sapper's subject was a *modern* cautionary, no no – warning ... to the future. Just as awesome attrition after-effects of industrial warfare was first realised in the Great War trenches as shell shock. The *real* documentary material of peacetime nuclear tests was worthy of a post-Hiroshima Kurosawa epic, and an English H.G. Wells social history.

It was good to be back home in London in the sharp cold, foggy wet winter of 1957, the dismal clinging damp as familiar as the lovely, big red trolley-buses, and cheeky cockney voices. So welcome, and safe. My brother was still serving out his National Service time in Paderborn, Germany. And I again tapped my roots, and visited as many relatives as possible. There was one episode worthy of recall. After my mother had finished her hellos; still in uniform, kitbag in the passage, my stepfather asked if he could chat to me 'privately' in the front room of that small terraced house in Stoke Newington. 'I know it has been difficult for you to accept me as a father', he began softly, 'But to be honest I find it difficult myself because...'

And in his strong Irish Dublin brogue Tom Dolan, my kind, but distanced, step-father, related what his reasons were; oddly a mixture of seemed middle-class differences from working class a list of data; of bro and I having attended Grammar School, being 'clever' – though this seemed to me untrue, as I had then, *no* valid academic qualifications, having left school early for economic reasons. His sincerity and my awareness of how difficult it must have been, earned a respect, I never lost for him over the next twenty years, until his early death in 1979. Unhappily, he would never again be able to be so open, so robust in his emotions until, with pain-filled lungs, he would voice his disappointments in life and especially of himself–to me, shortly before his demise.

It was late September 1957. I was twenty years of age and back from Christmas Island. And after leave, posted to H.Q. Royal Engineers depot at Chatham. Shortly afterwards I was posted to serve remaining time out, until formal discharge one year later, working as a storeman tech in charge of bridging equipment, based in a small detachment out at nearby, Upnor Hard on the bank of the River Medway – where regular R.E. demonstrations of light assault floating bridges (aka LAFB) and lightweight ferries, powered by multiple Rolls Royce engines, as I recall. Advanced bridging equipment performed for delegates of the United Nations and their military representatives. A good and last posting.

Back in Blighty, Christmas Island and its Nuclear Tests quickly receded in my youthful memories as I found myself down with a dose of dubbed Asian Flu, rampaging about the country and Chatham at that time, in the winter of 1957. I remained wholly ignorant of the being unleashed horrors as Grapple nuclear H bomb tests escalated on Christmas Island – and on a global scale amongst so-called civilised nations, well into the 1960s. And so I was able to maintain past iconic images of untainted *Paradise* on a tropical island in the Pacific, and in the populated West Indies.

The Hydrogen Bomb 1957

Civil defence pamphlet issued by Her Majesty's Stationery Office, published by the HMSO in 1957...

Nuclear

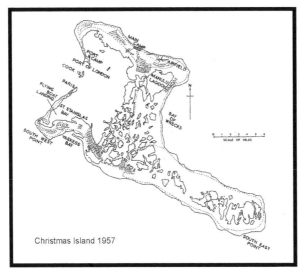

Christmas Island 1957

A coral island (over 100 miles circumference) discovered by Lt. J. Cook (Third Voyage) on Christmas Eve 1777 :–*Christmas Island, lat. 1 degree 55 minutes N., long. 202 degrees 40 minutes E, a low, barren, uninhabited island, with anchorage on the west side. It abounds with turtle, but has no fresh water.'* ... Its length, from Port London to the southernmost point, about 30-35 miles. Here follows a 'selection' from numerous photos, a cache of 28 FER b&w photos taken between 1956 and '57–before the H bomb, before the Atomic Tests over the Island and its coral shore. (Map Source: Adapted from *Christmas Island Cracker*, by Air Vice Marshal Wilfred E Oulton, Publ. Thomas Harmsworth 1987)

Christmas Island pictures – 1956-7

Two months before *The Bomb*. On a welcome leave at Oahu, Fort DeRussey, Honolulu (via aircraft carrier H.M.S. Warrior) March 1957 with 64 Field Park Sqn–Stores Troop. We could only afford one beer each in the night club; poor in contrast with wealth of some U.S. marines we met on their way out to Tokyo. That's me, second on the right.

After 13 months on the atoll, I left on an LCM with 71 Transport & Plant Troop of 28 Field Engineer Regiment. We left Christmas Island on Sunday August 25th 1957 on the T.S. Empire Clyde– arriving at Liverpool docks Sunday September 29th 1957. I was into my third year with the sappers. (Unknown to all of us squaddies, on the 8th November a 1.8 Megaton massive H bomb would be exploded just to the south of Port London in clear view from the beach of Christmas Island–bigger bombs to follow.)

LEFT: Typical flat landscape. View to south of the island - over which, next year, bombs would be mushroomed; with the implications... **RIGHT:** Village at Port London. (Villagers were taken off the island during the active experiments.)

LEFT: Copra spreading coconut husks. **RIGHT:** Village lagoon.

LEFT: Gilbert and Ellice islanders. **RIGHT:** Camp near Port London, at the northernmost part of the coral atoll.

LEFT: Vintage toilet facility - Toilet at the end of the pier (hole, in its floor) **RIGHT:** 1957. Veteran Nobby, left, myself centre, at Doghouse Bar, Colon, Panama (on the way home) about or after midnight. (and then found by MPs, and 'escorted' back to our ship...)

LEFT: 71 Transport Troop POL stores. Petrol, oil and lubricants for all army visits - I was in charge of this facility. **RIGHT:** Port London Village

LEFT: 28 FER Sappers at work, 1956. **RIGHT:** RC Church, built by sappers, on beach by Cassidy Camp.

LEFT: Arrival of stores, 1956. Site of 64 Field Park Sqn - most Sappers were national servicemen. **RIGHT:** Port London sappers at work.

LEFT: Mates of 71 Transport Troop and civvie matelots at Doghouse Bar, Colon, midnight.1957. On the way home, off the Ts Empire Clyde. en -route for Liverpool. **RIGHT:** Port London villagers.

Preparing dinner at Port London Village 1957

LEFT: Booby Bird - cannot fly? Many would die from fallout, etc., after the blasts.

RIGHT: Villager

LEFT: View of Port London village. **RIGHT:** RE 64 Stores Troop, on day off in 1956

LEFT: Cookhouse Site - Main OR's Camp, near Cassidy.

RIGHT: Port London Road to Cassidy Airfield - from where the bombs were loaded up.

LEFT: One of millions of hornet and land crabs.

RIGHT: Under the bed... One night, a scuffle under my bed revealed a Land Crab devouring a rat. Good job no snakes on the island!

LEFT: Old South Pacific Airline pier (SPAL) Troops island Rest Camp (St Stanislas), on the north west of the Island. **RIGHT:** 71 Transport Troop - Aussie Sunday papers. Main Camp

LEFT: Off limits! J.O.C. (Joint Operations Control) site. Where boffins pressed THE buttons for detonation? Out of bounds to all except if on duty. ... And that means YOU sapper. **RIGHT:** One of our two sapper built churches, adjacent to the camp, in 1957.

LEFT: Young Port Camp villagers (and pet) waiting outside its singular shop, to the north of the island. **RIGHT:** 1956. Fishing in lagoons, and off the sea beach - self, and Mike, of 64 Stores Troop. In 1957, I also fished with Len, Derek and Nobby of 71 Troop, catching Tuna, and other edible fish - cooked and eaten by us (but Sharks and Rays were also about us - at times.)

LEFT: Port London. **RIGHT:** On our first arrival at Christmas Island, in 1956.

Rest at S.P.A.L. site. 1957

LEFT: Me at Cassidy Main Camp, 1956. **RIGHT:** Partially hidden. Hush hush! buildings, 1956-7. Off limits, I don't know its function.

LEFT: New arrivals on Hastings, from US Hickam airfield, Oahu, Hawaii. (Most army 'squaddies' arrived by troop ship; RAF, and civilians by plane - via Hawaii, and USA.) **RIGHT:** Old American Pier at SPAL Point, from wartime occupation.

LEFT: Inside one RC Church, at the main camp. **RIGHT:** R.A.S.C. (Royal Army Service Corps) POL office tent.

LEFT: Port London village lagoon. **RIGHT:** Vacated native community house

LEFT: Posing beside a Port London native outrigger canoe house. (Months later, troops sat, with their backs turned, here - as bombs were exploded less than 25 to 30 miles south.)
RIGHT: Me and a caught Sand Shark, from one of the lagoons fed by the ocean.

LEFT: Line Islands District Police, Immigration, Customs and District Office Post Office building, located at Port London village. Our H.M. Forces postal address was B.F.P.O. 170.
RIGHT: Lifebelt (no use for nuclear fallout!) - site of main camp.

LEFT: Port London family. **RIGHT:** Port London LCM on standby.

LEFT: Port London. Gentleman in foreground helped me in fishing off this jetty. Later, 1959, the Duke of Edinburgh visited the Isle via this pier by Britannia, the Royal Yacht; he didn't drink the water or eat local food... **RIGHT:** One of 28 FER ten ton lorries! Collecting freight from Port Camp - or, the airfield. I'm the runner bean on the left.

LEFT: Port London Copra Pier. Islanders waiting for a visiting trade vessel. **RIGHT:** 64 Stores Troop day out.

LEFT: Port London Village. **RIGHT:** On the beach, evening at NAAFI - Cassidy Camp. Myself, centre, with 71 mates - relaxing, with Tennant's Export beers.

LEFT: A Hastings from Hickam OAHU routine delivery, at Cassidy Airfield. (No pictures of Jet aircraft or RAF personnel allowed - viz... passed by our formal military censor). **RIGHT:** Bogged down, on day out on Island with 64 Stores Troop, 1956.

LEFT: Visit to deserted village. **RIGHT:** Helicopter (possibly from HMS *Warrior*) arrival on island.

Tide out. Main Camp, known as The Wreck. American World War Two transport remains, from when they left the island in the late 1940s. Danger. 1957.

LEFT: Inside second home of 71 Transport. L to R: Len (fellow Londoner), Derek (Hampshire), and Nobby (a Geordie). Len and Nobby were veterans. **RIGHT:** Inside my first home with 64 Stores Troop. Yorky, Edge and Swede (west country; we gave each other friendly regional nicknames – I was cockney).

LEFT: Close by Cassidy Main Camp. The Wreck; an abandoned line of old American transport, c.1945-46. Tide well out. A very dangerous swimming site – at high tide, I recall one moonie drowning (and myself close to drowning) caused, at that time, due to the very strong undercurrents, as well as a *very* deep Pacific shelf, but a hundred yards or so out.

LEFT: Landscape view of 1956-7 transmitting site – with numerous masts apparent.
RIGHT: J.O.C. Generator's site.

LEFT: Old plantation dynamite storage shed. Nearby, I found trees with brittle wooden slats nailed on, dating from the old US wartime occupation, presumably for sighting enemy aircraft. **RIGHT:** Early, primitive, Cassidy Airfield low radar and receiving buildings, 1956.

LEFT: Port Camp Sunday sailing club. We'd recently finished putting the gear away after a trip to Paris. I pose with towel around my neck. **RIGHT:** Off duty sport at port Camp, cricket hockey football ... natives played with bare feet, very thick skin soles. Coral sand beaten hard for pitches.

LEFT: A flock of hundreds of birds in early 1957–most are frigates about SPAL point. Later. After one to-be later nuclear explosion, considerable bird-life were scooped up, killed by the blast of a megaton plus burst fallout, and ground stripped bare. The above seen greenery was prickly grass–toxic to any cattle or sheep. I poisoned a pricked foot on one occasion, foolishly going barefoot through the grass–no thick skin as our Gilbertese native friends, **RIGHT:** Young Frigate Bird kept as a pet by a local villager. Many would die from the blast and fallout of future bombs.

LEFT: 71 Transport Troop party, in 1957. I'm back row second from right, friend Len is third from right–Nobby is in front of me–both of them were ten ton lorry drivers. **RIGHT:** Pic taken by street photographer at Waikiki Honolulu, left to right ... Mike Myself & Griff of 64 Stores Troop. Thursday 14th March 1957

A favourite picture, my Gilbertese help on a fishing rod, at the end of the pier; watching the launching of a new outrigger canoe. My picture was used as one of a set by Central Press Photos in 1957.

Atomic Warfare

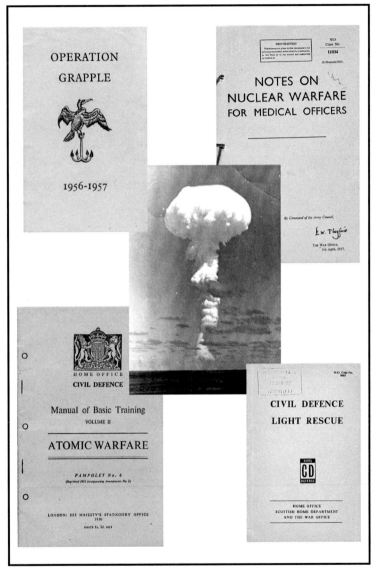

All available published (for military & civilian) support on nuclear material during postwar years 1950s and 1960s was essentially based and illustrated by, so called dirty (ground burst) A bomb 1945 Hiroshima Japanese exposure and recorded fallout results. H Megaton experiments (air bursts or other) were new business . And naturally could not, at least initially, anticipate short or long-term H-bomb genetic effects on human beings.

Five censored domestic photos (mine) of 28 FER's 64 Field Park Sqn Stores Troop sappers, okayed for Central Press Photos Fleet Street, published in '*The Illustrated London News*', May 11 1957. Four days *after* this publication, U.K's first Mid-Pacific experimental air burst H-bomb test, aka *Operation Grapple,* was exploded – for me, then, out-of-sight, but not out-of-mind.

The Mid Pacific News SPECIAL

SOUVENIR EDITION

BOMB GONE!

H-BOMB PUTS BRITAIN ON LEVEL TERMS

Wednesday 15th May 1957

A flash, stark and blinding, high in the Pacific sky, signalled to the world today Britain's emergence as a top-ranking power in this nuclear age.

CHRISTMAS ISLAND

SOUVENIR EDITION

No one saw it! No human eye could survive the hellish glare of white-hot air brought to incandescence by the fantastic heat.

But those who were present on this historic occasion, backs turned to the explosion nearly thirty miles away, could sense the brilliant intensity of the flash through closed eyelids. Even through thick clothing a flush of warmth penetrated to the body.

Ten seconds after the burst, spectators turned to see the dying explosion still threshing with the mighty powers that had been unleashed. High above the sea, and rising rapidly, was an enormous ball of fire that changed swiftly into a bubbling cauldron of coppery-red streaked with grey. A feathery white cap spread over the top of the cloud, extending downwards to form a gigantic snowball poised on a white stem, that appeared in sections between cloud and sea.

The minutes that passed while waiting for the following sound seemed endless. All eyes were fixed upon the fantastic yet familiar mushroom, bridging sea and sky like some giant waterspout. And when it came, it came as a double boom like distant gunfire.

As the cloud rose up and penetrated the tropopause, it flattened off into a round disc, while the stem leaned over drunkenly, and disappeared.

Hours of Preparation

The 24 hours prior to the release of the bomb were tense and dramatic. Long before dawn on the day before D-Day, the first aircraft roared off the runway on a met. flight; and as faint streaks of daylight showed, the ground crew of Valiant 818 and scientific teams began comprehensive preparations for bombing-up. One after another, aircraft were ordered off on their allotted duties. Shackletons of 206 and 240 Squadrons, and Canberras of 76 and 100 Squadrons broke the still morning air with the thunder of their engines as they took off from Christmas Island on weather reconnaissance — with

From our local produced and distributed newspaper dated 15th May 1957 an excellent anonymous first hand report of the first (of three) Grapple Bomb experiment over Malden Island 400 miles south of Christmas Island. I later wondered if there was much contamination about Malden as a consequence of the tests. Of course I (we) would never know, anyway?

Front page, *News Of The World*, May 19th, 1957; after the 1st Grapple Test on Malden Island on May 15th; and, with Australian Maralinga Nuclear Tests in progress, (cover supplied via The Sunday Times, 10/07/2011). I was still a resident sapper at that time.

I found investigative journalist John Pilger's written works *very* helpful. In *Heroes* (1986) he recalled the infamous *News Of The World* headline above, from May 19th 1957, *Tests Will Harm No One. Churchill's War-Time Adviser Condemns 'Scaremongers'*.

And, other British newspapers agreed with the NoW, the *Daily Express'* Chapman Pincher one such critic. The *Daily Graphic* published an open letter to Dr. William Penney, physicist in charge of the tests for Great Britain and Australia in the 1950s – praising the test results.

The scientific advisor to Churchill was Frederick Lindemann (Viscount, Lord Cherwell). At this time, in 1957, top secrecy prevailed: In fact, Penney himself had already objected to the continuation of the H-bomb tests for Grapple and Australia. He later identified with the similar fate of the American scientist Oppenheimer – who, too, developed an aversion , as had Einstein, Russell, et al – expressing considerable fears, resulting for the continuing advocacy of the USA and Britain, bigger and bigger atomic bombs, especially competition for higher thermonuclear yields, and subsequent inevitability of increased global fallout, cancers, etc. (*Churchill's Bomb. A Hidden History of Science, War and Politics,* by Graham Farmelo. UK. 2013).

In retrospect, at the outset of the A bomb 40s and 50s race between East and West, there was a real belief that a Nuclear War was imminent – at that time; and, of course, a cold war, before thermonuclear stockpiles of H-bombs, and nuclear headed rocket drones: *Blue Streak*, at Woomera in Australia.

But, Penney was consulted and, in future, would be overruled by Churchill (so advised), who wanted Britain to remain independent as a nuclear club member – regardless of the now critic (Penney) who witnessed so many of the awesome WMD (weapons of mass destruction), and deemed MAD, mutually assured destruction, atomic tests. Tests that would harm no one...? No winner is possible from atomic tests, everybody loses. Crazy.

I remain unsure (of course) now; did *any* of those leading politicians, including Churchill and the US presidents, *ever* witness close quarters nuclear test bomb explosions? Penney witnessed many of them, and later was convinced that to continue stockpiling them was 'madness'.

In London, large street demonstrations took place outside the British Embassy, on May 16th–17th 1957, in protest against the nuclear tests at Christmas Island: some 10,000 students were dispersed by the police, trying to break into the embassy compound. (*Keesing's Contemporary Archives* May 11th-18th 1957: page 15440). The protests of many were, as ever, ignored. Ten years on, similar protests outside the US Embassy, over Vietnam, were favourably received by the public. But, *no way* did the British government express any concern over the military and civilians involved in the oxymoron, Cold War years.

Fissionline

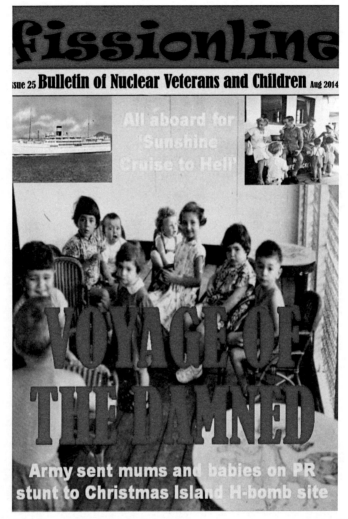

Fissionline, Issue 25. Bulletin of Nuclear Veterans and Children. August 2014. Editor, Alan Rimmer.

The troop transport, *TT Dunera*, left Southampton on New Years Eve 1957 with some 1000 troops; which clearly must have been much larger than our grubby *Charlton Star* in mid-1956, with under 500 army personnel.

The Dunera also collected 31 wives and 33 children to meet their respective husbands (of 25 Regiment, and other personnel due to return to Blighty). The Dunera arrived at Port London on Christmas Island on 1st February 1958, and after my 13 months residence, only five months since departure with the 28 FER. Dunera then returned home with servicemen, and the delighted contingent of women and children... on holiday.

Now, only weeks before their arrival, the first nuclear bomb of the Operation Grapple X test (with a yield of 1800 kilotons – Hiroshima was about 12 kilotons!) exploded only 30 miles south of Port London (less distance, still, from the airfield, and our main campsite).

The holiday 'excursion' of the wives and children, in retrospect, was a wrongful propaganda exercise – to ensure the USA and the World that only clean bombs (?) were to be exploded on and off the island base. And, any after-effects of radiation, etc., were negligible, which, in itself, seemed madness. The Windscale fire in Cumbria had only recently erupted, and abroad, in the USA – Rocky Flats, and in the USSR, more disasters were all hushed up in seven-plus veils of secrecy.

Missing... and Found

A friend sent me this cutting, featuring one of the Daily Mail's *Missing... and Found* media searches; of Grapple Tests in 1958 (exact date unspecified), resident Sappers on Christmas Island (Source: *Daily Mail* Saturday March 22, 2014):

THE DAILY MAIL offers readers a unique opportunity to re-establish contact with long-lost relatives and friends. Each week, MONICA PORTER features the story of someone trying to find a missing loved one, as well as a tale of people reunited. This column is produced in conjunction with the voluntary tracing service, Searching For A Memory, run by Gill and John Whitley.

AT 79, Tynesider Ron Taylor is running out of time to find and be reunited with his Royal Engineer mates.

During Britain's detonation of five H-bombs off the Pacific atoll of Christmas Island in 1958, he and fellow sappers sat facing away from the 'horrendous explosions', the heels of their hands pressed into their eye sockets to prevent blindness from the laser-like flashes and searing heat.

He writes: 'As one of many young National Servicemen at the sharp end of the H-Bomb tests, I enjoyed a close camaraderie with the others sharing this stressful experience.

'It would be tremendous were Alan Clack (then a West Ham supporter), Ray Bromwich, Tommy Sands from Buckie in Scotland and Derek Brown — left to right in the picture with yours truly in the middle — to hear of my quest and get in touch after all these years.

'If good mates Sergeant Stray, Ginger Dillon and Gerry Woods (a Taff from Bridgend) were also to learn of my search, it would be even better.

'Of course, it wasn't all doom and gloom on the Rock, as we called the barren outcrop of Christmas Island.

'One June, Sgt Stray, Alan Clack and I flew 1,200 miles north to lush Hawaii on seven glorious days of leave, when even the Sarge, for once, let his hair down and forgot that he was messing with lowly sappers!'

H-bomb veterans (l-r): Alan Clack, Ray Bromwich, Ron Taylor, Tommy Sands and Derek Brown

No way, back in 1956-57, when I was on the Island, could an 'unaccompanied' trio of squaddies have visited Hawaii on a seven day's leave. Good for them... well deserved.

Duke's visit 1959

I have a pleasant memory, as a seventeen year old Central Press messenger, of accompanying a duty photographer (my press pass still survives) to the Thames as the new Queen and consort on return from one of their many world cruises (as our leading national citizens): seeing their arrivals, back in 1954. Unknown to me, just a few eventful years on, in 1959, the Duke of Edinburgh, on one of these ongoing world cruises, stopped and visited Christmas Island, arriving at the pier I had left only two years before: it was an *interval* during the British nuclear tests, the royal yacht, *Britannia*, anchored not far off the coral reefs corralling the island shore, but the Duke not sleeping on the island, but returning to his royal yacht.

National Geographic Magazine, (Vol. 35, 1962, pp 181-189) published an illustrated article by Sir John Gutch, KCMG, OBE (high commissioner for the Western Pacific, 1955-60). On occasion of his royal highness, the Duke of Edinburgh, to Christmas Island and the Gilbert and Ellice Line Islands (later renamed Kiribati). The duke was himself a serving naval officer and no doubt enjoyed the stop off from 25th March to 5th April 1959. Amazing... the British tests on the island were from 1956 to 1958, and resumed with the Yanks in 1962, as the Dominic series. I left in 1957 – as these memoirs record. The Duke and his party were not permitted to drink any water on the island (only from Britannia): it is not recorded what foodstuffs he enjoyed; but, no doubt top precautions were made during his visit to the British colony.

It had only been months before – in 1958 – that Britain exploded a huge series of (Grapple) H-bombs thirty miles or so south of Port London, where the duke landed; he was subsequently escorted, in a restricted area, in a military Land Rover. Radiation? Whilst clearly the authorities were aware of fallout, and that radioactive matter from the 1957-1958 detonations were still about the island and its waters they chose, rightly, to protect the royal party: *Not* so for all the indigenous villagers and forces personnel who lived and were settled on the island – and at risk, from the residue of the fallouts aggregate radiation.

The Duke of Edinburgh arriving on Christmas Island. (Photo by Sir John Gutch, 1959. See references in *Colonial Servant* by Sir John Gutch, Chapters 40, 41, 44. *Prince Philip's Visit,* and *Gilberts Again and South Pacific Commission.* Private Publication 1987.)

Sappers – Christmas Island

After we of 28 Field Engineer Regiment, who had arrived in mid 1956, left in 1957; we, being 'squaddies' of 55 Squadron – our Korean vets; 12 Squadron (known as HQ), 71 Transport Squadron and 64 Field Park (stores troop) Squadron; and 51 Port Squadron – I served time with 71 and 64.

From late 1957 till 1958 we were replaced by 25 Reg, 37 Squadron, 51 Squadron, 59 Airfield Construction Squadron, and 73 Squadron, who experienced the first Christmas Island Grapple X tests.

From early 1958, 38 Corps Engineer Regiment took over, with 63 Squadron, 48 Squadron, 51 Squadron, 73 Field Squadron. Looking back, I wondered if the 'core' of 51 was the same Port detachment of 1956-57? They would witness the Grapple Y.

In 1958 to 1959, 36 Regiment replaced the 38th – with 24 Squadron, 46 Squadron, 61 Squadron, 73 Squadron and 17 Field Squadron. It appears that, from 1959 to 1960, 73 Squadron, 17 (ind) Field Squadron served from 1961-1964, known dates of explosions correlating with these dates. When the Yanks took over, the UK supplied 'detachments' to work with the US forces and chosen civilian workforce, in the 1962, Dominic Tests.

In retrospect, I have little personal knowledge of most of the atomic tests, or later work by Royal Engineers. And, inevitably, no formal written data on their personnel. There are, of course, published tables of 'results' of the estimated technical 'yields' of the atomic bomb tests, on and about the island. The work is still shrouded in secrecy... and propaganda.

The Bomb

Chapter Four - The Bomb

The Grapple 'Y' Bomb test.

' A   B.B.C. cameraman once told me that he found it really difficult to film atomic veterans   because the film didn't pick up our eyes properly and the final shot also showed a strange redness on the skin of the person who was being interviewed. He said it was probably something to do with the radiation inside us ...' [1]

Home, 1957

I was back in England, on a bigger island than Oahu, or Christmas Island – but, still, home. The climate was wet, cold and a little less foggy than the toxic sulphurous smog about, before I left Blighty; in contrast with the tropical heat of the South Pacific that I had become familiar with as a squaddie, these past fourteen months – since we sailed away on the shabby *Charlton Star*, from Southampton, Hampshire.

The loud, constant, noisy rustle and bustle of London, in great contrast to the relative silence experienced on the coral island in the mid Pacific: at this time (and for some years) I did not know of the potential toxic clime and the loud, loud big bangs of further nuclear tests, and of the fallout (or not) of the much bigger American nuclear tests. I'd thought that they'd ceased with Hiroshima and Nagasaki, of WW2, and the USA now tested in the pacific, and in the South West America Nevada Desert, and hills. Of course – well, they were 'only' similar military tests as our Grapple tests? They, too, were but extensions, of the 1945 world war – no more (or less) than that. A pejorative cold war, to my naïve twenty years meant, really, little political change – all my life I had only known blitz, aftermath of one conflict after another.

Home Station, 1958

After dis-embarkation home leave, and receipt of some £50 or so, paid in large white £5 notes (the only time I ever owned these fiscal sheets of paper), and briefly placed in the RE's HQ, Chatham barracks, awaiting a new posting (dealing with a nasty bout of Asian influenza). I received my last posting, from January 1958, to another test site, albeit minute, permanent staff; (thankfully, not a nuclear test site).

It was an experimental new bridging and ferry equipment site, used for United Nations demonstrations, located at Upnor Hard on the banks of the River Medway and sited across the water from Chatham naval dockyard. I was posted once again as a storeman tech, this time, not for POL, but in charge of substantial bailey bridge, and LAFB (Light Assault Floating Bridge), materials and ferry making with Rolls Royce engines (one to a corner – bit like the flying bedstead I witnessed in the Farnborough Air Show of 1954).

And, soon, I could tell you, identify every part of a 400ft plus Bailey Bridge, and LAFB and ferry parts. The bridge stores were adjacent to the Medway, on one side of a large pond/lake, and we were next to the other lake side. Our motor tug boats, et al, were kept in another large shed, on the concrete hard, Medway bank.

Windscale

Windscale, now Sellafield, in Cumbria. Built 18th December 1945.

After disembarkation, we heard of a nuclear power station called Windscale in Cumbria, producing plutonium – for the making of atomic bombs. There was a fire, and leak of radiation, and fallout. Nine days after our return, October 8th, the Windscale nuclear plant, a top secret accident, was very much, much more dangerous than reported, and Prime Minister Harold McMillan refused to admit the seriousness of the event, and held it top secret, so the Americas would accept Great Britain was still a nuclear partner. Physicist Dr. Penney's alarming report on 10th October remained top secret for over fifty years. But after Grapple, also *top secret*, it seemed a minute hazard to me, and I settled down for the rest of my time – till demob in December 1958; (no way, my CO attempted to get me to sign on, and offered some promotion, which I thought of as some con; and insisted I was out of full time soldiering). In America and across Europe, the media reflected a possible nuclear war with Russia, till recently a major ally during WW2 – and, there was a substantial British civilian movement, demonstrating its aversion to the American and European nuclear tests – bigger, bigger – bugger off... bangs...

Of the Windscale conflagration on October 8th, 1957, the event passed me by. But, on the 15th October, the *Daily Telegraph* p.1 (and other media) reported a much 'watered down' version of the disaster in Cumberland, Lake District:

ATOM MILK BAN ON 150 FARMS
200 SQUARE MILES NOW AFFECTED
SLOW DECLINE IN RADIOACTIVITY
SUPPLIES TO BE POURED DOWN DRAIN

By Anthony Smith, Daily Telegraph Science Correspondent.

The much muted report (top secret) was accompanied by a picture of the toxic milk churns being emptied, poured away into the Irish Sea.

Upnor Hard

On February 27th, 1958, I celebrated my 21st birthday, on guard duty at Upnor Hard, near Chatham in Kent. It was a good day; our NCO in charge allowed me to go up the road to the local pub, with my mates, and (oh!) with the rifle – of course, there was no ammunition, at all, on our outposted site.

The day also registered exit from childhood – still, taking pictures with my small Agfa Isolette – always on Ilford film, black and white, only.

The recent end of World War 2, and the Korean campaign, and so secret happenings of the atomic tests – since 1945; Hiroshima, Nagasaki, by America, Russia and Great Britain. Photographic film records, especially in colour, already hid from the general public growing effects of what became later known as 'the Downwinders' and the American, Atomic Energy Commission (AEC) military regime, with its official 'Cold War warriors', condoning human casualties on its own home turf (what a terrible reality).

As resident Upnor RE Staff, we lower squaddies had no cook for two days, two dinners per week. For those two days, we took it in turns to cook our own midday meals. My turn. Midweek. Morning tea break. *'What do you want?'* I asked amiably of my mates. *'Oh, erm! We thought bangers and mash. Ok?'* *'Sure'*, I glibly replied, *'No problem.'*

A couple of hours later, they returned for another cuppa, close to dinner time. *'Erm! Sorry...'* They looked across to me, through the kitchen hatch. *'I'm having a little problem... delay.'* Concerned. *'What?'* they replied. *'It's the spuds'*, I said. *'They're taking a long time to cook.'* (I'd peeled enough of them in my time.) *'I peeled them, but...'* Even as I spoke, a loud echoing, crackling noise came from the small kitchen behind me. I didn't know you are advised to *prick* the uncooked sausages, first... Bang, bang – Pop!

I had to join in with their good natured laughter, at my ignorance. And added, *'I did try to mash the spuds up* before *cooking them...'* Behind, the loud sausage bangs were *not* secret atomic nuclear mushrooms, though the incident was loud enough. We all guffawed, as I was put right what to do. I well recall that 1958 memory, and cherish their passing comradeship!

There was an added bonus. I suppose, at 21 years, I would, in the future, be allowed to vote. In the HM Forces, we were discouraged from voting at the polls.

1958. Upnor Hard, near Chatham, Kent. A small detachment of Royal Engineers permanent staff. I am back row, centre. (Colleagues were National Servicemen, most men qualified Thames lightermen/watermen, and occasional old soldiers nearing retirement.) Evenings and weekends (when not on weekend leave) in very spartan accommodation. Each evening. I recall a TV series, *The Army Game*, and TV news with Cliff Michelmore... And, many bottles of beer – and laughs.

1958 pictures, of a UK military demonstration, for United Nations, at Upnor Hard, Kent. Pictures show public stand; sapper bridges; and an experimental ferry, can be seen, as well as a three-masted old ship, used for naval cadets, on a bend of the River Medway, in the background. This was *not*, at all, toxic H bomb tests. (Source, pics by author...)

CND

A legal, democratic body of peacemakers, marching against nuclear bomb and weapon testing. The pressure group, from all walks of life, formed after a meeting in London, in February 1958. The protest movement called the CND, an acronym for Campaign for Nuclear Disarmament – and began to gather many sympathisers, eventually to go global – its icon banner, its flag to lead the first, of many years ahead, marches against the AWRE (near Newbury), and other nuclear establishments.

Left: Danger, Radiation! **Middle**: Toxic. **Right**: Example of a CND lapel badge.

LEFT: Early 1958 CND pics, of public protesters on the march for peace: An early rally, one of many to be such demonstrations, often meeting at Trafalgar Square, and marching on to the AWRE Aldermaston site – or other nuclear sites. (Source. Press Association Images. PA/PA Archive / Press Association Images. Used in Daily Mail.) **RIGHT:** A section of an Aldermaston CND led march, passing under the M4 Motorway, at Coinbrook, Middlesex. (Source. Press Association Images. PA/PA Archive / Press Association Images.)

Bomb

"Well, Billy's dad works for the Ministry of Defence."

Left: From *The Bumper Cartoon Book*; Over 3,000 cartoons from the Daily Mirror, p.331. Scientists... (Pictures from the 1960s. Published by Wolfe Publishing Ltd., Daily Mirror Newspapers Ltd., 1970. Lampoons and cartoons – like Daily Express Giles – cartoonists display day to day happenings... including gallows humour. **Right**: Grapple Y, the mushroom cloud, April 28th, 1958... (Source: nuclearweaponarchive.org)

Operation Grapple Timeline

		Minimum Yield (kilotons)			Type of Blast
Grapple 1	Short Granite	300	15/05/57	Malden Island	Air Burst
Grapple 2	Orange Herald	720	31/05/57	Malden Island	Air Burst
Grapple 3	Purple Granite	200	19/06/57	Malden Island	Air Burst
Grapple X	Round C	1,800	08/11/57	Christmas Island	Air Burst
Grapple Y	Yankee	3,000	28/04/58	Christmas Island	Air Burst
Grapple Z (1)	Pendant	24	22/08/58	Christmas Island	Balloons*
Grapple Z (2)	Flagpole	1,000	02/09/58	Christmas Island	Air Burst
Grapple Z (3)	Halliard 1	800	11/09/58	Christmas Island	Air Burst
Grapple Z (4)	Burgee	25	23/09/58	Christmas Island	Air Burst

NOTES: * The device was carried to its detonation altitude by Barrage Balloons. To put the yield figures into some perspective, the bomb at Hiroshima was 12 (not 20) kilotons, and Nagasaki 21 kilotons... One kiloton is one thousand tons of TNT. A megaton is one million tons. 400 or more kilotons referred to as megaton range. All A and H bombs produced toxic fallout... Nagasaki a Uranium bomb. Hiroshima a Plutonium (from Uranium) bomb...

Cassandra

I left Christmas Island on August 25th 1957 by troopship, the T.S. *Empire Clyde*, after being stationed on the island since 1956 – thirteen months.

I knew of three local *'Operation Grapple'* bombs, which had been exploded on Malden Island – south of us on Christmas Island. On the ship *HMS Alert* , stationed but 35 miles from the dire explosions, an English media press representative, William Neil Connor (aka Cassandra), of the *Daily Mirror*, one of the few press witnesses to this awesome event. I had been a regular reader of this eminent gentleman, an excellent investigative journalist.

Unlike island-based squaddies, Cassandra was kitted out with white protective clothing, with hood and goggles. He produced a few photographs depicting their *HMS Alert* observations. His graphic description from the Alert included:

> *'A thin, snake-like stem appeared at its base, as steam and water were sucked up from the sea below! The horrible pudding in the sky became a diseased cauliflower, and then changed into the familiar mushroom.'*

Cassandra (like colleague James Cameron before him, in 1946 and 1953) was informed by one of the on board scientific directors of this operation, Mr WJ Cook, a member of the British AWRE Team, back at Aldermaston (one of the *HMS Alert* commentators for the VIP media representatives). Cassandra included in his report:

> *'Mr WJ Cook – the brilliant scientific director, who is not only the stage manager and producer, but also the part author, of this grim and terrifying performance – was at lengths to emphasise the safety of the nuclear device from the point of view of 'fallout'...'*

And, with Cassandra's integrity, and journalist skill, added that Mr Cook *insisted* nuclear tests in the Pacific, Australia, Japan and USA, were unlikely to cause *'any after-effects from this, as it seemed,* hygienic *weapon.'* What?![2]

Grapple Y

On January 31st, 1896, shortly after the Victorian 1880s birthdays of my maternal grandparents; a meeting of scientists took place at the Chemical and Physical Society of University College, London: Their meeting demonstrated a series of experiments on *The New Photography*, discovered by Professor Rontgen in 1895. The photographic impressions were otherwise unseen by the naked eye; and demonstrated pictures which recorded internal images of bone injuries, helpful to a surgeon in a war hospital. This was the unique discovery of X-Ray photography.

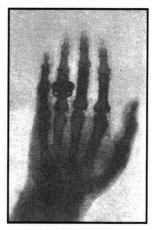

Early Xray (n.d.) *Daily Telegraph Centenary Supplement*. 1855-1955. January 1955 p.30

Attending the Grapple Y atomic weapon test on Christmas Island, on April 28th 1958, Sapper Ken McGinley, of the Royal Engineers, sat down on the Port London beach, and witnessed a three megaton atomic bomb detonation, only thirty miles or so to the south of him and his colleagues. A number of the witnesses, mostly boffins, were issued with dosimeters to record the discharged Roentgen rays – but not the lower ranks, and squaddies...

> "'Cover your eyes!' *bawled the voice, from the loudspeakers*",
> Ken recalled. *"There was a moment's pause, then it happened."*
> *"I had my fists shoved into my eyes and my back to the area*
> *where the bomb was going off. At that moment of detonation,*
> *there was a flash. At that instant, I was able to see straight*

through my hands. I could see the veins. I could see the
blood. I could see all the skin tissue. I could see the bones
and, worst of all, I could see the flash itself. It was like
looking into a white-hot diamond, a second sun. Then the
heat came... " (*No Risk Involved,* 1991)

And, Ken's back was turned *away* from the detonation flash... The landscape of the whole island behind him, and to his south, was flat, like a billiard table. No hills, no close trees in proximity, so the 'brute force' of the burst, followed by the wind force and advancing sight of the overhead fireball was, twenty seconds or so after the detonation, uninterrupted...

Another witness of that same event recalled:

"I think we had sunglasses on, you know, dark glasses. We
had to cover our hands over our eyes. We were backs to the
blast. And, you could actually see through your hands. You
could actually see, y'know, bones and everything."(*Just Testing.*
Derek Robinson. Tiplady. 1985. p55)

Ken's experience was of the *Grapple Y* test on Christmas Island, which yielded an immense 3.4 megatons – greatly underestimated by its advocate, Sir William Penney.

Less than one year before, the first British Grapple test was sited eight miles over Malden Island, about four hundred miles south of Port London on Christmas Island. On board the flat aircraft carrier *HMS Warrior*, monitoring the test, was a team of military and civilian personnel. The estimated yield of that first bomb was about 24 kilotons only (still, more than Nagasaki); the weapon exploded as a high burst, over the ocean adjacent to Malden Island itself, with full military preparations...

Just before that first Grapple test, all the hardware used by the Sappers in its construction work was buried – along with their personal belongings; this action a *precaution* against the expected blast and heat. One of five sappers who had worked on the island, Spr Gillman, was picked up by helicopter and returned to HMS Warrior to witness the event – and, to be sure no human was left on the island at the time of the due detonation.

On later interview, he recalled being on the top flight deck of the ship – and quite vulnerable. At countdown, Gillman recalled:

*"sitting there with our backs to the blast... hands over the
goggles. And, like everybody says, fair enough, you could
see the bone structure in the hands...!"*(Robinson. 1985 p.41-42)

Many witnesses to the detonation' *nanosecond* flash, and the heat aftermath,
are recorded (though, for many years, these records remained top secret).
Accounts of participants in the Hiroshima and Nagasaki explosions: the flash,
then *delay* of seconds followed by the noise, burst *after* that precise explosion,
and conflagration with the fireball, and over one hundred mile per hour blast
wind.

Existential flash in nanoseconds preceded the mushroom. Many, many
witnesses able to remember – in detail – and after photographic evidence.
Observers – participants – of the USA Operation Crossroads tests in 1946;
(and a plethora of USA Bikini and Marshall Islands atomic tests), as well as
the British (in Australia and New Zealand, participants in Monte Bello, Emu
and Maralinga tower bursts) who could differentiate between flash and
mushroom, fallout etc. The witnesses who experienced the explosion flash
itself would suffer from split second *over exposure* to the X-rays caused by
the atomic bombs. The USA experienced thousands of wilfully exposed troops
and civilians – exposed to the flash itself – let alone the horrors of the Bursts
and Fallout results. Many more of these 'guinea pigs' were exposed from 1951
onwards, in the Nevada Desert of the USA. (*Countdown Zero,* Saffer and Kelly. 1982:
Killing Our Own. Wasserman and Solomon. 1982. et al.) And who gazes into the sun directly?

Wasserman and Solomon, in their classic exposure of the betrayed USA
citizens, devoted a whole chapter on *X-Rays and the Radioactive Workplace*.
(Ibid. Part II. p.125-165)

In Alan Rimmer's excellent investigative work, *Between Heaven and Hell*
(2012), he interviewed hundreds of witness accounts of the Christmas Island
tests, especially the neglected, but now infamous, Operation Grapple Y test,
on April 28th 1958 – of which Ken McGinley presented considerable evidence
(though, unbelievably, the UK government continues to deny it).

Rimmer refers to an informed report by Captain C.D. Bridges, of the
Royal Army Medical Corps (R.A.M.C.); how so called 'volunteers' were used
– abused – as guinea pigs, during the Australian bomb tests. On at least one
test, the men were exposed, *deliberate blinding*, to discover the '*visual*

incapacity in human beings following exposure to a nuclear explosion'. Bridges reported that (as evidence) rabbits could be blinded by a nuclear explosion of forty two miles away: and that their *'scientists had calculated the human beings would receive burns to their eyes following exposure to a nuclear explosion'*. Bridges then supplies case histories to prove his case...*(Between Heaven and Hell*, Rimmer. 2012.) Christmas Island (Kiribati) is only thirty five miles in length, end-to-end.

There are numerous records of animals, especially birds, in their hundreds, blinded and killed by the flash or the burst of the experimental bombs. Records are replete of these findings: Monte Bello, Marshall Islands, Emu and Maralinga, Nevada Tests and, as Ken reminded me, especially noticeable in the aftermath of the Grapple Y test on April 28th 1958. Ken recalls one of his tasks was to collect the dead birds, as debris after the explosions. I recalled one year before, taking many pictures of the flocks of birds about the island.

Grapple Y was the fifth of nine tests, and biggest of the British H-bomb tests held in 1956-58 on Malden and Christmas Island coral atoll: and certainly in retrospect the most deadly. I recall the norm tropic weather patterns from my thirteen months on the Island, 1956-57, before Grapple Y: the tropical rain was mostly in brief but very heavy showers and deluges, plus quite brief, before the heat of the sun reappeared; the ground soon drying out under the sun's heavy rays. We squaddies regularly watched the Met boffins release their daily orange balloons, to gauge the direction of the winds at any time. We were informed (where so) by mouth, and in writing reports, that the prevailing winds, in the upper atmosphere where the bombs would be exploded, were always easterly (crosswinds were never considered) directed and, ultra safe to our population, from the H-bomb test explosions and, their potential radioactive fallout, cloud formations. So, what went wrong then?

Notes on the Bomb

From a teenager, until retirement in 2000, my personal knowledge of the past, and the plethora, enormity of events, during the Cold War bomb tests, remained fragmentary. Knowledge began to increase as I learnt how fortunate I had been during this period of time. And the soon to be birth of my grandchildren: a relief and a blessing. Ken McGinley's accounts (and my conversations with

him) of his experience of the Grapple Y Test in April 1958, encouraged me
to explore more of those latter day Cold War years.

One of our senior military British Officers from 1956-1957 until November
1957, and just exploded Grapple X H bomb, was Air Marshal Wilfred Oulton
CB CBE DSO DEC, a truly honourable gentleman, as his records concede.
Oulton was the designated Task Force Commander. British Thermonuclear
Tests 1957 – Pacific.

In Oulton's autobiographical book, *Christmas Island Cracker* (1987), he
relates his experiences, in preparations for and execution of the H-Bomb tests
on Malden Island and Christmas Island, in 1957. His fascinating, matter-of-
fact, good-humoured book discloses the plans and machinations of the
detonations up to and concluding at Grapple X on November 8th 1957, when
a 1.8 megaton bomb was dropped in an 'Airburst Freefall', given as approximately
2.5 kilometers (1.6 miles), and exploded zero site, off a south east point of
the coral island. It was estimated as 'officially' exploded 2,350 metres height,
the figures given to him for his book by a W.N. Saxby and Director of the
Atomic Weapons Research Establishment (A.W.R.E.) at Aldermaston, in 1987;
thirty years later.

It was a record of the then, explosions of the A and H bombs, during his
tenure. No way could it begin to disclose the results of those tests, in any
graphic detail. Such data was, rightly, not his concern – his job was delivering,
the Vulcan (et al.) RAF team's droppings.

Oulton's duty was concluded with Grapple X: the Grapple series continuing
under Sir William Penney, physicist i/c; and his masters, the politicians, back
in London, England. But, the *Table 1: UK Overseas Atmospheric Nuclear
Weapons Tests 1952-1958: and Table E1 (A) UK Atmospheric Nuclear Weapons
test in Australia, October 1952 - October 1957*: was supplied for publication
of Oulton's book by the AWRE.

The formal data supplied by AWRE (in 1987) for Oulton's *Postscript*,
also included information on *Grapple Y Christmas Island* and *Grapple Z
Christmas Island*; being the last British 'only' H-bomb atomic bomb tests. Of
vital importance there is, was, no information of any of the tests aftermaths:
only that they were all successful in preparations and execution of the
detonations.

According to Glen Stewart, an RAF pilot witness to the Y test explosion,
given in early evidence to Professor Rothblat's inquest of the event; the 3
megaton bomb had exploded at only 800 or so feet (not 8000, as the government

insisted). The detonation would have been only a quarter of a mile from the south east of the coral island. In retrospect (and much checking) the actual detonation of the bomb had been considerably lower than previously predicted and reported. If so, then the explosion's fireball must have been close to the beach, more like ground zero: a very dirty bomb with the evaporated fabric of the bomb, coral, in water – and off the beach: a very dirty detonation and a quarter of a mile (0.4225km) from the south east of Christmas Island. If so, with the beach and tide a consideration, I'd say it rated a ground zero rating. It was about thirty miles south of the Main Camp, and thirty five miles from the Port London beach, where Ken and his colleagues were sat down on the coral sand beach. If one considers this as fact then it would have been only twenty five miles from the Cassidy Airport – from which the bomb had been despatched: again, three megatons of an H bomb?

After Ken and his colleagues had been blown over by the seconds after blast, even as they began moving away back to their tasks (Ken to his bulldozer); about ten minutes later a friend of Ken's, Ken Taylor, recalled ten minutes or so later observing a:

> *"...very thick black cloud approaching inland from the sea. It was as black as pitch. The cloud came over part of the island then retreated out to sea again. By that time, we had all been showered in rain which was as big as 'ten pence pieces...'"*

It was clearly evaporated matter, rainfall, from the mushroom – the black rain – blown across (like a squall); a direct assault by the Fallout of the Y test blast, of the bomb's explosion. There were of course, then, numerous witnesses, participants of this proven awesome phenomena... a disaster.

With an incredible understatement they recalled, *"it was clear that something had gone far wrong..."*

Truth

Dr. Johnson had lived, in the 18th century, in Gough Square, Fleet Street –
close by my old place of work, Central Press Photos, in the 1950s. He wrote:

> *"Among the calamities of war, may be justly numbered the*
> *diminution of the love of truth, by the falsehoods which*
> *interest dictates, and credulity encourages."* (Johnson, Dr Samuel
> (1709-1784). The Idler 1758-1760, Vol.1 p.169. See 1797 edn. - War p.281)

I felt George Orwell would certainly concur, in his classic, *1984*.

You didn't need to be a physicist – or physician, to experience Grapple H
bomb tests. But, in Establishment 'politics', whatever background, fiscal
investments, shortcuts – in retrospect, that old war truism: *"First casualty of
the Cold War is truth"*. *Truth* during Cold War activities might become
redundant – or suspect, surreal in Orwellian terms. Anything and everything,
participants and civilians, may be expected to deny awesome real experiences
– NOT viable, not to be measured, recorded in official published statistics.
Anecdotal evidence, witnesses might not be acceptable – except as breaking
current top secret acts...

These past happenings, questions, became obvious. Where is the precise
site, location of the detonations? The identity and type of nuclear bombs being
used in the military experiments – estimated yields – and individual components?
And, intended geographical areas anticipated to be affected by the intrusions?
And at what 'height' from the below ground zero was the telemetric release
of the intended detonations?

Most crucial to be anticipated, the then crucial meteorological weather
pattern, clouds, winds – upper and lower directions – and strengths: where
and when the blasts, and winds blew... its fallout. And, important, the ecological
environment, the explosions would be detonated on – to be fragmented,
vaporised, and sucked up in the inevitable rising mushroom clouds. Was it
over terra firma, rock and earthworks, on towers, or low-burst bombs over
desert sands; at sea over oceans, or measured shallow lagoons – not oceanic
depths; and, water, rivers, any exposed water courses and aquatic reservoirs
for drinking purposes.

Most important, the place and inhabited area: sparse population, or exposing dense occupants in towns and cities. Military viewed collateral, to use the dreadful realities. And, *who* actually decides the validity of any population for extinction (man, beast or vegetation). Most vital – nuclear tests were supposed to be scientific – their laboratory and equipment, NOT perhaps the reality where empirical gauges – and sterile statistics betray human involvement – deliberately or accidentally. All the foregoing had been scientifically investigated by the USA, since 1945 – but human equations remained, too, top secret.

The *Empire Clyde* left Christmas Island on Saturday August 25th, 1957 and, five weeks later, arrived at Liverpool on Sunday September 29th, 1957. On departure we believed that the recent British tests at Malden were the last H-bomb tests to be exploded: But, not so; the last bomb we knew of was fired on June 19th 1957 over Malden Island – the third bomb test known to us squaddies – known as Grapple 3, coded Purple Granite, with a detonation estimated at 200 kilotons, considerably less than the Grapple Two, Orange Herald, with 720 kilotons, detonated on the 31st May 1957.

Back home, after success of three Malden Island tests (which left the island itself uninhabitable and likely contaminated for some time), the RAF Commander in charge was informed he had to return to Christmas Island to continue further tests – but over Christmas Island itself (erm! – just off it – he was informed): This was crucial, to impress the Yanks, and gain the largest H-Bomb, more megaton explosions. But, there was little time: and, he was informed, it would save time and money. This next test would be Grapple X, then another afterwards, Grapple Y and , finally, Grapple Z...

Researcher Alan Rimmer and others uncovered considerable data of the Grapple Y test after a number of discovered official documents were released after thirty years. Freedom of Information, and other declassified acts – releasing Top Secret records pertaining to the 1950s tests. But most, it safely removed the gags and threats of the previous Establishment (whatever political persuasion) on Nuclear Veterans and their families; who had suffered deaths or disablement subsequent to Fallout and exposure to the detonations.

What they, the researchers, also discovered was some of the apparent falsification of data on the atomic tests, recorded data – as opposed to genuine missed miscalculations in the scientific predictions of yield, etc. The latter would have been unfortunate (but still admitted, in retrospect) but, after all, they were 'tests' – 'experiments' with nuclear energy detonations.

As above described, the height of the Y test was possibly below 8,000 feet, the intended telemetric zero point of explosion. Due to a faulty mechanism, it misfired, and dangerously exploded below the intended air burst prediction. But, *if* so, not only was this fact a disaster – but, more so, the dreadful meteorological predicted winds, which carried contaminants over the island; these errors, facts, denied by the Establishment top secret recordings – for generations.

After the RAF pilot dropped his Grapple Y bomb, he recalled seeing a series of thunderstorms caused by the bomb's detonation blast so high at 46,000 feet. The rain quite clearly (note the oxymoron) heavily contaminated by the radiation. The dubbed 'sniffers' (*Oulton 1987*) were assigned to fly into the mushroom clouds and collect samples for analysis – to be flown back to the AWRE in Britain. Some pilots and crew were subsequently heavily irradiated by the pollution – some soon to die directly from their dreadful missions – or, at least, suffer later cancers, from their invaded DNA body tissues. And, other dire consequences. All supplied fallout data would be included in the top secret findings of the AWRE and politicians... and denial.

Grapple X recorded up to a 1.8 megaton yield – almost twice the hoped for measure by Sir William Penney. Detonation was triggered in a 2250m (7382ft) high air burst. Ground zero, below, gauged for the uninhabited area, the southeast point of the coral island. Though, I believe, I read that a forward thick steel bunker – for observation – was located close enough to that location. Oulton was one of the persons occupying that bunker who, with his staff, immediately then flew off the site after witnessing the bomb; thus not to be affected by subsequent, and inevitable, fallout. The principal fuel of this weapon was high-grade uranium – very expensive – probably flown in from Windscale nuclear power plant in Britain.

And so, fallout would have contained particles of this contaminating element – to settle on the land and sea by the blast, and wind of that time, about the island. The black rain clouds, mist, in the X fallout, was recorded within three to four hours to have dropped *all* over the Main Camp, and airfield constructions – and, of course, personnel. This, most surely, has been so, as

so-called collateral damage resulted in demolished buildings and equipment
– and, erm, blown over personnel.

If the achievement of Grapple X was deemed highly successful at 1.8
megatons, how much more so was Grapple Y, at almost double that detonation.
But, this explosion was, in retrospect, a disaster for the RAF and troops on
the island at that time. I read estimates of 3 to 3.2 megatons yield – an incredible
event. The intended height of the bomb (with an improved devil's cocktail)
was to have been at 8,000ft, 2350metres (1.46 miles) but, due to an unexpected
'delayed fuse' problem was to be well below that target – to the chagrin of
the personnel involved. I read that Sir William Penney and his 'gentlemen',
concerned staff, flew 400 miles off to the safer Malden area before the dire
explosion *(Rimmer, 2012)*. Y's low burst fallout travelled all over the island;
structural damage, at least 30 miles upwards, to the main camp – with its
fallout proving subsequently fatal to many of its participants – but which H.M.
Government denied ever took place – the fallout, that is!

Among the many declassified documents of the Y bomb test, Rimmer
(Fissionline, April 2013, Rimmer) revealed previously secret meteorological
office data. I read an item:

> *"29. Operation Grapple Y, the greatest and only measured*
> *value (of 150 microcuries per square metre) was obtained*
> *at the uninhabited site at Vaskess Bay..."*

Vaskess bay is (was) located close by the South West Point of St. Stanislas
Bay – and nearby, north, the narrow peninsula with Paris, at its end.

St. Stanislas Bay and the Flying Boat landing to the north, and Vaskess
Bay south, with a narrow spit of coral reef in between the waters: little distance
between them – contamination for how long – what... where? No doubt the
top secret, hidden Met records could answer such details. But, of course, it
was enclosed, they said, uninhabited! And the personnel, air, soil and water
would be cleansed – in time. Washed away, and decontaminated. But:

This area was previously in use by the SPAL (South Pacific Air Line)
USA troops and as R and R (Rest and Recreation) for us, its building – and
narrow wooden pier – used by occasional officers and squaddies as official
breaks: I visited this luxury with our two national service officers, and several
other servicemen, in 1956-1957: and photographed our visits – which included

some fishing and swimming. It was a regularly used bay for flying boats – and easy travelling distance from our Main Camp, and Port London Camp... In short, a usual occupied site for relevant troop luxury and, within weeks ahead, to be kept heavily contaminated (with what... uranium, plutonium?) from Grapple Y in 1958.

Demob

And so, I was back home, in North London, demobbed in December 1958 – very little appeared to have been, as yet, rebuilt after the Blitz...

How well I recall that day, mid morning, 6th December 1958. As I left a small rear gate, out of the Chatham Barracks, RE, dressed in cheap civvies. Officially, I had another month's time to serve, but this was owed to me as annual leave. On paper, I would have to serve (ready to be called up if needed) seven years on reserve colours: but, I was now a civilian, aged 21 (and nearing 22).

Before catching my train up to my beloved London and still blitzed plains: I stopped several hundred yards down the adjacent Chatham road, at an almost empty transport, working cafe – and, enjoyed my first 'cuppa char' as a civilian.

Only seven years before, in 1951, I'd experienced final departure from Spurgeon's Orphanage, in Reigate. The emotion of being free (in care, all my young life till that time); discharge from the sappers felt just like that, a marvellous day of release – into a new world I knew very little of... Free!

A small mid-terrace three bed house, and new, now, stepfather from Dublin. No more lodgers. And, it was so very, very small. My grandparents' (even smaller) terrace at 2 Baxter Grove, Islington, in north London – only a walking distance (cycling) – still had glass, gas mantles, and a penny (now shilling) meter, to pay for supply. No indoor toilets at home – or at my grandparents... where my mother, one of eight siblings, had been brought up, in the early 20th century. No longer a need of a toilet in coconut plantations, or woodland.

For many years, I had only experienced large dormitories in the orphanage, and in army life, and the immense spaces of the coral island and huge oceans, travelling abroad. But, to adopt that cliché, our small home was beautiful, in the 1950s of postwar London.

Out of the orphanage, I shared a bedroom with my bro, and would do until I was eighteen, and away in army life. Not until I was twenty one years old would I (albeit briefly) experience a single room to myself, at Dynevor Road, N16. And, my mother's cooking, so good; now, fresh milk, real potatoes (not powdered) and, a wonder, fresh eggs. Rationing was almost over, though shortages abounded in post war Great Britain. And, wages were quite frugal. But, freedom was great!

For a while, I found it difficult to sleep on a mattress, after the canvas bed and coral sand floor of Christmas Island in the 1950s. Flies and mosquitoes were prolific – as on the island – but the sticky, tacky, yellow anti-fly papers still hung down from the low ceilings, in our close knit little house. I had saved money from the Christmas Island NAAFI to purchase our first refrigerator: no more depending on milk, kept in a wood and wire hanging box, or put in a bowl of cold water, as if camping, instead of being in a home, with modern electricity and other conveniences though even, as yet, no bathroom.

Discharged home, to war-damaged North London – homecoming, Christmas and New Year, into 1959 – I went into finding a job. (Ex-National Servicemen were, by law, expected to have their old job back, upon application, but, Central Press Photos apologised, not possible etcetera; much like (I assumed) thousands of other ex-servicemen post WW2, and post war years, now redundant squaddies out of work and finding some army trades were not applicable in the market place). Used to getting up at the crack of dawn, for years, now 21 coming 22 years of age. I walked, or cycled, up to the West End – in search of work. Often up at 4 o'clock each morning – and off. Eventually, I located an Employment Agency up-west, and I was engaged as an Enquiries Clerk for Moss Bros, at Covent Garden. I recall conversations with other to be demobbed servicemen, that it would be a dream to earn £12 per week – in fact, £7 per week was a norm in 1958 (in 1955 it was £4 per week).

Moss Bros

Moss Bros, in 1959, early sixties, presented a whole new way of life – of real Generals, Upper classes, and a whole department under a military (new and second hand) heading. I learnt that very few of these individuals (and I was a query clerk!) appear to ever, wholly, settle their fiscal accounts, with not just many uniforms and accessories, but a very large trade in riding habits and top hat (etc.) on hire, evening dress.

Further, it was a large, very large in those days, department on a number of levels (much as M & S, etc., today – but more so). In the basement was the packing despatch; and then – each upper floor, in charge of a floor walker; with separate ladies (where I found Janet, a blonde, ladies' assistant) and gentlemen's attire, each with their own manager. Upstairs, I was attached to a typing pool – encircled, and in the charge of a retired young naval commander RN: I was one of two to three clerks – outside the corral – and I moved, connected, with all department heads and, Moss bros themselves.

I quickly latched onto becoming an establishment photographer, taking passport photos, attending their sports functions and occasional dances and presentations. In retrospect, when I later on watched a popular television serial called '*Are You Being Served?*' I always thought of the firm (though I believe their scripts were based on other large west end stores). Several of my domestic photographs were published in their journal, '*Bits of Moss*'. I enjoyed a sophisticated way of life, and I made my first trip to France on a Moss Bros outing to Boulogne in 1959, my first, albeit brief, encounter with our cousins in Europe – who happened to speak French.

LEFT: Cover of 'Bits of Moss' magazine. **RIGHT:** One page of a number of my photo contributions. An in-house dance – centre of picture, the young group, included friends of mine – right, centre Barrie had a Vespa, and I, a Lambretta.

But, the shop world was not for me. And I moved on, first leaving to be a dance teacher for Arthur Murray based in Oxford Street, W1, in which I was quite successful, winning a prize or two, and joining occasional acts of cabaret – but, most enjoyable, the Escort duties, in my then evening dress, to numerous night clubs / shows and dinner dos, at West End hotels (often adjacent to debs dos, as held at the Dorchester).

On leaving Arthur Murray, at the end of 1961, I had been offered a post in a USA, Californian Arthur Murray's dance studio. After politely declining the offer, I explained that I had decided to go on a tour to Europe on my own – although it was winter – for a few weeks, mostly hitch-hiking my way from Paris down to Marseilles via Lyons on the Route 7 south highway, and east towards Nice. I had been given a letter of introduction (the custom still existed in the sixties) by my friends and dance students Doc. F. and his wife.

Grand Tour

On my first journey to Paris, France, in 1961, I accepted a lift by an acquaintance, leaving me (at my request) somewhere in Montmartre. I noticed the entire journey, driving from Dover to Paris – the flatlands – miles and miles of farmlands, green fields, and most roads – and villages marked with rows, and rows, of trees.

No way could I, at this point, imagine the rude devastation of the so recent WW2 geography – or; more so, my grandfather and other relatives fighting at the Somme, in muddy, bloody trenches – but it was France, and Europe. I had a little French (and Latin?) from several years of grammar school.

Perhaps, it was a cultural thing; from the outset, I liked the French people – felt related to the Parisians.

But, social reality, after finding digs for several nights at a pension in Montmartre – I did the sights (well, some of them). First was to the top of the Eiffel Tower, and, then down to... what the? The entire area around the bottom of the tower was ringed by uniformed gendarmes, all heavily armed and clearly looking for something or other. It was my brief introduction, as a tourist, to the Algerian war and the OAS.

Afterwards, I enjoyed a walking tour of the arts and architecture of northern Paris.

Colourful, apparently little changed from the war, on appearance: Paris' buildings were spared by the Nazis. I did go to one of the night-time cabarets, risqué, but enjoyable – though, I understood little dialogue or the need to. And a fleeting awareness that my Aussie father had been a vaudeville performer on the stage of 1930s and 1940s; and an aunt an English actress, filmed in 1930, down in Nice.

Early morning, I put my too-full haversack on my back and, after riding to Versailles, began to hitch lifts, down the route N7, south for Lyon. It was cold – and, before long, began to snow. Several, lucky lifts; one a lorry, then a car of tourists en-route to Switzerland.

I soon responded to an urgent need to stop, and have something to eat. It was a road cafe off The River Saône and, in my appalling French, I managed to order, and enjoy, a fantastic six-eggs omelette. But, arriving in Lyons, a large city, and previous centre of Vichy France, I located the local YMCA.

It was, for me, horrible. Food was a dish of sheep entrails (not lamb meat, per se) and, for me, inedible, dormitory bed was fine – but, ugh, the toilets facility! I never could get used to the habit of placing my feet in concrete steps over a hole in the floor; clearly I had been spoilt on Christmas Island and back home in England.

Eventually I arrived, via Marseilles and Nice, but not before exploring a Roman amphitheatre above Lyons, the dire weather allowing me to ramble at ease – alone. After some enquiry, I located the large caravan site in Nice, where my two to-be new friends resided: Dr and Mrs Foster, acknowledging my friendship with Dr and Mrs Franklin, back in London.

I had a small tent, and set it up close to the Fosters' long caravan and, adjacent to another tent, with a family of Italians, who treated me to a glass or two of Vino. The air, though mid winter, was cold – but not damp, as back home – The Med had what they called a mistral wind – cold but dry.

After a sumptuous meal, and a real introduction, they asked if I played bridge. I replied sorry, but I didn't know how, so they proceeded to to try and teach me – a little. I learned that Doc had several practices at home, in London, and he was a homeopath and gynaecologist – which I thought an odd combination at the time. His base his clinic at Walthamstow, a Harley Street practice – and, a station here in Nice.

Quite recently, Doc. Foster had been asked to visit Monte Carlo, and examine Princess Grace (Grace Kelly) as a gynaecologist, but I gained the impression he was probably one of a number on call, to attend the royal charge.

I had no exact plan, or a precise timeline. Very, very naïve (in retrospect), I'd packed an evening dress, shoes to give dancing lessons, socks, etc., a book of poetry given by a student for my travels – she'd offered me (no strings attached) an MG car left in her garage – her father, a major, had recently passed away; I, of course, politely thanked her, and declined the offer. One idea was to proceed east – working my way (how?) ho ho, towards Australia.

I learnt that the idea of travelling by the Burma route was off – and common sense prevailed. Any overland trip was a no no – based on my zero knowledge and small budget.

Doc offered me a means to make some pocket money – to paint the whole of his forty foot caravan chassis. I agreed, somewhat relieved. What then? Exploring the local scene – nearby was Cannes, East, at the end of the Promenade des Anglais, adjacent to the Med beach, was the old town of Nice; and up a nearby hill I surveyed the mountains of the Alps and hill road; eastward at the end of the winding coastal road to Monte Carlo.

I realised this whole area was traditionally a part of the education 'The Grand Tour', of former Victorian gentry, Dickens described it, I recall.

My new friends had an interesting hobby, playing a system at the casino in Nice and down the coast at Monte Carlo. They enrolled me in as a temporary club member for Nice and Monte Carlo casinos, and I learnt a little *trente et quarante*, whilst they enjoyed their investments. But, it was still winter, and my birthday was due on February 27th. Tongue in cheek, Doc suggested with my youth and talent I could easily court one of the many grass widows, ex-military, etc. No way. I'd the full experience of Arthur Murray's recently behind me.

Several weeks had passed and, reluctantly, I realised that I needed to return to London – by train. After a four hour wait outside Paris, I eventually continued, by ferry, home. And unemployed. A very cold winter, in 1962.

I kept in touch with Doc and his wife Pat (who, sadly, had cancer and, shortly afterwards, passed away). Doc Foster offered me a trainee job in his Walthamstow clinic pharmacy, but I wasn't ready yet to settle down.

For several years on, Doc Foster visited me, as I linked up with our two friends in common, Dr Franklin and his wife in London.

A real lesson learnt. No way should I have embarked on such a trip, so unprepared, but the travel bug persisted in my juvenile ambitions.

Nice and Monte Carlo casino membership cards, 1962.

Home County Travel

We met, I recall, about the time I left Arthur Murray's. I had recently broken
with Jackie, a girlfriend, a fellow teacher, and was foot loose and fancy free.
Keith B. and I enjoyed the company of the ladies and, based in Earls Court,
well acquainted with overseas visitors, tourists and students from abroad. We
identified a current need, to form a club – meeting at regular parties at our
digs in Earls Court, held for potential customers, Commonwealth and European
visitors.

Calling ourselves *Home County Travel*, together we purchased a large
secondhand Dormobile van as its transport. And, mostly on weekend trips
down South, and west country on average, about six guests at a time: my bro
joining our group (whilst he still lived at home in Elm Gardens, Mitcham).

Still in vogue in the early Sixties, we charged so many guineas per trip
– including accommodation, at boarding houses. Great fun. No profit, since
the income barely covered the cost of the outings. Keith, slightly older than
me, was also an ex-serviceman, he served in the Australian armed forces (an
ex-medical student) – sometime in New Guinea.

Home County Travel organised, on request, several trips abroad; one
holiday was a two week overland journey to the Costa Brava, in Spain. Keith
and I booked a villa, and soon filled our quota (my bro included). By agreement
I went, by train, in an advance party (of one), provisionally camping in a field
just on the outskirts of town. Slightly bizarre in a way, after checking out the

villa we hired was OK. It was a large, old building, owned by two elderly ladies – both of whom were widows, after the recent Civil War in Spain. Franco was still very much in charge. The large, mostly stark, empty isolated building to the previous existence, occupied by the two widows, had dark hanging pictures with solid frames, of bearded males, and bleak, black lace veiled younger women folk; visibly pleased at our stay – giving life to it for a short while. 1961; the year that the Berlin Wall went up.

From the outset, very little fresh water was available, so Keith and I purchased a largish supply of cheap white wine to clean and rinse our teeth with.

We enjoyed evenings out at a local nightclub (more of an upmarket pub); where, as a recent ex-dance teacher, I enjoyed drinking tequila and lively dancing – latin cha cha and mambo; and especially tango when possible – but, mostly, we jived to the juke box in one corner... on holiday of course...

Over the weekend, we enjoyed the long custom of promenading along the seafront – as in Nice, or English seaside resorts – a clearly Catholic town, with a dour overhanging legacy of war.

The weather was quite warm, and the seafront easy walking distance, the holiday going well. On one day, the girls wanted to visit a bull fight and Keith agreed to take them. I politely declined: perhaps childish, but I had an aversion to killing bulls, whatever their entertainment level.

And, time off, I went climbing, yes, climbing, along the face of a low ridge of hills around the bay. I had a fear of heights and was trying to subdue it. Weeks before, on the visit to Paris, I went to the roof of the Notre Dame Cathedral, and looked down, much like Quasimodo, very aware of my latent fears – and, determined to tackle them.

At the time, here in the Costa Brava, one afternoon at the beach, dressed in my swimming trunks, I crossed the road to a nearby shop, when, horrors, two Spanish policemen blocked my path, brandishing their rifles. Little English (no Spanish on my part) but, clearly, I was not allowed to leave the seafront dressed only in swimming trunks.

It was a huge success, the holiday, and soon Keith and I drove our guests back across Spain – heading for France. But, on impulse, we decided to explore Andorra, on the way back.

It was quite misty on our arrival at the small town on its summit, but the fog became impossible to risk the safety of our troop. We stopped at the top of a hill, just down from Andorra. Stopped, we used the van and camped outside; the sound of running water, like a waterfall, was easily identified. Few of us slept well, cold and damp, but, streuth! on awakening, the mist clearing, we found ourselves perched just on the lip of a waterfall, at the edge of a cliff.

Thanking our lucky stars, we decided to immediately descend the hill, and reach the French border at its bottom. But, we had run out of petrol – and so, on a whim, Keith and I felt it safe to (brakes sound) cruise all the winding way down to the border below; police, French and Spanish, all armed, were on duty at the border. Fortunately, a garage was close by and we stopped, filled up, then had some breakfast. Though, time was short, the rest of the journey was uneventful.

All commonwealth colonial visitors – re-designated Aliens, 1962.

Danger abroad

And, erm, there was a number of (in retrospect) odd contacts – and, journeys contracted for Keith and me. One occasion, we were hired by a West End Russian translator, writer, A.F., living in a flat over a shop, at St. Giles Circus, who had a most interesting book of young au-pairs for hire. Anyways, we agreed to one job, where it meant driving across Europe (this was the Cold War), in our Dormobile, to a book fair: I think it was in Romania, make a delivery of his books – and return – via Hungary, where Keith later recalled horrific evidence of poverty and disabled citizens – and, of course, a cautious military presence. Well, we agreed that he would take our vehicle (I couldn't drive) and I would 'hold the fort' at this end, from my then Mitcham London home. And... I received a night-time telephone call from a certain British Embassy where they were confirming some details – and would I back up his return, etc. How? Why? It appeared, that whilst going through some forest or other he was held up and robbed of the van, etc. - and, eventually, the van was discovered, burnt out; and the bandits (whatever) had been shot, on discovery of the papers & effects of Keith (passport, etc.) Bare details.

Home County Travel - To Russia, with love. 1962

Notting Hill Gate

Later, I left my parents' home, and Keith and I took lodgings at Earls Court; then moved to Notting Hill Gate. We had our respective girl friends, my new lady, Jill, a South African, and Moira, an Irish girl et al. of course – and we enjoyed many a party, and theatre visit to the West End. Keith later married

Audrey, a nursing sister, and soon moved out to New Guinea, and my bro Emil married a South African, together moving out to Cape Town.

I vividly recall one of our evenings at Notting Hill Gate, in October 1962, listening to the radio account of the USA and Russian confrontation and incident, of the 'Bay of Pigs' and a stand-off between Kennedy and Krushchev over Cuba; the discovered rocket sites (aimed at the USA) and moving of ammunition and potential troops... Whoops! It was most dramatic: but, we had long-time followed the antipathies of the WW2 Cold War – and Korea... and... And, we moved on... numerous adventures at home and abroad. But, for many years, I (we) knew nothing of the thirteen days – till Oct. 27th – when nuclear war was just averted...(See Documentary *Kennedy's Nuclear Nightmare*, TV, More4, 1040pm Friday 22 November 2013)

Left to Right: Emil, my bro, Aussie Keith, Jill, a South African, (whose friend Lettie would marry Emil – and move to Cape Town, a way of life foreign to me). I am end right. Home County Travel, 1962.

Exploration

After Keith and Audrey left for New Guinea, I worked for a City commercial firm called International Factors, whose work meant buying up the entire portfolio of various companies – and paying all their debts – getting a regular return for their investments. It was/is the only time I lied to get a job: on application I said I had a number of A levels and didn't, but got the post. In fact, it would be less than a decade before I did obtain those A levels. My bro had married in the city, Dutch Afrikaans church (where only Afrikaans was spoken).

Handing in my notice, I was due to fly out and join Keith and Audrey in New Guinea – funded, potentially, by a travel firm called Micro Tours – on the strength that a *Daily Mirror* contact secured a small contract with me on my arrival. But, Micro Tours went bust, and I was unemployed for a short while. And, meanwhile, I met and married Sara, my first wife (of two) – living in Mitcham, in South London.

Irish

1963, I was courting my first wife, Sara, who was living in Earls Court, and working in St. James. A good catholic, with several young female friends, Irish Catholics, all living in Camden Town.

On one vivid visit to her friend, Moira, recently courted by an RAF war veteran (years older than herself) and, on one night's courtship, since become pregnant: her first sexual experience.

Moira (not her real name) was from Belfast in Northern Ireland. Innocent; and vulnerable. As an unmarried Irish Catholic it was anticipated (by the authorities of the day) that, on delivery, her new born child would be *forcibly* taken, adopted – as being illegitimate. It was a massive Irish crime and stigma. In the 19th century, illegitimate mothers were admitted to houses of correction for their licentious criminalised status – whatever the origins.

Six years before, on the way back from Christmas Island, I recall squaddie sapper Paddy, a veteran of Korea and Atomic tests, leaning over the ships' rail, and telling us mates of his resentment; of his awful, brutal treatment as a child by his strict Catholic school. I remember that experience. And, with my new Irish stepfather and his relatives, all from Dublin, settled in London: I knew absolutely zero about their previous life in Catholic Eire: and developed a strong affection for all those abused victims of such callous child upbringing (as, it had nothing whatever to do with the IRA!).

Now, Sara, my then fiancée, asked me to visit Moira with her, in hospital at Camden Town, to see her newborn. The visit was for me to pretend to be a grateful boy friend, engaged to marry her soon.

I took a large bunch of flowers onto the ward, and made an approach as the beloved father of the newborn, hugging and displaying much delight and emotion. The ward staff reported the visit – and Moira safely returned to

Belfast with her child, with all the inevitable hardship a single parent would experience in the 1950s and 1960s. A good mother.

It was 1964 – now married, Sara became pregnant while we lived in our rented one-bed flat in Mitcham. For sometime I had, on occasion, visited the British Museum library on different enquiries of interest. One was actually quite amusing – I had a passion for WB Yeats, myths, legends and magic tales of yore; I left research slips at the museum desk, for a series of books of a writers' Welsh legends. To my surprise, I had delivered a pile of books – all in Welsh and beyond my capabilities! Lady Gregory, and the Mabinogion.

It was about the time I began a course of journalism. At first, I appeared to be doing quite well until, after submitting a piece for examination I was, albeit politely, informed that no way would everything be accepted by a paper.

In particular, if it did not fit the policy of the magazine, then it was a no no. More so, I was being encouraged to invent, as facts, complete untruths – unaware it was a very common currency with certain writers and publications. Yes, I was that naïve – I believed in only telling the truth – though how had to be considered. Or remain silent – as appropriate.

Worse, when I read one of my submitted pieces in a journal – word for word – well, I was so disgusted I withdrew from the course – would never make a writer. (In fact, I had almost completed a book, for New English Library (NEL) on 'Teach Yourself Sixteen Dances' – encouraged by my Daily Mirror contact. It was shelved, and I never completed the work.)

Early in 1964, I married Sara in Shoreham, West Sussex, and lived in a flat in Mitcham / Streatham, in South London. My bro had married a South African, Lettie, from Cape Town; back in 1962, he'd met her at one of Keith and my Home County Travel club meetings at Earls Court. I was settled working in the Agfacolor Processing labs, in Wimbledon, since my return from Nice in 1962.

In 1964, I spied a newspaper advertisement for anyone interested in 'exploration', world travel, etc., an advert placed by the International Anthropological Exploration Society (I.A.E.S.), director general Mr. S.Z. Ahmed – with numerous travels all over the world, and reports published.

The advert invited interested persons to contact him, at a London address. I applied. And, in a short while, was hooked into the link's possibilities – supported by Mr Ahmed himself, a recent participant in African and Himalayan expeditions.

Mr Ahmed asked members to submit illustrated articles for its quarterly journal, '*Exploration*', and I submitted two pieces, on Christmas Island, and Panama, both articles later published in 1965. The organisation was not in the league of the *National Geographical* magazines and travels, but it did still attract a number of contributors.

I met up with one experienced traveller, not known like the explorer, Wilfred Thesinger, but of equal experience, as I soon learnt. Middle-aged Mr Stanley Kupercyn B.Sc., of Polish origin, was the organisation's current leader of (the) exploration, known as director expedition division. Stan asked me to join in his research and planning for two potential new travels abroad; both expeditions well worth a BBC documentary series. Stan (with Ahmed) planned:

> One, to South America, by the Greyhound Bus route, south from New York, down across Mexico, and Panama – to Peru, Lima – then eastwards through the Amazon, via Inca, Maya, Chimu, Moche, et al – remains... For which the British Museum supplied an abundance of information from numerous past explorers.
> Second, A backup expedition across the Western Sahara route, south through Algiers and French Colonial, Sahara, Mali, desert. Known as the Mauritania route... An enormous amount of research.

Stan befriended us, and invited me, potentially, to share his next expedition abroad. He'd recently returned from a tour to Indonesia and Bali, and met with President Sukorno, one of his many fascinating interviews.

Stan invited me to go with him and his party on the expedition. Of course, my work was only academic.

Dept. Date	Dept. Day	From.	Arr. Date	Arr. Day	Destination	Dist- ance M.	Night Stops	Remarks
AFRICAN ANTHROPOLOGICAL RESEARCH EXPEDITION								
1964 - 65								
ITINERY								
29 Dec.	Tues.	London	29 Dec.	Tues.	Paris	240	2	Flying
31 Dec.	Thurs.	Paris	1 Jan	Fri.	Dakar	3,200	14	Senegal
15 Jan.	Fri.	Dakar	15 Jan.	Fri.	Koumpentoun	294	1	
16 Jan.	Sat.	Koumpetoun	16 Jan.	Sat.	Tambacoumba	66	3	
19 Jan.	Tues.	Tambacumba	19 Jan.	Tues.	Nayes	176	1	
20 Jan.	Wed.	Nayes	20 Jan.	Wed.	Kita	260	1	Mali
21 Jan.	Thurs.	Kita	21 Jan.	Thurs.	Bamako	160	2	
28 Jan.	Thurs.	Bamako	28 Jan.	Thurs.	Sikasso	229	2	Up.Volta
30 Jan.	Sat.	Sikasso	30 Jan.	Sat.	Bobo-Dioulasso	235	1	
31 n.	Sun.	Bobo-Diou.	31 Jan.	Sun.	Ougoudougou	222	7	
7 Feb.	Sun.	Ougoudougu	7 Feb.	Sun.	Thiou	143	2	
9 Feb.	Tues.	Thiou	9 Feb.	Tues.	Bandiagara	102	2	Mali
11 Feb.	Thurs.	Bandiagara	11 Feb.	Thurs.	Mopti	75	3	
14 Feb.	Sun.	Mopti	14 Feb.	Sun.	Ke Nacina	240	1	

An extract from one of the plans, drawn up with Stan.

One thing I had learnt of many professional explorers, that they became serious loners: married life was not for them – Stan was no exception. But, Sara was almost due with our first born: I thought it through – she knew how much I wanted this journey, and said, Go; surprise, I made my choice – didn't fancy becoming another such loner, however passionate, and leave the family.

Well, Stan *did* go on his trip, making good use of my maps and data. On his return, some months later (I was working at Agfacolor Processing at Wimbledon), he met up with us and relayed aspects of his fascinating Sahara expedition. Invited to his flat at Barons Court in London, tongue in cheek he related how the person (or persons) who rented his premise whilst away, was one of the circle of then political scandal who had been heavily involved (I think, not sure, it was a doctor something or other); it was the Christine Keeler affair – the Profumo scandal.

But, what really interested me was his adventures in the Sahara and West Africa. Fortunately, he spoke good French (I believe) and he stumbled on a French nuclear test site in the middle of the desert. After checks, etc., he wasn't treated as a spy and enjoyed their hospitality. France first exploded an H bomb nuclear test in Algeria, Sahara in 1960.

Shortly after these events, I had published articles in *'Exploration'*: And, one article on 'Plamil', Plant Milk, working part-time with Doctor Hugh

Franklin (a biochemist) and his wife Winifred Franklin, of Kensington, who had been regular dance students of mine, several years before.

More events. We shortly left Mitcham, and I left Agfacolor Processing, Wimbledon, to move down to the south coast. After more adventures (as it were), later including a time working in New Scotland Yard press office. I eventually became, in 1967, a full time registered mental nurse student, at Graylingwell Hospital, Chichester and, later, a career in Psychiatric Social Work in West Sussex (see my book, *Better Court Than Coroners*, 2012) for over forty years.

No Bombs

From the time of demob, back in December 1958, till fifty years later (see Google), I had not read of, or been aware of, any 'detailed' information about continuing global nuclear tests, let alone been aware of the many undisclosed nuclear human guinea pigs... that is right up until after I retired in 2000. Still no awareness of the continuing H-Bomb tests, in the air, under water and Underground tests – and, their victims, nuclear veterans. Clearly, the very secret records with HM Government were (and still are) very closely hidden, or censored, depending on whose definitions... Google had yet to emerge!

Revelations, at first a trickle then, after, an increasing flood – after the infamous 1983 Cold War confrontations, published data on past nuclear tests – including those on Christmas Island in the Pacific. And, in the UK, the 1991 publication of Ken McGinley's experiences – and, gathering frustration of world nuclear veterans and their families; attempts to gain some compensations – at least government responsibility – for the infamous treatment of its troops and civilian casualties (as in USA), involved, subsequent fallout, after exposure to legion radioactive explosions.

Forensic Photos

I recall, as a child in the early 1950s, being given a cheap plastic 127 kodak film camera. At 16 years leaving school, 1953, first job I worked at was in a Fleet Street photo press agency, the Central Press Photos where, as runner and assistant to the Press Photographers, I was introduced to processing of black and white photos and 5"x4" glass gelatine plates, and flexi 5"x4" film

– as from Saturday football matches and making up chemicals for processing in the Darkroom. No way was colour an option, far too expensive anyway; the press papers, for illustrations, like the small televisions, only did black and white pics. I worked many Saturday day shifts.

On callup for National Service in 1955, I had just started in the firm's darkroom – working drying and glazing machines (see earlier, in these memoirs). And, then entered a new occupation in HM Forces, in August 1955. Before leaving Central Press, at 18 years old, I built a makeshift darkroom downstairs, in our small London terrace home's cellar. I engaged private photography in outside hours, weddings, celebrations, passport photos, etc. all, of course, in black and white. In the Royal Engineers' sappers, photography remained a hobby.

On Christmas Island I purchased an excellent Agfa Isolette one, 2¼ x 2¼" camera; used in black and white – from the NAAFI shop. Only used for domestic work, not at all intended for picture 'installations', etc. And took hundreds of Ilford pictures – a few sent off to my old firm Central Press (after passing censorship) who printed a number of pics (all black and white) in the *Illustrated London News*, and a number of provincial papers. They were only black and white, holiday snapshots.

I was well aware of not taking pictures which could be misused, i.e. ending up in, erm, the enemy's hands. However, it was taken for granted that, for the tests, many (in fact thousands) mostly 'reels' of black and white movies.

Later, pics for the tests in colour... pics and films from overhead aircraft, off ships, and sundry 'official' personnel, wholly anonymous. Secret.

Berlyn Brixner was an official photographer for the Trinity Manhattan project. The bomb detonated at 5.30am, July 16th 1945. Incredibly, he had fifty cameras in operation – some running up to 10,000 frames per second. This gave a record of that first test, at Los Alamos, New Mexico (he used black-and white 35mm, eight millimetre film, and Panatomic X Film (Pan-atomic!) ASA30 speed – some used Super Double X). Protected cameras in lead lined boxes were sited as close as half-a-mile from the blast. He said in an interview:

> "My first impression was of a 'brilliant white light out of the initial part of the explosion' then the formation of a ball of fire that becomes an immense ball of white-hot material..." (All in Black and White) [3]

On release of further de-classified material, author Stephen Walker published in 2005 more detail of the photography of that first atomic explosion in 1945, the bomb on the top of a 100 foot tall steel tower, which vaporised during the explosion, on Apache territory near the river Rio Grande.

> "There were the three concrete bunkers to the north, south and west of the tower, and lead-lined photographic bunkers, housing batteries of cameras, some of them mounted on army airforce machine-gun turrets. There was a radar unit to track the fireball and four high-speed Mitchell 35mm motion picture cameras to film it, in slow motion, and innumerable spectrograph's to record its radiation." [4]

I presume that colour film was used for the spectrographs, though this detail was not recorded in this most excellent book of the inaugural event.

And, to the joy of the then British Tory government – Mr Macmillan MP, our prime minister; stated publicly on a UK newsreel, 'we' could now be classed, rather re-instated as world leaders – with the USA and competitors in the USSR – at the declared success of the British and Commonwealth, Operation Grapple, atomic tests. All good stuff... But, always buts.

After demob, still taking b&w pictures (see early in these memoirs), I was now well into colour slides, preferences for positive Agfacolor transparencies in 1963, and employed by Agfacolor processing laboratories, based in Wimbledon, South London.

At Agfacolor, I was employed on two floors: The main chemical processing floor machines – developing and drying cabinets, with an inspector (senior on the floor) at the end of the completed then boxed transparencies.

The unprocessed films were joined (with labels) by metal clips, joined together in total darkness – a job I enjoyed for some time.

And, second occasional appointment, to work in the upstairs analysis lab; measuring ph with pipettes, and other sundry work. Our lab manager was a Scots Phd, and there were also two very likeable BSc men from Pakistan. I was the only assistant who was unqualified, in this post. I enjoyed that work.

Agfacolor

The author at work at Agfacolor, Wimbledon, 1963.

The Agfacolor lab inspector on quality control (or an assistant) observed if something was wrong with a slide - first (the obvious) was it one roll, or was there a whole batch damaged (disaster!). If the error was obvious, and a batch emerged damaged, then it was 'stop everything', take samples up to the analysis lab to examine the chemical makeup: this was usually the first check (after correct temperature, etc.). But, if it was one person's roll of 24 or 36 exposures at fault – why? Was the whole roll black, or unexposed; if blank and black, was it the camera, or other cause; were such sun spots, blur apparent; or – the fault was not discovered, and returned, with a note, to the addressee... And, there were occasional unknown sources of contamination.

In later years, I settled on a Nikon kit, with interchangeable lenses, etc; but continued to use the box film process. Agfacolor had (they asserted) an industrial secret for its success; this was a film base – based on their use of the reds in their spectrum. Black and white had shades of grey – but, colour, whatever make, had its own, possible secrets... well, potentially... endless?

Red, orange, yellow, green, blue, indigo and violet. And, out each end of the spectrum, X-rays and ultra-violet – thickness of angstroms. As with musical wavelengths, sound waves (noise) and, other measurements and, if possible, (to be) seen – felt – or enjoyed: Numbers, key measurements, the physics and biology of applied chemistry in – photographs. Electron microscopes, x-ray photos – since the early 20th Century.

Photography changes and records, changes with technology, I admit to experiencing problems, as these years rolled by. All phenomena can be identified as and by its, mass shapes – and colours. (Digital photography was a long way off.)

At Central Press, in 1954, printing the pictures for press delivery, I learnt about shading, cupping with ones hands. And fading out unwanted detail.

Years later, when using Photoshop, I engaged a home tutor, a middle-aged, award winning photographer, who travelled about the country to judge competitions. He had a penchant for art pictures, eliminating, rather than shading out, unwanted detail (of course, well known in press pics). He severely criticised some of my pics as being 'far too busy' – 'too noisy', he said. After one visit to Paris with friends, I brought back a few pictures to show him.

I protested that his supposedly 'superfluous' details – things on a portrait, action or play of some sort, were needed. Like a Brassai, Capa, or Hardy, I liked my pictures to tell a story – not just an artwork.

As an amateur, I'm sure I was often wrong – well, not always. Like a crime-scene picture, one could easily remove evidence on a pic, rather than losing it altogether... or delete, lose the pics. This approach would later be dubbed forensic, in the police.

Due to the advance of technology – inevitable cultural lag, past archives, hidden (or forgotten) records were able to be deciphered. And, after, over, thirty years – and a new generation; previous classified, top secret, documents, text and photographic records of awesome historic events began to emerge, as they were (though limited) de-classified. And a boon for museum artifacts, and cold criminal cases in the police detection units.

Day-to day, in the 1970s, I found austere living conditions (four day weeks, etc.) uncomfortable. On a personal level, and in a squaddie perspective, I found the total removal of the British imperial monetary system – of pounds, shillings and pence. And, subsequently, confirmation of the end of the British Empire – forever, in extremis.

In 1971, our government formally introduced the European (mostly French) metric system of space, measurements etc. Kilometres, kilograms, kilotons, megatons. New coinage, with 100 new pence to a pound; equal to old coins and notes, of twenty shillings to the pound – and, one pound and one shilling to a guinea.

For me, as a Blitz child, I never learnt by rote or experience, instant conversion from sterling to metric. This was rigid, mostly for commerce, economic conversion became most confusing, in measuring cause and effect – keeping in touch with technology, especially in relation to aspects of the Bomb, and emergence of atomic nuclear power plants – which produced and converted extreme heat into steam, thence into essential fuel, of electricity... with uranium, plutonium as its fuel rods – equated to past black coal.

Whilst a squaddie on Christmas Island, working for the Grapple sequence of atomic bomb tests for the UK, I used black and white Ilford film. It was then, in the 1950s, uncommon to see coloured pictures in the press media, and they were rarely used for general recording by the public. Colour photography, though well in use – as in Kodak and Agfacolor. I found it (and, then, probably too the public media), too expensive for general use. And this was, it seemed, for many official 'secret' film records by the professionals, officially recording on camera the sequence of explosions (the mushrooms); and recorded violence presented in the initial yield of each blast.

Before the bombs in 1956-57 I joined, on the island, a small photographic club, and made brief use of a van for developing negs and prints. But, I was too inexperienced at this level, and the excessive tropical climate ensured that, at its heat, the film was overdeveloped, damaging the surface. And so, my film rolls were later sent off, via the NAAFI, to Oahu for processing. In the media, many incredible pictures would appear of the mushrooms, and used to establish what yield, et cetera and, on ground (or at sea) level, physical damage to buildings, transport, and anything else. But it all remained very secret – from us squaddies, indeed, from all the rank and file observers; and folk back home. I assume, and it is only not knowing different; the same for American, Australian, New Zealand, Soviet and French servicemen.

In the next decade, in the 1960s, coloured photographs, and their cameras, became more available. In fact, this was the case, coloured pictures, in recording, would and did provide new phenomena; such as heat variance, chemical changes, tracing meteorological vapour trails, spectrography, spectrobolometer apparatus, etc. In fact, science must have had a ball, with all this physical recording... pure science.

From the very first atomic tests, in the American Nevada Desert in 1945, photography was recording some dreadful phenomena, as evidence, on flora, fauna and the elements exposed to blast and fallout. Even so, the results would remain classified, held for many years, top secret. They (the Atomic Energy Commission) were caught out by the use of what could be deemed forensic photography, given that it provided evidence, of possible wrong doing – deliberate harm on the human indigenous population. Of course, they were deemed tests, otherwise known as scientific experiments; so that was OK, then....?

A colour photograph of the Trinity Nuclear test, taken by Jack W. Aeby, a civilian worker at Los Alamos laboratory, working under the aegis of the Manhattan Project on July 16th, 1945. (As a work of the US Federal Government, this picture is in the public domain.)

In 1945, but more likely in 1946, one result of the Trinity nuclear tests (Manhattan Project) was the discovery of discharge of fallout nuclear waste into the nearby Wabash river, in Indiana. If it was on record, the data remained top secret with the USA Atomic Energy Commission (AEC) and the government of the day. But inevitably the radiated sediment settled on shore farmland, with civilians in residence, and entered the food chain; grass and vegetation.

Photographic evidence was, in 1945, already available. At the Rochester location of Eastman Kodak Company, in New York, an employee reported unwelcome spotting, like raindrops; white spotted snowflakes of radiation, fogging, even wiped black, affected photographic stock. On investigation, it was found that it was caused by the recent nuclear tests in Nevada. The vegetative cardboard, used to pack their stock, was radioactive, and its source was realised, and reported to the, then, Atomic Energy Commission (viz. government); who demanded this detail would remain top secret, but at a price...

A secret agreement was made between the AEC and Kodak, that they would be informed, in advance, of future relevant tests, allowing the processing laboratories to install state of the art filtering air apparatus. But, in no way was the general public to be informed of this fallout information. The top secret classification was agreed upon in the USA.

Documentary

In 1964, the English BBC produced *The Great War* television series, an incredible black and white war documentary, Sir Michael Redgrave as its narrator. And, years on, again the BBC produced in 1973 a wonderful documentary series, 26 episodes, on WW2, *The World at War*, with Sir Laurence Olivier providing the voiceover.

In retrospect, *The Great War*, with its gripping original (no 'talkie' movies in 1914-1920) footage – but, edited, with many survivors, memories of those men who fought in that unhappy global war of attrition... in future, I found this too sad...

My maternal grandparents (never knew paternal lineage), had lived through the Boer War, the Great War and its aftermath. And many relatives (as with all families) fought, and died, during horrendous battles of the first World War. And, again, now, *in colour* – the documentary *World at War* 1939-1945 series of campaigns. And, my own generation – National Service and regulars – in the Cold War years of 1945-1989... As these recorded memories in my own time reflect – *The Blitz and The Bomb* – as a squaddie. Most memories are black and white; and, like the Great War episodes – mostly quite dour.

On the 8th September 1985, ITV3 showed one of the many re-runs of the *World at War*, all 26 episodes. But, with the new computer available, I recorded (on VHS) an additional awesome, sad documentary (in black and white) as 'Episode 27' at that time. Its title, *A Painful Reminder: Evidence for All Mankind*. This footage included a 40 year old British documentary, previously top secret (it was not allowed a showing); a black and white documentary, taken at the opening of Belsen, one of the diabolical, thousand and more, Nazi concentration camps. The black and white documentary, made in 1945 by a British Army group of filmmakers, followed the Brits, and later Yanks, working with them, on the clean-up of the camp and its zombie survivors; including mass starvation, typhoid, and other numerous horrors.

I noticed (still in the 2000s) initially, the *World at War* would repeat, again and again, but that *black and white* episode seemingly *disappeared*; in fact, the World at War episode '*Genocide*' (often shown at a later timeslot because of its content) contained material from that Sidney Bernstein original. The '27th episode' itself, in terms of viewing, became one of the 'not to be shown' documentaries, like *The Sorrow And The Pity* (1969), and the almost ten hour long *Shoah* (1985).

One of my uncles, an older half-brother of my mother's, was Len Ayres. Len was a chauffeur for a British general (don't know his name) and opened the gates of one of the infamous Nazi concentration camps. A kind, quiet, dignified gentleman, his dark hair was recorded as going white overnight due to that dark episode, shared with his, whoever General.

In 1946, with Hiroshima and Nagasaki (like Europe) still in utter ruins: its occupants, both indigenous people and new, resident, American marines, were, years on, to develop long term experiences, numerous diseases, and disorders from nuclear radiation and its clean-up attempts (in evidence about the devastation). A US Army Air Force squad was ordered (permitted) to document the results of its aerial bombardments in the Japanese cities, and a US photographer shot twenty hours of documentary film footage in Hiroshima and Nagasaki, in early 1946 (a member of a special US military unit). But, due to its authenticity and revelations in his copy, like the British documentary of 1945, in Europe: it was deliberately hidden for over 40 years.

The cameraman was (is), Herbert Sussan, and, uniquely, it was all shot in *colour*; twenty to thirty hours of evidence which, in future years, could be described as *forensic photography*. Evidence of wrong doing?

It contains footage of Japanese sufferings, including those with healing (or not) keloids. But, despite many, many years attempting to gain the film a public showing – he never succeeded. Sussan died in 1985 – but, his film survived. I have yet to see any printed 'photos', stills taken from his vital evidence. (Lifton, Mitchell, et al. 1995).

In recent times – yes, from the 1980s, USA and British politicians have allowed a degree of declassifications – but, still few of the many human fatalities have surfaced of those first days of the 'Cold War'.

And, five or so years on, in 1951, when the awesome, new series of atomic bombs were being tested; with thousands of American troops used as unprotected exposed victims, as witnesses; and any indigenous citizens living in the compass of South-West USA. Their own people deliberately exposed, as photographic films, by Kodak, confirmed, but, hidden from the general public.

Dosimeters

Official policy insisted that any dangerous level of presented radioactive fallout which settled on anything, any object, would be registered by all scientific personnel, by button-holed dosimeters; these were like litmus photographic papers (and, as birds had been used in mining coal, to locate toxic gases). But, and it is a *big* but, most squaddie personnel had never seen, or heard of, these life saving badges. I recall that no squaddie I knew, on Christmas Island in 1956-7, had heard of this benign instrument. I had never heard of them. And did not know of them for many years.

Years later, there appeared numerous reports of wanton discarded dosimeters by senior personnel – if they registered too much radiation exposure. But, even worse (and, agreed, the knowledge was yet to be realised), the dosimeters only measured the instant effect of the mushroom blast, and external body burns, or other primary external exposure, and did not record internal ionisation.

No admission, and nothing, in writing or photographs, to the public, was reported; of any individuals risks of subsequent internal damage, caused by the ionisation. Yet there was, already, a substantial amount of data available, from the rank experiences of 'atomic disease', fallout effects, due to the twenty or so kilotons dropped on Hiroshima and Nagasaki in 1945 – and, the years that followed.

Before dosimeters, I was acquainted with geiger counters, boxes that, with batteries, reacted to the presence of any material that was radioactive. I recollect many children's comics and black and white fiction in the 1950s that featured the use of this detection apparatus. More advanced was the commercial and hospital use of X-rays, post-Madame Curie. And microscopes and telescopes – all apparatus of detection long around, before WW2, domestic use and forensic, and a 1971 book on DNA genetics by Crick and Watson.

In WW2, and early 1950s, the value of uranium became more valuable than gold – and, miners equipped with geiger counters researched ground and underground for this valuable element. Initially, ignorant of, to be, awesome powers of radioactive material, after effects on their miners, by exposure. Which came later...

British Nuclear Tests in Australia

Date/Start Date	Name	Where	Yield
October 3rd 1952	Hurricane	Monte Bello - HMS Plym	25kt
October 15th 1953	Totem 1	Emu - Tower	10kt
October 27th 1953	Totem 2	Emu - Tower	8kt
May 16th 1956	Mosaic G1	Monte Bello - Tower	15kt
June 19th 1956	Mosaic G2	Monte Bello - Tower	60kt
Sept. 27th 1956	Buffalo	Maralinga (One Tree) - Tower	15kt
October 2nd 1956	Buffalo	Maralinga (Marcoo) - Ground burst	1.5kt
October 11th 1956	Buffalo	Maralinga (Kite) - Air dropped	3kt
October 22nd 1956	Buffalo	Maralinga (Breakaway) - Tower	10kt
Sept. 14th 1957	Antler	Maralinga (Tadje) - Tower	1kt
Sept. 25th 1957	Antler	Maralinga (Brak) - Tower	6kt
October 9th 1957	Antler	Maralinga (Taranaki) - Balloon air burst	25kt

A symbol of all that remains at the Maralinga test site, 1987 (Source: *A Secret Country,* by John Pilger, pp178, 1989) A posed picture of a broken toilet pan, with no visible evidence of previous waste disposal. A grim but excellent metaphor for the unseen radioactive wasteland of Emu and Maralinga Australian atomic nuclear tests in the 1950s. One result from numerous low level tests which, thought static in detonation, ejected radioactive matter in easterly winds across Australian territory... and has left to this day 'hot spots' in Western Australia, forbidden territory. Australian Len Beadell (1923 -) talented, engineer, surveyor, explorer – and cartoonist, was engaged during WW2, serving with an Army Service Corps in New Guinea until 1945. Beadell later became a significant explorer of Australian Bush and desertland – the Australian government employing him in the 1950s, to construct nuclear based sites, For Woomera, Emu, and Maralinga – with British Dr. Penney. Ironically, Beadell's book, *Blast the Bush* (1967) concludes (p.212) with a description, dated October 15th, 1953, watching the detonation of *Totem One* atomic explosion – *before* subsequent fallout!

Shot Priscilla USA

Shot Priscilla – 37 kilotons, June 24th 1957 (note that Nagasaki was 20 kilotons) – a de-classified American military film, from 1950s. This was a sanitised public film, made for both the general public and military distribution. An army chaplain reassures two Yank squaddies, about being exposed to the close ground zero Los Alamos, New Mexico nuclear sites, as close as 2500 yards (just over one mile!). The chaplain says it it perfectly safe.

'Actually, there is no need to be worried, as the Army has taken all the necessary precautions to see that we're perfectly safe here. First of all, one sees a very bright light, followed by a shock wave, and then you hear the sound of the blast. Then you look up, and you see the fireball, as it ascends up into the heavens. It contains all the rich colours of the rainbow, and then, as it rises up into the atmosphere, it assembles into the mushroom. It is a wonderful sight to behold.'

In her 1993 book, Gallagher comments:

'After witnessing the shot, soldiers returned to Camp Desert Rock bleeding from the eyes, ears, nose and throat...'[5]

Gallagher sets the tone for her incredible published work, recorded live survivors, damaged witnesses of the many USA bomb tests in the Nevada desert – since 1951, and references to existing evidence – much of it forensic *photographic* (in possession of the survivors – or their families) – but, *they* would not be seen, due to the top secret, AEC, politics; would not allow to appear in the public arena: banned, and denied, for many years to come.

Dominic Tests – 1962

Meanwhile, back at the ranch, in 1962, at the time of the infamous (Bay of Pigs) Cuban missile confrontation, a new series of tests was being carried out on Christmas Island with the Americans, and a detachment of British military personnel. All now in colour, glorious technicolor...

Between 25th of April, and 11th July, 1962, there were 38 explosions, up to 7.65 megatons each, on an almost daily basis, including 'Weapons related Airdrops', which were as close as ten miles south of Christmas Island. The US test name was 'Dominic', the UK name 'Brigadoon'.[6]

USA. Operation Dominic
Timetable

Yield (kt)

Dominic (1)	Adobe	190	25/04/62	Christmas Island		Air Drop
Dominic (2)	Aztec	410	27/04/62	Christmas Island (S)		Air Drop
Dominic (3)	Arkansas	1,090	27/04/62	Christmas Island		Air Drop*
Dominic (4)	Questa	670	02/05/62	Christmas Island (S)		Air Drop
Dominic (5)	Frigate Bird	600	06/05/62	Johnston Island		SLBM**
Dominic (6)	Yukon	100	08/05/62	Christmas Island (S)		Air Drop
Dominic (7)	Mesilla	100	09/05/62	Christmas Island (S)		Air Drop
Dominic (8)	Muskegon	050	11/05/62	Christmas Island (S)		Air Drop
Dominic (9)	Encino	500	12/05/62	Christmas Island		Air Drop
Dominic (10)	Swanee	97	14/05/62	Christmas Island (S)		Air Drop
Dominic (11)	Chetco	73	19/05/62	Christmas Island (S)		Air Drop
Dominic (12)	Tanana	3	25/05/62	Christmas Island (S)		Air Drop
Dominic (13)	Nambe	43	27/05/62	Christmas Island		Air Drop
Dominic (14)	Alma	782	08/06/62	Christmas Island (S)		Air Drop
Dominic (15)	Truckee	210	09/06/62	Christmas Island (S)		Air Drop
Dominic (16)	Yeso	3,000	10/06/62	Christmas Island (S)		Air Drop
Dominic (17)	Harlem	1,200	12/06/62	Christmas Island (S)		Air Drop
Dominic (18)	Rinconada	800	15/06/62	Christmas Island (S)		Air Drop
Dominic (19)	Dulce	52	17/06/62	Christmas Island (S)		Air Drop
Dominic (20)	Petit	2	19/06/62	Christmas Island (S)		Air Drop
Dominic (21)	Otowi	82	22/06/62	Christmas Island (S)		Air Drop
Dominic (22)	Bighorn	7,650	27/06/62	Christmas Island (S)		Air Drop
Dominic (23)	Bluestone	1,270	30/06/62	Christmas Island (S)		Air Drop
Dominic (24)	Sunset	1,000	10/07/62	Christmas Island		Air Drop
Dominic (25)	Pamlico	3,880	11/07/62	Christmas Island		Air Drop

Notes: Christmas Island (S) – drop took place to the south. * This drop was slowed in flight by a parachute. ** This was the only US test of an operational ballistic missile with a live warhead.

Nuclear Testing Timeline
Significant Series from Trinity to Starfish Prime

Date/Start Date	Name	Country	Where	Yield	Fallout
July 16th 1945	The Gadget	USA	Manhattan Project	18-20kt	
August 6th 1945	Little Boy	USA	Hiroshima, Japan	15kt	Toxic
August 9th 1945	Fat Man	USA	Nagasaki, Japan	21kt	Toxic
1946	Operation Crossroads (Able & Baker)	USA	Bikini Atoll	up to 23kt	
April 1948	Operation Sandstone (3 tests)	USA	Eniwetok Atoll	18-49kt	
August 1949	First Lightning/RDS1	USSR	Semipalatinsk, USSR	22kt	
January 1951	Operation Ranger (5 tests)	USA	Nevada Desert Test Site	0.5-22kt	
April 1951	Operation Greenhouse (4 tests)	USA	Eniwetok Atoll	45.5-225kt	
October 1952	Operation Hurricane	UK	Near Montebello Islands	25kt	
October 1952	Operation Ivy (2 tests)	USA	Eniwetok Atoll	0.5-12mt	**
August 1953	'Joe 4'	USSR	Semipalatinsk, USSR	400kt	
March 1954	Castle Bravo	USA	Bikini Atoll	15mt	Toxic
May 1956	Operation Redwing (11 tests)	USA	Eniwetok Atoll	0.2-360kt	
September 1956	Operation Buffalo (4 tests)	UK	Maralinga, South Australia	1.4-12.9kt	
1957-1958	Operation Grapple (9 tests)	UK	Christmas Island	24-3000kt	
September 1957	Operation Antler (3 tests)	UK	Maralinga, South Australia	0.93-26.6kt	
1958	Operation Hardtack (26 tests)	USA	Eniwetok Atoll/Bikini Atoll	0-2000kt	
February 1960	Gerboise bleue	France	French Sahara	70kt	
October 1961	Tsar Bomba	USSR	Novaya Zemlya	50-58mt	
1962	Operation Dominic (25 tests)	UK/USA	Christmas Island	2-3880kt	
1962	Operation Fishbowl	USA	Johnson Island		
1962	Starfish Prime	USA	Johnson Island	Outer Space	

** NOTE: Due to secrecy issues, these tests were not reported until 1954 (and often shown as occuring then),

Gerald Rice

Gerald Rice, a nuclear veteran, contributed in 2013, for me, a list of all the Dominic detonations on Christmas Island, in 1962, which he witnessed, and took coloured photographs of eleven of 24 bombs. Gerald told me:

"As part of 'Operation Dominic', twenty four bombs were dropped at Christmas Island, with five at Johnson Island, some 1,200 miles to the North West. We saw the flash of this detonation from Christmas Island. The first two bombs I sent you information about are 'Adobe' and 'Aztec', which were dropped ten miles away, to the South East of the island, and the last one I included was called 'Bighorn' and was the largest of the tests dropped at Christmas Island, yielding 7.65 megatons ('Housatonic' was the largest of all the tests, at 8.3 megatons, dropped at Johnson Island on 30th October 1962 – the culmination of the Dominic tests). These are the only ones I can remember the names to, as there were so many in a short time.

The first three bombs we had to parade for on the football pitch under the supervision of a Sergeant and the rest we were able to stay in bed wearing our high density goggles as they were mostly detonated in the early morning. We were issued with film badges to register the radioactivity and these were taken off us after the first four bombs and we were told they hadn't registered anything. We weren't monitored at all after that.

Then, they dropped much larger bombs, up to 7.65 megatons. We used to send our film to Hong Kong for processing and, after about the 6th bomb, pictures were being leaked out to others, with photographs showing up in Russian magazines. At that time we were ordered to register our cameras and hand them into the squadron office prior to a detonation. Being an avid photographer, I risked a court marshal by not registering mine and continued to take some of the remaining detonations, including Bighorn. Fearing being found out, I sent my films home to my mother, in Creswell, who took them to the local chemist for developing and sent the slides back to me on the Island. This made the later shots unique, as I was the only one with them. Most of the detonations were dropped in the darkness of the early morning and some of my shots were taken using the flash of the bomb and in order not to overexpose them I altered my camera speed to the fastest and the aperture to the smallest. I was very lucky that I obtained such perfect exposures.

I was a sapper in the Royal Engineers and passed out as a Carpenter & Joiner from the Chatham School of Military Engineering and posted to 38 Engineer Regiment in Maidstone Kent. My next posting was 40 Advanced Stores Regiment in Willich in Germany where I put in for postings to 1st Singapore, 2nd Hong Kong and 3rd Christmas Island. I was detached to the Island four weeks later, in June of 1961. Unbeknown to me, there was to be a worldwide unilateral test ban treaty to become effective in 1963, and the Americans had not completed their tests, so they asked the British government for permission to use the Island. They came out in March 1962, with a 2,000 strong civilian task force called Holmes & Narver, along with 150 American servicemen and a few service Police, and set up installations around the Island. At that time I was detached from the joiners shop to work in the boathouse, looking after twelve yachts, relieving the outgoing boathouse man.

Yes, there were around 300 British servicemen on the Island as a maintenance force since the British tests of 1958. Approximately 150 R.A.F., 150 Army and 20 Royal Navy with a civilian running the N.A.A.F.I.

There were 3,000 civilians in the works party; about 200 American Army and about 20 American Police personnel with an unknown amount of Test Professors and Engineers. They were billeted at main camp which was 12 miles away from us at Port London so we didn't see much of them. It was from there that the tests were conducted and they had a tannoy address system through to us at Port London which they called Mahatma. They used this to count down the detonations of the bombs, every five minutes for an hour, then every minute for five minutes, then the last ten seconds to detonation. American Destroyers and other various war ships arrived and anchored off the Island at Port London.

Shortly after the American task force arrived there was a fatal road accident involving four American Army Personnel; apparently they were on the wrong side of the road.

Four youths killed – Brits drove on the left, Yanks on the right.

Some of the British forces worked alongside of the Americans and found them very friendly and generous, some made close friends and visited them in America on their way back to Britain. The good thing that came from the massive influx of Americans was the food, as ours was of a very poor standard. If we were working near their camp we were allowed to visit their mess and it was big steaks, warm bread and milk, ice cold orange juice with delicious sweets.

When the outworkers came back to our camp and told us with their distended stomachs that they'd never had food like it. The next day a land rover with six lads went for a feast, four days later two three toners went up packed with hungry British servicemen signing in as Dick Barton, Donald Duck and other alias names. This lasted for a further week with more and more men travailing the twelve miles to the American mess. A week later the base commander received a bill of over £1,800 for the meals taken by all these fictitious men. From then we had to have a pass issued by the squadron office. Fortunately I made friends with an American and every Saturday he brought a load of food to Port Area and we loaded it up in the boats with the beer and sailed over to Cook Island for the week end barbecuing, fishing, snorkelling and enjoying ourselves.

Before I went into the Army I was an avid photographer and with my brother set up a small business taking photos of weddings, developing and printing and making up albums. At that time I had a Topcon RE 2 single lens reflex camera and mainly did black and white photographs as colour was a little bit more difficult and more expensive. When I arrived on the Island my room companion ran a mail order business with a company in Hong Kong and I ordered a Werra 5 with a built in light meter and Carl Zeiss Tesser lens, which at that time was the Rolls Royce of all lens and probably still is. The film I used was mainly Kodachrome 2 colour reversal and on occasions Agfa which produced some good results.

When we knew the Americans were coming to do their tests the electricians painted a ban the bomb sign on their 2ft. 6" wide door which got a few of the lads going, so when I went up to the joiners shop the next day and saw it I went back to my boathouse and painted one on the double doors 6ft. high. Two days later and not to be outdone the Plant section painted one on the end of their sectional building 20ft. high. There were ban the bomb signs going up all over Port Area and the base commander had to put an order up that they all had to be painted out because it wasn't good for Anglo American relations."

'I was posted to Christmas Island (Pacific Ocean) from the 17th June 1961 to the 6th of December 1962 where I witnessed all 24 of the American Dominic Nuclear bomb tests between the 25th of April to the 11th of July 1962. I also witnessed the detonation flash of Frigate Bird which was shot and detonated towards Christmas Island from a submarine positioned at Johnson Island 1200 nautical miles to the North West. I knew and served with Roy Prescott on the Island and later found he had successfully made a compensation claim with the aid of other vets I served with. I personally know of five other veterans I served with that have also made successful claims but cannot name them without their permission. Every year I organize a reunion of 15 veterans I served with at the time of the tests and with their permission I could name them. Two years after I left the Island my wife gave birth to our son Iain and when he was 8 years old we noticed that his right leg was shorter an thinner than his left. the doctor referred us to a specialist in Sheffield. After he had examined him I asked if his condition could've been caused by my involvement with the tests and he said he was not qualified enough to say. He did say that

> *he'd only experienced this same condition once before in*
> *all his practiced life.'*

Gerry had been but one of the 300 British Servicemen attached to the American Task Force at Operation Dominic. On my previous departure of Grapple in 1957, I never met or heard of any of my peers again, or the fate of those who remained on board, but, Gerald Rice did keep contact with other British Sappers – and American personnel – indeed, did so for many years, after 1962.

As he recalls, in his memoirs of Dominic, of the 150 British army personnel he knew, not only of Roy Prescott (who died of lung cancer in 2006), but others who, too, were acknowledged as definitive fallout casualties, by the American administration – but never, ever, by any British government. One ponders, that surely the 'lists' of stationed HM Armed Forces personnel were officially held somewhere. Secret, or lost in archives – somewhere. Why?

Christmas Island Dominic Tests
(Photos by Gerald Rice)

From 24th April 1962 to 27th June 1962.

American warships, anchored off the Island at Port London. 1962

B52 bomber, of the same type as dropped the Dominic Bombs.

LEFT: View of minute *Cook Island*, between *Port London* and *Paris* and *SPAL*; and, in the south west, *St. Stanislas Bay*. **RIGHT:** American and British soldiers sometimes sailed to, and had picnics on, *Cook Island* – before the tests. Source: Photos from Gerald Rice.

Picture of the wharf and sandspit of *Port London*; preparing for the airborne tests (to the south). The red floating buoys on the left were to be towed to the places of detonation – as markers for the aircraft drops. Pictures taken from a Hastings aircraft. Gerald Rice, 1962.

Bomb 1 - Adobe
25th April, 1962 - 190 kilotons (NB: Hiroshima was only 20 kilotons)

The first of the Operation Dominic Tests, on Christmas Island. (In nearly all pictures, of all the bombs, the 'mushrooms' are clearly seen.)

I took this photo while we where being accounted for and waiting for the countdown to the first bomb Adobe, under the section sergeant Wilson. The RAF and Naval personnel to the rear. Note the only protection we had, goggles, on floor. (The Grapple lads didn't have these, only hands.)

Front row L to R: Space where I was sat, unknown, unknown, Brum Dewsbury, Bill Barker RS. **Second row:** Barry Firmin, David Rawlings RASC, unknown, Alan Miller RASC. **Third row:** John Evans, Bert Leighton. (Postal) The rest unknown.

Taken from Daily Mail *Missing… and Found* column (Gerry's picture from Daily Mirror)

and FOUND!

Posting: Royal Engineers stationed on Christmas Island, in the Pacific, in 1962

LAST November, Rayland Peace was looking for his mates from 1961-62 when they were members of 73 Squadron of the Royal Engineers, stationed on Christmas Island in the Pacific, watching the American H-bomb tests

'On completion of our posting there, we went our separate ways,' said Rayland. 'I was posted on to Singapore.

'I'd love to locate my friends from that time. I was known as Charlie Peace throughout my Army service.

'Many who served on Christmas Island have died of cancer. I have skin cancer and have had a chunk of my leg cut out, but the MoD is in denial about it.'

Reg Read emailed in response: 'I was delighted to read your item on Christmas Island. I was a sapper in the Corps of Royal Engineers doing my National Service there in 1960-61. I worked as a clerk in the RE Stores. Every two weeks, it was my job to receive and replace worn out personal kit and clothing for 73 Squadron personnel.

'During this time, I met all personnel as I was the only one doing this particular job. Many thanks for your interesting column.'

John Wallin also got in touch. He served on the island with the RAF, and wrote: 'Reg might recall me as I was an announcer on the island's radio station and also connected with the island church. Thanks for bringing back many memories, mostly happy of my stay on Christmas.'

"Many who served on Christmas Island have died of cancer. I have skin cancer, and have had a chunk of my leg cut out, but the MoD is in denial about it." (Rayland Peace)

Black Cloud

Gerry recalled, after one explosion:

> *"This great cloud was approaching, and people started to panic. There was nothing I could do, so I just carried on clicking away. It was an awesome sight and passed right over our heads. I was told it was too high for us to be affected, but it would have been a different matter if it had rained. I realise how close we had been to disaster when I was told of a coded message by a wireless op."*

On this explosion fallout was high up in the atmosphere; fortunately, there was no rainfall, thus no 'black rain' to contaminate: unlike many other tests, which did suffer from lower atmospheric fallout, and black rain; USA, Australia, France – and the Grapple Y tests.

Bomb 2 - Aztec
27th April, 1962 - 410 kilotons

The second of the Operation Dominic tests, on Christmas Island.

Bomb 3 - Unknown
1962

Part of the Operation Dominic tests, on Christmas Island.

Bomb 4 - Unknown
1962

Part of the Operation Dominic tests, on Christmas Island.

Bomb 5 - Tanana
25th May 1962 - Fizzled

I think this was codenamed Tanana and it resulted in a fizzle, the first of the failures of the Dominic tests. At the time there were rumours round the camp that it was a trigger unit and as the information came out much later, it was, as it didn't ignite the secondary stage.

Bomb 6 - Unknown
1962

These shots were taken in the early hours. We were told that the flash of the detonation was roughly ten times stronger than the sun, so I set my camera with the fastest speed and the smallest aperture, and was very lucky to get the first shot. (With a film speed of 200 ASA, a normal sunlight exposure setting would be a 60th of a second shutter speed and an aperture of F8. To compensate for the flash of the bomb, I made the following adjustments to my camera settings: I increased the shutter speed five times and reduced the aperture five times; the results were incredible for someone aged 21. For the rest I reverted the camera back to the light meter settings .

Bomb 7 - Unknown
1962

This photograph was given to me, by a veteran pal, at the time.

Bomb 8 - Unknown
1962

I missed the detonation shot this time.

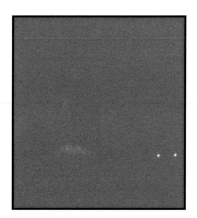

Bomb 9 - Unknown
1962

Unknown name and got this one spot on. Taken in the early morning utilizing
the light of the flash for the first photograph. Note on the first shot the light
in the cookhouse bakery (the bread was made on the night shift). Also on the
other shot the small light to the right of the fireball which is the light on top
of the water tower.

Bomb 10 - Unknown
1962

Unknown name and as before flash of detonation, available light of the fireball
and back to the early hours. Note on the first shot again the cookhouse light.
This was dropped approximately 50 miles away and yet it lit up the corrugated
buildings of the cookhouse. These shots are unique and at a time when all the
cameras were handed in.

Bomb 11 - Bighorn
27th June, 1962 - 7.65 megatons

This was Bighorn, and the largest of the 24 Christmas Island USA Dominic tests that were dropped on Christmas Island. These shots were taken from my barrack room doorway when I knew the patrolling sergeant wasn't looking. This is the reason why I was unable to take the flash and fireball shots.

Starfish Prime

Russia, and the USA, agreed to suspend, cease, airborne atomic weapon tests near the end of 1962 (underwater and underground OK – out of sight): stalemate, in the cold war chess match. This was ratified in August 1963.

The last series of the US Dominic tests was scheduled for the end of the year 1962, and though most tests were on Christmas Island, an additional high level US Series was launched by Thor missiles, off Johnson coral Island, named *Fishbowl*; one prominent on July 9th known as *Starfish Prime*.

The detonation of *Starfish* was 250 miles high, about 890 miles southwest of Oahu, Hawaii; and 1200 miles north-west of Christmas Island – the flash light (into cloud) of the bomb explosion was seen from Hawaii, and Christmas Island – as Gerald Rice recorded, he saw the light of the flash, but heard nothing.

But, heavens, what of all the personnel on or about Johnson Island: still too high to hear the explosion – but what a sight: scary, as this was in outer space; the Soviets had exploded a gigaton H-bomb, called *Tsar Bomba*.

During the 9th July 1962 explosion, the electro magnetic pulse (EMP), caused by the precise flash wave (received as a blast heat wave) of the *Starfish Prime* nuclear test, made at least 300 street lamps on Oahu, Hawaii (500 to 800 miles away) shut down; and other electronic appliances, as well as communications monitoring facilities – off their safety ranges. Many burglar alarms and air raid sirens went off, and other electronic equipment was affected.

This event was reported by an *Honolulu Advertiser* article, dated 9th July 1962, and *The New York Herald Tribune* (European Edition) 10th July, 1962 p2... A Tale of Bell, Book and Candle; and opening of Harry Potter' series... Magic, Witchcraft... Physics.

Circuit breakers on the Island of Maui went off the scale due to the unexpected magnitude of the EMP burst of *Starfish*. The radio flash wave, communicated considerable scientific information (telemetric traces) sufficient to predict, prevent subsequent megaton detonations – and potential of unimaginable global – starbursts etc...

Any metallic object, wire, can collect energy (from the EMP), detected in the electromagnetic field, and measured, detected current and voltage pulses to a hand-detector. The larger or longer the conductant, the greater the amount of immense energy collected... some battery?

Published date, April 1962 – viz before *Starfish*, and other to be recorded huge detonations, in 1962, *The Effects of Nuclear Weapons*. Edited by Samuel Glasstone: prepared by the United States Department of Defence, and published (officially) by the United States Atomic Energy Commission, in April 1962. In this most helpful Glossary, defined on page 703, I found:

> *Electromagnetic radiation: A travelling wave motion resulting from oscillating magnetic and electric fields. Familiar electromagnetic radiations range from X rays (and gamma rays) of short wavelength, through the ultraviolet, visible and infrared regions, to radar and radio waves of relatively long wavelength. All electromagnetic radiations travel in a vacuum with velocity of light.*

Dominic CND 1962

CND icon, one of a number on Christmas Island.

This sign, a symbol of a nuclear peace, was painted, in good humour, not in defiance, on the door of the Port London boat club. A few other 'wits' painted a number of the icons about the island; until the station commander asked them all to be removed. They were, and no other action was taken against the jokers. Officially, they were removed not to upset the Americans – with whom 'all' personnel, especially Yank squaddies, had well befriended the Brits. True bonhomie: sappers were on very good terms, amongst rank and file; as Gerald Rice confirmed, in his memoirs: much evidence, yet to be declared.

Gerald Rice, et al – through the global network – numerous witnesses; American, European, Asian, Commonwealth; whatever nationality, or written language; found a common bond of friendship and legitimate indignation, at politic denial of scientific evidence; cautionary and often deadly denial, of their own countries' experimental 'facts', families' legacy during the cold war years.

I was reminded that, as a wartime child, the V for victory had – two fingers up of Churchill – become a global icon (as doves of peace – hawks of war). In the late 20th century (and the start of the 21st), the V sign has been adopted by some of the Asian nations, including Japan. In an opposite, the thrusted single digit up gesture a negative from the individual.

No caption needed...

Sappers on Nuclear Tests 1955-1962.

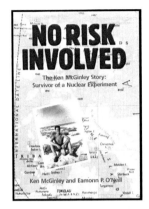 

RIGHT: Sapper Ken McGinley, 1958, his book (shown left) written by Eamonn O'Neill and published in 1991. Ken was a founder member of the BNTVA (British Nuclear Test Veterans Association) in 1983.

LEFT: Sapper Danny Perriton, in 1957, by the British Forces Post Office, BFPO 170 (attached to 28FER). Danny would later be promoted to a Captain, in the RE TAVR... **RIGHT**: Sapper Gerald Rice, 1962. Gerald, a talented carpenter, and photographer, supplied invaluable coloured photographs – and text.

LEFT: The author, in 1957. **RIGHT:** A recent photo of Danny, of the 1957 Grapple tests, and Gerald of the Dominic tests 1962, after they met over 10 years ago at a reunion in Weston-Super-Mare. They've become inseparable friends ever since, spending many holidays at each other's homes. (Source: Gerald Rice)

Graylingwell

Married, two infant sons; in 1967, we moved south, into West Sussex. I had worked as a civvie clerk for the Metropolitan Police and New Scotland Yard. Whilst at the Yard in the press bureau I developed an interest in psychology.

Finding wages from the Met as an unqualified clerical officer inadequate to support the family, I supplemented my income by working occasional weekends, in 24hr coverage, as a security guard for London Securicor services; posted as needed in West End offices, factories, wherever required.

And, in addition, I worked as a civvie telephone switchboard operator in the Met's Twickenham police station. At this 'nick' I enjoyed the company of the London bobbies, a great bunch of guys – men and women officers, most chaps ex National Servicemen, or servicemen retired after WW2, Korea or Middle East posting. They were great carers, as I soon found out – as well as experts in upholding the UK statutory laws. Not all were rigid supporters of the famed local Twickenham Rugby Team, as I discovered, over weekend duties.

At the Yard, I'd joined up with John, a colleague, as part-time Territorial in the Harrow branch of the Royal Army Medical Corps (RAMC). And in the Summer of 1967, served a two week compulsory placement with the RAMC, in West Germany. Our course of training was to be a wartime casualty military base – in a Nuclear War. Our unit to serve as a 'Decontamination' Casualty station, following a recent Nuclear attack – or 'incident' involving radiation poisoning, etc. None of us knew anything about Nuclear, the 'behind the scenes' of the secrets of Cold War...

Despite my three years in the Sappers, thirteen months on Christmas Island, 1955-1958, I knew absolutely zero about atom bomb tests. However, it was during the Six Day War in 1967, in the Middle East – and, we were warned we might 'not' be going back home, but be on standby transfer to the Canal Zone. Relief. I rejoined my young family in Teddington, and moved south to West Sussex, And would sign on as a student registered mental nurse (RMN), at Graylingwell in Chichester, West Sussex – and, a career in psychiatric social work, till retirement in 2000 (*See. Better Court Than Coroners. 2 Volumes, 2011 and 2012*)... I remain totally ignorant of the ongoing intensity of global nuclear peacetime tests, for many years, but, learned by experience much about life after shell shock and traumas after two world wars... and the Cold War.

Black Gold

The European Cold War is generally accepted, at least in theory, as concluded by the removal of the Berlin Wall, separating East and West Germany in 1989, after which a few, dark state secrets soon started to emerge in the mass media. Every country, I learnt, in every state, each community and in every Babel-like language; all had (indeed always) in place, Official Secrets Acts. As a squaddie in civilian and military ranks, on a number of occasions, I had had to sign documents forbidding disclosures as a witness to job-related occupations. And, certainly, the media, especially paper press, rigidly toed the line in this aspect. To my knowledge, I really had had nothing to declare in this aspect. But there was, in retrospect, plenty of buts... perhaps.

My grandparents were born in the wake of Victorian England, in an age of candles, gaslight and steam power – generated, mostly, by the fuel of coal and wood-burning industries.

In early 2000s, with an interest in aspects of local history, I attended a book fair in Lewes, where I located an original folio of a local church's churchwardens accounts, 1602 – 1835. After checking out the legal aspect of provenance I obtained a short-term loan from my bank and purchased this original source of history.

Much to my surprise, I found many, many folios (pages) of dated entries of Poor Law claims for coal; regular requests from the parishioners. Page after page, parish clerks recorded, signed 'X', claims of both paupers and tradesmen; most people, then, could not read or write and so made their marks.

Hundreds of repeated applications for coal fuel (and/or blankets, clothing, etc.) appeared. It was clear that possibly, probably, everyone in the parish depended on their Poor Law funds, via the churchwardens; for limited fuel (coal or wood) supplies.

This was before gas lamps became available: people still had but charcoal (wood) or a wax supply of candles. Here, there, was where for centuries the tribe, manor, or parish church. What was not always recorded was what mines supplied the coal fuel, to the parish poor law stores.

Whoever owned and managed the coal mines – the energy sources – in essence, controlled the nation's industry and domestic supplies, and every form of government, depends on our 'black gold' – or nuclear?

In early days of the Manhattan Project, in the 1940s, General Groves, the senior officer on the project, was given almost bottomless government funds for the atomic bomb tests; and so, with the growing high value of uranium (essential in producing plutonium, for the fabric of the atomic weapons) and its sources, Groves purchased sources in the Belgian Congo of Africa – and other 'sources', thus ensuring the necessary fuel would be available when needed, on the project – the product produced by the new nuclear plants (as Windscale/Sellafield) in England.

And, as diluted coal had produced the smokeless fuel of coke and, blessed, greatly aided the removal of the awful smog, of fog, falling rain plus sulphur and other clinging, choking matter; I vividly recall this fallout in the early 1950s (see Chapter 2)...

The establishment began to use a bi-product of the atomic waste, called depleted uranium – and, so allow nuclear rocket shells (with radiation?) in future global conflicts.

Two hundred of so years on, the system, in the 21st Century, is the same; whichever body controls the energy supplies of the village, state or nation, remains in charge – and, can hold to ransom its own indigenous people or exported, energy sources – in times of peace and war. In times of war and poverty, coal has always been 'rationed' scarce or unavailable. A candle *alone* produces little heat.

All affluent politicians and high income earners, too, must be dependent on this fact... and, to date, in the 20th century, nuclear power energy prevailed, as new atomic energy, supplies, with their own awesome fiefdom – and bonds of secrecy. And new problems of dangerous waste disposal – of nuclear waste.

Gas, electricity, oil, even water supplies remain dependent on this awesome fact of life – or death, all our domestic and industry dependent on these energy supplies. But, always, I found out that with electricity or coal strikes – at the turn of a rogue switch or nuclear power station – accident – all computer records, cooking and heating appliances, are off – and, once again, depend on black gold, or coal – or wood supplies (if obtainable) to date remain the only substitute. Solar heat, per se, has yet to be industrialised.

In the late 1940s, WW2 over, the USSR threatened to sign a separate peace pact, with the eastern zone of Berlin; to further the intended occupation of Europe, previously occupied by the Nazi domination of European nations.

A physical wall began, with the attempt to isolate, to starve into submission, the people of Berlin.

The millionth bag of coal to be delivered during the Berlin Airlift handed down from a US Skymaster to pilot Sergeant Clyde Peterson and Group Captain B C Yarde (commander of Gatow Station) at Gatow Airport, Berlin. (Photo by Keystone/Getty Images)

And, so, the Berlin Air Lift took place – fuel, coal sacks and foodstuff were parachuted into the isolated city, under siege, in 1948 – and over a million sacks of coal dropped by air into Berlin from western nations. (Not until 1961 was the wall completed, and existed until 1989.)

Moi, all I recall, at 11 years old in 1948, the year of the London Olympics. And a brief holiday out of the orphanage. Of world events 'outside' – I knew, mass media or otherwise – zero?

Not Just Money

The cost of ongoing atomic tests and, so called, little wars – and, occasional consideration of domestic budgets... too often meant cooking the books. And, to outright lying, denial or worse, in recording the fallout effects of the kiloton, then megaton atomic weapons. Sometimes wrongly recorded or, worse, the so-called scientific evidence (of results) on cost to the human populations – just not a real consideration at that time.

But of course, during the 1940s, 1950s and 1960s and, yes, up to the 1970s – with the continuation of nuclear tests and nuclear power stations – costs in human, flora and fauna became absurd a justification – if denied evidence.

In the early 1980s, state domestic secrets began to be unmasked, as Top Secret, classified, government records became declassified – and less became more ... This fact was especially true in democratic USA, where the declassified details of past atomic testing effects on its own indigenous civilian and military population became known.

But, our British successive governments remain, to date (2013), in total denial – few declassified documents, and insistence that no British Servicemen (or their families) – to which the paper media, press and digital, were unable to insert level of declassification; as in the USA. British governments glibly insist that no British and Commonwealth personnel suffered at all in the participation of any nuclear tests: no proven evidence of toxic effects internal or external, could be proven in evidence given at a British court of appeal...

Secret

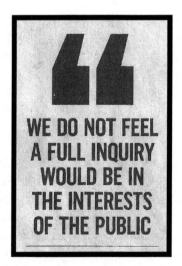

WE DO NOT FEEL
A FULL INQUIRY
WOULD BE IN
THE INTERESTS
OF THE PUBLIC

Taken from the Sunday Times, July 14, 2013.
Quoted, ad nauseum, by all government press releases

Revelations

Early in WW2, George Orwell (*All Propaganda is Lies,* 1941-1942 eds., Secker and Warburg, London. 1998 p.39) in an insightful BBC October 1941 broadcast spoke on the weighty subject of 'propaganda' as a weapon in war and peace: of *deliberate* projection of fiction (as fact) misinformation, and disinformation, in his text; of non-fiction writers, and fiction material projected in our awful state of war – its cause and effect – however painful. As a child, I was too young, and could not identify with such patriotic writings, or carefully chosen tones, in his speech. But, in the 1950s, I did learn of Orwell in *1984*, and *Animal Farm*.

Two public figures, American film stars John Wayne and James Stewart, were mythical figures in my lifetime – then, icons, of freedom, honesty and Perseverance. One winning gritty line: In *Rio Grande* (1950) expressed by excellent actor Ben Johnson, playing Sgt. Tyree, says to the new squaddie (son of the C.O., John Wayne), *"Get it done, Johnny Reb,"*, a line I often said to myself in facing unpleasant situations in need of resolution. The half-full, rather than half-empty, metaphysical bottle – which, in later life, meant one's body as the bottle.

Two other examples of Wayne. One, the unseen background hero – supporting the seeming helpless James Stewart – who, in the film, would become an iconic lawyer and statesman. A journalist heard the lifestory of the senator in the film *The Man Who Shot Liberty Valance* (1962, the years of Nevada and Dominic atomic tests). Asked if he would print this new truth, he replied *"No Sir, this is the West: When the legend becomes fact, print the legend"* – a moral oxymoron.

Last John Wayne quote is on the controversial film *"The Green Berets"* (1968) – at the height of the proxy overseas war, in Vietnam. Americans, drafted (like British National Servicemen, who had been fighting in Korea), out to fight a war they could not win, as it would mean all out nuclear war, with the USSR, China, and Communist Europe: No sides wanted that awesome atomic campaign... no way! Whatever the merits and demerits of the Vietnam war, John Wayne offered his support to the armed forces, the squaddies sent out to this unpopular, fateful conflict. A true USA patriot – war and politics apart. Ironic, The Duke was a Cold War victim, a *Downwinder,* at the time of the USA Tests in the 1950s – he contracted cancer from the nuclear fallouts, whilst making a Hollywood Film, *The Conqueror*, in the Nevada Desert. They killed their own American hero.

I heard of abuse by the MKULTRA (M-K-ULTRA, an American Secret Service experimental brainwashing project) by USA, USSR, and British politic misuse, as *Ipcress File,* fictionalised by Len Deighton (1962) indicated, malpractices – most politically motivated. But, no way had I personally seen or heard of such awful evidence-based black science accounts, by the USA and USSR.

I followed, with interest, press cuttings on the iconic mushrooms, Hiroshima – and the benign British Nuclear Test Veterans Association (BNTVA).

In 2011-12, for some months, through *Google* and emails, I was accepted in a 'loop' of ex-nuclear vets sustained by their current solicitors. In addition, for some months, I enjoyed regular, very friendly, telephone communication with Grapple Y witness Ken McGinley - until I experienced two major heart attacks at the end of 2011.

Early in 2012 , I was recovering from two heart attacks... and housebound. I discovered via the *Google* Web – *new* sources of incredible (to me) revelations, most data of which came from recently de-classified information – in America and the UK... and, new contacts.

I felt frustrated that most material , whilst all fascinating, it was/is still and, newly re-classified (in the *Google*) viz copyright of de-classified – valid citations. But, recent new book titles appeared during routine searches... of great interest; books not printed in the UK...

Three early pre Google publications, for me, at that time, stood head and shoulders above other, fascinating non-fiction books on Cold War nuclear tests. First was Ken McGinley's 1991 Grapple book; second was an American investigative journalist and photographer, Carol Gallagher, her publication dated 1993. And, third, was a Russian work by Vladimir Chernousenko published in 1996.

McGinley's book was mostly based on the British Grapple Tests on Christmas Island in the late 1950s. Gallagher's' work was on research of the USA Nevada nuclear tests in the 1950s and 1960s. And, the third by Chernousenko, was an awesome account of the Chernobyl disaster and its consequences (he died from it one year after the book's publication).

All of these foundation books present concrete evidence-based accounts of the many individuals, and their families, who experienced the burns and toxic fallout exposures to the many top secret, *Cold War* Nuclear Tests.

Royal Prerogative

In 1940, the blitz demolished our home in north London. My mother, then single with two infants to home and care for, received a government billeting allowance of eleven shillings – for all of us – to survive on. In modern coinage, this would be 55p total, per week, to survive. Any work (with the infants in tow) was attempted, but even charity was taxed; any loan from the state had to be repaid. And, with the rank fiscal depression which followed the costs of WW1 – poverty was endemic in the twenties and thirties and, still, in 1939-40. The *Beveridge Report* helped provide for 'all in need' as the Welfare State was born in 1946 – instrumented in 1948 – as the benign *National Health Service* was formally introduced; with all its new provisions from birth to death, backup provisions in place.

After *National Service* and short-term as a regular in the army, I joined the territorials (See *Chapters One and Two*) till 1967, when I enrolled as a student mental nurse in Graylingwell Hospital. I learnt that until 1946 with the NHS, it had been one of many registered 'special' workhouse asylums. And it also ended – though years before I discovered the anomaly – historically, all the public buildings and staff protection in principle were covered by the (then) *Royal Prerogative*, with the reigning monarch nominally as head of State. This prerogative had been well in place since the 16th Century, and King Henry VIII. After the 17th Century civil war, modern parliament was born in its wake. And the *Royal Prerogative* diluted – but later still in place... and became the *Crown Proceedings Act, 1947*.

All the following, I learnt socially, and by experience, as a matter of fact. I was employed by the NHS and, later, working in our community as a psychiatric social worker till 2000. But, it was only by my gathering interests, soon passion, for social history that I researched the origins of the hospital, and NHS systems and began to learn that by introducing the new government authority of the NHS establishments, the *Royal Prerogative* no longer existed, as such – with all its subsequent (who's responsible) problems when things go wrong.

True, that individual's criminal behaviour remained indictable – but, the hospital authorities, for many years, could no longer be held responsible, as a body, for the treatment of its employees – and human patients. After 30 years, I produced a non-fiction book, '*Better Court Than Coroners*', in two volumes in 2011 and 2012... albeit in a very limited edition; but, a record no less. But, of course, the 1948 NHS, and its establishment, also applied to 'all' previous public institutions – included the military.

Since working as a civilian at New Scotland Yard press office, in the sixties, I continued to gather (out of interest) press cuttings of anything of interest to me; workhouses, police, science, experiences in the army in the 1950s and early sixties. I retained an interest in anything to do with the 'goings on' at home and abroad of the Nuclear weapons industry – still much in use in this time, being ill-named Cold War. In retrospect, I very, very slowly, became aware of the media and government 'only' reporting the global mushrooms, as iconic images of technical and political achievements but, very little of the 'boots-on-the-ground' squaddies, and air infantry. Who, and how, catered for their needs? Clearly, the *Royal Army Medical Corps* was, as a military body, totally controlled by the state, and any wartime happenings, controlled by an elected government – still (but unseen) top secret under the mandates of the *Royal Prerogative* – and its Principle of 'who cares for' the armed services (and their families) health and welfare – and pensions were clearly applicable.

I read more and more of the failed attempts, in the 1980s through to 2000s, of the *British Nuclear Test Veterans* to obtain a valid hearing by this government. To no avail. The press and media mostly gave lip service to the pleas of numerous casualties of the many atomic test victims. An inevitable singular iconic image of a mushroom usually marking one test (of hundreds) and, perhaps, a brief interview with local press, and a local identified individual – often a widow, or other close relatives who had suffered as a result of attending one, or many, nuclear tests in the 1950s and sixties.

In reckoning, I was one of at least 20,000 British and Commonwealth military, who took part in servicing these wartime – *Cold War* awesome nuclear experiments. But, whilst I had been servicing the first three Grapple tests – 1956-1957 – I did *not* really consider myself a nuclear veteran: that unhappy identity I designated for vets who witnessed the mushrooms, blasts and fallout radiation. It never occurred to me that many veterans (since declassified top secret documents confirmed) had *not* necessarily seen a mushroom – though, horrors, RAF personnel were often sent into the mushroom clouds of radiation to do their duty.

I was piqued in following the enormous (and justified) frustration of the Vets clearly being treated like criminals for producing evidence of wanton abuse of its military personnel – and, families whose children and members, evidenced awful, terminal, slow deaths and forms of disability during the past 40-50 years. And, I enrolled in the loop of those who supported the claimants for compensation – and, more so, their evidence of total 'official' denial, ongoing by all British governments, of the veterans.

I was *not* a claimant, nor intended to be but, by God I supported those who were truly abused by the state, using the now defunct top secret law of *Royal Prerogative*. And, for the next few months, I connected via *Google* and email with involved bodies.

It was during this time I learned of Ken Mcginley's book, *No Risks Involved* (1991). Then began a fruitful few months exchanging phone calls with him (he lived in Scotland, and I in Sussex), and I heard of many abuses. The solicitors' loop sent me regular emails on the progress of the vets' claims.

Not till the late 2000s did I read, off a *Google* search, data on the BNTVA ongoing attempts via a London based firm of solicitors. I had heard of the *Crown Proceedings Act, 1947* which in theory, for the first time, allowed civil actions, torts against the crown - but 'reasserted' the time immemorial, common law of Crown Privilege. I found this definition most confusing on hearing of this proposed change to the statutory laws.

The Act received the royal assent on 31 July 1947 – but, not till 1 January 1948 did it come into force. Coincidence? The proposal of the new NHS act was written in 1946 and came into force, you guessed it, 1948. But, criminal acts were still indictable – it remained on statute that the crown itself could *not* be held accountable. Thus, in NHS and military law the 1947, post WW2 aftermath Section 10 of the Act, was still in force in the 1950s and sixties.

Whereas both Reagan and Gorbachev (post Chernobyl) acknowledged the effects of radiation exposure, Thatcher, and the Tories, did not. In 1987, Section 10 of the 1947 Act, which referred to the Military, was rescinded, and would allow (in principle) nuclear vets and others who suffered toxic damage during the Cold War, to sue for compensation – and recognition.

Feres Certiorari

The USA, too, in parallel with the UK, had its own *Crown Proceedings Act*, which was enacted from the end of WW2 – and continued into the years of the Cold War. The US law was referred to as the *feres certiorari*; in both countries, UK and the USA, top secrets were absolute. Any infringement was deemed potentially as an act of treason.

In 1950, the US was challenged by an individual, the widow of Lt. Rudolph Feres, who died while serving as a soldier on active military service. Lt. Feres died in a barracks fire at a base camp, at Pine Camp, New York. His widow sued the government as responsible for providing the unsafe conditions which caused his death; rather than a specific individual, on a criminal charge.

The US Supreme Court denied any legal responsibility under the current *Federal Tort Claims Act* – Feres v United States – but his widow lost the case as the country remained totally immune from any statutory responsibility. Just as the UK *Crown Proceedings Act 1947* was still in force in the 1950s, Sixties and Seventies. Both countries could legally at any time, peace or war, do literally anything to and with its armed forces and not be sued as wilful acts of abuse... or otherwise.

Certorari is defined by my *Collins English Language Dictionary* as:

> "Certorari, n. Law. An order of a superior court directing that a record of proceedings in a lower court be sent for review. See mandamus, prohibition – from legal latin 'to be informed'."

In other words, forbidden, blocked, barred from challenging the state: in origin this suggests the imperial head, representative of the state – or empire. And pre-American, British Royal prerogative (aka, Crown Law), seems, vaguely, imported into the 18th century United States rights of independence in the US constitution, vested in the president... so research indicates.

Whatever the etymological origins in post WW2 parlance, this *'Feres doctrine'* implied that any claimed injuries *could be* obtained in circumstances other than indicated origins from serving in the military forces. And, to rebuke that law, could imply treason – against the state. To reiterate: In the United Kingdom, the foregoing *Section 10* of the *Crown Proceedings Act* of 1947, remained firmly in force as law, and political policy: even when 'evidence based' such as forensic, and found proven – would be denied by the state prosecutors. McGinley's excellent account (*No Risk Involved*. 1991. c7) details events up to 1987 which indicated previous exposure to toxic radiation, during the atomic, nuclear bomb weapons of destruction is, *not* was, proven as probable.

Thanks to the backing of President Reagan, who approved new legislation, in 1987, which allowed US nuclear veterans to automatically qualify for a veterans' pension (and their family dependants), consolidated in the USA, new legislation that *'Presumptives for Disability Compensation'* – would include all vets – including subsequent vets exposed to toxic chemicals, etc., in times of conflict – Vietnam, Gulf Wars, et al.

In the United Kingdom, successive governments since WW2 remain intransigent, using policy rather than evidence of wrongdoings by government employees, during the *cold war* years.

In 1990, Prime Minister Margaret Thatcher declared that the proposed *'Radiation Exposed Crown Employees (Benefits) Bill.'* was *not* proved. This despite the USA and President Reagan's compassion, and post-1986 Chernobyl findings which enabled President Gorbachev to acknowledge the associations of nuclear (toxic) radiation and subsequent sufferings, due to abnormal exposure to radiation and fallout.

Despite the British Section 10 being altered, it did *not* acknowledge the clinical, albeit proven, scientific evidence of association of radiation and subsequent deadly after effects of *The Bomb*, but, the absolute ruling of the past government refusal under the *Feres Doctrine* to accept the military, human costs during the hundreds of nuclear tests.

BNTVA

The *British (*and Commonwealth*) Nuclear Test Veterans Association* (BNTVA) was founded by ex-Sapper Ken McGinley, who became its first chairman in 1983. Before this important date, legally it could *not* exist because of the *Official Secrets Act*, and its full gagging powers – *whatever* abuse or proven neglect could be established.

Before the ex-military BNTVA in 1983, an American similar organisation was established in 1979 by Orville E Kelly of Burlington, Iowa, USA which, legally, allowed membership by any proven USA atomic veteran survivors (and their family descendants). Known as NAAV – the *National Association of Atomic Veterans, Inc*. As with European Cousins in the British Commonwealth the USA, too, is a non-profit charity – not an entitlement of service – guaranteed to unite in recognition of a fair court hearing relating to their developed radiogenic health issues, caused by excessive exposure to fallout from nuclear weapon tests, past explosions, or associated events. (This would later include any future toxic conflict or domestic members, in the 1980s until the 2000s, as well as Vietnam and Iraqi wars.)

Other English speaking nuclear veterans associations include the Australia and New Zealand (*NZ Vets*) and neighbouring protectorate Pacific Islanders, and Fijian inhabitants.

It's imperative to include the non-English-speaking nuclear survivors, from Hiroshima and Nagasaki, and their subsequent disorders.

The exposed survivors were labelled, in a pejorative term, *Hibakusha* (translated: bomb-affected people) by their fellow Japanese, though under the new protection of the USA, as a protectorate, it would be many painful years before (like a leper community), being integrated in a, mustn't speak of them, shunned, unclean human victims of the nuclear war – then known as atomic disease.

My knowledge of the other non-speaking English societies, Asian and others, is largely, even today, virtually non-existent, as squaddie or other: my elementary research finished with Alexander Solzhenitsyn's *The Gulag Archipelago* (pub. 1974) and Andrei D Sakharov *Memoirs* (pub. 1990).

But, to update, the tragedies of the 1986 Ukraine-Soviet power station at Chernobyl provides more than enough evidence of unsafe nuclear power stations – their wastage and, accidental or not, fallout. To be continued...

Black Rain

It was August 6th 1945; an atom bomb, *the Bomb*, had exploded early in the morning in Hiroshima, Japan. Dr Michihio Hachiya, medical director of the Hiroshima Communications Hospital, had been on night duty as an air-raid warden in the hospital.

Suddenly, a strong flash of light, and all that had been so bright and sunny became dark and hazy. Through swirly dust he could just see the wooden column of his house, in the act of 'leaning crazily and the roof sagged dangerously', so his diary notes of that horrendous event began.

He became aware of being completely naked (the clothes blown off him), and badly cut and injured from the debris. It was the beginning of a horrendous nightmare.

Amongst the damage, he tripped over a decapitated head – as the blast of the bomb continued to demolish all the buildings about him; and an intense heat, incinerating all about him, as fires whipped up by a vicious wind (from the blast) began to spread.

As he attempted to move, an overpowering thirst overcame him – but no water was to be found. The heat of the bomb's initial blast was so severe it sucked out the body's tissue – all dehydrated, internal organs losing fluid. He was severely burnt, as were other survivors about him; they, too, mostly naked and dazed. Flash burns from the thermonuclear heat appeared, at first, limited by whether the skin was naked (as face) or covered by black clothing, caps, etc; or if diminished by white garments, which reflected a portion of the intense white heat. But, this was only the beginning for those injured survivors (at the time), who had to endure the continuing intense fires, which kept spreading across the crumbling city centre.   Heated flash burns led to thickened skin scars, called *keloids*. But, these skin 'tattoos' inevitably hid injuries from uninvited observers.

Dr Hachiya described how the outer burnt skin would be peeling off to expose soft tissue – open to further infection. And these were primary symptoms. The naked faces and skin swelled up, totally removed body parts, like ears, noses – with huge swollen features hiding previous identity.

Secondary symptoms were soon apparent, apart from the inevitable dehydration (with only available black rain puddles, or ionised / fallout particles in the hot ground or dark water courses). Survivors (including the good doctor) vomiting, and experiencing bloody diarrhoea stools – initially thought to be caused by bacillary dysentery. And excessive vomiting, the internal damaged organs unable, with the dehydration, to sustain any intake of food or water. And there were people suffering from partial blindness, later designated cataracts. A whole range of internal organs were also damaged, though, as well as anorexia (loss of appetite), thyroid and other problems, leukaemia, and many cases of cancer.

Subcutaneous haemorrhages were appearing as skin eruptions, and in many sufferers with excessive sore throats, bloody ulcers emerged as thyroid infections, etc; Another symptom was a low white blood count, and vulnerability to disease; these deemed symptoms of atomic disease – caused by the aftermath of the bomb blast.

A few days after the explosion, in-patients and out-patients disclosed increasing petechiae, eruptions on the skin, and other dire symptoms, of unknown origin. And many patients began to lose all their hair (epiliation) which just fell off on contact. As a symptom of this new 'atomic disease', it was suspected that a new toxic gas might be its origin.?

All the foregoing infirmities were, without question, derived from the blast and fallout, black rain of the Hiroshima and Nagasaki atomic bombs... the Bomb.

But, in the years ahead, full forty years and more – WW2, into the infamous Cold War period, till 1991; thousands of massive atomic tests – tests, purported to be scientific, revealed equally fatal fallout effects due to multiple exposures of world-wide explosions up to many megatons – and their fallout. These fatal side-effects were caused by the ionisation infection of the internal organs.

For some time, Dr Hachiya believed that a massive, at least 500lb, conventional incendiary bomb had been dropped by an American bomber above his city, and its dense population. Evidence of a severe conflagration was all around him, with carbonised, shrunken bodies about him. And so, as he became aware he, too, was badly burnt about his person (much as casualties of the London Blitz – and English cities during the burning Blitz: and, the later destruction by fire of Dresden; and deaths of thousands of indigenous inhabitants).

Two Englishmen were allowed to watch the Nagasaki bombing: Group Captain Leonard Cheshire, VC, DSO, DFC, authorised by Churchill, and physicist Dr William Penney, who had been involved with the Americans in the Manhattan Project. Many years later, as a student in the early 1960s I visited one of the Cheshire's homes for the disabled in Hampshire. In fact, our hospital, Graylingwell, at Chichester, donated a substantial amount of beds and furniture, freed from wartime evacuees returning home. I was most impressed by the Cheshire Homes for the handicapped and disabled.

And, Dr Penney – well, after Japan, he remained as a principal English advisor for the duration of the Cold War. It was possible I saw him on Christmas Island, though I would not have recognised him – indeed, I'd never heard of him, at that time.

And, so, Dr Hachiya's incredible Hiroshima Diary '*The Journal of a Japanese Physician*' recorded, in his diary notes until September 30th, 1945, evidence of the aftermath, and so-called atomic disease, unremitting in its devastation. And, his own injuries self-evident.

Of that first day, he would record:

> 'Huge raindrops began to fall. Some thought a thunderstorm was beginning, and would extinguish the fires. But these drops were capricious. A few fell and a few more; that was all the rain we saw.'

Obviously, this telling account was in his Japanese. In an eventual English translation, a footnote was added;

> 'There were many reports of a scanty rainfall over the city after the bombing. The drops were described as large and dirty, and some claimed that they were laden with radioactive dust.'

It was a description of black rain, aka acid rain, rain out...

Only ten years on in America, about the Utah desert, since 1951, thousands of American military troops, and indigenous citizens, frequently witnessed (sometimes close up) numerous atomic bomb tests – aiming for megatons, *many times* more than those of Hiroshima and Nagasaki. This was only months after I left Christmas Island, in 1957: months before the later, infamous, Grapple Y test, in April 1958, only twenty five miles south of where the troops still lived, in the Main Camp, RAF Camp and Port London...

Though frequently denied by the British MoD, there were many witnesses amongst our Christmas Island squaddies (including upper ranks – also sworn to secrecy); witnesses who experienced the first deadly vapours from the Grapple Y bomb, which would certainly have been black rain (the evaporation, cooling of heated clouds saturated with ionised matter, the fallout debris).

Official British MoD de-classified published records stated Grapple Y was 3.4 megatons – which was very high. But, after declassification, and *The Freedom of Information Act*, and 50 years on, other alarming facts were realised. An RAF officer, Flight Lieutenant Joseph Pasquini, navigator of a Canberra bomber, whose aircraft was one of the, by then regular, gatherers of toxic matter, sniffers, high up in the mushroom cloud, fed up by our self-centred politicians, had personally experienced his dosimeter recording levels of 10.4 megatons, a devastating yield.

Another nuclear survivor, RAF officer Flight Lieutenant Eric Denson, another RAF sniffer, was ordered not once, but *twice*, to fly into the Grapple Y mushroom cloud and collect samples of the ionised debris. He never recovered from injuries from the inevitable overdose of radiation. And, after immense suffering, he died from his wounds in 1976.

Again, the British MoD and its government totally denied their men and dependants, whose absolute loyalty was (is) ignored; though following Lt. Denson's death, after legal battles, his widow, Shirley Denson, was finally awarded a grudging pension.

In the years after the awesome Grapple Y test on Christmas Island, in April 28th 1958 many other RAF (Navy and Army) personnel would suffer ill effects from overdosing on radiation. And all casualties, witnesses and their relatives were sworn to total secrecy, to the ignoring of the HM governments in the next fifty years and more.

I recall, in the 1950s and sixties that the armed forces were completely divided: Army, Naval and RAF detachments had their own camps and domestic facilities – often miles apart (as in World War 2) – rarely coming in contact with one another, at least at squaddie, on ground level. Upper echelons with their civilian boffins led their own superior, comparative lifestyles.

It became inevitable that without day to day contact – even socially – the troops' personnel (of which I was a member) would know nothing of their peers in the other services. Despite all of us being engaged on *Operation Grapple* nuclear tests in the 1950s.

It is hardly surprising that despite mass media brief reports, and with absolute secrecy, taboos were in situ. We army squaddies referred to our RAF peers (mostly ground crews) as '*Brylcreem Boys*', friendly rivals, but not in the pejorative. And, to the naval juniors, well – contrary to the media, most of us respectfully referred to the navy as the true *Senior Service* – never rivals, per se. Again, not negatively pejorative, but, sometimes, our sailors might refer to all other military, including the *Royal Marines*, as '*pongos*' – or, erm, like apes.

And as for the high fliers of the RAF – well, in all ways we viewed them as well above us, in the social scales (our generation recalled the World War

2 Blitz, etc.) – and, where lifestyle was wholly unknown, except in books and recorded on film. The RAF regiment (like our red caps) were the police of the RAF – we'd known of them, but rarely had contact: they were with the ground crews – still RAF personnel.

It was hardly surprising that by 50 years and more, our unseen RAF colleagues on the *Grapple* 1950s tests' exploits remained wholly unknown – and secret. And so the immense dangers they were exposed to in any real contact with the weapons, and associated aftermath of the tests were again unknown to us. Until technology advanced, as our offspring generations were born, and, slowly, we read declassified data of the past, and some gags were removed.

And, worse, the civilian boffins mis-predicted the direction of the wind, which blew toxic black rain 'over' the mostly unprepared military below, on Christmas Island. Sapper Ken McGinley was at the *Grapple Y* tests and recalled, with many of his companions, heavy black rain following the air bursts, and fallout blowing over their heads, but the official records refused to recognise these 'live' witnesses and any maladies subsequent to this event. And, over the next twenty to thirty years, casualties suffered many severe ailments (as did their children and grand-children) – wholly denied as impossible to legally prove.

Yes, the tests were successful, for both politicians and the military, but at what price?

Black Rain Continued

In 73AD the Roman towns of Pompeii and Herculaneum were destroyed and buried, with their population, by the active volcano Vesuvius. The massive falling detritus spewed up by the immense blast waves of the energy, combined with very toxic gases, completely buried the two prosperous coastal towns. And this was no way triggered by martial or otherwise human activities, but through natural phenomena; as with all volcanoes, through millions of years (it is a warm planet) in common with earthquakes, flood inundations, tsunamis and massive storms.

But, the coming of the new atomic nuclear age (unless, we realise, we humans are natural phenomena too) would soon discover that the fallout and massive conflagrations caused by any – all nuclear bombs, were yet to be discovered, from Trinity, Hiroshima and Nagasaki. And, it could have been much worse, in August 1945 – and afterwards.

At the instigation of US General LeMay, et al, more atomic bombs were already planned to deliver '*total destruction*' of at least ten Japanese cities; this was demographic population. Surely an act of genocide – only averted by the complete surrender of the emperor, Hirohito, effectively bringing WW2 to an end.

In retrospect, it was probably necessary to make those drastic plans. Stalin's troops were only 700 miles or so from Tokyo – situated on the maritime east coast. But, and it's a huge but – why was it necessary to continue atomic tests immediately *after* Japan surrendered?

And so, to the world-at-large (perhaps not Stalin?) total joy was the order of the day, in August 1945.

Initially, the awful '*after effects*' of the bombs detonation – aided by the unpredictable caprice of earth's weather patterns over the next (at least) 40 to 50 years, were not envisioned...

Shortly after the Americans occupied Japan, the USA military authorities authorised studies of '*the survivors*' of the two A bombs. And, inevitably, this could only have been, then, primary results of the initial blast, and exposure to the fallout effects of radiation on the population. When the fallout was still detected, after the mushrooms had long-gone, they (the authorities) were soon forced to realise that delayed secondary side effects had begun to kill off many of the exposed individuals. This was radiation sickness.

I believe it was decided the military should properly '*only*' record found dead '*casualties*' among enemies, called *precision bombing*. A body count equated only deaths.

I knew by experience, and other sources (of course), an awesome pre-war military and social history, set the scene for potential *mass extinction* of any opposing faction – from current conventional weaponry in the fiscal early 1940s – to awesome, new, means of mass destruction by atomic warfare in 1945 and post-war WW2 years .

The recent 'Blitz' of 1940-41 Nazi Germany's military superiority maximised its assets and, initially, exercised precision bombing destruction (Blitzkrieg), with its full armament and polarised acrid politics, but, it didn't defeat Great Britain and its benign friends in the Colonies of those times.

Hitler decided to bomb, burn and destroy (if he couldn't enslave) and declared the maxim of *Total War* against civilian populations, domestic and military, and occupy their countries. *Total War* to destroy, annihilate all allied forces – *genocide* – to name the ghoul. And, in retrospect (so recent) in 1940-1 he declared all civilians (even his own countrymen) were legitimate targets, starting with the *Baedeker Blitz/raids* upon us, in Great Britain.

And, in 1945, the US military, in the event of *No Surrender*, planned its own *Baedeker* raids on the main Japanese towns, ports and cities – in total war *against* the Japanese nation – first, by jelly napalm bombs to burn all principal towns and cities, then by Atomic Bombs.

Keloid

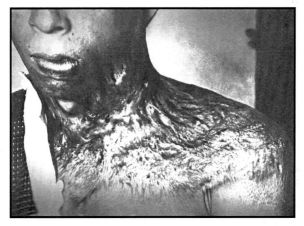

A survivor of Atomic bombing, from Hiroshima or Nagasaki. The 'healed' scars – called keloids.(Picture source: *The Devils Repertoire, or Nuclear Bombing and The Life of Man* by Victor Gollancz, 1958. His source for the photograph taken from Fernand Gigon's *Formula for Death*. Published by Allan Wingate Limited, 1958)

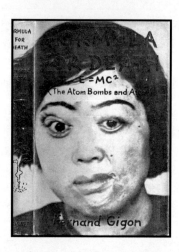

The cover of *Formula for Death*, by Fernand Gigon, published in 1958.

One of the graphic photographs of a survivor of Hiroshima shows a man, with thick ribbed keloids, as tattooed by fibrous tissue. He'd experienced severe flash burns, caused by direct exposure to the immense heat, in the blast of the dropped atomic bomb. Also above is a woman, disfigured by the explosion. Their wounds would be a primary symptom of that extreme explosion. Closer still to the ground zero, centre of the atomic bomb site, there was soon to be estimated hundreds, thousands, of black, carbonised, shrivelled, anonymous burnt human corpses.

Fallout 1945, and After

After the formal signing of the Japanese unconditional surrender on September 2nd 1945, on board the battleship *USS Missouri,* anchored in Tokyo harbour, the US Marines advance party disembarked, the to be thousands of US occupying forces (to remain so for six years). By the end of September 1945, marines were arriving at Kure and Nagasaki harbours, initially, to aid and instruct the Japanese in cleaning up the (not yet realised) radioactive debris – and drinking contaminated water supplies. Toxic waste was, unknowingly, thrown into the sea. The men were unprotected, thousands of them.

'The Arrival of the Occupation Forces. Four aircraft carriers and 20 transports accompanied by American destroyers steamed into Nagasaki Harbour on September 23, 1945, less than two months after the atomic bombing. The soldiers standing on Dejima wharf in this photograph are probably members of the U.S. Marines Special Landing Brigade.' (Source: Photo and Caption, '89 Municipal Centennial Nagasaki 100, p18.)

In the above picture (considering the quality) three ships can be seen; the centre vessel is named *US Navy Hospital Ship, Sanctuary*, the context obvious. And, adjacent, other dockside white painted vessels, likely of a similar navy red cross facility, the other ship, out in the harbour, identity unknown...

Published unclassified pictures of Hiroshima and Nagasaki, of a wide compass of buildings and utter demolition of physical environment: a pattern long established, be it London, Hamburg, Dresden; a flattened landscape.

Whereas the purpose to eliminate the enemy, militant and general population en-masse – from 'predicted' human statistics (five hundred and fifty thousand, a million), too numerous to estimate. Only a few non-classified pictures of *keloids* apparent – recording the maximum extreme heat from 'blast' effects on human beings – anything, *any evidence* – short or longterm, of people affected by ionised matter – *Plutonium* refuse, radiation, remained wholly top secret, classified. And be so for the next fifty years or more... Denial.

But, witness evidence from the first visit, was readily available from the US Marines sent in to clean up the mess as preliminary to full occupation. The underestimated fiscal cost of the Bomb, exploded, would, in *future* time, cost billions of dollars, pounds, roubles, whatever: clean-up of toxic nuclear waste year on year to be solved as an ongoing major problem. And, of course, the human equation, the statistics in human life.

The American social historian, Studs Terkel (1912-2008) in his *The Good War, An Oral History of World War Two,* published in the USA in 1984, included interviews with marines who were among squaddies sent in to clean up the mess at Nagasaki then, later, at Hiroshima.

V.T. was a member of that September 23rd, 1945 landing at Nagasaki harbour. Previously, he was one of many personnel who had endured the awful Pacific War with the Japanese military machine.

> *"I'll never forget August 6, 1945. I'm standing in a chow line on Saipan... I heard... that a terrible new weapon had been used on the City of Hiroshima, Japan. It'll be a hundred years before anybody will be able to enter that city."*

And, further in the interview, a few weeks later, he questioned the one hundred year prediction – on a troop transport:

> *"How can we occupy Nagasaki... when they told us, it would be a hundred years before."*

He asked a young lieutenant of the Second Marine Division – informed they were going in to Nagasaki. And came to hear the knee jerk reply:

> *"Marine, you don't have anything to worry about. The scientists have gone in there. It's very safe"*

Which later proved wholly untrue.

On September 23rd, 1945, the US ships pulled into the harbour of Nagasaki. The following day, marine troops were able to explore at their leisure, And V.T., with five buddies, acted as tourists, exploring the recently atomised ruins of Nagasaki – and, awful, occasionally seen, damaged survivors... and death.

He, V.T., and his US marines remained three months, to tear down buildings, and clean up the rubble. By then, twenty thousand troops of the Second Marine Division occupied the town.

> *"We were instructed not to touch or go near any Japanese that we saw dropping in the street...*
>
> *We had no idea what it was all about. I was on the deck one day, doing duty, and here's the beautiful white ship in the harbour. On the side was painted* United States Scientific Expeditionary Force. *I turned to my buddy and said, 'We've been here a week and now they send in this scientific force to check this damn city over. We'll probably be sterile.' We kidded and laughed about it. We never took it seriously. Hell, we drank the water, we breathed the air, and we lived in the rubble. We did our duty."*(Source: Studs Terkel).

Still with the marines; marine L.Q. remembered, years later;

> *"We walked into Nagasaki unprepared... it was a grisly scene. Corpses were still being burned in the open air. Women's hair was falling out, the men all had their heads shaved, and all of them had running sores on their heels, ears, all over."*

Totally unprepared for their awesome experience in Nagasaki. No protective clothing (for thousands of marines) deemed necessary. No warnings whatever about potential contamination. L.Q., and his marine buddies of Company C – a 150 strong clean-up contingent, billeted at a partially destroyed concrete schoolhouse up the hill from the spot over which the atomic bombs had exploded. (*Killing Our Own. The Disaster of America's Experience with Atomic Radiation.* Wasserman, Solomon, et al. 1982)

L.Q. and his buddies drank the city contaminated reservoir water, and worked in the midst of the most heavily damaged area without any protective clothing. And, when he got back from Nagasaki, he felt burning, itching, running sores on the top of his head, and the top of his ears – just like the observed sores on the Japanese survivors. The radioactive underside would not become apparent to him for decades.

Almost a thousand or so of those Navy Seabees (Engineers) were billeted in the core area around the blast centre. Assigned clean-up duties:

> *"Press releases announced that scientists had found no*
> *lingering radiation worth worrying about in Nagasaki."*

Presumably referring to gamma rays, from the post-blast after effects of the bomb. No serviceman was observed wearing any dosimeter.

In later years, ex-marines suffered from multiple cancer myelomas, including a high incidence of terminal bone marrow disease and, symptoms of blood-related afflictions – such as Hodgkin's disease, myelofibrosis and leukaemia, well documented by the clean-up veterans and their widows – and other painful debilitating illnesses, contracted during the marines military service at Hiroshima and Nagasaki.

They recorded radioactive illnesses of occupying marines in September 1945 – and, afterward, correlate with the medical diary of the Hiroshima doctor Michico Hachiya and his colleagues, at the time of that first bomb blast, and effects. Blast *Keloids* would, of course, not be observed in the marines, and clean-up operatives – but, all other nuclear radioactive illnesses, short term and long term, would inevitably correlate, despite the US government and AEC denials.

War goes on

The very word *War* became a misnomer, with atomic bombs A and H, weapons of mass destruction, after the politic, conventional weapons of World War 2. And from day one (as Orwell predicted) after VJ day, both the USSR Stalinist' armed forces (viz. led by their politicians – Uncle Joe i/c); and the USA with their respective allies and existing 'other' protectorates, used as resources.

Russia had conquered the vastness of the Asia continent, from Latvia in the west to Mongolia in the east; and established hundreds of nuclear armed fortifications on ground, and underground, bunkers – even purpose built top secret towns...[7]

America, in opposition, developed its huge western nuclear based, top secret nuclear plants, bases and silos...:

> *"Anything you can do, I can do better than you..."*

As the 1946 Yankee wartime musical (with lyrics by Irving Berlin) *Annie Get Your Gun*, (followed by the 1950 US Film, with Howard Keel and Betty Hutton starring) expressed in song and praise. After the end of the Cold War in 1989; a number of declassified documents, and photographic evidence, were revealed – but, it would take many, many years for most, relevant historical facts to emerge...

Pacific Proving Grounds

After America's success exploding atomic bombs on Hiroshima and Nagasaki. Success, in *technology*, and contributing to the end of the Second World War – in August 1945. The USA military planned on exploiting their, then, global monopoly, in owning the secrets of atomic nuclear power.

The Yanks had fought, since 1941, the war machine of Japan, including the conquest of many of the islands in the Pacific. And, after occupying the territory of Japan (instead of the Russians) they approached the United Nations, who agreed in 1947 that the USA assume government, control, over some 2000 islands – to also occupy and secure their populations, against any alien hostile takeovers.

And, so, in order to protect island populations – and for the good of mankind (in opposition to the aggression of Stalin's USSR, seizure of European Territories, after conquest of Nazi Germany) – America began to bomb (aka tests) many of the Pacific Islands in their care; to further 'their' knowledge of atomic nuclear bomb weaponry, and what it could do.

Biological Weapons

To *deliberately* infect a person with mediaeval like plague; or anthrax, arsenic, typhoid, sarin, dioxin, plutonium, depleted uranium, strontium-90, et al – any chemical substance which can, probably will, kill human beings is a biological forensic invasion. In WW1 the terrible gas bombs, mustard, et al., were intended to kill, or at least disable, opposing enemies. And, in time, at the end of the second world war in 1945, the deliberate use of atomic bombs was (it appears) as 'conventional' weapons; as bigger and bigger bombs of TNT – instruments of global war – *not* deemed chemical killers, per se?

I often read in the media that weapons of mass destruction are but sophisticated conventional weapons. But, the evidence of atomic weapons being 'biological'; whether exploded on ground zero, or otherwise delivered; is really overwhelming. Even if denied by politicians, or global governments in power and the military.

The force, and material destruction, by the detonation is self evident, but any squaddie or civilian on the receiving end is unlikely to treat it as the equivalent of metallic 'shrapnel' from high explosions. It is the ionisation (deliberately fired) of radiation, by fallout, which destroys the biological constitution of living beings, most in long-term half-life (how appropriate), destruction of body tissue, as inevitable inner destruction, poisonous effects on the life-giving blood system, etc; Biological weapons of war – individual Cold War nuclear invasions.

Crossroads, Redwing...

The Trust Territory of the Pacific, the USA governed protectorates spread over three million square miles (seven million, eight hundred thousand kilometers) is an incredible resource for the USA to protect, all in the Pacific Ocean.

This action was formalised on July 23rd, 1947. It followed two more atom bomb explosions after Hiroshima and Nagasaki, and the Manhattan, Trinity test, in July 1945; the subsequent fourth and fifth 'tests' were exploded about Pacific Atolls – codenamed *Operation Crossroads* – in 1946.

A single atoll is a circular coral reef; or, a string of coral islands, surrounding a lagoon or plural, lagoons. And, further helpful definitions: a lagoon is described as a body of water cut off from the open sea (ocean), by coral reefs or sandbars, any small body of water, especially one adjoining a larger one (a pool).

Bikini tests identify a single small island of that name – *and* plural coral islands and lagoons called Bikini. Christmas Island is the largest mid-pacific coral island of some thirty-five miles in length with numerous small, and large internal lagoons – as I discovered on my limited perambulations, in 1956-1957.

In July 1946 – less than one year since Hiroshima and Nagasaki – the USA exploded two more bombs (in future called tests in the 'Cold' War) at Bikini

Atoll and Marshall Islands in the Pacific, located about 2000 miles south west of Hawaii. The two tests were of the same 'yield' as Nagasaki – about 21 kilotons, with a toxic base use of Plutonium. The first test was named *Able* in an airburst; the second, three weeks later, an underwater (attached to an LCM barge) test – called *Baker*.

These were the two (first) explosions watched by the British journalist James Cameron, and physicist William Penny (later Sir), I read in our English newspapers. It was a deliberate showcase of American achievement – but, wholly, denying the myriad of civilian and military potential victims of the deadly wide radioactive fallout.[8] There are other detailed accounts available most in the plethora of the 1980s, printed in America...

The US military declared the two tests as a great success, *but* there would be many casualties caused by fallout – the plutonium, et al, maiming, killing, *in the future*, many US Navy military witnesses; but, this data was *top secret* for many years – as, piecemeal, ten, twenty, thirty years on, the atomic debris fallout took its toll. (Terkel, Wasserman and Soloman, et al).

Operation Crossroads, I learnt, was mostly a US naval operation. Hiroshima and Nagasaki, despite the devastation, *did not* provide enough evidence as to just what the bombs (later, warheads or rockets) could do to warships in an occupied port; as well as the effects on any and all forms of life and physical constructs such as buildings. And so the war went on.

And, more so, how big a bomb did you need to 'win', if success was to be predicted by their producing local earthquakes, tsunamis, and controlled contamination of a local designated enemy – presumed stationary targets – since the easterly winds, whatever, would dilute any high irradiated matter and produce only 'clean' explosions (there's a contradiction!), the fireball in a bubble above ground, to reduce immediate fallout contamination.

The US Navy assembled a fleet of ninety-two (or so) redundant ships as targets, around the Bikini lagoon, in the Marshall Islands of Micronesia. The vessels included captured German and Japanese ships with, by the end of WW2, no longer needed US 'battle wagons'. The act, as a byline, released enormous military manpower, saving millions of dollars – which could better fund the coming Cold War facilities.

Officially, that is publicly, *Able* was treated as a relative failure given that no huge 'showtime' catastrophe, like causing a fissure in the sea bed or other such visible man-made destruction, occurred.

But, the second test, *Baker*, was deemed *very* successful, when all but nine ships were eventually sunk by this underwater nuclear test, and even those surviving became so contaminated that (with their contaminated crews) the vessels were dispatched to Hawaii and San Francisco, where they proved much too dangerous to clean-up, and were sunk in the ocean waters' depths.

The USA had demonstrated the awful potential of nuclear warfare and, once again, declared to the world (especially the USSR) that they were its master.

US Army sergeant major Orville Kelly, a commander of a signals detachment, based on a small island mass (coral?) called Japton, witnessed 22 atomic bomb tests (obviously, with his other army buddies) on the Bikini, Marshall Islands tests. He recalled wearing a fallout dosimeter during the Redwing Series, in 1958, but, no consideration of beta ingested Plutonium matter gathering inside his body and, as it were rotting it slowly away.

Back, at the time of August 1945 Dr Hachiya, a damaged survivor of that A bomb burst, in his Hiroshima 'make do' hospital, soon realised (and recorded), that the impact of the radiation was to damage, even destroy, immunological balance of the inside body tissues, thus – according to the dosage – causing a person to be very vulnerable to toxic diseases and disabilities: this was to be diagnosed from the black rain, radiation contaminated water and food, and lack of medical attention, so badly needed, after the fallout.

Operation Crossroads in 1946 and then the Bikini tests in the 1950s. Sgt. Kelly subsequently developed cancer, 'lymphocytic lymphoma', twenty years on. He and his wife, Wanda, founded the US National Association of Atomic Veterans (NAAV) in 1979. Sgt. Kelly died in 1980...[9]

J.S. was a seventeen year old sailor on board the destroyer *USS Alan M Summer* when he arrived on July 1st, 1946, to attend the two tests – *Able* and *Baker*. One of many young men, John would later, after Kelly, become a president of the nationally US formed, *National Association of Atomic Veterans (NAAV)* – one of (then) fifteen thousand disabled survivors of the to be numerous US atomic tests. It sounded strong, but, in his interview with Studs Terkel, he stressed that (at least) *'Forty two thousand veterans that had participated in Operation Crossroads – already'*, [thirty years on], *'twenty-seven thousand of 'em are dead'*... and that was from 1946 onward.

In his interview, John said he, and all his fellow crew members, '*were advised there would be nothin' harmful. Just a lot of excitement, and have a lot of fun'* (sic.) However, shortly afterwards, they were summoned (en masse) to attend the US flagship, *USS Mount McKinley*, before they witnessed the actual bomb testing. The crews had to legally swear, on oath; '*not to disclose or talk about any explosion of the bomb or any of what he saw on the Island. If we had why, of course, that could mean time spent at Leavenworth'* [US Military Prison], '*or a huge fine.'* All the brass and scientists were appropriately covered and dressed, aboard the flagship. But, back on his ship, they were exposed 'downwind' from the aftermath, contaminated fallout from the *Baker* explosion. John was a designated fireman, and sent on board a ship to put out one fire, dressed '*standing in shorts with a t-shirt on'*, and cleaning up results of the nuclear explosion; he, one of 2,000 sailors detailed to scrub (standard decontamination technique) some metal parts, on board the *USS Independence*, and other vessels, with 'volunteers' – to put out the fire: just one of the, then, seventy-five surviving target ships. They fought the fire for one hour on and two hours off. '*Maybe sixty, seventy guys.'*, all without any protective clothing.

It was a special exercise, as they had to check out the tethered animals that they had on board. On departure, after three hours of exposure, they returned via an LST checkpoint, where a scientist scanned them with Geiger counters '*to see if we had picked up any radiation'.* Which they certainly had. It transpired that plutonium ionised particles had attached, stuck to, metal, and proved too difficult to wash, scrub down. The cleaning up (called decontamination) wash down and shower, became standard procedure; just like removing dirt after an energetic rugby match, in pouring rain and mud, one presumes. But, deadly.

John's health deteriorated, and his 'lymphedema', the blockage of the lymph system, caused his legs and arms to swell. He had both his legs amputated, but when the VA medics offered to sever his arm (but *not* to admit the military was any way responsible) he declined; stoically refused.

There is a photograph of John, taken on July 31st, 1983; he appears to be in a wheelchair and, notably, his gigantic swollen left hand is clearly visible, showing his infirmity. On September 11th 1983, he died, of cancer of the colon, liver and spleen (*see Tredici, Schell, 1987*). Nuclear fallout! Sad, but in 1985 the USA *General Accounting Office* (whatever that was) published a document entitled *Operation Crossroads Personnel Radiation Exposure Estimates Should be Improved.* John's medical history was well noted. I read that a senior Lt. General contributed (it says it all): *'Almost all the exposures were well within internationally accepted radiation exposure limits...'* And the damning error of predictions (not science); *'No firm evidence exists to show that exposure to low levels of ionizing radiation would cause adverse health effects...'* (Ibid).

Monte Bello

In 1952, Australia allowed the UK to expand its nuclear arsenal, by a series of nuclear tests, initially on the islands of Monte Bello off the north-west coast of Australia. And then, in the mostly low populated deserts of the Australian continent; at Maralinga and Emu Field: where they continued until 1958 – despite considerable later opposition (justified by the Aussies), due to the intensity of the top secret operations. There is little doubt that – as with the American programmes, abuse of the civilian and military population would later be uncovered by events, the authorities 'refusing', as 'policy', to admit damage and longterm images on its manpower and indigenous natives, despite considerable witnesses, casualties and radiation sickness from fallout after each test – and, by dismissing an aggregate due to the heavy number of atomic tests. But such data remained top secret...

The winter of 1946-47 was awful, especially the deep snow and blizzards, which, I recall, lasted for months here at home – approaching spring. In the orphanage we were – as most of the nation – often very, very, cold. But the other side of the globe, in July 1946, the American nuclear tests were underway, hot in the Pacific. And in 1947, angry at the UK for an English named Russian spy, Fuchs, the Yanks closed ranks, and from then on denied *any* person 'not American' access to their ongoing atomic nuclear weapons database. This was ratified, shutting out all previous allies into the cold – including us limeys in the UK, on our own, again...

We were still in denial, after the devastation of WW2 – and, our bankrupt finances, politicians and people still living in the past of the 400 year old British empire – it, too in ruins. However, most still loyal subjects of the (then) previous occupied colonies gained freedom. (Which, unsurprisingly, allowed the USA and USSR to expand their growing Empires.)

Despite the American withdrawal of co-operation with Great Britain in 1946 (the Fuchs episode), the Brits formed their own nuclear establishment, Aldermaston, near Newbury, in Berkshire, the *Atomic Weapon Research Establishment* (AWRE). Britain made approaches to both Canada and the USA to 'share' their immense sovereign territory: and, jointly, for them to fire the British nuclear bomb tests.

America in 1951 was still considering testing the British bombs in the doomed Nevada deserts of the West Coast USA. The Bikini, Marshall Island tests of the states had become a risk, escalating up to 1954. Inhabited Pacific Island indigenous natives, ocean fishermen, were found suffering from the American nuclear bomb tests, wind blown, and polluted seas, on the east coast by proven nuclear fallout. Which, of course, wasn't really happening... top secret, you know. (*Joan Smith* 1985: Lorna Arnold and Mark Smith.)

In 1952, the Brits, with colonials' collusion, commenced their own series of tests. Though unable to trace my father, or Australian relatives, I felt historically close to the Aussies and Kiwis... *Operation Hurricane* was the title of one of three UK atomic tests, sited at the Monte Bello islands of North West Australia; kicking off with at least twenty five kilotons of plutonium explosions. From Monte Bello, the UK tests moved eastwards into mostly desert hinterland, outposts of the Australian mainland, to continue the tests. The Brits and Commonwealth squaddies, as well as those previously stationed in Korea or Australia, were being transferred to Christmas Island – where I, too, arrived in 1956.

The first of the UK Atomic 'A' tests were exploded on Monte Bello on October 3rd, 1952 – introducing *Operation Hurricane*. The objective was to further the military knowledge of what damage could be inflicted, on ships and harbour ports of a potential enemy. (Was it coincidence that Christmas Island's port – was named Port London?) A naval vessel, *HMS Plym*, had a plutonium bomb planted in its hull – just as if saboteurs at work, etc. The test was a replica of the American Crossroads 1946 Bikini test. *Plym* was at anchor only 400 yards off shore. The experiment was deemed a success – proven, with the totally vaporised vessel given as evidence... total destruction.

The British detonated a total of 21 atomic explosions; eleven in Australia; and then, ten off of Malden and Christmas Island in the Pacific. These tests (known as series) took place from 1952-1958. The first, as described, was Operation Hurricane in October 1952, when the *HMS Plym* was sunk, off

Monte Bello. Whilst Sir William Penney, on his return to England, described the test as a resounding success, no casualties, all engaged personnel provided with dosimeters, etc... Politics!

Sheila G. met her future husband, Frank, on his return from *Operation Hurricane*. They married shortly after, in July 1953. Sheila described losing their first baby, which emerged; "*just a triangular piece of liver-like substance with a small round knob at one point. I presume the head...*" And, two months later, she recalled; "*Frank was discharged from the Marines, discharge papers said,* 'Fundamental Dyspepsia of the Stomach'." And, in common with survivors of Hiroshima and Nagasaki; "*his hair began to fall out, his teeth went bad and he had constant stomach pains.*" Sheila's memories then recalled the awful sequence of future illnesses, and dire events, for them *and* their family, from 1957. In 1987, he had his blood analysed in New York(!) which confirmed he had been irradiated serving in the Marines, back in 1952. Her catalogue, case history, of the dreadful consequences on the children is but one story, from hundreds of atomic nuclear tests, and the servicemen exposed during them.

Thomas W., a sapper in the Royal Engineers, was one of the 'first' re-entry party to step ashore *after* the Monte Bello detonation. He recalled that the only protective clothing he had on was '*an overall and a bush hat*', whereas, spokesman Sir William Penney, physicist in charge, had back home in England declared to the politicians how well protected all of W.'s party were. Yet, from the outset, as they arrived on the island, it was 'crackling' with radiation. He had only been issued with a small hand held dosimeter...

Royal marine Frank G., in a separate interview, confirmed Thomas W.'s findings. Rather ominous. He and his small detachment of 'specially trained' men landed from a dinghy, across the highly radioactive lagoon where *HMS Plym* had just been vaporised. Thomas' detail was to rescue a group of scientists who had been left in a 'forward area bunker', to monitor the effect of the detonation. He said; "*I saw two men in protective clothing, and several others wrapped in blankets. They were only wearing sandals, shirts and shorts with no headgear*":which seems so irresponsible, or truly naive. The marines had arrived at the bunker, which was sited into the side of a hill; "*we found it charred, and smoking...*".

"*On returning the men 'in deep shock' back in dinghies to their ship, the scientists had to be helped up the gangplank, and a couple of them collapsed onto the deck. I believe they were taken from the ship later that night, and that was the last anyone saw of them...*"[10]

On Dr. Penney's jubilant return to England he declared, to the politicians, the total success of *Operation Hurricane*. Of the evaporation of *HMS Plym*, which precluded – by nanoseconds – a mushroom with a *great greyish-black upheaval*, followed by a *great sandstorm over the islands* of Monte Bello. Of mud-and-water rising up to 1500 feet high... contamination.

In the aftermath, a serving British marine described how the 're-entry' group had returned from their followup examination of the contaminated island. All clothing was discarded, and thrown into the sea. The marine was on board *HMS Zeebrugge*, one of two waiting ships – the other *HMS Tracker*. He was one of the men who disposed of a number of sealed toxic steel drums, filled with atomic waste matter (how were they packed?): several of the drums were retained and sent back, for chemical analysis, but the rest were to be thrown overboard into the ocean.

But, the marine was unfortunate when handling one of the toxic drums; it was leaking, and leached onto his arms and legs. A waiting scientist, monitoring the disposal, said; *'You will regret that one day,'* as the drum was thrown overboard. Within weeks, he had a skin psoriasis, and... and their ships, still radioactive, returned to England. (*Robinson, 1985*)

From the end of 1952, the British began a new series of nuclear tests, at Emu Field, 746 miles north west of Adelaide. The test area was in the Great Victoria Desert. And, by August 1954, the tests were expanded to a more permanent territory, Maralinga, in the South West of Australia. All tests were in the low yield kiloton range and, unlike the *perceived* clean high-burst explosions, they were deemed safer (that is, more controlled) due to the low bursts of their detonations, from erected towers. And so, with the fireballs considered... Ground Zero detonations were normal in the desert. Penney, et al, believed the desert totally uninhabited, ideal for atomic tests.

The official MoD list was deceptive, as the hundreds of omitted small ground burst tests – 5-600 at least, of them, using toxic fuel made (from uranium) element plutonium, with its half life waste residue, to remain for possible thousands of years. (*Robinson 1985, Overon 1987*) The foregoing were 1950s nuclear events. I was but a teenager for most of these cold-war years – and, fortunately, unaffected by such (myself, and most young squaddies). Day to day life. Kept in total ignorance... I was unable to emigrate to Australia under the £10 only fares for Pommies. I had not yet qualified in any wanted skill or other such qualification (this would come in later years).

Empty Spaces

Employed at Moss Bros, Covent Garden, in 1959, I enjoyed a brief 'belonging' to a group of co-workers; clerical and floor staff. One of our group (like *Are You Being Served*) met daily in the staff canteen, and sometimes outside in the nearby Soho restaurants. One lady in our group, a blonde as I recall, was tall and enamoured of a Notting Hill Gate West India immigrant (shortly to be married). With an interest in photography, I was asked whether I would be interested in being their wedding photographer: of course, I quickly agreed. No problem.

Though many West Indians from Jamaica were (like Windrush) taking up residence and experiencing abuse from some quarters, the immigrants were (to me) no different from the many refugees from Poland and Western Europe: they were all willing, and did work hard in our midst. At 22 years of age, I had no prejudice through experience. After all, wasn't my father born an Aussie (who I had no memories of); and his parents, my grandparents, immigrants, in the late 19th Century, from war torn Europe to Australia and New Zealand.

Another member of our small gathering was a clerk, who had his sights on entering London as a stockbroker. One visit to Soho with, call him John, he introduced me to Italian food, spaghetti bolognese and cold lager. Both of us had no ambitions of remaining in the shop world at Moss Bros. At that memorable lunchtime Soho visit, I recall John suggesting, with my background, emigrating to Australia, in particular the Northern Territory to work, learn, at a sheep farm, etc. The newsreels often included commercial film of Aussie cattle and sheep farms, and so, interested, I visited Australia House at Aldwych, and requested an interview with a view to possible emigration. But, this idea was blown out of the water – I did not have the qualifications (including marriage, etc.) to be considered. It was but two years on that I befriended Keith B., my Aussie mate, at *Home County Travel* in Earl's Court, and Notting Hill Gate (where we rented accommodation). We met as dance instructors for Arthur Murray in Oxford Street in the late 1950s. I left Murray's in 1961 – for a trip to France – and met up with Keith, about this time.

I knew nothing about the demography or politics of Australia and the preference for White Europeans only. In the mid-Fifties, it meant nothing to me, through experience. I knew nothing of consequence.

Empty, clearly inferred – no or little demographic resident occupation. As to the word *Desert*, this indicated little likelihood of any (or very little) settlement – but, trade routes, nomads, indigenous folk. The very name of *Empty Quarter* (and *Sahara*) in the middle-east of Arabia; self evident of such little to no demographic settlement – of mankind and their domestic sources of food – vegetarian and livestock, sheep, goats, cattle, swine. I as any infant, and school age child, grew up with this fact of life. And, as a boy scout and young sapper in my teens in the 1950s – all facts self evident. As the postwar metaphor would have it, you didn't need rocket science to be aware of such truisms. Since 1952, and Monte Bello, Australia experienced top secret, atomic, nuclear bomb tests – in its empty spaces (aborigines did not count).These Aussie nuclear tests produced enormous fallout radiation which drifted east across the continent, to Adelaide and beyond.

Hibakusha

Human beings were becoming a nuisance – even nomads – in a believed uninhabited desert. And the weather, well, it would become more and more a handicap. However, at first, indigenous deemed primitive people did *not* count – unless you (the establishment) were caught out. It must have been annoying for the inclement weather to harass, pursue folk – outside the nuclear zone. Fallout, and its aftermath, after the initial blast and burns exposure, was *not* really an admitted option. And, like any squaddie, we became indigenous for a while, during those tests. Boring; politics, polemics, truisms. But, the aftermath of such inhuman tests did not disappear. Such was the very marrow of Orwell's *1984* work, written back in 1949, when lies and denials became recorded history. It submerged in amnesia.

The USA switched its main nuclear testing grounds to its own domain, in the west American desert. No more cowboys and indians, except in films. Native Indians in the USA were being called, indigenous, like the aborigines, an anthropological term of dismissal. The awful fallout, far and wide, of the Pacific *Castle Bravo* 1954 series of nuclear tests; its explosion too big to be hidden under the usual carpet of secrecy. Both the Pacific indigenous natives – *and their own US military* – were known to be experiencing radiation sickness.

In the same timeline, the British, with staunch allies Australia and New Zealand, switched, after *Monte Bello*, to the desert and scrubland of south west and central Australia. Its rockets at Woomera, and about 600 nuclear *minor* trials, at the Emu Field and, shortly afterwards, to a more permanent base at Maralinga; both nuclear based sites, built from scratch under the formal direction of (to be) Sir William Penney, physicist. Fallout from the Atomic tests (many of them) moved eastwards across Australia from Monte Bello (north) and from Emu and Maralinga, across Australian desert, and cities. (Pilger, 1984, et al)

In the immediate aftermath of Hiroshima, there was no possible 'analysis' of the casualties – living or dead – of the radiation sickness after effects: symptoms from ionisation, internalised, radioactive particles in toxic food chains; or from breathed in intake of unseen (let alone unknown, and not realised) minute flesh clinging contamination, which took years to emerge.

A Japanese name, term, was introduced to the dubbed victims, of the first Atomic bombs – *hibakusha* – which translated as *'explosion-affected persons';* this described living survivors of the atomic bomb (Lifton & Mithell 1995: Paul Ham 2011) and its aftermath. And soon, globally, the term came to be, by association, applied to all atomic test experiments, those affected socially, and medically, treated like lepers, untouchables, of past history – to be avoided. Worse, to be denied as existing. Horrendous, the divisive term would become a racist faction. Analysis – at a village to village level in an anthropological: identified as, *not like us*; tribal divisions, separated from then dominant regime – waffle, waffle, waffle. A past reality referred to as *White Man's burden*, very much in place during the World Wars...

After the end of conventional World War 2, Japanese *hibakusha* were denied recognition in Japan and the US for at least a year on. The reason by then, equally appeared many, 'other' nationalities, caught up in the fallout of the new atomic tests bombs. Their own civilians and armed forces exposed.

And, in dire subsequence (to the shamed chagrin of politicians) *hibakusha* and nuclear veterans of whatever country (the Bomb itself had no means of such selection) would be denied existence throughout the Cold War.

After the muted successes of the US, British and, later, French atomic tests in the Pacific proving grounds (neither the Atlantic or India continent, owned as many, coral or volcanic islands – many occupied, in distance, from the tests. It was the windblown (most easterly) fallout, increasing as the tonnage increased – kilotons, megatons, even gigatons (in USSR): and, inevitably, increased the uncountable minute windblown contaminated particles in a polluted star dust distribution. The heavier toxins lodged, monsters in the deep, in sediment of rivers, lakes, layers and, always most obliging for waste disposal, the global seas and oceans.

In 1951, the USA began to move away from the infected Bikini, Marshall Islands in the Pacific. And, Britain, after Monte Bello, moved to the huge deserts of Australia. Whilst the phenomenal white technological achievements became self-evident. The unexpected, occasional casualties of the many tests were recorded, but rendered top secret for up to fifty years. My bro and I from an early age (viz teens), though attached to London by our mother's ancestry, both felt totally neglected by our paternal father, and our Australian white ancestry; petty, though in retrospect it now seems in old age.

The whites only political philosophy of the Establishment, in the continent of Australia certainly, up to the 1960s, branded the indigenous natives, the Aboriginals arrogantly dismissed as 'savage' or 'stone age', measured by the technology of the whites. Yet, as Arthur Upfield, Aussie detective writer, defended (and Aussie Neville Shute, and South African novelist Wilbur Smith, in Cape Town) the so-called native savages were more knowledgeable than ignorant immigrants. And, retrospect, since ancient history, classical times – conquered in wars became slaves as the occupational race considered its spoils. Thus, in South Africa, (yes) North Africa – Arabs enslaving the blacks; USA a slow genocide of its own native Indians, indigenous... a global vice.

Despite the huge deserts of South Australia, publicised as *Empty*, of all nomad indigenous people, even camel stations, sheep and cattle stockman's farms and mission schools. There were again (like Bikini) fallout casualties from the many atomic tests. Even the city whites across to Adelaide and Queensland were polluted but, as predictable, such data became top secret – few were informed of such politic realities. The aborigine and white nuclear radiation casualties of the Australian continent became like the Japanese victims – new, Hibakusha. (*We don't talk about them.*) As, even more so the people in Nevada, USA, the USSR/Russia remains a totally unknown area.

AUSTRALIA'S EMPTY SPACES

to profitable mining in the Territory. By the provision of roads and better means of communication to promising mining centres, assistance to prospectors and miners, and the granting of free assays, and by the establishment of an ore sampling and buying department at Darwin, the Government has already helped very materially towards a better state of affairs.

The main handicaps to industry of any description in North Australia are, and will remain, the impossibility of obtaining a supply of native labour[1] and the unreasonable demands of white workers, for the whole of the Territory lies in the tropics though for the greater part of the year it is arid.

[1] This must not be taken to mean that the author advocates the introduction of coloured labour of any sort into Australia. He does not. Australia should and could be kept for the white race, and the British in particular. The day will dawn when it will be possible for large areas of tropical and semi-tropical Australia to be effectively occupied and utilized by a healthy, indigenous race of white stock. But generations must pass ere such a race can be evolved, and applied science must be enabled to show how water can be brought down from the clouds as rain and/or otherwise ere those areas can be utilized. Meanwhile, Australia has to be held by the white race, and it can so be held only by the cooler and better areas of the continent being more intensively developed and settled with white people in the next few years.

124

Australia's Empty Spaces, by Sydney Upton, 1938. *'At a time when empty cradles were contributing woefully to empty spaces, it was necessary to look for external sources of supply. And if we did not supply from our own stock we were leaving ourselves all the more exposed to the menace of the teeming millions of our neighbouring Asiatic races': '37 Catholic Boy Migrants Welcomed...' (Humphreys, 1994. See p.233)*

Aborigine Hibakusha

There is no entry for Hibakusha in my *Collins English Dictionary, Second Edition, 1989* though, if modern 2000s *Google* search is entered, its answers are certainly prolific, and most refer to survivors of the Hiroshima and Nagasaki Atomic Bombs in 1945. Only.

In 1795 (at the time of the American War of Independence, and Prussian, French and European Wars) an eminent geographer, William Guthrie (*System of Modern Geography*. Sixth edition), described the European discovery of New Holland, a portion of the vast unknown (to Europeans) continent of Australia. He described it:

> '*The largest island in the world, and formerly supposed to be a part of that imaginary continent called* Terra Australis Incognita.'

Viz the unknown land of (New Holland) Australia... Guthrie expanded his introduction, written in 1788:

> '*At the first landing of governor Philip on the shore of Botany Bay, an interview took place with the natives. They were all armed; but on seeing the governor approach with signs of friendship, alone and unarmed, they readily returned his confidence by laying down their arms. They were perfectly devoid of clothing, yet seemed fond of ornaments, putting the beads and red baize that were given them, on their heads or necks, and appeared pleased to wear them...*' (Guthrie, p.1038)

Two hundred years later, twenty seven years after the Emu *Totem One* second detonation (15th October 1953), the first of the minor trials, an aboriginal nomad, Yami Lester, recalled as a young South Australian boy at Wallatinna station near the opal mining town of Coober Pedy, in South Australia. Lester said about 7 o'clock one morning, all of the inhabitants of the campsite heard a loud bang, curious as to its cause:

Some time later – perhaps the next day, they saw a black, greasy, shiny smoke rolling up to them… it stayed for a while. Later, he said people became ill, and some, he thought, might have died. The symptoms were sore eyes, sickness and diarrhoea…' (Britain, Australia and the Bomb. The Nuclear Tests and their Aftermath. Lorna Arnold and Mark Smith, 1987, p.70-71)

That 'first' Aussie atomic explosion, from a tower (which evaporated), was a 10 kiloton estimated yield. The low fallout cloud, which blew a black mist over the campsite, radioactive debris, drawn into the convective boundary layer – 'the layer of air close to the earth's surface'. The more dust – the worse the fallout.

Squaddie (could include senior ranks) searches, in addition to Japanese, British, Australian, New Zealand, American, French and Pacific Islanders: and, citizens of the USSR (though impossible to quantify). Any place on Earth where, in the 1940s to 1970s, atomic bombs and their fallout patterns, produced radioactivity, and ultimately caused cancer borne deaths. These casualties (victims) all correlate with the new premise, Hibakusha (not to be mentioned), *delayed* after effects.

No way, over future years, would I meet (or know of) squaddies who *voluntarily* requested a nuclear posting – *knowing* something about the post-effects to exposure to radioactivity. This would, of course, preclude many personnel who (with top secrecy in place) believed they were to be in a tropical posting of a halcyon paradise.

And, if the premise is an equation of radioactivity harmful to man, then *any* weapon, or source nuclear plant, which produces (knee jerk) ill after effects: especially, growth of hydroelectric, nuclear plants, producing and discharging *waste* into nearby rivers, or dormant in stagnant ponds – or, worst of all, stored in steel diesel drums. Inevitable, metal fabric will deteriorate (whether stored or buried): such a plant is certainly not green or cheap energy!

American and British Hibakusha

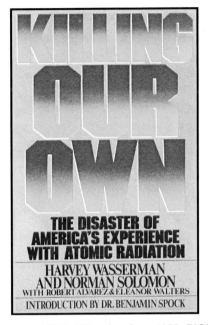 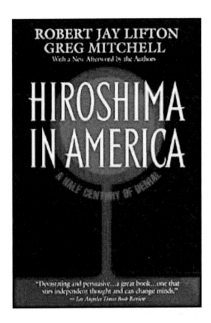

LEFT: *Killing Our Own,* 1992. **RIGHT:** *Hiroshima in America,* 1995.

Nevada Desert Tests, a 'still' from the 1959 US Army documentary *Atomic Bomb Blast Effects.*

Soon after the US Nuclear Tests, *Operation Crossroads* in 1946, and *Bikini* Tests in the Pacific, America began, in 1951, the long series of tests in the Nevada Desert, during the 1950s and 1960s. Many military army personnel (and there were civilian casualties) were wilfully exposed – at the face – to a long series of tests; to record adverse effects, from their explosions, and aftermath fallout. *With deadly effect.*

And so, slowly, disabled, killed uncounted troops, with casualties of forthcoming cancers – wilfully caused by their government of the time. The first victims were sheep, cattle and ranch hands and native, hopi Indians – indigenous peoples infected by the white snow of fallout.

Aftermath 1957

We disembarked at Liverpool docks on Sunday 29th September 1957, having left Christmas Island some 10,000 miles away, back on Sunday August 25th, 1957. I returned on a wet, dark but welcome journey to my home in north London. Unbeknown to all of us (at home), squaddies, whatever rank – on that same day, *the same day*, of the 29th September, almost 4,000 miles away to the east of us in London; an awesome nuclear accident/incident had occurred, in Soviet Russia, 1,000 miles east of Moscow, at Mayak, a top secret, town, nuclear plant – Chelyabinsk (Ozyorsk), in the Southern Urals... not mapped... aka Kyshtym... (knowledge of Rocky Flats 1957 - many years on)

Inevitably, such data would remain top secret for many years to come. Its cause was an explosion in the water cooling plant, throwing up massive radioactive matter, ionising a clouds formation, which winds blew across hundreds of miles overland, across north east Asia and caused many deaths.

The Russian peoples were to pay a devastating self-inflicted cost, in the aftermath – surely, many times more than the casualties of Hiroshima. All, again, such data would remain Top Secret for many years. Its nuclear waste site would, in later years, be recognised as the most polluted, toxic place on earth.

And four days after our return, on Thursday 3rd October 1957, three hundred or so miles north of London, fire broke out in the Windscale nuclear power plant, which was situated by the small coastal village of Seascale, in

Cumberland (Cumbria). The fire lasted three days and was, at the time, a major disaster; the plant situated at the foot of the beautiful Wordsworth mountains, in the Lake District. There were numerous farms, woodland and, of course, local village populations. In retrospect, I understood that the plant's function was to process uranium into plutonium for the British atomic tests (no mention of, erm! the plant as a source of electricity on the cheap).

Sure enough, the discharged debris of the fire produced considerable radiation fallout about the district – and blew across nearby counties. The black rain saturated the farmland, and affected the flora and fauna. Crops were rendered 'dirty', and sheep and cattle livestock soaked in the radiation – milk and produce grossly infected by the ionisation. Inevitably people, too, were affected, and a cause of numerous to be cancers, and other physical traumas – many taking years to emerge.

Space Age

I had long been an avid reader of science fiction, reading Wells, Verne, Bradbury, et al, and, space travel technology was a major feature of its content. And so, when Soviet Russia achieved the first space craft to circle the earth, though unmanned, the launch of the Sputnik was recognised as the first artificial satellite to leave the earth's atmosphere, launched on Friday 4th October, 1957.

In just two to three generations, during our 20th century, mankind' technology, and transport advanced from balloons, flimsy aircraft, and zeppelins – to the early WW2 blitz-raids, whereby the war zone (by air) remained limited by the range (and weather) of its bombers – to and fro, for both sides of the east, allies and axis opponents. Obvious facts as I and every schoolboy knew – even from our comics – during the war.

So, for the first years of the recent WW2, the USA was safe from *direct* aerial invasion by Germany or Japan – and vice versa. Not till the development of unmanned drones and nuclear rocketry, and numerous silo based unmanned massive rocket bases, in USA and the USSR, would that barrier be dissolved. And early science fiction would become science fact, in peace and war.

The space age was truly under way. So sad that, instead of sharing the scientific triumph of the Sputnik, it only speeded up the animosity between the West, viz US, and the East, viz USSR, both feeling threatened by the potential of launching explosive rockets, including nuclear weapons, across the globe. USA now, well within reach of its orbit – as, of course, the opposite directions.

Cosmonaut

In 1961, the USSR, the first cosmonaut, military Yuri Gagarin rocketed from Vostok, as the first man to travel in outer space – and return to earth. Again, sadly, the USA saw this as another threat of potential war in space. And, within one year, the Cuban Crisis just averted nuclear war...

A Russian contemporary writer, with Tolstoy and Wells, a Soviet physicist named Konstantin Tsiolkovsky (1857 - 1935); a notable non-fiction and science fiction writer back in 1903 designed what he named, and illustrated, a *'reaction-propelled vehicle machine'*: certainly, in tandem, with the Wells and Jules Verne's journeys to the moon. Tsiolkovsky's book, *The Call of The Cosmos*, was, despite Stalin (who died in 1953), allowed to be published an English translation published in Moscow, printed in early 1960. Notably, the translator added in a final chapter – of Mother Russia's achievement with the Sputnik. And, a decade on, in 1969, the USA's success in making journeys to the moon. The animosity, mostly political, culminated in the *Star Wars* scenario – and, horror subsided at the time of Gorbachev and Reagan in the 1980s.

Nuclear Accident

Disasters, in non-fiction and fiction storylines (time shift tales) have always been with us, those singular events prompted by individual human beings, with greed, power – whatever the motive for their dire actions. And then there are accidents, aka incidents, throughout history – *'for want of a nail'* in the classic metaphor.

And, gigantic terrestrial and cosmic, massive earthquakes, aeon shift of tectonic plates, rearranging our planet's ecological strata – of water and terra firma. Late 20th century disaster books and film recording updated technology. In our post war period: the 1951 film, *The Day The Earth Stood Still* demonstrated the relative ease to interfere with all human communications – arrest nuclear, electricity and other energy sources – at the touch of a switch. And, post war 1950s, *War of the Worlds*, a 1952 film version of H.G. Wells fictional classic began with a machine's laser-like rays that annihilated man and any solid, vaporised matter, atomised into oblivion. The appearance of the nuclear weapons drones advanced this previous, science fiction invention.

And, during the Cold War real nuclear accidents – as Windscale (1957); Kyshtym (1957); Rocky Flats (1957, 1969) Three Mile Island (1979); Chernobyl (1986) – lately the Fukushima (2011) incidents. Innumerable atomic weapons, nuclear tests and atomic energy plants – fatal incidents. Most such 'accidents' were predicted through *cutting costs* in poor or lacking appropriate safety equipment. As ever, appearing to want cheap energy, mass-murder (millions of deaths and illnesses) technology, at *cutting cost* exercises - for profit.

Three Mile Island, USA

In 1979, even as the Cold War started to thaw, affluent America experienced the *near* meltdown of another nuclear power station, at Three Mile Island, Middleton, New York State, Pennsylvania. It was a near thing – there were casualties. But, this incident, unlike Rocky Flats in 1957 and 1969, went public. A full page advert from the American state-run energy plant, the AEC, highlighted the USA radioactive dilemma, and denied there could be any subsequent casualties. The AEC advert followed the recent 1979 near-meltdown of Three Mile Island, and the increased USA awareness of its previous official stance (politic) of invulnerability in the Cold War.

Ever an avid film fan, I recall, in 1974, the Hollywood movie epic, *The Towering Inferno*, a man made disaster film. A corrupt electrical engineer ignores the safety margins of the cables, as expected by the architect's plans and buys inferior jerry-building electric wiring, installing it in the new skyscraper; to secure a substantial personal profit from this criminal action.

That was fiction. But, globally, too many accidents, incidents, occur with huge loss of life, due to jerry-building in real life. Nature itself often causes fatal human disasters. In between, there are many disastrous incidents caused by fiscal cutting corners, in cutting costs. Low budgets (huge profits) at the expense of public safety. The introduction of radioactive atomic nuclear plants (factories) in the 20th century began a most deadly new source of potential disasters. And, fifty plus years on, over 400 such molochs exist throughout the globe.

Another Hollywood film epic, *The China Syndrome*, was released on March 16th, 1979, about a fictional malfunction at an American nuclear power plant. Incredibly, a real life such incident occurred only twelve days later, at the Three Mile Island site in Dauphin County, Pennsylvania, USA. The cause, trigger of the near meltdown was believed to be a stuck safety valve, which controlled the flow of the essential water coolant for the nuclear fuel rods. Result, with no water coolant the plant became overheated, releasing radioactive gas into the air; and, subsequently, toxic wastes into the nearby river, its sediment flowed to infect nearby farmland. This near thing, of a nuclear meltdown, would have devastated huge tracts of heavily occupied territory in the USA, but, nevertheless, it did have proven dire after-effects on the flora and fauna, human population. The event exposed the vulnerability of any of the 100-plus American nuclear plants, and potential risks of over 400 nuclear sites across the globe. (J Samuel Walker. pb. 2005)

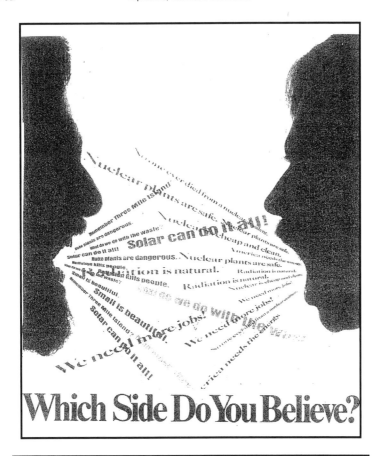

Which Side Do You Believe?

There are two sides to the issue of nuclear power. Both sides feel strongly that their position is correct—which makes it difficult for Americans to form a responsible position on whether our country needs this source of energy.

Americans are bombarded with conflicting views and statements from numerous self-proclaimed energy experts. Some have even said that nuclear power—which currently provides 12% of the nation's electricity—should be halted altogether.

But consider the *sources* of the loudest anti-nuclear noise. Among those leading the attack on nuclear power are a host of actors and actresses, rock stars, aspiring politicians and others who think America has grown enough.

The Issue Isn't Just Nuclear

Nuclear power is not the only thing they oppose. These are often the same people who have been against development of geothermal energy in California . . . stopped new hydro-electric plants in Maine and Tennessee . . . blocked a new oil refinery for southern California . . . opposed new pipelines to deliver natural gas to the East . . . fought the building of more coal-fired plants. And they're the same people opposed to President Carter's plan for developing a synthetic fuels program. One wonders what they are *for*, and how they propose meeting America's energy needs?

For many of these people, stopping nuclear power is but one part of a political objective to slow growth across the board in America.

This no-growth philosophy of the anti-nuclear leadership was clearly expressed by Amory Lovins, one of the world's leading nuclear critics, when he admitted, "If nuclear power were clean, safe, economic . . . and socially benign per se, it would still be unattractive *because of the political implications . . .*"

Support For Nuclear Widespread

On the other hand, consider the many organizations that have *endorsed* nuclear power for America's future. They include: the AFL-CIO . . . the NAACP . . . the National Governor's Conference . . . Consumer Alert . . . and many more. These groups recognize that America's need for electric power is growing at a rate of 4% each year.

Consider also that the health and safety record of nuclear power has been endorsed by a vast majority of the *scientific* community—including such organizations as the National Academy of Sciences, the World Health Organization, the American Medical Association, and the Health Physics Society.

We're not saying that nuclear power is risk free. The truth is that risks are involved in *all* energy technologies. However, the overwhelming scientific evidence is clear: nuclear power is at least as clean and safe as any other means available to generate electricity—more so than most.

Where will Americans get the electricity that is needed if not, in part, from nuclear power? That's the real question in the nuclear debate. It's the one for which the anti-nuclear leaders have no answer.

Nuclear Power. Because America Needs Energy.

America's Electric Energy Companies. Department 13, Post Office Box 420, Pelham Manor, New York 10803.

The above New York Times, 1st February 1980 caption reads:

'There are two sides to the issue of nuclear power. Both sides feel strongly that their position is correct – which makes it difficult for Americans to form a responsible position on whether our country needs this source of energy. Americans are bombarded with conflicting views and statements from numerous self-proclaimed energy experts. Some have even said that modern power – which currently provides 12% of the nation's electricity – should be halted altogether. But consider the sources of the loudest anti-nuclear noise. Among those leading the attack on nuclear power are a host of actors and actresses, rock stars, aspiring politicians and others who think America has grown enough.

The Issue Isn't Just Nuclear

Nuclear power is not the only thing they oppose. These are often the same people who have been against development of geothermal energy in California... stopped new hydro-electric plants in Maine and Tennessee... blocked a new oil refinery for southern California... opposed new pipelines to deliver natural gas to the East... fought the building of more coal-fired plants. And they're the same people opposed to President Carter's plan for developing a synthetic fuels program. One wonders what they are for, and how they propose meeting America's energy needs? For many of these people, stopping nuclear power is but one part of a political objective to slow growth across the board in America. This no-growth philosophy of the anti-nuclear leadership was clearly expressed by Amory Lovins, one of the world's leading nuclear critics, when he admitted, 'if nuclear power were clean, safe, economic... and socially benign per se, it would still be unattractive because of the political implications...

Support For Nuclear Widespread

On the other hand, consider the many organisations that have endorsed nuclear power for America's future. They include: the AFL-CIO... the NAACP... the National Governor's Conference... Consumer Alert... and many more. These groups recognise that America's need for electric power is growing at a rate of 4% each year. Consider also that the health and safety record of nuclear power has been endorsed by a vast majority of the scientific community – including such organisations as the National Academy of Sciences, the World Health Organisation, the American Medical Association, and the Health Physics Society. We're not saying that nuclear power is risk free. The truth is that risks are involved in all energy technologies. However, the overwhelming scientific evidence is clear; nuclear power is at least as clean and safe as any other means available to generate electricity – more so than most. Where will Americans get the electricity that is needed if not, in part, from nuclear power? That's the real question in the nuclear debate. It's the one for which the anti-nuclear leaders have no answer.

Nuclear Power. Because America Needs Energy.

America's Electric Energy Companies.'

Source: New York Times, 1st Feb 1980.

Three Mile Island, near Middletown, Pennsylvania, 1979. (Source: Photo from the Public Domain *Public Health Image Library* of the *Centre for Disease Control*)

Reactor four at Chernobyl, during construction of the '*Sarcophagus*', 1986. After an awful two days delay, the entire population of Pripyat, 49,000 persons, were evacuated by a fleet of buses. And, after including surrounding villages and towns about Chernobyl, at least 100,000 were initially evacuated... This count, naturally, precluded the hundreds, thousands, yet to be affected by fallout... The devil's count to grow in the years ahead, not just 31 fatalities. Source: *Chernobyl: Insight from the Inside* (1991) by V.M. Chernousenko, p128, picture reproduced with permission from the publishers, Springer Verlag, Berlin.)

Lake District

In the 1950s and sixties, I had an 'odd' awareness, a blot, of Sellafield/Windscale nuclear factory on the coast of Cumbria. I came to believe only the extremely well off could afford to live amongst those wild, picturesque green hills and clear lakes. It was cheaper, easier, to cross the channel to the continent, than visit, let alone holiday, in them-there-hills of Coleridge, Wordsworth and romantic places: but this was to change.

During the 1970s, I had close relatives move to Cumbria: initially to Papcastle, near Cockermouth and, later, north of Keswick near the Solway Firth. I soon, in the 1980s, developed, cherished, a love of the Buttermere lake, and Borrowdale and its surrounding hills. There, close by, were high fell walks up to Scafell Pike and Scafell mountain peak (highest in England, in the Lake District). And, from Scafell, along the crests, hill walks over and down to the coast – overlooking the Irish Sea – and Sellafield.

One year, we booked in at an inn in the small town of Boot, Eskdale, located south of Wast Water – south of the Buttermere lake. Our site was only a short-distance from the old Roman fort of Hardnott and Wrynose Pass, with its very steep winding snake upward road eastwards. Close by our digs, five miles or so, was a miniature railway from coastal Ravenglass to Eskdale Green, which took us to the coast and, nearby, Seascale and Sellafield visitor centre (as it was called). Also nearby, off the A595, was Calder Bridge, where The Queen would open the Calder Hall nuclear power station in 1956, the first electricity nuclear power grid plant in the UK. I vividly recall our travelling down to the pebbly beach – with Sellafield just north of us – and briefly wondering, what if...

Sellafield was sited on the Cumbrian north-west coast; adjacent to the busy waters of the Irish Sea. Just a newspaper memoir; no reason to believe any possible 1957 residue of (what?) 'fallout' existed in any sediment or soil in the vicinity. And, from the early 1980s, and once a year for the next ten years, we would, with great pleasure, enjoy the fells, hills and walks of beautiful lakeland. Water and hills everywhere – rivers, lakes, streams, fed from above by constant heavy rainfalls.

On lakeland holidays, I was well, *well* used to the long wet days, the constant heavy rainfalls. And, the Lakes, water sediment beds, fed by constant waters cascading down from the hills above them. Wrapped up, always ready for yet another heavy rainfall – it didn't, after a while, seem to matter when on holiday. It was, after all, *our* holiday.

One day, towards the end of April, the papers were headlining a nuclear plant catastrophe at somewhere called the Ukraine in the USSR, at Chernobyl. It seemed a massive steam forced plume of radioactive matter adhered to then collective falling rain drops, being blown over the continent – and, we read in the papers, around our lodgings south of the Buttermere valley; radioactive residue settled on the hills, and affected the local farmland, cattle, especially sheep. The unseen nuclear waste had polluted the grassland, and the livestock – gallons of milk to be disposed of – and corrupted flesh, meant destruction of the farm animals. But, we saw nothing, and nothing registered of faraway catastrophe, on our holiday in August of 1986. Ignorance and holiday bliss prevailed.

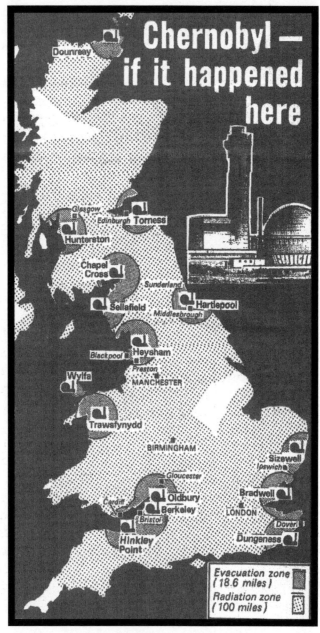

From *The Guardian*, 6th June 1986, p15

Chernobyl

In the early morning of 26th April 1986, an explosion occurred at Chernobyl, a nuclear power plant in the, then, Soviet Socialist Republic (SSR) of the Ukraine – north of Kiev. The event took place when an operator was due to test a 'safety' emergency water cooling feature, instigated by a switch on/off electric circuit. It took a one-minute gap, a possible then safety risk, which proved unsafe and disastrous. In fact, less than twenty seconds – too long? Reality – what nanoseconds – to switch off, even then? The accident took place in Reactor Four: a steam power surge blew the concrete roof off altogether – and meltdown had begun, releasing a massive cloud of radioactive dust.

At the moment of breakdown, two on duty operators, Akimov and Toptunov, were to switch off a safety switch to test the backup systems. But, it failed... Later, when the state, kneejerk, looked for naming the guilty, both personnel were to be formally tried as responsible for the yet to be magnitude of the disaster.

Moscow accused them of; '*Unpreparedness, negligence, and violation of the rules that guarantee the safety of the plant*', for which they were unable to defend themselves. The two men answered their inquisitors; '*Why did it happen? We followed all the procedures correctly. How could it have happened?*' But, before the unfortunate two scapegoats could be imprisoned, they died a few weeks after the event of (surprise), *acute radiation syndrome*. And, eventually, the state had to admit that the nuclear plant itself was unsafe. (Chernobyl. The Hidden Legacy. 2007)

One living survivor, Oleg Genrikh, 30, an operator working in the central hall of block 4, gave a witness account to the physicist V.M. Chernousenko in Moscow, in April 1990:

> '*I was just starting a second shift. It was hot. I took off my jacket... You know how we used to dress. I had a dosimeter hanging on my jacket. My pass was in my pocket. I went into the little room – and right then came the explosion. A mighty crack. Then a hissing. The lights went out immediately. Water started gushing...*'(V.M. Chernousenko, 1991)

When the event was first reported to President Gorbachev of the USSR at Moscow, and discussed with physicist Andrei Sakharov, it was interpreted as a possible fabrication by the west, and not believed (Sakharov Memoirs, 1990). And, it was stated that only 31 personnel had died at the scene. But, with a crucial two days delay, the state eventually realised that a major disaster was underway, and reacted to a maximum. Thousands of its citizens were in immediate jeopardy, so mass evacuation of the Ukraine local townships' population ensued. If the reactor on site problem of the Chernobyl No. 4 nuclear plant wasn't bad enough, the worse, cloud borne black nuclear radiation worsened by the day, as the winds enveloped central and northern Europe in its path...

With the not black, but grey rain and white snowflakes aftermath in the first days close to Chernobyl, the town of Pripyat, the population of which mostly serviced the ongoing needs of the plant, were speedily evacuated from the vicinity: In the short term after the explosion, the black rain emissions had discharged, initially for ten days. Within three days, by 29th April, the countries of Poland, Austria, Romania, Finland and Sweden received the black rain of radiation: 30th April, Switzerland and Italy reported the wandering radioactive cloud, and, by the 2nd May, six days on, the radioactive clouds unleashed upon France, Belgium, the Netherlands, Great Britain, Greece and Ireland, third of May, to the south, Israel, Kuwait and Turkey received the massive nuclear fallout. Then, in the days ahead, across the northern Hemisphere, to Japan on 3rd May (one week on): China on the 4th May – and across the globe the USA and Canada on the 6th May. *(Dr Rosalie Bertell, 2014)* It looked like, if it intensified, as in Australian writer Neville Shute's fiction epic *On The Beach*, 1957, that it would infect the whole of the northern hemisphere.

All points of the compass were affected, almost concentric a whirlpool, with Chernobyl and the Ukraine at its centre – a massive global ripple pebble burst of unknown proportions. When the multiple weather patterns of Europe, north, south, west, further north – and across the north east, across Asia to the USA. (Chernobyl. The Hidden Legacy. 2007)

About Great Britain, by the 2nd May, fallout descended onto the hills of north Wales, Scotland and the Lake District. April, and spring showers were exacerbated by a then incoming Atlantic storm. According to T.S. Eliot: (to paraphrase:)

> *'April is the cruellest month, breeding lilacs out of the dead land'* (T.S. Eliot, The Wasteland - 1922)

Invisible ionisation, a radiation-spotted picture taken in Pripyat, a local town adjacent to the damaged Chernobyl Nuclear Plant. This picture was taken only a month after the explosion in May 1986. The camera film negative acting as a dosimeter. The lower half of the picture is inundated with 'the snow', invisible to the human eye, recording radiation fallout from the explosion... (Source: *Chernobyl: Insight from the Inside* (1991) by V.M. Chernousenko, p51, picture reproduced with permission from the publishers, Springer Verlag, Berlin.)

Invisible Radiation

Example of film spotting (shown in this picture of a Chernobyl truck) caused by ionised matter in the air. Washing down newly ionised matter, the snow, was the same for any surface, including man. But, inevitably, the water itself carried a residue of the radioactive matter – just as river courses and, of course, black rain. Humans and animals were used as bio-robots. Attending the immediate aftermath of every nuclear exposure, essential washing down facilities for staff and equipment was a priority – be it personnel, aircraft, ships decks, et al... But, what happens to the running, ionised, soaked 'wet' matter is debatable. (Source: *Chernobyl: Insight from the Inside* (1991) by V.M. Chernousenko, p188, picture reproduced with permission from the publishers, Springer Verlag, Berlin.)

Water, Water Everywhere

Nuclear plants – factories – were initially constructed as atom bomb providers, for uranium into plutonium, etc; A and H bombs. Few such sites existed in the late 1940s; the USA, Russia and Britain... But, with the phenomenal profit making of private corporations in producing 'components' of the new industry (and Arms race). At some point, the same factories (of death) would be converted to produce apparent cheap sources of electricity – as opposed to depending on oil, coal, gas and other traditional sources. And so, these huge mega factories, hundreds, sprung up like mushrooms across the globe, in the coming decades.

In 1957 the Queen opened Calder Hall, adjacent to Windscale (Sellafield), in Cumbria, as the first nuclear plant producing electricity and connected with the national grid (*UK Pathe News*). The Irish Sea was nearby, to receive its 'waste': a not infrequent cause of concern. Was unwanted atomic waste but raw sewage?

Most, if not all nuclear plants depended on immediate access to flowing water courses; rivers, lakes – mostly sea water of the world's oceans. Inland? As with South Australia, inventiveness, tapped even below the desert for artesian wells to contain in their fabricated water coolant towers. But, all such coolant water sources became, thus, polluted – irradiated with toxins.

And, though initially cheap, even (deceptively) 'clean', the 'waste' polluted products, produced clean up costs of billions of dollars, pounds, roubles. And, water, water everywhere – with not (a little) a drop to drink. As the nuclear waste products leached and leaked into river courses – and foolishly stored in leaking steel drums, or buried deep – anywhere. Lethal.

The word water (whatever language) remains a metaphor. Two hydrogen molecules combined with one oxygen, produces a water droplet. Colourless, clear, tasteless and odourless – in its pure form. But trite it sounds, life itself, its water, essential to whatever elements it combines with.

But, any contaminations and water damage transform – or kill its host. Such truisms applied to water coupling with any radioactive matter... still retained in the sediment, laid in lakes or collective, stilled, undisturbed: or any and most essential moving courses of life giving water, absolutely vital to continuation of life – shifting the polluted water sources.

Nuclear Plants

Top Left: Fukushima Daichi, Japan, 1975, *before* the tragedy of 2011. This plant was one of 50 in Japan – with the island (like Great Britain) surrounded by water to supply the coolants for plants. At risk of earthquakes, tsunamis, and human elements.(Source: National Land Image Information (Color Aerial Photographs) (http://w3land.mlit.go.jp/WebGIS/), Ministry of Land, Infrastructure, Transport and Tourism.) **Top Right:** Oi Nuclear Plant Unit 3 & Unit 4, Oi District, Fukui Prefecture, 1993. (Source: KFI at ja.wikipedia) **Bottom:** Rocky Flats, USA, one of over 100 US nuclear plants, after the clean-up in 1995. (Source: USA DoE via Wikipedia)

Top Left: Bruce Nuclear Generating Station, Ontario, Canada, 2006. (Source: Chuck Szmurlo, Wikipedia) **Top Right:** Dnieper Hydroelectric Station, Zaporozhye, Ukraine, 2007. (Source: A1 via wikipedia.) **Bottom Left:** Paluel, Upper Normandy, France, 2010. (Source: Bodoklecksel, Wikipedia) **Bottom Right:** Palo Verde Nuclear Generating Station, Wintersburg, Arizona, USA, 2010. (Source: Cuhlik at Wikipedia project.)

North America built hundreds of nuclear plants in the postwar years: so too Europe and, albeit secret, Russian plants. All, too, shared the common problem of dealing with their nuclear waste; and need to access considerable water supplies as coolant. No yet global solution in disposing of their waste products in the 21st century.

Vietnam and Two Gulf Wars

It would be many years before I read, heard of, disenchanted nuclear Cold War veterans, and civilians of the 1950s and early 1960s. And fallout, governments in denial.

The press, television and other mass media seemed to have almost forgotten all people – whatever country – who suffered from toxic effects of exposure to the Cold War peacetime price tags of death, and slow death disorders. What was evident, very much, in the growing visual catalogue of conflicts and casualties of the late 1960s and through the Seventies was war; USA and Vietnam. Initially Australia, too, was in support of this anti-communism, but later withdrew. I recall one Australian doctor, in particular. He was a casualty of Vietnam, a disenchanted physician. One of his symptoms was alcoholism, with other mental health problems. I had professional contact with the ex armed forces welfare SSAFA (Sailors, Soldiers and Air Force Association) workers. We discussed a number of local ex-RAF Spitfire (and other) pilots, who were suffering from mental and physical problems. As a mental health, psychiatric social worker, I was able to offer some assistance. This welfare group also included contact with ex-POWs, and those personnel with missing limbs, etc., and blind veterans. I visited various places in Rustington, Storrington and Worthing, as well as residences in Brighton and Rottingdean, in East Sussex. And there were others, in need of post war support; on offer to WW1 and WW2 veterans.

Our prime minister at the time, Harold Wilson, kept the United Kingdom out of the awful wasteage of Vietnam involvement. But, in retrospect, for over a decade after 1963 the 'transparent' truce between America and the USSR, banning airborne nuclear weapon tests. After thirty years, and from the 1970s, 80s, Cold War veterans were displaying morbid real symptoms, from their past contact with atomic nuclear tests; at home and abroad. The colloquial nuclear veterans, nuke vets, became a still hidden cauldron.

The first Gulf War of 1991 effectively meant a conflict between USA and Iraq in the Middle East. Iraq had aggressively invaded its neighbour country of Kuwait and the US went (with United Nations approval) to defend its numerous oil wells... It was estimated that 200,000 Iraqis died during the war (*Pilger Documentary)*. I recall being afraid that if the United Kingdom became involved in an escalation of the war, my two sons would be conscripted – as my bro and I in the early Cold War of the 1950s.

The US, with the UK in support, had a strong armoured force – with, from the outset, control of the air defences. Both sides used rocket missiles. And, very effective, the tank shells of the US (and projectiles from aircraft) had – like steel arrowheads – housed the powerful tank penetration of the enemy's armour, to deadly effect. The tank bullets were tipped with the poison of depleted Uranium (the same substance used in nuclear weaponry); depleted atomic waste, radioactive waste – being recycled.

Enemy tanks were penetrated by depleted uranium shells, like the proverbial 'hot knife through butter', and left heavily contaminated metal, which remained. In time, too, unexpected, devastating effects on the 'handling' of the shells were experienced by the *winning* side, as well as the enemy. Once again, in retrospect, whilst relatively few of the US personnel were killed by the Iraqi's forces, hundreds of the winning side would be affected by radioactivity from the depleted uranium. And as to the civilians and Iraqi military?

The US Vietnam war (1961-1971) used chemical weapons, called Operation Hades (hell), during its war against the Vietnamese population. In the Great War mustard gas was used by both sides, chemical warfare supplanting so-called conventional weaponry. Before Japan's capitulation in August 1945, the US used chemical napalm jelly: this napalm burning everything it touched. The use of polystyrene in napalm-b in 1965-6 ensured that, on contact, Vietnamese would likely die in agony: it did *not* differentiate between military and civilian, man woman or child – just as in total war in WW2. Napalm with gasoline ensured absolute conflagration, destroying wood and paper and thatched dwellings with their occupants. But that, of course, was again in total war. I was aware that during the Blitz of England, Europe, and USSR, WW2, incendiaries could initially be extinguished – not so napalm. (Green. F. *Vietnam! Vietnam! Prelude to Genocide* (1967) US: Ham, Paul *Hiroshima and Nagasaki*; of proto-napalm. GB (2011)) The military were fighting unseen rather than unknown combatants, indigenous Vietnamese. In no way was everyone a malignant Vietcong. A principal, up front offender, toxic herbicides, dropped from US helicopters, known as the defoliant, *Agent Orange*: the object to destroy or diminish the protective flora of the Vietnam highlands, which gave support in hiding the enemy. In fact, many of the population lived in a maze of tunnels underground – and survived; many did not.

I recall that on Christmas Island, we had no thick woodland, no tall bush (or highlands of foliage), only scrubland and cultivated plantations of coconut palms. The local populace mostly depended on fishing in their basic diet, Daily, I observed overhead a low flying Auster airplane, with a smoking cloud of DDT being sprayed – to suppress the mosquito 'menace' of the tropical heat – especially in the static lagoons. No problem – though shades of Rachel Carson and *Silent Spring* (1962), any added danger to nuclear fallout seemed academic. But, in the decade following entry of the Vietnam war, the *Agent Orange* aircraft drops were very, very much more lethal, toxic to friend and foe alike.

Agent Orange, like nuclear fallout, became a collective term for negative effects on flora, fauna. Indeed, local rivers and sea water were affected, after spraying of the herbicide. Fish, contaminated vegetation, vital parts of the food chain, for man and beast, were poisoned, much as nuclear waste fallout, which later destroyed large tracts after the late 1986 Chernobyl disaster, in the northern Ukraine; large forests were killed – along with tracts of farmland and local exposed population – man and beast, and fish in the rivers – with dioxins.

Depleted uranium; and toxic herbicide compounds, were but two devastating man-made toxins. Dioxins and furons were but two of the herbicide deadly PCBs – polychlorinated biphenyls, manufactured by USA private chemical manufacturers; albeit contracted by the US government for use in Vietnam by its designated conscripted military forces. Many US forces were doing what we British knew as compulsory National Service. The British media, daily press, as I recall, gave regular progress reports on the US forces in Vietnam – but, the defoliation was received as but a weapon of that war. Dioxins would hit the headlines in later years. The controversial label of *Gulf War Syndrome* referred to this new hibakusha, servicemen and indigenous inhabitants, to suffer from the use of depleted uranium, recycled bomb fuel; with florid, unrecorded radiation sickness and unseen fallout horrors.

Approaching Closure

In 2011, I enjoyed telephone contact with 1958 Nuclear Vet, Sapper Scot Ken McGinley, in six months or so friendly telephone conversations; and receipt, from him, of a number of fascinating (and legal) DVD compilations.

Ken was happy to comment on various local and global experiences, enlarging, with grim humour, encounters with eminent politicians, on the trials and tribulations of surviving nuclear veterans (forces, and their families). Ken had been to America, Germany, Japan and Russia to meet kindred civilians, and service veterans who had suffered, often massively and slowly, over 10, 20 and 30 years after first experiencing blast gamma and beta radiation, and then hidden; they already knew in Japan, through Hiroshima and Nagasaki: atomic bombs ionised internal damage after effects, due to fall-out radiated debris.

Even after long denials by officials, condemning cold war nuclear veterans, as casualties (collateral), had been denied and, finally, confirmed by most global authorities; *two generations* since the nuclear events the UK government continue to strongly deny, to press and media, that (any) evidence could be proven that our British forces had experienced any damage due to the many nuclear tests during the existence of the Cold War period. Propaganda... unbelievable... but true. Worse, as hibakusha, our own British media and politicians (shame) buried its veterans – much as I uncovered in post WW1, lack of care for shell shocked squaddie armed forces; the hibakusha, victims often condemned as malingerers (see *Better Court Than Coroners,* 2011 and 2012), during the early 20th century...

Fukushima

It was on one of those days when, in retrospect, you would live through a life defining moment which marked you, and your memories. Birthdate is definitive, but that is more your mother's. The day the European world war officially broke out on September 1st 1939. I was being, for the first time, evacuated, an infant, out of London; a photo recording departure at north London, N1, Canonbury railway station, in Islington (and no, I do not recall it). And, whilst I was aware, as an eight year old in a Surrey orphanage, in 1945 – I have no precise memories of the VE day's celebrations. Neither, till eight, did I recall the time of the formal end of the VJ war, by the first atomic bomb explosions, at Japan's Hiroshima and Nagasaki.

I recall, years later, Windscale, Three Mile Island, and Chernobyl nuclear disasters. But, now retired, and a fragile disposition in old age, a new nuclear disaster in Japan.

Saturday, March 12th, 2011. I was with friends, visiting an exhibition of Thesiger's expeditions of desert photographs, at Pitt Rivers Museum in Oxford: Big Chris (as I know him, from his height) himself a distant blood relative of the great explorer, and I, with his wife Alison, were touring the museum, and passed an interesting event taking place on site.

The museum had a tele monitoring cubicle, with a TV and was printing out updated handouts of a very recent, awesome nuclear plant global tragedy – just underway.

Only hours before, on March 11th, a dreadful off shore earthquake and a tsunami had badly damaged the plant at Fukushima. At the time, the magnitude of the disaster was still unrealised. The horrors would soon be comparable to the Chernobyl incident of April 26th 1986. But, at the time, this nuclear event was only just beginning...

Fukushima Nuclear Power Station, situated on the north east coast of Honsu Island, was owned, managed, by the Tokyo Electric Power Company (TEPCO); supplying much of the electricity, public network in Japan. As with other global 'incidents' of the past, the enormity of the ongoing tragedy (for surely, it is – not was), was hugely underestimated: and the authorities grossly underestimated tsunamic, and nearby earthquake risks – as followed offshore, Japan's underwater 9.0 earthquake.

Given that the whole of the island's buildings and facilities were built over a known, near ridge of active volcanoes. And the 40 foot (12.1 metre) high tsunami wave response to a recent earthquake; not only destroyed local coastal towns, but devastated three of the Fukushima nuclear plants – and released unknown quantities of poisonous windblown (and seaborne) nuclear radiation.

There are many, many casualties yet to be realised. As late as the 19th of March 2011, a US military aircraft measured radiation within (at least) a 15.5 mile (45kms) radius from the site: much as the event at Chernobyl was first globally observed by a US military aircraft, in the Ukraine back in 1986 – one generation before.

When the reaction stopped, fission turned off – the plant continued to produce (and dispose of) considerable amounts of heat , and demanded flowing water coolant to remove the decayed heat – but the water then contaminated as nuclear waste remains a problem: with Fukushima, there was of course the Pacific ocean on its eastern flank and the discharge of wind driven radioactive matter – an unsolved problem. Unresolved.

When volcanic eruptions are underway, the local population needs to be evacuated from the immediate toxic fallout: be it Etna, Vesuvius, Krakatoa – or any other location. So, as with all nuclear plant disasters, the local population needs instant evacuation from – to date – at least a twenty to forty mile radius. So, Chernobyl, Three Mile Island, evacuated thousands of its close population. But, the aftermath, the atomic waste, polluted earth and water courses would increase with devastating toxic effects in the flora, and fauna, especially the food chains...

I recall the media press (as *Daily Mirror*) back in 1954 and first reports of the Castle Bravo nuclear tests fallout devastation, gauged by a 100 mile radius from ground zero. Thirty years on, with Chernobyl such a UK based disaster in, on our island would, as the USA versus USSR, Cold War had realised no City or town was immune from the bombs, or nuclear explosions. I had a special interest in the ongoing Fukushima disaster, as my eldest son, a musician, is married to a Japanese lady, and living in Osaka. And, with awareness of fallout, and especially pollution of the seas and food chain (Japan thrives on its fishing industry – much as Great Britain, and other island communities)?

Sailor – Under Water

In November 2011 I had, at age 74 years (living alone, a widower since 1996), two massive heart attacks, and lost contact with Ken – but, despite circumstances, a total wave of detailed email information, and incredible photographs of various tests sent to me from *other* vets as I very slowly made a partial recovery.

Just after the (for me) black hospital Christmas and New Year period, I met a neighbour from down the road, who was recovering from losing his wife to alzheimers and cancer; he then diagnosed with advanced lung cancer, from many years serving in the Royal Navy, exposure to asbestos; many long term exposures to this element, working in the docks at Portsmouth, and ports in Malta. Two years younger than I, we befriended and offered support to each other, using 'gallows humour' (as ex-servicemen). But most, most important, I learnt he was a Cold War veteran, sailor, one of that special breed, a submariner who had experienced the post war conflicts on submarine patrols. He, R.S., asked to be known as Sailor. It was serendipity.

LEFT: On patrol, HMS Orpheus, 1963. RIGHT: Sailor. Photo source, 'R.S., Littlehampton'.

Sailor, a Royal Navy squaddie, leading seaman, joined the navy in 1956 at the age of 17.5 years, initially entering for nine years. After training, he joined a frigate in 1957, then transferred to a submarine: his total service from

September 1956 to discharge, in 1966 – in submarines from 1958 to 1966. His first sub was a 'T' Class, the *Teredo*, a relatively small vessel, run by electro-diesel fuel. Earlier, it was of the same Class 'T' class as used in the classic John Mills films, *We Dive at Dawn* (1943) in Sea Tiger, wartime adventure into the Baltic, and *Morning Departure* (1950), of war and postwar H.M. Submarines – a similar gray submarine. He then transferred to the *Orpheus* from 1960-1963.

Returning from a tour in the Far East in 1960 in the *Teredo*, he transferred to a new sub called the *Orpheus*, one of the then called hunter killers. His new base in the Firth of Clyde, NW of Glasgow was in a British area known as Faslane - not to be confused with the USA's Polaris nuclear navy base at Holy Loch, also in Scotland – local towns of Dunoon and Greenoch. The *USS Nautilus*, the first Atomic submarine, was completed in 1955. (In the future, three or four Trident carrying nuclear submarines would be stationed at Faslane in Scotland, as an ultimate deterrent.)

Sailor married quite young, and was allocated married quarters, south of his sub base, where he and his wife remained till 1963. They then moved south to a new posting, until demob in 1966.

It took special training to constantly endure life deep down under the waters of the Med, and very much deeper oceans of the world. On patrol against the 'threat' of a possible Russian submarine (as they were doing the same 'self defence' duties); and surface disguised fishing trawlers of the possible cold war enemy.

He experienced many hazards, including spending ten whole weeks under water, with no surfacing, in the region of the Arctic cold waters, deep and seemingly bottomless. He recalled lying still for ages, whilst a Russian sub (it made quite a lot of noise, he thought) passed overhead. This was well into the Cold War face to face encounters. but not, fortunately, nuclear powers, as they were in the near future. Sailor's main duties were as the torpedos and explosives man – the torpedos, twenty one feet long, their gyro guidance (not necessarily so in recent wartime), by electric.

I asked Sailor if the subs had ever come to rest on the sea's bottom, as in some dramatic films; he remarked that, in the Med, vessels could generally be viewed from above by flying craft, but not the oceans of the Atlantic, Indian and Pacific, which arc far too deep – a number of subs, and complete crews, had disappeared this way, never to be discovered.

Britain, for decades, emerged as an Allies' base; an aerodrome and European port for Americans – and, for WW2, a world-wide base for nations opposed to Nazi domination.

Sailor recalled nuclear 'Polaris' navy submarines, rocket bombs. From day one there were CND marches at Aldermaston and Holy Loch in Scotland (the home of the American nuclear subs) in protest at their very existence that whereas the subs' missiles could reach most Russian targets so, too, in mutual self-destruction, could the cold war enemy target the UK – cities and ports. Hence, stalemate – neither side could win (he, himself, was never employed on any nuclear submarine). Lung cancer killed him. He sailed away, end of September, 2013. But, thankfully for me, dear Sailor would *not* let me die. '*Not on my watch*', he emphasised – and watched me evenings for months in early 2012, when I was mostly bedridden and alone. A good man now departed, also a Cold War veteran.

Waste not

Chapter Five - Denouement

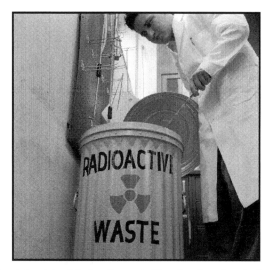

A student uses a lead-lined dustbin for disposal of local radioactive, toxic waste, at the new-ly-built Ford Nuclear Reactor Project, at the University of Michigan; licensed by the USA Atomic Energy Commission in 1955. In retrospect, one asks where was the infected waste then disposed of? (Source: Getty Images)

Denouement

Shakespeare suggested *Seven Ages of Man*, expected during one lifetime. Certainly mine, and yours, and your family members too. In our fragile species, one generation... (*Collins' Dictionary* defines, suggests, a normal (average, statistic) lifespan, between two generations – of about, 35 years for human beings, averages 30 plus years.)

Generation gap? Only one generation separated WW1 from WW2: not so our next two generations – spanning seventy years, 'officially', perhaps more visible, than the distance of the latter: defined as an unofficial, an 'invisible' wartime generation in the Cold War (1945 – 1989), the Cold War better described as an atomic war, its substance not heavy metal, shrapnel, but like its new elements – plutonium, fuelled by uranium – more valuable than gold. And invisible, and more deadly.

Our generations Cold War supplies were engineered, privately contracted, by the countries government Nuclear Energy Plants: their factories which (for great profits) produced plutonium through the processing of uranium, and protected by keeping production lines top secret – regardless of ethics, real or moral ground, towards their own indigenous population (if the cap fits...).

I recall reading, in the aftermath of the Ukranian Chernobyl disaster in 1986, of the terrible unpredicted loss of life, principally by dreadful toxic radioactive fallout, spread by noxious winds and rain, and damage to the then Russian plant – one of then sixteen or so USSR nuclear factories: three years before the fall of the Berlin Wall – clean up cost in millions of roubles.

Eventually constructing the sarcophagus around the melted down buildings, it was reported to Gorbachev that it would relatively restrict the further discharge of radioactive waste – sludge and minute air-blown particles. But, thirty or so years on, the cement monument would need replacing – *one generation after* the dreadful and unprotected nuclear accident.

After Blitz years; halcyon memories of Hawaii; of Laurel and Hardy (*Honolulu baby , where'd you get those eyes*) of twenties and thirties: to wartime, and cold war military activities; and, subsequent, glam, luxury years scenarios, as excellent, fun loving (with gangsters) films, of *Hawaii 5.0* and *Magnum PI* (don't mention the Cold War – only 1941.)

So too, the USA movies changed totally, for me, the previous, pioneer days of American history of indigenous cowboys and indians. Of course, so too, diminishing our British colonial empire, of some 400 years history, which would change forever in extremis.

The 1960s

One Sunday supplement in the mid 1960s, an English media newspaper (I think it was the *Observer*) recorded a special occasion to remind us... It was June 5, 1966.

> *'What is so special about today's date? Until now, June 5, 1966 has not had any particular significance. Yet it may well find its way into the history books.*
> *Between the end of the First World War and the beginning of the second, there were 7601 days. Between the end of the Second World War and today there are 7601 days too. We have now drawn level with the 20 years of uneasy peace that separated November 11, 1918, and September 3, 1939.*
> *This peace, our peace, has been as uneasy as the last. They had Abyssinia and Spain; we have had Korea and Vietnam. All that can be said is that at least we have avoided all-out nuclear war. Every day, from today onwards, is a kind of bonus.'*

The words *Cold War* were not eluded to in the text, though one sentence said it all; '*at least we have avoided all out nuclear war*'; emphasis on avoided. In the early 1960s I worked at Arthur Murray Dance Studios in Oxford Street and close-by Carnaby Street, where we often went to lunch in the Soho area... the Swinging Sixties in London. Yes, personally a good time (the Cuban Crisis just avoided in 1962): a very fragile global agreement to cease overground (that is, airborne) nuclear tests was underway.

After leaving Arthur Murray, and my Lambretta scooter, for several years in the early Sixties, I shared a flat with my Aussie friend, Keith Buxton. Keith was an Australian veteran of New Guinea, and entertained me with tales of New Guinea; and working on the Snowy Mountain Projects of Australia (See *Home County Travel*).

For me, pleasant years; memoirs recording a number of non-nuclear 'live' events. But, I/we knew nothing of the awesome cancers, and atomic diseases, of decades earlier atomic tests, and aftermath, fallout consequences. And neither did our general public – secrecy prevailed. To admit their presence was tantamount to treason and prosecution by Her Majesty's Government... Orwell's ghost.

And, globally, horrors continued. Apartheid in South Africa (my bro emigrated to Cape Town and, for a while, helped in the outer black townships); In the States, the slave, now racist coloured, divides prevailed. Australia, their 'whites only' policy. Russia though not (it seemed) as mortal as Stalin's terrorist regime. and Mao's mass starvation in China... and, and, well: in the UK, it was still happier times in the Swinging Sixties, in London.

War and its victims: *Guardians of the Asylum*. 1798

Legacy

For more than twenty years, I scoured bookshops – new and second-hand, rare and antiquarian. I doggedly searched for material, especially illustrated – data, on *Shell Shock* from the WW1 casualties, and found very, very little *non-fiction* material. But I underestimated the growth of contemporary fiction, its writers well representing evidence, knowledge, of shellshock, exposing the denial, political myth – all war casualties; shell-shocked veterans accused of malingering – not dead heroes? And so concluded two volumes of non-fiction on sanctuaries, *Better Court Than Coroners* and *Lest We Forget*: not specifically of the Cold War 1945-1989 – which remained, by definition, and still sustained only in text books as invisible, and only for (more dishonest) politics. After two heart attacks in my mid-seventies and two years surviving, absent from constant pursuit of material on *the Cold War*, its veterans, *two generations*, denied or airbrushed out of global history – despite millions who suffered – and still, into grandchildren and even great-grandchildren, certainly *not* malingerers: Cold War veterans denied by 'so-called' Establishment, official Orwellian case histories. Denied. Hidden. Hidden from two generations...

Deserts in the WW2 postwar years, 1950s, 1960s and afterwards, were sought after as ideal testing grounds for moribund thermonuclear drones – of A and H bombs; from a few (deadly enough) kilotons to millions of tons of TNT, exploded over earth and sea. And, worse, the potential of thermonuclear rocket missiles – *all* of which, at the touch of a switch, could exterminate millions.

And, all left a future legacy of radioactive land and sea, saturated, dormant, from those past nuclear tests. Islands, hotspots in a diseased and polluted planet. All living things were – are – still surviving of these past misadventures. I learnt more and more from published and declared unclassified government and military sources, and from survivors.

In 2000, Hutchinson published a delightful travel book by Martin Buckley. I read its paperback of 2001 Virago. Buckley spent over 18 months to two years, circumnavigating the deserts of the globe – driving main trunk roads across the barren wastes. His adventures included one journey along the West Coast of the USA, passing through territory of the desert near the Manhattan atomic project site, exploded back in 1945. He described:

> *Driving through flat and dusty scrubland just beyond the*
> *perimeter of the bomb site, I came into a two horse hamlet*
> *called Bingham (Bangem?), and pulled into the driveway*
> *of a shop selling rocks, gems and 'bomb souvenirs'.*

Buckley was shown one relic, the glistening chunks of quartz and amethyst, a piece of gen-u-ine 'trinitite', taken from the bomb site! Fused at Ground

Zero (the shopkeeper said) – the nuclear pendant was set in 22 carat gold, to be worn as jewellery: *'Actually, it's hardly radioactive at all'* the shopkeeper enthused. Buckley handed over twenty dollars for the grim relic and, in addition, was introduced to an old man who was witness to that historic event. The shopkeeper described his predecessor of the souvenir shack...

> *'Well, the old man discovered he was fatally ill, and there*
> *was nothin' he could do about it. So he sat right there on*
> *the porch. And he shot himself in the head.'*(Grains of Sand.
> Martin Buckley, 2001. pp.281-2)

Fuel

I recall reading an old mid-Victorian *West Sussex Gazette* newspaper: in court reports, it described a sad old woman who alone entered a gentry's estate, in search of some twigs for her cottage fire. She was arrested by the local gamekeeper for stealing '2d of wood' off the private estate – formerly, a parish waste – and threatened to be transported abroad to Australia. The outcome was not reported...

Parish churchwarden's accounts (I own an original volume, with two hundred years entries) listed regular charity records for its parish poor (not only the poor) who were allocated a coal ration, on a regular basis, and signed for with an 'X'.

Times have changed since the early Victorians, and before: local fossil fuel, coal mines, and wood fuel, have added gas, oil and electricity, hydro-electric heating facilities. And, in the mid 20th century – introduced nuclear plants (steam into high energy) – but, such plants depended on atomic energy as this book of memoirs described at length. And nuclear fuel is deadly – but, if coal mine tips were bad enough, atomic waste is proving more and more deadly.

Mark Twain Wrote

> *'The very ink with which all history is written is merely fluid*
> *prejudice'* (Source: *Pudd'nhead Wilson and Other Tales*)

In childhood Blitz and post war adolescence, no way did I observe, let alone appreciate, not wearing shoes (ouch!) and advisable clothing in others' climate. Missionaries (and travel writers) often showed pictures of natives, hitherto being unclothed – or, sparsely so, and insisted that first and foremost 'they' be hidden in clothing and learn to wear European footwear (so necessary on concrete or other grounds). But, as I would later learn from overseas service – in no way did being clothed or not, really equate civilisation, in style and behaviour as children and adults.

On Christmas Island in the 1950s I noticed islanders barefoot and wearing brief sarong garments: all required in a hot equatorial climate. Watching the islanders play football (not soft ball) in their bare feet, each time they kicked it into the air I winced. But, as I would later write for a publication, I noticed the thick skin soles of their feet so hardened from infancy, their layers of skin, like leather skin soles. But, in poor and war torn countries, going barefoot was not a choice – nor such rags their people could gather about them. And, certainly demonstrated whole peoples living in hot climates, with mostly sand underfoot, have no need of clothes, in need of constant washing in valuable water, and replacement. They were dressed for culture, not practicality. (See, for example: Illustration and Text; 'Clothing a native for his entry into civilization'; *The Passing of the Aborigines*. Daisy Bates: pp190-196, John Murray. pb. London 1966 edn. (first published in 1938)).

1971. I decided to move sidewards, from hospital based, professional work. After a series of advertisements in the *Social Work Today* in the mid 1970s, and nursing journals, I was accepted at the North London Polytechnic (now university), School of further Social Work Studies – culminating in a diploma of social work.

London, once again, became a focus for college research and work experience in the field, spent on the Isle of Dogs. One historical project referred to the exploration and support for poor (at home and abroad); especially for generations of pauperised children, in the East End in the 1880s, about Whitechapel, an area quite familiar to me during the 1950s and 60s.

Almost 100 years later, I qualified in generic social work, including working in child care and care and welfare of children in need, in London and the UK; with my own experiences – in care, in WW2 and post war years.

In the early 1980s, established as a senior social worker, I was placed in Worthing, West Sussex. My warrant card (all qualified workers had to possess one) included the full care range of children, old age, mentally ill and mentally handicapped, and disabled, with compulsory emergency work in after hours, night-time, and weekends, and bank holidays, etc. By rota.

Qualified Social Worker Warrant Card (details removed for security...).

It was a fact of life, in these close fields of social work, as a professional: '*You were damned if you do... and damned if you don't...*' became a cliché. If you sectioned a patient; or, had to take a child into care...

One routine, albeit a pleasant one, was to work with foster parents, and children up for adoption. I recall the enquiry from someone abroad, asking if a parent, or relative, could be traced. If I could not resolve such a request, I routinely passed it on to colleagues working in the Salvation Army, in the 1980s. I never could trace my own Aussie father and parental relatives. No trace. Retired in 2000, I continued occasional acts of writing non-fiction on domestic and social history. Unaware of the magnitude of the revelations to come.

At the time of my grandparents' youth in the late 19th and early 20th century a substantial percentage of immigrants to Britain fled from Russian and Polish politics; many of White Russian background (viz not yet Communists):

a substantial amount of refugees and emigres, lived and worked in the East End of London. George Sims (1847 - 1922) a social historian, referred to the East End as *Slum Land* (1903). Slum was the supposed unwashed, Dickensian poor -people of London: poor perhaps in monetary status – but clean, not dirty, in homes and habits, as Jack London established in his *People of the Abyss* (1904) documentary. Poor, yes, but not dirty.

And as writers Bernard Shaw, Thomas Hardy, George Orwell and other writers described, the working classes had generally clean domestic habitations; families well cared for – *within their means*. Aliens (viz foreigners, refugees, immigrants, exiles, not-born-here) what's in a name? To be British born – English, Scots, Welsh or Irish, of the British Isles of Great Britain, and nationalised citizens.

St. Jude's, Commercial Street, Whitechapel, London, 1888.

St Jude's

In 1866, accompanied by Lord Shaftesbury, Dr Thomas Barnardo visited London's East End, and uncovered a number of starving 'Street Arabs' (nomads – homeless); all were orphans. No less than seventy-eight street urchins, boys and girls, were found shoeless, ragged and uncared for (as if in a war zone). From that time, the history of Barnardo's homes began – his first boys home (orphanage) opened in the Commercial Road, close-by *St Judes*. And my great uncle, Rev Joseph Manton Smith, with Rev. C.H. Spurgeon, opened his first boys home, in Stockwell (before Barnardo). (And, in which, evacuated home my bro and I would live six years, from WW2, as this memoir recalls.)

The Victorian 19th century work of what became known as Toynbee Hall, based on the work and staff of Rev. S.A. Barnett, and his wife, Henrietta Barnett, based at St. Judes, Whitechapel. Apart from charity work, it was an education facility, for a new breed of social workers in the making. I purchased a bundle of old pamphlets on St Judes, Whitechapel. The bundle included a pamphlet, *The Ethics of Social Reform. A Paper Read at a Meeting of The Fellowship of the New Life, London, by Maurice Adams.* (Price twopence). Published by W. Reeves, Fleet Street London, 1887.

Dear God! The pamphlet, 1887, by Maurice Adams, quoted a fiscal suggestion made to import slaves for a plantation owned by the charity to pay for needy children in their care, in Georgia, USA, the aftermath of the American Civil War:

> *'A striking example of how much evil may be brought about by this system, is furnished by the fact that slavery in Georgia was introduced through the efforts of George Whitefield. "When he went over to the colony of Georgia to preach the gospel, all the people were free. A strong feeling against negro slavery was entertained by the founder of the colony, General Oglethorpe, by the Moravian Ministers, and settlers, and by others. For the benefit of large numbers of helpless and destitute orphans in the colony, Whitefield founded an orphan house, and from the large congregations in England and America he collected large sums of money for their support. According to the ideas of most colonial agents in those times, he believed that his property could never prosper, unless negro slaves were imported to work on a plantation for his orphan house. He and others persuaded the trustees of the colony to legalise the abominable practice of slave owning." Georgia afterwards became one of the worst of the slave states. It was the governor of Georgia who offered a reward of 5000 dollars for the apprehension of Garrison, who strangely enough was born in the very town in which Whitefield died.'*

Migrants and Evacuees

As I look back to 1939-1945 experiences, I compare all those older evacuees who could recall a before, middle and an end to being evacuated..

I was an infant during the East End Blitz. When mother, bro and I first returned from Northampton billet, in response to the Phoney War of 1939-40; only to be present in the worst Blitz of 1940 – a return to our billet in Northampton; and, an incendiary totally demolished our end of terrace home.

In 1986, a Nottingham Social Worker, employed by the Social Services Department (SSD) was engaged in child care. *Mrs Margaret Humphreys* included problem families and vulnerable children in her caseload (just like myself). In an excellent memoir of those times, she recorded as non-fiction *Empty Cradles*; and, later in a film, a fictionalised documentary, *Oranges and Sunshine* (based on a true story), Mrs Humphreys described uncovering numerous British child migrants sent off abroad to the, then, colonies and fraternal dominions: *not* to return. My bro and I were lucky, we missed that boat of *no return*, during our long years of evacuation, from 1939-1951, as I have earlier described in some detail in this memoir.

Histories of evacuation and settlement in foreign parts is reflected in world history, of wartime, and natural disasters, going back centuries, no, thousands of years. I learnt any invasion, and subsequent occupation by the victorious, introduced *their* own language and culture. And, in time, the immigrants compete with indigenous peoples... and, slowly, the indigenous disappeared – absorbed in a new nation.

The 19th century saw the rise and rise of Germany, the war machine. Its military used the fact that 'their' language was to be spoken – and provided justification for military invasion. In WW2, Germany invaded in the Blitzkrieg, the Blitz of European cities, including our Britain in the 1940s – Napoleon had intended to invade over 100 years before: both attempts failed.

Looking back as adult, to post war years, the word evacuee, to me, reflected those of us – in Great Britain – who were displaced by the actions, and demolitions, of World War 2. and temporarily billeted in foreign parts, somewhere more rural. Us Blitz kids in London, and other large cities and towns, lived amongst industries of war production...

As an evacuee, I conjure up images of Richmal Compton's (1890 – 1969) *Just William*, a lovable rascal of an English eleven year old, with short grey trousers, white shirt, with tail hanging out, woollen socks (slack, without garters) black-boots (or was it shoes); most prominent, a striped-skull-cap with peak, untidy, tussled hair, and a short-striped-tie – always loose, from an unbuttoned, dirty shirt collar: And, his gang member, pirate dust-and-grime face – painting of whatever wide-game of the moment. William's two-button undone grey-jacket, stuffed with old sweet papers, catapult (yes, we had them – although quickly removed on inspection). Sweets soon unavailable.

Released in 1948, I call to mind the film *Just William's Luck* – when I, too, was eleven years old. *Not*, as William, a model middle class family, with at least one housemaid and cook in attendance. As Americans imagined all English families in illustrated parodies, in film and literature of the time. The same respectable family imagery of the black-and-white 1942 film 'made for USA' of 1940 Jan Struthers' *Mrs Miniver*; a model middle-class family, in a detached rural house – albeit close to our river Thames; through London – and 1940s – Dunkirk escape. A well crafted 'made for USA', complete with maid, cook and servants.

But, no way was *that* the stark imagery of the London East End blitz. I recall, The British Government censored the real East End War for public consumption. Yes! Young as I was to this day, those Miniver and Just William sketches were comic illustrations of the British evacuee: *not* church halls. Orphan homes I experienced... homeless displaced refugees – bombed out. Kids, often had FUN – as most children of countries in turmoil, still managing to manufacture childhood games (of course, in rank contrast of Nazi Concentration Camps – killing the children).

What larks! *Fun?* In his introduction, Robert Westall's *Children of the Blitz* (1985), an excellent collection of 'true' anecdotes of children who grew up, and survived the Blitz and after WW2 years. His selection recalls how we kids – some of us – lived, during those displaced years; as evacuees , and those who remained in their broken homes... the war ruins about them. Westall wrote in his introduction:

> *What the Children of the Blitz have shown me is that they found the war fun; the best game anybody ever invented, unless you or somebody near and dear got killed...*

Our BBC Light Programme wartime broadcasts were dominated by, Tommy Handley (*ITMA*), Flanagan and Allan (*Crazy Gang*), George Formby (ukelele), Arthur Askey, Tommy Trinder, and numerous loved British comedians, who never failed to keep up our otherwise stiff-upper-lips, during the Blitz and throughout the war years... fun against adversity. And, for us children, we had our comics, Children's Hour on the radio. And, J Arthur Rank's British films (John Mills) and, USA American, cowboy and indian features. Distant cousins far away in the USA, in 1939-41, were very much against involvement in the war, despite the excellent support of their President, Roosevelt – for Britain. And, how did the Yanks propaganda most depict European Brits in particular on screen? An example comes again to mind; the delightful, but sanitised, middle-class film of *Mrs Miniver*.

Vera Brittain (1893 – 1970) known for her poignant memoirs of WW1, *Testament of Youth*, published in 1933, also produced an excellent memoir, *England's Hour* in 1941, written during the London Blitz of 1940; Brittain writing her diary notes often under fire from the Nazi bombers overhead in London. One of her many tasks was to organise vital interviews for suitable potential carers of children evacuees; as escorts; conducted in the Mayfair district of the West End of London.

It was during 1940 that her own two children, Richard and Shirley Catlin, were evacuated to the USA, where they remained for three years. In time. Atlantic submarine warfare soon sank ships to and from Europe and the USA; although America would not formally be at war till the end of the following year, after Pearl Harbour in December 1941.

With the collapse of France in 1940, our British government endorsed 'official' schemes to send thousands of British evacuees to the dominions of Canada, South Africa, Australia and New Zealand. And, the United States (initially) agreed in principle to a rescue of Europe's children, for one hundred thousand boys and girls of British stock to America (Brittain, 1941. p63)... But...

Since the 17th Century, Britain had, under its Poor Laws, exported criminals and non-conformists abroad to the colonies. A probationer nurse's notes of 1906 (in my possession) emphasised the Poor Law as best remedy for the poor and needy children of this country – sent abroad to prosper.

So. Charles Dickens saw the British Colonies as lands of opportunity, Australia and America, et al; a certain remedy for destitute and criminal classes of the British poor in the 19th century (*Martin Chuzzlewit: Great Expectations*).

Great Britain, in 1940, offered a selected escort's bonus, for each person out of pocket appointed carer, £5 for Canada, £12 for South Africa and £20 for Australia – return fares – to selected escorts of migrant children. Certainly, *no* FUN element was included in such packages of export care. Even *Barnardo's* exported goodwill, could *not* determine the aftermath fate of thousands of child migrants, once they arrived at their unknown destinations. There was *no* formal feedback of thousands of absent children sent overseas – severed roots from their homeland.

The British Isles is in the north east of the Atlantic, only 21 miles off the shoulder of France, in Europe. At the outbreak of World War 2 in 1939, our British native indigenous population approximated 40 million or so census souls, soon alone, against the immediate threat of Nazi invasion on our south coast, by the Channel in 1940. But, even before that fateful time, in late 1930s, the *Spanish Civil War* had evolved under the Nazi-supported General Franco, and his Republican (anti-royal) armed military regime. For me, the writings of Hemingway, Koestler and Orwell, and surrealist artist Salvador Dali. And, paella...

An international rescue of exiled Catholic children, of Basque refugees, was shipped to Britain, Belgium (not yet invaded) and the USSR – even some to Mexico. Many refugees then sent from orphanage to orphanage. Nationalists soon to be defeated by Franco; exiles first went to Portugal, Italy and Germany, Holland and Belgium. One can only guess their fate as the Nazi's brutally, in turn, overwhelmed all countries. Meanwhile, in relative terms, my bro and I were safe, evacuated from 1939-1951: most in English orphanages and foster homes.

At least 4000 Spanish children arrived at Southampton Docks, in Hampshire, on 23rd May 1937, two years before the declaration of World War 2 in 1939. The contingent, arriving on the steamship *Habana*, which was only designed for 800 passengers; that trip, it carried 3840 children, 80 teachers, 120 assistants, 15 catholic priests, and two doctors. The Spanish refugees and their *Los Ninos* – child exiles, arrived at Stoneham refugee camp, before being moved to various refuges for evacuees about the country. And, this was to be just one of many such fleeing refugees to precious Albion. Since Adolph Hitler's ascendancy in 1933, persecution of all European Jews became anathema, due for ultimate annihilation. Not only European German Jews, but *ALL* of the Jewish Faith – and, in time, *any* human being – whatever faith – murdered. Over 10,000 refugee Jewish children, and escorts (where possible) were exported from Nazi Germany in the last nine months of 1939 – before they closed all German borders – and, then sent such children to the infamous death camps about Europe – till 1945... Britain welcomed the children.

The *Kindertransports*, German name of child transports (mostly trains), allowed by Nazi-officials – payment at a fiscal 'price' for each 'fare': this was, thus, a facility only for those fortunate for child exiles (over two million, at least, of children would die in Concentration Camps...) who escaped to Great Britain before September 1939.

In an incredible work of scholarship, Karen Gershon (1923-1993) wrote up detailed first hand interviews with over 300 Jewish refugee children, between two to sixteen years of age, who had survived during this incredible exodus of child refugees from Nazi Germany. Gershon personally interviewed thirty of her contributions – and recorded many recollections from other child refugees. In retrospect (reading her book) I was impressed by the benign distribution of thousands of free child Jewish refugees – and marvellous reception by our British population of late 1930s, and early 1940s. Despite the already incredible demands made by the war in occupants of Great Britain, during those Blitz years. (*We Came as Children*. Karen Gershon. 1965) Good will was in abundance...

From an early date, the 17th and 18th Century, numbers of 'offenders' from Newgate, or other British Gaols could be spared, from a life of pauper-crime and a lifetime of one-prison-after-another, *if* they accepted transportation abroad to the American or Australian convict settlements. First to serve out an awarded term of servitude – a veiled apprenticeship; '*Indentures*', specific training for an occupation – attached to a free person, or trade, for seven years: then, if not re-offended, free to make a living in that country or given place on their own. A new migrant. Abroad.

These selected criminals, or dependants on the Poor Laws – since 1601 – were a substantial contribution to whites of British or other European stock. For centuries, poor whites were unpaid servants and slaves, as worse off unpaid imported black slaves. The system, Poor Law workhouse children, discharged (or contracted out – like *Oliver Twist*) and imprisoned from child to adulthood...

Not-a-lotta-people-know-that, (including many journalists?) Poor Laws existed until 1948; and the coming era of the NHS and British Welfare State, support from birth to death existed. With the 1948 Childrens Act till the late 1960s, our Poor Law system prevailed: Compulsory School raised from 12 to 14, then 16 years of age in the 1950s. And, I was part of it; as child, young adult. And, poor law possible; apprenticeships for up to seven years (viz to 21 plus); low-paid semi-employment. For a chosen few, very few, a substantial term and a university scholarship...

The early *Child Migrant* systems were most dependent of charities (as the COS – Charity Organisation Societies of the 19th century) the Poor Law providing legislation, but not fiscal support, for costs. And most schools, most orphanages and linked foster care homes continued to be based on the hundred-years-plus Poor Law models: including, where sent abroad, the *indentures* – cheap labour or unpaid post-sixteen 'trainees', further education, as such, mostly non-existent – exist, by subsidy of a backed charity, person or organisation. If the new country accepted responsibility, at least in some measure, for its involuntary young migrants, birth to 16 years old...

It was during the 1980s, 1990s and 2000s; exposés were realised, of past, historical 1950s and sixties overseas child migrants, abused by harsh treatment of new migrants 'hosts' – slave labour, or cheap labourers at least; and a number reported being sexually abused by their caretakers. Mrs Humphreys discovered that child evacuees – migrants' signal belief they were orphans but, in 1940s, 50s and 60s, falsely regarded as no parent or relative to care for them at home. The migrants grew up, (especially in Australia) in the belief that they had no living relatives back in the home country of origin, abandoned by previous kith and kin! But, as Mrs Humphrey's diligent detective work uncovered; many now grown adults (with children of their own) found they still had surviving relatives back in Britain. A plethora of publications on the subject: London (1904), Goffman (1961), Parr (1980), Wicks (1988), Bean, Melville (1989), Holman (1995), Robins (2004), Mann (2005) – all complimented Humphreys' now classic work on child migrants – and new, British, immigrants.

Institution Continued

Orphanages, until 1948, *received* children into need-for-care. *Workhouse* systems still run by the Poor Laws (whatever malady of age or need): no public funding – so the staff and inmates had to pay then for their own survival – aided by charitable trusts: Many of religious, or mercantile origins – excellent in formation; but very difficult to administer abroad – child migrants, as fodder. I experienced living in wartime, in British institutions; evacuated and fostered (never adopted); living in a closed orphanage (see Chapter One): Institution.

Mrs Humphreys excellent work as social worker, and co-founder of the *Child Migrants Trust;* a charitable organisation to support orphans of the 20th Century; British survivors of overseas; uncovered *Child Abuse;* by country, and, now, by numbers of carers, who *abused* their young vulnerable charges. She concentrated mainly on two settlements in Australia; both supplied and maintained by Catholic brothers on very limited income by their charity. Children from as young as three years of age, up to sixteen – and, then, with poor education possible, up to the farm: most in the relative outback of Western Australia and New South Wales: The farms were, are, Binoon and Fairbridge; both of charitable Catholic origins, with very, very little fiscal support.

From mid-1960s, when I was working as a student in a psychiatric hospital (asylum), I learnt, in time, of the sad neglect of pre war; of neglected shell-shock of rank and file (not officers), casualties and families wholly dependent on ongoing media change, as public malingerers... all sufferers branded with this infamous, historic treatment of its years later, hypocritical, in death real heroes; but in life, Malingerers... I stayed working in health and welfare employment for the next 40 plus years...

   Child abuse has always, sadly, been with humanity, and measured from birth to child bearing possible late adolescence. As a qualified social worker, specialising in psychiatric, mental health – and child abuse – well, we were always busy, busy, busy. In the *Home Counties*, any orphanages and care homes were, relatively, about the size of ours – two-hundred-plus children in residence. But, these were no way, far away, from village, towns or cities; and *not* as *Binoon* and *Fairbridge* examples, farm communities. And there were collectively, over the decades, many thousands of child emigrants: full count not possible – records sparse, and certainly not really possible to calculate.

I was at first surprised to read detail about Binoon and Fairbridge clothing; young children all working bare-footed on rough terrain: and there were (don't mention) indigenous aboriginal nomads... eh! Somewhere across Australia?

The child abuse was not rampant (it was hardly a qualification). But, added to the indifference (to them) of the outside world at large. My bro and I, though 'alone' in the home, were lucky we suffered no such abuse.

But, as the years unfolded, one area of rank abuse and neglect, since World War 2, has been the British rank indifference, abuse, of thousands of people involved during the Cold War atomic tests. And, ignored by our government.

Cold War Aftermath

M. and Mme. Curie finishing the preparation of some radium. (Source: *Strand Magazine, Illustrated Interviews. LXXX. The Discovery of Radium,* by Cleveland Moffett, Jan/June 1904.)

Cold War over, back in 1989? '*US Starts $1 trillion upgrade to Cold War nuclear arsenal?*'(The Times. Saturday 15th November, 2014, p44) The item enlarged on the ongoing, growing, pile of '*who has the most strategic warheads: US and/ or Russia, to date...*' As ever, it will only take one final missile to ensure world oblivion... *One* fired weapon of mass destruction. I look back at the now distant generations of nuclear tests, and nuclear plants...

I recall the Windscale Fire Disaster of 1957, when it was producing plutonium for the A and H Bomb atomic tests – and now, forward to the 21st Century Windscale, renamed Sellafield, still serving some 250 buildings or so, in a relatively minute two-square-mile area. Location, still in North West Cumbria, off the coastline of the English Channel and Ireland.

Thirty years on, in 1986, the awesome Ukranian Chernobyl disaster occurred. *The Guardian,* 6th June 1986, p15, published an article, headed '*Why you can't get away from it all:*'. In it, David Fairhall illustrated a graphic map of Great Britain, with its then *nuclear geography* – and plotted British established nuclear plants, all on the coastline, around the country, including Sellafield; over a dozen of them. (See Chapter 4, p442)

The Guardian's graphics revealed that, due to the limited size of our island, an evacuation zone of 18.6 miles (minimum for each Nuclear Plant); and minimal, immediate radiation 'danger zones' of 100 miles circumference, meant that *any* Chernobyl type disaster – well; no-one of our island would, could escape its aftermath.

Nuclear plants, bombs, missiles... a similar prospectus may be drawn. Yes, of course, *this* is only theoretical.

But, another generation, 30 years on, The Guardian (30th October 2014, p10) headed: '*Photographs show perilous state of Sellafield Storage Ponds: Radioactive fuel rods lie in cracked concrete dock: Nuclear safety expert warns of 'significant risk'. (Article by John Vidal and Rob Edwards).*' The two toxic 'ponds' (viz static), were commissioned back in 1952, and fell into disuse in the 1970s – and have remained in situ since that time... Disposal of the highly radioactive waste has become an economic minefield, as any programme for a 'cleanup' is deemed too dangerous...

Estimated '*Cost of clearing nuclear waste at Sellafield rises to £56bn in a year*' quotes The Times March 5th, 2015. And, the Independent, 12th March 2015 (Business) expands; '*Ultimate cost of Sellafield clean-up 'cannot be forecast*'(Mark Leftley, Associate Business Editor); informed the Independent, of current (update) '*estimate for decontaminating the Cumbria site – £88bn to £218bn...?*' Pause... 218 *billion* pounds to decommission one site! Reality!

The word 'cleanup', I learnt, is a misnomer, as any contract means removing toxic nuclear waste, highly radioactive,and guaranteed to 'spread' abroad – out of Sellafield and there is, to radioactivity, *no* present known effective antidote for elements (viz eg plutonium) that require hundreds, thousands of years to degrade. And this data is about the *hot spot*, as Sellafield nuclear plant, not a site of past nuclear explosive tests, but, more than enough to provide forensic evidence of all global, nuclear waste toxic sites. And, that despite British politicians (Margaret Thatcher, Tony Blair et al) constant denial that no British serviceman could have contracted radioactive illness; or any civilian any leukaemia, from radioactivity.

Our Britain, fortunately, never experienced any nuclear bomb explosions on our island, but *hotspots* are easily found abroad: Manhattan USA, Nevada USA, Australia, Chernobyl. *Cleanups*, a metaphor for '*Pass The Parcel*' storage and removal, site-to-site of any affecting atomic waste. And, still politicians wish to build new toxic lavatories: preferably financed in other countries – so *they* have theoretical profit, but not the waste produced in production. This is a problem – not a solution. A world problem, not privately of politicians, denying our Cold War veterans, inheritance of radioactive waste.

In denouement, a published letter in the *Daily Mail*, January 8th 2015: Subheading '*Having Atomic Kittens*'; as a well informed letter, about the nuclear plant realities; by F.N. of Essex. Good for the *Daily Mail* to publish and, especially, the dire, truthful content. I quote, for its honesty, the last two paragraphs of this forensic, fiscal narrative:

> '*I also asked if they could tell me exactly how much a complete decommissioning has cost. The answer surprised even me: there is not, anywhere in the world, a single nuclear plant which has been completely decommissioned.*
>
> *All those that have been shut down in the past 35 years or so are still going through storing and/or processing of spent fuel and hardware, and the water being used is still too radioactive to let loose into the environment. Get the picture?*'

And so, it goes on... *Independent on Sunday*, 15th March 2015, p30, reports: '*Nuclear Waste Workers fear for their safety (Pic). Dounray decommissioning staff, hit by injuries and concerned about equipment, express 'no confidence' in management.*' (by Mark B Fley)

After a fire at Dounray Plant resulted in a serious radioactive leak in late 2014, justified concern was aired by engaged staff in the decommissioning, ongoing project. *'Fears over the protective outfits, known as airline suits, were allayed when workers were told how to handle them properly...'*

The Dounray site is at the northernmost of Scotland. It is easily viewed isolated in the 1986 nuclear geographical map. Unsurprisingly, the Star Trek protective looking suits, remnants of the radioactive risks of bombs, today in 2015. No detail on what, how, they decommission the new disused plant – and its waste. (See Chapter 4, p442)

Another recent *Times* header; (The Times, Thursday February 5th, 2015 p.39) *'NATO to build six bases as 'Cold War' defence...'* Awful memoirs of the late 1962 confrontation at the Bay of Pigs, and Cuba conflict, so very close to total nuclear war between USA and Russia. The USSR threatened by nuclear rocket bases, was it Turkey – aimed at their countries: and Cuba aimed at the continental USA: so horribly close to annihilation.

And. *On the same Times* page, a theme close to my heart and experience. I read: *'Germany curbs 'church sanctuary' for migrants...'* For me, *Sanctuary*; its charity: *Sanctuary*; safe – church, mosque, temple, hospital; whatever the place of safety, its use and abuse.

Booklet published in 1997.

Gerry Rice, major contributor to this memoir, sent an update email to our narrative, on *cancer* from nuclear test origins...

> *'In the past 17 months (September 2013 to February 2015) of the hundreds of lads who witnessed the 24 Dominic detonations a mere 5 lads known to me (meaning there could be many others) have contracted it. I also know of widows whose husbands have died with compensatable diseases that have not bothered to claim. One being a lady whose husband was an RAF policeman who died with a brain tumour at the age of 49 whilst still serving. Only yesterday my veteran pal from Portsmouth rang me to say he'd got it in his bowel. It is a secondary one, after he made a successful £43,000 claim from the American Nuclear Compensation board two years ago...'*

Children of The Bomb

Much is written, memoirs and film documentaries of the 1945 A-bomb explosions of Hiroshima and Nagasaki. The bulk of material on the ruins of the towns, and resident population, living on the site at the time. But, little public data is to be found on *the aftermath* of the nuclear bombs, subsequent black clouds, and wind distribution of the fallout radiation, distribution about Japan itself and, say, the Pacific coastline. But, whatever later disclosed records, I found little, initially, on the Hibushka's descendants, children of these infected survivors.

In 1972, a Japanese author published a collection of essays and personal accounts, by children of atomic casualties, *Will you still be alive Tomorrow.?*'The sufferers viewed as 'delayed victims of the bomb', who first exhibited radiation injuries years *after* the bombs' explosions, known later as *kibaku nisei*... (*Children of the Ashes. The People of Hiroshima After the Bomb*. 1995 edn. Robert Jungk.)

I was acquainted with the classics of Hersey (1946) and Dr. Michito (1955) – which were too early for *their* generations' children and grandchildren, to contract *inherited* radiation symptoms, well after the original detonations. Jungk (1985) described a youth called Fumiki Nagaya who became a martyr, example of the new, *hibakusha nisei*, as he wasn't born until August 1960: before his fifth birthday he developed leukaemia, and died in 1968.

But, despite mounting evidence of Australian, British and American participants, of which I was one on Christmas Island for 13 months, in the 2000 or so nuclear tests in the 1950s to 1960s, victims' legacy of extreme ill health was slow to be recognised, as many died over a 30 year plus period – and, indeed, the legacy passed down to grandchildren...

I, too, was slow in learning of this toxicity; it has taken over 30 years, one generation, before declassified material acknowledged even the possibility of participants passing on mutations through their DNA, and is still being realised today in their descendants.

'Cancer risk for nuclear veterans' Children.' (*Independent,* 18th October 1991. By Sharon Kingman.)

> *'Men who took part during the 1950s have left their children a legacy of ill health, the British Nuclear Test Veterans Association said yesterday.'* The piece continues... *'It claims that studies on its behalf show that veterans' children are more likely to develop cancer, or be born with physical deformities...'* (Documentary: *Children of the Bomb.* 17th October 1991. Tyne Tees Television. It suggested adrenal cancer is eight times more common in veterans' children.)

From the outset, British Press *might* negate such evidence produced as 'claims to' (for legal reasons no doubt... hmm!) – setting many journalist speak, knee jerk, in future statements from the BNTVA nuclear vets and their relatives. Years ahead, the USA, Australia, New Zealand, France (even USSR) would acknowledge that atomic fallout radiation could, indeed would (after DNA discoveries) confirm offspring of Vets and their wives giving birth to malformed children.

After the conclusion of the USA, British, Dominic atomic tests on Christmas Island and Johnson Island in 1962, the American president John. F. Kennedy, ratifying the milestone, Nuclear Test Ban Treaty in July 1963, said: '*The malformation of even one baby, who might be born long after we are gone, should be concern to us all...*' (Quoted . *Fissionline* August 2013. in Bulletin of Nuclear Veterans and Children.)

Denouement - Continued

I have come a long way since austere, grey but happy days of the 1950s. It was the norm to see only black-and-white minute television. On the box, most formal, the male presenters; dressed in bow ties, such formal rainment, speaking with a mouthful of plums, all white-skinned and, likely, upper class in origins. Very few smiles, stiff-upper-lips – opening, with usually slow, slow crisp Oxford and Cambridge accents. The so called kitchen-sink dramas had yet to begin – introducing how our other half of the English population' toiled and spoke, worked for an elite, and... and... changes.

What's that old saying. When ignorance is bliss, 'tis folly to be wise... hmm!! *Singin' in the Rain* remains a firm film favourite, resonating with the early 1950s. Wonderful USA' musicals in full technicolor, 'glorious technicolor'... Dozens of, so wonderful, escapist happy, musical comedies, that the States made so special: they continued into the early 1960s.

In retrospect, that whole fifties period of cinema history underneath, hid under black clouds, (now infamous) hundreds of global nuclear tests (in the land of cowboy westerns); hidden, many to today, in the 21st century, their results kept in the militant hell of secrecy.

What a delight I see nowadays in the 2000s; colourful, taken for granted, new ethnic, now so British males and females, interviewers and presenters: with rainbow names, reflecting parental origins from Africa, India, Middle East, and many others now integrated; sons and daughters of immigrant, new British citizens. True, it will take a generation or two, or three, to consolidate present day cultures as Christian cultures took hundreds of years to accept differences in origin, abroad, Buddhism and other faiths.

Abroad, too often we experience opposing political parties – killing each others' competitors: We British do *not* hold elections (however banal) where we assemble hustings to shoot, kill and maim our politic differences: Labour, Tory, LibDem etc: Instead of different parties and politicians allowed to change in a democracy (which can never be perfect), without violence to any new contenders for parliament: again, hustings which sad, could become more hate-ins, then potential love-ins.

What Cold War?

In late 2014, I visited a Lewes Book Fair at the local town hall. One book stall, with its focus on military and technology books, and illustrated material, I asked what he had on the Cold War; expecting at least stuff of RAF employed during the fifty odd years. The proprietor looked puzzled and said *'Nothing, nothing at all, nothing happened...'* Nothing in print; nuclear tests, radiation, hundreds did not warrant a paragraph or two in one of his stock items...

And I visited a clothing shop in Worthing, and had an interesting conversation with the young manager, who recently completed an honours degree in British history. I asked him, casually, did he cover the Cold War; he replied *'Of Course. There was Hiroshima, and the ongoing politics between*

USA, Europe and Russia, culminating in the 1989 Berlin Wall removal!' No, he did not recall *anything* about nuclear tests in the Pacific, never heard of Christmas Island.

In hospital for Cancer treatment in 2015, on my 78th birthday, there was an 84 year un-named patient opposite me, who had his birthday next day. To my surprise, he said (albeit briefly), he had been a nuclear scientist based at Harwell in the 1950s: Bill explained he'd attended the Emu tests and Maralinga, and Nevada Tests – close up! And then a close friend of Dr Penney, and his family. But, Bill had never visited Christmas Island and its battery of H-bomb tests. He said he had been trying to forget much of the years – he'd lost a younger brother with leukaemia some years ago. Bill believed all aftermath of the explosions were 'cleaned up' – so he was informed. His own ongoing injuries were not explained to me.

And so I recalled a brief journey in 1956, passing Harwell at 4am on my way back to my RE Camp – shortly to embark for Christmas Island, Operation Grapple and the ongoing Cold War – hotting up...

Stop Press

As I prepared this manuscript for its limited print, I was amazed, pleased, to read a current budget presentation (*Daily Mail* Thursday March 19th, 2015) which (at last) clearly recognised the Cold War Nuclear Veterans justified decades long claims for recognition. Much praise to John Baron, the MP for Basildon and Billericay in Essex, for being a champion of this decades-long attempt to recognise the medical claims on H.M. Government.

Quoting from the article:

Help for nuke test veterans.

A new £25million fund will pay for medical care for older military veterans, including nuclear test veterans.
Around 22000 British troops were sent to witness nuclear blasts in the South Pacific in the 1960s. Studies have suggested their children have around 16 times the normal rate of birth defects.... The cause of the nuclear test veterans has been championed by John Baron, the MP for Basildon and Billericay.

The *Daily Telegraph* also reported this (to me) astonishing revelation, the admission that British troops suffered nuclear radioactivity illnesses due to exposure (ignore 'suggested') in the 1950s, and 1960s... Supporting the BNTVA. (*Daily Telegraph*, Tuesday March 19th, 2015, p11.)

Acknowledgements

Institution and Blitz memoirs, contributed by relatives in London – all deceased. The Bomb and nuclear tests detail was contributed by Sapper Ken McGinley; Sapper (later Captain) Danny Perriton of the Royal Engineers on Christmas Island and his friend, Sapper Gerald Rice, who witnessed and recorded the Dominic series of nuclear tests (with the USA) in 1962. Gerry later made a significant contribution to this pot-pourri of memoirs – from 1989 to 2015. In addition, I thank Lee Cooke, my computer engineer, for invaluable work on these non-fiction memoirs.

Barone Carl Hopper,
Littlehampton, 2015.

Notes and References

Notes and References: Chapter One.

1 Aunt Lil, several years later, opened a wartime workmen's café in the Balls Pond Road, and in Homerton, E8.

2 Unigate Dairy in Warren Road, Reigate.

3 Oak Road

4 Off Wray Park Road (the Address of the Homes) – St Davids, Reigate.

5 Colloquial for lone fights between German and British aircraft overhead trails blazing visible and very noisy

6 Holmsdale Road leading into Doods Road, Croydon Road was the fourth road enclosing The Homes Estate behind The Dingle & Dell leading to Wray Common.

7 Brooklands School (aka Infants), enlarged still existed in 1981

8 Spurgeons Homes' house journal was called *'Within Our Gates'*.

9 The Parish Church of St. Mary Magdalene Reigate.

10 Bro and I met Sam Costa at Hackney Empire several years later. A lovely man.

11 See for e.g.: Newspapers called my aunt, mother's older sister, Lillian Manton (b.1911) aged 17 years the 'London Cinderella', *Islington & Holloway Press,* Sat. 19.1.1929. *World's Pictorial News* Jan.27 1929. *Star* 29.8.29. *Poppy's Paper* 16.4.1929. Film shown at the *Tivoli* theatre Strand Aug.1929. and *Alhambra* theatre Mar. 1930.... History. 'Monty Banks ... was looking for a girl to portray his fiancée in the comedy, *The Compulsory Husband*. He had seen dozens of young actresses, and had selected from among them a few to whom he proposed giving a final test. But on the night before the test he visited a (West End) theatre, went into the bar during the interval, and there saw the ideal girl for the films. ... Lillian Manton, programme girl and usherette, walked through those gates of hope with fame and fortune within her grasp.' *(The history of the British Film. 1918-1929* by Rachel Low. Published. London. George Allen & Unwin Ltd.. 1971. See pp.263-264. And p.319)

Notes and References Chapter Two:

2. It all sounded to me like a Dickens' Bleak House storyline. But the sad facts were true and further outlined by extent family witnesses at the time.
3. *Crippen & Manton*, whol, tea & coffee dealers, 8 Eastcheap–listed in *Post Office London Directory,* 1846. p176.
4. When I later attempted to unravel the genealogy of our branch of the Manton lineage from Dr Thomas Manton D.D. (b.1620-1677) 'for family' (my mother and Great Aunt Lil) in 1980.   In pursuance of this search I first visited Stoke Newington St Mary's, and subsequently wrote to various record services. Unbelievable. There was on record Eleven children born to his wife Mrs Manton nee Mary Morgan of which three were stillborn. And of these eight, two died in infancy–Nathaniel b.1649 d.1651.and James b.1655. d.1656. ... And as to traced survivors. Oldest son named after his father and First born was Thomas Manton b.1645, his death date unknown and burial place not known (the year of 1645 when his father, then but Twenty years old, was ordained–and, at Oxford University–and recently married ; surely an eventful year indeed). There were five other recorded surviving descendants; Second was a Henry b.1648 death date and burial place unknown. Third was Mary b.1651 d. 1701 ; Fourth was Anne b.1654. d.1689 (married John Terry) ; Fifth was another Mary (which had me puzzled) b.1658. d.1689 or 1690 ; Sixth was another Nathaniel who was born in 1657. His death and burial place unknown.

    In searching for any roots, noting the obvious, the Great Fire of London in 1666 (and preceding Great Plague) took place during this period. But what effect, if any, this had on our ancestors' 17th century Mantons' history, I had no way (or resources) to detect. Aware that only the male line carries the Surname forward. I established that only Three male descendants appear to have survived; in order, the eldest was another Thomas Manton; Second was Henry Manton and youngest Third was Nathaniel Manton ... But it remained wholly unclear which Manton our branch (on my mother Maude Susie's side). Backwards I was stopped at my Great–great- grandfather George Manton (1806-1856) and his sibs, their father was Joseph Manton (1772-1856) who had moved to London from Long Buckby in Northampton, but was born in Warwick. In one census Joseph was registered as a tailor. ... But who *his* father and grandfather were remained a mystery. Only threads remained.

Great Aunt Lil had had a family tree dating back she recalled, to Dr Thomas Manton D.D.–but it had 'disappeared' (she did then have a number of relics) . This gap was vital as it would have disclosed who and which of Dr Thomas Manton's (1620-1677) surviving sons–especially the eldest was, following their father's death; and of course who his, and our, descendants were–on that side of *The Family*. But I was not successful and the gap–and mystery–remained. ... Just as much t'other side, as our own, paternal Australian–Austrian–whoever ... wherever, our absent father's paternal lineage and roots disappeared back into, remained shrouded–in mystery. ... But, at least, bro and I felt we really belonged, by birth–to London itself.– As it was in those tender post-war years.)

5. On discharge in 1918
6. Ugh! Rats were a common diet in The Trenches. When tinned bully beef and other normal tuck became difficult to obtain.
7. *A Child of the Jago.* by Arthur Morrison. Published in 1896. Penguin paperback.1946.
8. *Handbook of London.* Bohn. 1854. p.612.
9. Quoted : *Round London.* Publ. Newnes.1896. p39.
10. Father remarried
11. *Wonderful London* ed. Adcock, Vol.2., p.419.
12. 1870-1922. Originally known as Matilda Alice Victoria Wood.
13. Ibid.
14. Board School, London, p.89. Sims. *Living London,* 1902.

15. Ibid. p.90.
16. Mother knew nothing of this gentleman when my brother and I were sent into the same *Spurgeons Homes– after* it was transferred to Reigate during the Second World War.
17. Charles Haddon Spurgeon's autobiography featured in Bibliography.
18. Ibid. p.88.
19. *Age of Austerity,* Ed. Sissons & French. Publ. Hodder & Stoughton, 1963. p.37.
20. See *Keesing's Contemporary Archives*, 1951.
21. Keesing's, 12759.C.
22. Ian Opie and his wife wrote the classic book on childhood games.
23. Adcock, Vol. I., p.73.
24. *Old and New London*, Walford, Vol-III., P-324.
25. *A History of London*, Ibid p.143. (*Old and New London*. Walford Vol. I., p.336)

Notes and References Chapter Three:

1. *All Quiet On The Western Front (Im Westen Nicht Neues),* written by Erich Maria Remarque in 1929.
2. *Picture Post,* May 2nd 1942, p.24; picture and caption.
3. Anthony Babington wrote extensively about this in his 1993 book, *For The Sake of Example.*
4. Nevada Desert test sites, see Chapter Four
5. Captain Cook, see Captain Cook RN later in this Chapter.
6. *Operation Grapple.* 1956-1957, p.33. 1957 published booklet.
7. Ibid. Grapple pamphlet. p36.
8. See published article 1964.
9. *Illustrated London News.* May 11th, 1957, p.761.
10. *Swiss Family Robinson.* Chandos Classics, translation by Mrs. H.B. Paull.
11. See *Keesing* 15540.
12. See *Keesing* 15468 B.
13. *'Manual of Basic Training'*, Volume II.   HMSO. No. 6. Civil Defense. *'Atomic Warfare'.*
14. *John Bull* August 17th,1946, p.8.
15. *Picture Post.* 18th February 1950 p.31-36.
16. *Mid-Pacific News. Souvenir Edition.* Wednesday, 15th May 1957.
17. Ibid. *Mid Pacific News, Wednesday 15.5.57.*
18. *Mid-Pacific News. Special.* Number Two. British Press. See *Second Test.*
19. *Mid Pacific News,* Friday 31.5.1957.
20. *Sunday Times.* 27.5.62 p.10-11.
21. In retrospect. *Any* minute discussion on the aftermath of the tests, reported in the media, on all three British Operation Grapple Tests : Grapple ... and from 8th November 1957 Grapple X, Y, & Z tests : and subsequent American nuclear tests–including Christmas Island -- in the Nineteen Sixties ... remained absolute taboo. And subject to a minimum of thirty years ban.   Nuclear tests held in Australia, America, French Sahara, Russia–and on other Pacific Islands. All detail was covered by each countries own *Official Secrets*

Acts ... for a *minimum* of thirty years. I knew nothing of ANY subsequent thermo-nuclear test experiments after the third all British Operation Grapple Test in mid-1957.–until the early 2000s.

22. The 1947 Act was repealed in 1983 ... But for a generation only D notices gagging the media. There would be no such access as free *Google* computer internet–or purported *Freedom of Information Act*. Yet always. There is Not In The Interest Of State Security– or deliberate denial, gross ignorance or politic misinformation. Such stuff remaining a possibility with any country's government in power. Or Orwellian interest..

23. *Sunday Times*. 27th May 1962. p.10-11.

24. Ibid.

25. *No Risk Involved. The Ken McGinley Story: Survivor of a Nuclear Experiment.* by Ken McGinley and Eamonn P. O'Neill. Published. Mainstream .Edinburgh. 1991.

Notes and References Chapter Four:

1. *No Risk Involved. The Ken McGinley Story : Survivor of a Nuclear Experiment.'* By Ken McGinley and Eamonn P. O'Neill. Published by Mainstream Publishing. Co. Edinburgh. 1991. p.120.

2. Source: *Like an Oil Painting from Hell: Christmas Island in the Pacific,* June 3rd 1957 – for the Daily Mirror.

3. Source: *At Work in The Fields of The Bomb*, Photographs and Text by Robert Del Tredic; Introduction by Jonathan Schell. Published Harrap, London, 1987 See p.90 (in b/w) and recorded interview on pp. 185-187. (This book took the author six years to research.)

4. Source: *Shockwave, The Countdown to Hiroshima*, by Stephen Walker, published John Murray, pb ed. 2006 p.15

5. Source: *America Ground Zero, The Secret Nuclear War*, by Carole Gallagher, 1993.

6. Source: *The Nuclear Option,* by The Reverend John Walden, pub. Atomicstamps, Norwich, 2009, p.496

7. *Russia - After the Wall, traces of the Soviet Empire.* Photographs by Eric Lusito, introduction Francis Conte – Dewi Lewis Publishing, 2009.

8. *Under the Cloud.* The decades of Nuclear Testing by Richard L Miller. US First Edition – 1986, Second 1991.

9. Wasserman and Solomon, 1982.

10. McGinley & O'Neill 1991. Rimmer 2013

Bibliography – Squaddie, Blitz and The Bomb

Encyclopaedia Britannica (1771). *A Dictionary of Arts and Sciences*. Three Volumes. First Edition. Bell and Macfarquar. Edinburgh.

Guthrie, William (1795). *System of Modern Geography. 6th edition.* London. C Dilley and Robinson.

Sims, George R (1883). *How The Poor Live. Living London.* Cassell. 3 vols.

Spurgeon, C.H. (1900). *Autobiography.* Four Vols.

London, Jack (1904). *The People of The Abyss.* Macmillan.

Barrow, John (1930). *Cook's Voyages of Discovery. 1768-1780.* A & C Black Ltd.

Upton, Sydney (1938). *Australia's Empty Spaces.* London. George Allen & Unwin Limited. Museum Street.

Nixon, Barbara (1940). *Raiders Overhead. A diary of the London blitz.* Scolar/ Gulliver

Beaton, Cecil (1941). *History Under Fire. 52 Photographs of Air Raid Damage to London Buildings, 1940-41.* B.T. Batsford.

Brittain, Vera (1941) *England's Hour.* London. Macmilland and Co. Ltd. 1941

Wendt, Gerald et al (1945). *The Atomic Age Opens.* US, World Publishing Co., Cleveland and New York.

Hersey, John (1946). *Hiroshima.* UK, Penguin Books p/b.

Orwell, George (1949), *Nineteen Eighty-Four.* Martin Secker & Warburg Ltd., 1949 and Harcourt, Brace and Company (USA Review Copy, 1949).

Clarke, Arthur C (1954). *The Sentinel. New Worlds Science Fiction.* Nova Publications.

Hachiya, Dr Michitko (1955). *The Journal of a Japanese Physician.* UK. Gollancz.

Hopper, Barone (1957), '*Ready for the Hydrogen Bomb Tests: Christmas Island in the Pacific*' (Pictures by Barone Hopper of Central Press Photos) – featured in *The Illustrated London News,* May 11, 1957, p761.

Oulton, W. E. et al (1957). *Operation Grapple, 1956-1957.* UK. p/b

Gigon, Fernand (1958). *Formula for Death: E=MC² (The Atom Bombs and After).* From French. Translated by Constantine Fitzgibbon. UK. London. Allan Wingate,

Goffman, E. (1961) *Asylums: Essays on the Social Situation of Mental Patients and Other Inmates.*

Glasstone, Samuel (editor) (1962). *The Effects of Nuclear Weapons.* US. United States Department of Defence. United States Atomic Energy Commission. April 1962.

Gutch, Sir John (1962). *Christmas Island. High Commissioner for the Western Pacific 1955-60.* UK. Geographical Magazine Vol. 35 pp 181-187.

Gershon, Karen (1966) *We Came as Children,* London. Gollancz (Republished Macmillan, Papermac, 1989)

Beadell, Len (1967). *Blast the Bush.* New Holland Publishers (Australia) p/b

Cameron, James (1967). *Point of Departure.* Oriel Press.

Greene, Felix (1967) *Vietnam! Vietnam!* UK Penguin Special p/b.

Cudlipp, H & Boyle, P. (1967) *Cassandra at his finest and funniest.* Daily Mirror p/b

Cameron, James (1968). *What a Way to Run The Tribe*. Macmillan.

Calder, Angus (1969). *The People's War. Britain 1939-1945*. Jonathan Cape.

Chitty, Susan (1971). *The Woman who wrote Black Beauty*. Hodder and Stroughton.

Longmate, Norman (1971). *How We Lived Then. A history of everyday life during the Second World War*. Hutchinson.

Cameron, James (1974). *An Indian Summer*. Macmillan.

Bailey, Eric (1977). *The Christmas Island Story*. Stacey International.

Lewis, Norman (1978). *Naples? 44. An Intelligence Officer in the Italian Labyrinth*. William Collins.

Cameron, James (1979). *Yesterday's Witness*. BBC.

Parr, Joy (1980). *Labouring Children. British Immigrant Apprentices to Canada 1869-1924*. Croon Helm. London.

Simone, Daniel De et al (1980). *The Effects of Nuclear War. Office and Technology Assessment. Congress of the United States*. US/UK. Allanheld, Osmum Publishers. Groom Helm, London.

Cameron, James (1981). *The Best of Cameron*. New English Library.

Longmate, Norman (1981). *The Doodlebugs. The Story of the Flying-Bombs*. Hutchinson

Saffer, Thomas H. and Kelly, Orville E. (1982). *Countdown Zero*. G.P. Putnam & Sons, New York.

Harvey Wasserman, Norman Solomon, et al (1982). *Killing our own. The Disaster of America's Experience with Atomic Radiation*. US. Delacorte Press, New York.

Halliday, Fred (1983). *The Making of The Second Cold War*. Verso p/b. Second Edition.

Terkel, Studs (1984). *The Good War. An Oral History of World War Two*. US. Pantheon Books. New York.

Jungk, Robert (1985). *Children of The Ashes. The People of Hiroshima After The Bomb*. Paladin p/b (1st Edition, 1961, Heinmann)

Robinson, Derek (1985). *Just Testing*. UK. Collins Harvill, 8 Grafton Street, London W1. p/b.

Smith, Joan (1985). *Clouds of Deceit. The Deadly Legacy of Britain's Bomb Tests*. UK. Faber and Faber. London, Boston. p/b.

Westall, Robert (1985). *Children of the Blitz*. Penguin. Harmondsworth. England.

Arnold, Lorna and Smith, Mark (1987). Britain, Australia and The Bomb. *The Nuclear Tests and their Aftermath*. Palmgrave (2nd Edition) p/b.

Oulton, Air Marshal Wilfred (1987). *Christmas Island Cracker. An account of the Planning and Execution of the British Thermo-Nuclear Bomb Tests, 1957*. UK. Thomas Harmsworth Publishing, London.

Tredici, Robert Del et al (1987). *At Work in The Fields of the Bomb*. US and UK. Harrap, London. p/b.

Bean, Philip and Melville (1989). *Lost Children of the Empire. The Untold Story of Britain's Child Migrants*. Unwin, Hyam.

Motoshima, Hitoshi et al (1989). *'89 Municipal Nagasaki 100*. Japan. Nagasaki Municipal Centennial.

Newhouse, John (1989). *The Nuclear Age. From Hiroshima to Star Wars.* UK. Michael Joseph.

Pilger, John (1989). *A Secret Country.* Jonathan Cape.

Gould, Jay M. Goldman, Benjamin A. (1990). *Deadly Deceit. Low Level Radiation. High Level Cover Up.* Four Walls Eight Windows. New York.

Johnson, David (1990). *The London Blitz.* Scarborough House / Publishers. p/b

Sakharov, Andrei (1990). *Memoirs Translated from Russian by Richard Lourie.* UK. Hutchinson.

Chernousenko, V.M. (1991). *Chernobyl. Insight from the Inside.* Germany, Berlin. Springer-Verlag.

McGinley, Ken and O'Neill, Eamonn P (1991). *No Risks Involved. The Ken McGinley Story: Survivor of a Nuclear Experiment.* UK. Mainstream Publishing.

Miller, Richard L (1991). *Under The Cloud. The Decades of Nuclear Testing.* US. Two-Sixty Press, The Woodlands, Texas (originally published in 1986 by The Free Press, A division of Macmillan, inc., USA) p/b.

Gallagher, Carole et al (1993). *American Ground Zero. The Secret Nuclear War.* US. MIT Press. Cambridge. 1993.

Humphreys, Margaret (1994). *Empty Cradles.* Doubleday.

Walker, Martin (1994). *The Cold War.* UK. Vintage p/b.

Fermi, Rachel, Samra, Esther, et al (1995). *Picturing The Bomb. Photographs From the Secret World of the Manhattan Project.* US. Harry N Abrams, Inc., Publishers.

Holman, Bob (1995). *The Evacuation, A Very British Revolution*. A Lion Book.

Lifton, Jay and Mitchell, Greg (1995). *Hiroshima in America. Fifty Years of Denial*. US. A Grosset/Putnam.

Isaacs, Jeremy and Downing, Taylor (1998). *Cold War*. UK. Bantam Press, London.

Pilger, John (1998). *Hidden Agendas*. Vintage p/b.

Harclerode, Peter (2000). *Equinox. Warfare*. UK. Channel 4 Books. Macmillan.

Henshall, Philip (2000). *The Nuclear Axis. Germany, Japan and The Atom Bomb Race. 1939-45*. Alan Sutton.

Buckley, Martin (2001). *Grains of Sand*. Vintage p/b.

Holdstock, Douglas, Barnaby, Frank et al (2003). *The British Nuclear Weapons Programme: 1952-2002*. UK. Routledge. p/b.

Munn, Michael (2003). *John Wayne. The Man Behind the Myth*. Robson Books.

Pilger, John (2003). *The New Rulers of the World*. Verso p/b.

Gavin, Adrienne E (2004). *Dark Horse. A Life of Anna Sewell*. Sutton.

Pilger, John (2004). *Tell Me No Lies!* Jonathan Cape.

Cross, Roger and Hudson, Avon (2005) *Beyond Belief. The British Bomb Tests: Australia's Veterans Speak Out*. Wakefield Press, South Australia. p/b

Gaskin, M.J. (2005). *Blitz. The Story of 29th December 1940*. Faber and Faber.

Harris, Michael (2005). *The Atomic Times. My H-Bomb Year at the Pacific Proving Ground. A Memoir*.

Walker, J Samuel (2005). *Three Mile Island: A Nuclear Crisis in Historical Perspective*. US. University of California Press. p/b.

Walker, Stephen (2005). *Shockwave. The Countdown to Hiroshima*. UK. John Murray. p/b.

Waller, Maureen (2005). *London 1945. Life in the Debris of War*. John Murray p/b.

Pilger, John (2006). *Freedom Next Time*. Bantam Press.

Hennessey, Peter (2007). *Cabinets and The Bomb*. UK. The British Academy. Oxford University Press.

Hayward, Anthony (2008). *Breaking The Silence. The Television Reporting of John Pilger*. Network p/b.

Hubbard, Group Captain Kenneth and Simmons, Michael (2008). *Dropping Britain's First H Bomb. The Story of Operation Grapple 1957-58*. UK. Pen and Sword. Aviation.

Isaacs, Jeremy & Downing, Taylor (2008). *Cold War. For Forty-Five Years The World Held Its Breath*. Abacus p/b.

Baggott, Jim (2009). *Atomic: The First War of Physics. And the Secret History of the Atom Bomb: 1939-49*. UK, Faber & Faber and Allen & Unwin.

Lusito, Eric (2009). *After The Wall. Traces of the Soviet Empire*. Photographs by Lusito... UK. Dewi Lewis, Stockport, England.

Walden, Revd. John (2009). *The Nuclear Option. A Philatelic Documentary*. UK. (Privately). Atomic Stamps, 11 Hemmings Close, Norwich. NR5 9EH, UK.

Gardiner, Juliet (2010). *The Blitz. The British Under Attack*. Harper Press.

Ham, Paul (2011). *Hiroshima, Nagasaki, The Real Story of The Atomic Bombings and Their Aftermath*. UK. Doubleday.

Hopper, Barone (2011). *Better Court Than Coroners, Memoirs of a Duty of Care, Vol. 1*. PV Publications.

Paterson, Peter (2011). *How Much More of This, Old Boy...? A Reporter's Life*. Muswell Press p/b.

Hopper, Barone (2012). *Lest We Forget. BCTC Volume 2, Memoirs from a Duty of Care*. Perseverance Publications.

Rimmer, Alan (2012). *Between Heaven and Hell* Amazon p/b

Rimmer, Alan (2012-). *Fissionline*. Online newsletter.

Iversen, Kristen (2013) *Full Body Burden. Growing up in the Shadow of a Secret Nuclear Facility*. Vintage Books. London. p/b

Schlosser, Eric (2013). *Command and Control*. UK. Allen Lane. Penguin Books.

Index